TURBULENT TIMES, CREATIVE MINDS

Turbulent Times, Creative Minds

ERICH NEUMANN AND C. G. JUNG
IN RELATIONSHIP (1933–1960)

Edited by Erel Shalit and Murray Stein

CHIRON PUBLICATIONS • ASHEVILLE, NORTH CAROLINA

Turbulent Times, Creative Minds: Erich Neumann and C. G. Jung in Relationship (1933–1960) is published in cooperation with Recollections, LLC. Recollections is devoted to promoting and supporting the publication of material related to the early development of analytical psychology. Through its partnership with Chiron Publications, Recollections has several projects underway.

www.ChironPublicatons.com
Interior and cover design by Cornelia G. Murariu
Printed primarily in the United States of America.

ISBN 978-1-63051-445-7 paperback
ISBN 978-1-63051-363-4 hardcover
ISBN 978-1-63051-364-1 electronic

Library of Congress Cataloging-in-Publication Data
Names: Shalit, Erel, editor. | Stein, Murray, 1943- editor.
Title: Turbulent times, creative minds : Erich Neumann and C. G. Jung in
  relationship (1933-1960) / edited by Erel Shalit and Murray Stein.
Description: Asheville, N.C. : Chiron Publications, [2017] | Includes
  bibliographical references and index.
Identifiers: LCCN 2016043905 (print) | LCCN 2017007586 (ebook) (print) |
  LCCN 2017007587 (ebook) | ISBN 9781630513627 (pbk. : alk. paper) | ISBN
  9781630513634 (hardcover : alk. paper) | ISBN 9781630513641 (electronic) |
  ISBN 9781630513641 (e-book)
Subjects: LCSH: Jung, C. G. (Carl Gustav), 1875-1961--Correspondence. |
  Neumann, Erich--Correspondence. |
  Psychoanalysts--Switzerland--Correspondence. |
  Psychologists--Israel--Correspondence. | Psychoanalysis. | Jungian
  psychology.
Classification: LCC BF173.J85 A4 2017 (print) | LCC BF173.J85 (ebook) | DDC
  150.19/54092--dc23
LC record available at https://lccn.loc.gov/2016043905

Cover image: Mordecai Ardon, *Big Clock* (1972-1973). ©Ora Ardon. Photo by Avraham Hay.
Hans Fierz and Carl Jung in front of the Dome of the Rock, 1933, reprinted with permission from the Jung Family Archive.
Mordecai Ardon, *Venus of Beersheba* (1962). ©Ora Ardon. Photo by Avraham Hay.
Photos for Rivka Lahav chapter by Marion Badrian. ©Neve Tzeelim.
The Moon Princess painting by Erich Neumann ©Ralli Loewenthal-Neumann.
Painting by Erich Neumann (1936) from his story *The Beetle Orchestra* ©Micha Neumann.

We are grateful to Fred Appel and Princeton University Press for permission to quote from *Analytical Psychology in Exile: The Correspondence of C.G. Jung and Erich Neumann* by C.G. Jung and Erich Neumann, Edited by Martin Liebscher, Translated by Heather McCartney. Copyright © 2015 by Princeton University Press.

Contents

Introduction

With the recent publication of the correspondence between C. G. Jung and Erich Neumann, the personality and significance of Neumann for analytical psychology heaves into view more sharply than ever before.[1] Although Neumann's classic works, such as The Great Mother and The Origins and History of Consciousness, have been widely read and appreciated inside and outside of Jungian circles, his full range of works and his vibrant qualities as an intellectual leader in the field fell sadly into the shadows following his early death in 1960 at the age of only fifty-five. Had he lived another thirty years to the ripe old age of eighty-five as Jung did, his name and contributions would be far more widely recognized among his analytic colleagues and in the world at large. Now with the publication of the extensive correspondence between Neumann and Jung and thoughtful contributions by scholars such as those included in this volume, the stage is set for a Neumann renaissance.

Neumann was clearly a star in the Jungian firmament during his last decade of life and was recognized as one of the most brilliant exponents of analytical psychology. Beyond that, he made genuinely original contributions in works that extended depth psychology's range

---

1 C. G. Jung and Erich Neumann, *Analytical Psychology in Exile: The Correspondence of C. G. Jung and Erich Neumann*, ed. Martin Liebscher (Princeton, NJ: Princeton University Press, 2015).

of application to areas of history and culture that Jung himself, as a pioneer, had not been able to work out in a systematic way. While the focus of many of the papers in this volume is on the relationship between Neumann and his mentor, others consider topics that represent original and groundbreaking expansions into territories such as cultural history, art, and religion.

The times during which Neumann wrote and his relationship to Jung was played out, 1933 to 1960, were immensely turbulent, and for European Jews like Neumann tragically so. As both men were engaged with their respective political situations to some extent, both also suffered from the tumultuous destructiveness sweeping across continents and engulfing the entire world in what can only be regarded in retrospect as a period of mass psychosis on a gigantic collective scale. Their small boats tossed hither and yon on these stormy seas, Jung and Neumann managed nevertheless somehow to remain in contact throughout the years of chaos (with the exception of the years during World War II) and indeed to deepen and extend their dialogue significantly in the years of continuing anxiety following the Holocaust, the founding of the state of Israel, and the onset of the cold war. Their correspondence reflects the background turmoil in their respective social and cultural climates while their discussions concerning analytical psychology and its clinical and cultural applications remain in the foreground. On all levels, as we can now see clearly, two brilliant minds were attempting to remain open to one another and creatively engaged throughout this period.

The relationship between Jung and Neumann can be compared to that between Freud and Jung. Both involved an older senior mentor figure and a young aspiring student. A similarity between the two relationships lies in the fact that Neumann never conceded his intellectual independence, just as Jung had claimed similar autonomy vis-à-vis Freud. A difference is that Jung, in the position of mentor, was considerably more encouraging and supportive of Neumann's individuation process, which inevitably included differences of opinion, than Freud had been of Jung's. Perhaps

Jung had learned something about mentoring from his painful experience with Freud. While tensions were definitely a part of the story between Jung and Neumann, they never led to a break. Whether this resilience was due to Neumann's ability to withstand Jung's sometimes abrasive expressions of opinion on sensitive emotional issues or to Jung's capacity to understand Neumann's psychological and cultural differences and to respect his genius remains open for discussion. Readers of the letters will form a variety of opinions as to what kept this dynamic relationship intact. Certainly the need to maintain close contact and to collaborate was mutual.

Jung and Neumann shared roots in a common culture in central German-speaking Europe, with a shared love of the poets Goethe, Schiller, and Hölderlin and an education (Bildung) among great German philosophers such as Kant and Schelling. But they were also each indelibly steeped in their distinctly different heritages. Jung was a Swiss Protestant Christian, quite secularized as an individual but bearing the religious influences of his culture and of numerous pastors and theologians in his immediate family background. Neumann was a Jew who grew up in Berlin in a nonobservant family, and as a young man he looked to elements in Jewish culture for his identity and sympathized with Zionist ideas about a homeland for the Hebrew people in Palestine. Upon discovering Jung—they met for the first time at Jung's famous Berlin seminar in 1933—Neumann quickly realized that Jung's analytical psychology and his discovery of the objective psyche could offer a means to recover more of the profound value and meaning of his Jewish heritage. They could thus each separately but also in fruitful dialogue share an appreciation of the depths of the archetypal layers of the psyche as explicated in their separate cultures and envision general trends in and threats to humanity. The basis for collaboration was present despite what would turn out to be quite sharp cultural differences.

A Brief Review of the Relationship as Reflected in the Correspondence

The personal relationship between Neumann and Jung began in earnest when Erich Neumann, age twenty-eight, arrived in Zurich en route to Palestine in the autumn of 1933 with his wife, Julie, and their two-year-old son, Micha. Neumann came to Switzerland with the intention of studying with Jung and becoming a psychoanalyst in the Jungian school. Jung was at the time fifty-eight, thirty years older than Neumann when Neumann first visited his consulting room in Küsnacht on the shores of Lake Zurich. By that time Neumann had earned a doctorate in philosophy from the University of Erlangen-Nuremberg in Germany (1927), with a dissertation on the mystical philosopher Johann Arnold Kanne (1773–1824), and all but the degree in medicine from the University of Berlin, which he did not receive at the time due to the virulent anti-Semitism that set in with the appointment of Hitler as the German chancellor earlier that year (he did receive it in 1959). His personal training analysis took place over the course of the next seven months, both with Jung and with Jung's assistant, Toni Wolff. As he entered upon this new phase of his life, Neumann was searching for a professional orientation that would suit him and his changing living conditions. He was also looking for a teacher, whom he found in Jung.[2] The letters between Neumann and Jung during the first years of their correspondence, from 1934 into 1940, at which point World War II created a hiatus, circle largely around questions of Jewish identity, Neumann's new professional life as a Jungian analyst in Palestine, and emerging intellectual passions involving analytical psychology and culture. This was anything but an easy time for him.

---

2 In Neumann's terms, he had wanted to find a *tzadik*, a Jewish teacher. In a letter to Jung, he writes: "Before I came to you, I was rather sad that I was not able to go to a Jewish authority because I wanted to go to a 'teacher' … . According to Jewish tradition, there are Zaddikim of the nations, and that is why the Jews have to go to the Zaddikim of the nations" (Jung and Neumann, *Analytical Psychology in Exile*, 35–36).

The troubled times in Europe intervened abruptly at the very beginning of their relationship. The first significant letter in the correspondence is a letter from Neumann to Jung that is undated, most probably sent in early 1934, that is, during the time when Neumann was in the midst of his analysis with Jung.[3] It concerns a stormy public controversy set off by an article written by the psychoanalyst Dr. Gustav Bally in the Neue Zürcher Zeitung in which Bally suggested that Jung was anti-Semitic. Jung defends himself vigorously in the press, denying all of Bally's allegations, but the heated public exchange set off very disturbing effects among Jung's Jewish students and colleagues, among them now the young Erich Neumann.[4] Neumann writes to Jung: "Dear Dr. Jung, When I spoke—in some dismay—with Miss Wolff today about the partial validity of Dr. Bally's article and she gave me your paper 'The State of Psychotherapy Today,' I could not have imagined what a controversy of such fateful personal significance was about to unfold!"[5] At the very outset of their relationship, as we see in this letter, Jung was aggressively confronted by Neumann with an issue that would haunt their days going forward, namely, the ugly and tragic relations between the Germanic people and the Jews in the Europe of the 1930s and 1940s. We do not find in the correspondence an immediate response from Jung to the issues raised in this letter; most likely they were discussed in face-to-face sessions while Neumann was still in Zurich and in analysis with Jung. But in this first letter we already get a taste of Neumann's fiery spirit.

In the summer of 1934, Neumann and his family moved on to their intended destination, Tel Aviv, where they would spend the rest of their lives. Soon after getting settled, Neumann wrote Jung several long letters, some describing his new place of residence, his reactions to what was now

---

3 Jung and Neumann, *Analytical Psychology in Exile*, 10.
4 C. G. Jung, "A Rejoinder to Dr. Bally," *Neue Zürcher Zeitung*, March 13–14, 1934.
5 Jung and Neumann, *Analytical Psychology in Exile*, 10–11.

his homeland, and his experiences with people in Palestine. He also raised questions about his developing psychoanalytic practice in Tel Aviv, and he asked for advice about troubling relations with fellow Jungians who were then living in Palestine (James Kirsch, for example). He expressed feelings of social isolation in this still foreign land. Along with these letters, he sent Jung lengthy drafts of writing that he was working on, asking for comment. He urged Jung to write about Judaism, to make a full statement, to write a book about this religious tradition.[6]

Jung, however, was extremely busy during this time with his presidency of the International Society for Medical Psychotherapists, the editorship of the 'society's journal, the founding of the Eranos conferences in Ascona, his full analytic practice, travels, and other responsibilities and interests. His research had turned powerfully to alchemy, and he was becoming passionately immersed in this study. He did not get around to replying to Neumann extensively until April 27, 1935, nearly a year after Neumann's departure from Zurich.

In Palestine, Neumann was soon busy writing and lecturing extensively on the subject of modern Jewish identity. This is a topic that interested Jung greatly. He was curious as a psychologist to see how Jewish identity would be affected by its new grounding in the ancient homeland of the children of Israel. "I know that the Jewish problem is, for you, a matter of the utmost seriousness—just as, for me, our spiritual condition and the psychic life of the individual's soul is the most important thing," he wrote in 1934. "You can therefore be sure that I will give my attention to this problematic issue using all available means, as it is for me of the utmost value to discuss the complex intricacies of modern culture and its psychic situation with a Jew who is expressly familiar with the European context and who is coming

---

6 Neumann eventually took this upon himself, writing *Jacob and Esau: On the Collective Symbolism of the Brother Motif*, only recently published, and a major, as yet unpublished, work on Jewish consciousness and Hasidism.

to this issue from a slightly different perspective, while residing on his own archetypal soil."[7] Jung was curious, too, about how Neumann's new life in Palestine might transform his thinking about analytical psychology.

Neumann expressed gratitude to Jung for taking the time to think through his burning questions with him: "I thank you very much for your letter that has shown me once again that you continue to have patience with me and once again have engaged with my problems … . I do not even believe that Palestinian soil is so important for the Jew but it will become so if ever this soil absorbs sufficient human beings to be a true ancestral soil once again."[8] In a later letter, written on November 15, 1939, which would be one of the last communications between the two men before the interruption of World War II, Neumann continues with his thought about the Jewish people: "Two things are colliding in me … the one namely the consciousness of belonging to a dying people, and the other is the knowledge that something new is emerging … . In the course of history, individuation is the consequence of Jewish development; at the same time it seems to be the abolition of the Jewish. My slogan: it is no longer about Judaism but it is about Jewish people, about the individual as revelation-center and realization-center of the Self—but it seems to me, along with the dissolution of the old Judaism, to require and to signify something like a new Jewish beginning."[9] Neumann was expanding his view of individuation from ethnic and religious identity to what he would later call "interiority" or "inner being," the conscious awareness of the ego-self axis.[10] This latter term would become the signature piece of his psychological theory, which offers a conceptual advance on what had been postulated heretofore in analytical

---

7 Jung and Neumann, *Analytical Psychology in Exile*, 53.
8 Ibid., 120.
9 Ibid., 148–149.
10 Erich Neumann, "The Psyche as the Place of Creation" (1960), in *The Place of Creation* (Princeton, NJ: Princeton University Press, 1989), 367.

psychology. This notion would announce Neumann's understanding of the stage of the individual in the individuation process, the next step in human consciousness beyond the stage of patriarchy.

World War II interrupted the correspondence for five years. During this time, Neumann kept busy in Tel Aviv with his research and writing: the manuscript for *The New Ethic* and *The Origins and History of Consciousness* (in progress but nearly finished). Jung too was deeply occupied with research and writing, mostly about alchemy and its meaning for psychology. Soon after the end of the war, they resumed epistolary contact, and letters passed once again back and forth between Tel Aviv and Küsnacht. In summer of 1947, Erich and Julie Neumann managed to visit Switzerland and were able to meet with Jung in Zurich and to attend the Eranos conference in Ascona. There, Neumann met Olga Fröbe-Kapteyn, the founder and controlling presence of Eranos. This would be a fateful meeting of minds and hearts that would bear much fruit in the years to come. At this conference, too, Jung introduced Neumann to representatives of the Bollingen Foundation, who were persuaded to consider assisting Neumann financially to write a book on the Great Mother image in myth and to cover the costs for his next visit to the Eranos conference, where he would lecture for the first time. Eranos and Neumann's concerns about the publication of his new books became topics for many discussions in the correspondence with Jung.

Neumann did give a brilliant inaugural lecture at the Eranos conference in 1948 titled "Mystical Man." Jung could not attend that year due to illness, but he got a very critical report from one of his followers, Dr. Jolande Jacobi.[11] This was the first salvo in what would become a heated battle between the Zurich Jungians and Neumann for Jung's favor and preference. The sharp and sometimes snide remarks and rebukes that passed back and forth, often over Jung's desk, resemble sibling rivalry

---

11   Jung and Neumann, *Analytical Psychology in Exile*, xl–xli.

for the blessing of the father. Neumann's style of presentation seemed too detached, too rational, and too systematic for the Zurich group, who had formed a tight circle around Jung. To Neumann they looked like a band of groupies who needed to be shaken up and exposed to a broader intellectual world. To Olga Fröbe-Kapteyn, however, Neumann's brilliance was convincing, and in time she would designate him Jung's successor as the central figure of the Eranos conferences. He was indeed the star speaker there until his sudden and surprising death in 1960 just a few months after he gave his last lecture, "The Psyche as the Place of Creation."

In the 1950s, Neumann's work took up problems of women's development as different from men's and the need to bring the feminine more visibly and powerfully into the patriarchal structures of modern society. About the stages of women's development, contrasting it to that of men, he gave a moving depiction in his interpretation of a classic fairytale in Amor and Psyche: The Psychic Development of the Feminine (1952). Another masterpiece on the archetypal feminine, The Great Mother, was published in 1955. Neumann and Jung shared the conviction that the time had come for the feminine to take its place as an equal partner with the masculine in modern society because they represented two distinctively different principles and attitudes, both necessary for wholeness as much in men as in women.

In July 1955, Jung was celebrated by people from all over the world in recognition of his eightieth birthday. Many friends and colleagues came to Zurich to honor him. A couple of weeks beforehand, he wrote to Neumann, who had sent him an early congratulatory birthday greeting, personally acknowledging his high estimation of Neumann's recent writings: "My dear Neumann ... I would like to sincerely thank you not only that you have taken to the pen for me in such a generous way, but also for that greater thing that you are achieving in your life's work."[12] This is another testament to Jung's high regard for Neumann's significant contributions to analytical psychology in his recent writings.

While Neumann's work was heavily criticized by the Zurich Jungians for being too rational and not suffused enough with the spirit of the unconscious, Jung himself knew better. He had after all been Neumann's analyst. In a late letter Neumann disclosed to Jung the source of his inspiration for writing Depth Psychology and the New Ethic, his first and most controversial and viciously attacked work. The inspiration was an active imagination, and it shows Neumann's deep spiritual connections:

> I seemed to be commissioned to kill the apeman in the profound primal hole. As I approached him, he was hanging, by night, sleeping on the cross above the abyss, but his— crooked—single eye was staring into the depths of this abyss. While it at first seemed that I was supposed to blind him, I all of a sudden grasped his "innocence," his dependence on the single eye of the Godhead, which was experiencing the depths through him, which was a human eye. Then … I sank down in opposite this single eye, jumped into the abyss, but was caught by the Godhead, which carried me on the "wings of his heart." After that, this single eye opposite the apeman closed and it opened on my forehead.[13]

This was a side of Neumann that he did not show to the Jungians in Zurich, probably for good reason: they would have found cause to accuse him of untoward psychic inflation if he had ventured to tell them of numinous experiences like this. To them, his personal life remained hidden. Today we can see it much more visibly, thanks to the publication of the correspondence with Jung and the research that has been done in previously undisclosed documents in the possession of the Neumann family.

---

12   Ibid., 310.
13   Ibid., 331.

Contents of the Present Volume

The present compilation of essays consists largely of papers that were presented at the Jung-Neumann Letters: An International Conference in Celebration of a Creative Relationship, held at Kibbutz Shefayim, April 24–26, 2015, in celebration of the publication of the correspondence between Jung and Neumann. Members of both the Jung and the Neumann families were present and made important contributions, of a more personal nature. The papers in this volume are grouped around themes that were discussed at the conference. They reflect the wide range of topics that Jung and Neumann dealt with, individually and in discussions between them.

In the first section, Martin Liebscher, the editor of the published volume of letters, discusses the relationship between Neumann and Jung in light of the correspondence. Nancy Swift Furlotti, who has been involved in the publication of the correspondence from the beginning, follows with observations about the friendship between the two men, and Ann Lammers, editor of the correspondence between Jung and James Kirsch, offers trenchant observations about the sibling rivalry that flared up around Jung among his students.[14]

In the second section, Paul Mendes-Flohr, professor of Jewish studies at the University of Chicago and the Hebrew University of Jerusalem, paints a vivid picture of the shared cultural backgrounds of the two men and considers the specific dilemma of the German Jews, who found themselves increasingly divided in their identities between their religious tradition and their secular loyalties. Ulrich Hoerni, Jung's grandson, draws attention to the history and culture of Basel, the city in which Jung grew up and was shaped by in his cultural assumptions and attitudes, including the proto-Zionism of Jung's grandfather, Samuel Preiswerk.

---

14   C. G. Jung and J. Kirsch, *The Jung-Kirsch Letters*, 2nd ed. (London: Routledge, 2016).

Erel Shalit discusses the emphasis by both Jung and Neumann on the significance of cultural differences and particularism in order to reach out to universal human values.

The third section, titled "Troubled Times," takes up the difficult issue of the time in which Jung and Neumann came to know each other. These were years of maximum stress in Europe and indeed in the entire world. Andreas Jung, a grandson, draws on family archives to describe a little known visit made by Jung to Jerusalem in 1933, just prior to his first meeting of Neumann at the Berlin seminar later that summer. Thomas Fischer, a great-grandson of Jung and presently the director of the Stiftung der Werke von C. G. Jung (the Foundation for the Works of C. G. Jung), extends this reflection on Jung's activities in 1933 to other new beginnings. Joerg Rasche, a Jungian analyst who lives in Berlin, offers the results of his recent research on Jungians in Berlin during the 1930s and through the war years.

The sections that follow pick up on various facets and interests shared by Neumann and Jung and offer some comparisons and contrasts between their approaches. In the fourth section, Henry Abramovitch and Murray Stein focus their deliberations on the problem of evil and explicate Neumann's bold proposals in *Depth Psychology and a New Ethic* and Jung's appreciation and reservations about Neumann's position as laid out in that work. Murray Stein compares this, as well, with Jung's discussion in *Answer to Job*.

At the Eranos conferences, Jung and Neumann shared a platform for several years following the war. In the fifth section, Ricardo Bernardini describes the importance of this European venue for Neumann and the reception of his brilliant lectures by the distinguished audience. Julie Neumann's poignant letter to Olga Fröbe-Kapteyn following the death of her husband underscores the central importance that Eranos held for Neumann.

One of Neumann's chief passions was psychological creativity and the arts. In section six, Gideon Ofrat, a widely cited authority on Israeli art, considers the prevalence of the Great Mother in Israeli art and relates this theme to Neumann's classic work on the subject. Christian Gaillard, Jungian analyst and professor emeritus at the Ecole des Beaux Arts in Paris, compares Jung's and Neumann's approaches to the arts and artists and discusses Neumann's writing on the famous painting, *The Virgin and Child with Saint Anne,* by Leonardo da Vinci, a work also famously interpreted by Freud. Finally Tom Kelly and Debora Kutzinski consider Mozart's *The Magic Flute* and Neumann's commentary on this opera.

While most of Neumann's writing concerns metapsychology and major cultural themes, he was also deeply engaged in the clinical work of psychoanalysis, and his contributions to this field are taken up in section seven. Rina Porat, Batya Brosh, and Rivka Lahav are clinicians who have worked in close relationship with Neumann's students and professional descendants in Israel.

In the next section, which deals with several of Neumann's writings on religion, scholar Tamar Kron takes up one of Neumann's earliest interests, Judaism and in particular Hasidism. Her contribution is based on research into some of Neumann's earliest works, much of this material still unpublished.[15] Here we get a glimpse into Neumann's deep penetration into his own religious tradition and his fascination with mystical elements so often overlooked in Judaism. Angelica Löwe presents the major theological themes that Jung and Neumann discussed, pertaining to the hostile brother motif, represented by Jacob and Esau, and the consciousness of God. In the final section, Joseph Cambray discusses Jung's and Neumann's views on synchronicity in their late letters.

The collection concludes with personal contributions by family members and people whose parents were in close contact with Neumann. One of the highlights at the conference was an evening that featured them on stage offering spontaneous reminiscences and memories from family life and stories passed down through the generations. The presence of

---

15 Ann Lammers is editing this major as yet unpublished work of Neumann's.

Erich and Julie Neumann as well as of Carl and Emma Jung was palpable on that memorable evening.

Erel Shalit and Murray Stein

Tel Aviv and Zurich

July 2016

PART I. THE CORRESPONDENCE
(1933–1960)

Uncertain Friends in Particular Matters: The Relationship between C. G. Jung and Erich Neumann

Martin Liebscher

The relationship between C. G. Jung and Erich Neumann began in 1933 and lasted until Neumann's death in 1960. Their correspondence covers the entire time span until 1959—with an interruption during the war from 1940 to 1945. The physical distance between these two men, which is part of the reason for the existence of this vast amount of letters before us, is a significant characteristic of their relationship. Berlin-born Neumann left Germany at the end of September 1933. The Nazis had seized power earlier that year, and Erich and Julie Neumann, both dedicated Zionists, did not hesitate to leave Germany for Palestine at the earliest possibility. With them was their two-year-old son Micha. The small family interrupted its journey in Zurich, where Erich engaged in psychological work and studies with C. G. Jung. The two men had met earlier that summer, when Jung was in Berlin to hold a much acclaimed seminar from June 26 to July 1, 1933. Whereas Julie and Micha left for Tel Aviv in February, Erich stayed in Zurich until May 1934. The Neumanns returned one more time to Zurich before the war, for two months in May and June 1936. During this time Erich, who had suffered from symptoms of exhaustion, worked analytically with Jung and with Toni Wolff, who also became Julie's therapist. The next meeting between Neumann and Jung did not take place until 1947.

Altogether Neumann and Jung were not in the same place for more than ten months between the years 1933 and 1947, yet in this same period we count twenty letters directly from Neumann to Jung and eighteen from Jung to Neumann. However, especially before the war, the letters differ significantly in length. Whereas Neumann's substantial letters went up to ten pages or more, Jung's letters—with a few exceptions—were kept rather brief. The reasons for this discrepancy lead to the heart of the relationship between these two men for the first half of their acquaintance.

First, there was a significant difference in age, which meant there was also a huge imbalance in professional and scholarly experience. Jung was thirty years senior to Neumann. Whereas Neumann was a young, promising psychologist-to-be, who had just finished his studies of medicine and several subjects in the humanities, Jung was at the height of his professional career as a world-renowned expert in psychology and psychiatry. International recognition for his distinct branch of psychology manifested itself during this time in invitations to conferences and presentations all over the world, several honorary doctoral degrees, a professorship at the *Eidgenössische Technische Hochschule*, as well as the presidency of various psychological societies.

Neumann, in contrast, was rather inexperienced. When he met Jung in 1933 he could hardly present himself as a scholar of any repute. Aside from the publication of his thesis on the almost unknown German Romantic philosopher Johann Arnold Kanne, he had written some poetry, published the beginning of his novel *Der Anfang*, and had written an unpublished commentary on the novels and short stories of Franz Kafka, who had yet been recognized for his literary achievements when he died in 1924. In the realm of psychology Neumann had no scholarly credentials at this stage of his life. It was only due to Jung's advice that Neumann put together his thoughts on the typology of Jacob and Esau in the aftermath of his review of Rosenthal's article on the subject of typology in the Jewish history of religion, though Neumann's article was not published at the time.[1] Jung's suggestion that he present his work to the Psychological Club in 1933–1934 was rejected by Neumann, who felt he was not up to the task at this stage.

The work that occupied Neumann most of the time during the 1930s was his two-volume study *Ursprungsgeschichte des Jüdischen Bewusstseins* [*The Origins and History of Jewish Consciousness*], which has not yet been published. Volume one is entitled *Beiträge zur Tiefenpsychologie des jüdischen Menschen und der Offenbarung* [*Contributions to the Depth Psychology of the Jewish Man and to the Problem of Revelation*] and volume two *Der Chassidismus und seine psychologische Bedeutung für das Judentum* [*Hasidism and Its Psychological Relevance for Jewry*]. In his study Neumann demands that the depth psychology of modern Jewry needs to be aware of its historical preconditions. Whereas the first volume deals with the apocalyptic prophetism around the time of the destruction of the Second Temple, the second volume is dedicated to Hasidism. According to Neumann, Hasidism is able to bridge the gap between the ancient God-principle and the earth-principle.[2] This link brings with it a new set of values: a joyful affirmation of creation and, at the same time, a rejection of melancholy and depression as world-denying emotions, an antipathy toward Jewish intellectualism, and a new appreciation of the feminine principle through a deeper understanding of the Shekhinah.[3] But, according to Neumann, Hasidism failed to renew the Jewish psychological condition by giving in to the rabbinate.[4] When asked by Gustav Dreifuss in the 1950s why he

---

1   Hugo Rosenthal, "Der Typengegensatz in der jüdischen Religionsgeschichte," in C. G. Jung, *Wirklichkeit der Seele: Anwendungen und Fortschritte der neueren Psychologie* (Zurich: Rascher, 1934), 355–409. Neumann's text was finally published as *Jacob and Esau: On the Collective Symbolism of the Brother Motif*, edited and with an introduction by Erel Shalit (Asheville, NC: Chiron Publications, 2016).
2   Erich Neumann, *Ursprungsgeschichte des jüdischen Bewusstseins* [*On the origins and history of Jewish consciousness*], vol. 2, *Der Chassidismus und seine psychologische Bedeutung für das Judentum* [*Hasidism and its psychological relevance for the Jewry*], unpublished typescript, 217.
3   Ibid., 118, 114, and 123, respectively.
4   Ibid., 126.

would not publish the manuscript, Neumann replied that it was not close enough to the primary sources and too much orientated around Buber.[5]

As his first letter to Jung after the war, dated October 1, 1945, demonstrated, the decision not to publish the manuscript was probably due more to a shift in personal interest than the closeness to Buber's work:

> After I had completed the large work on Jewish antiquity— on the Soul History of the Jew—(it is now obsolete and only useable as source material), I wrote a book on the psychological meaning of Hasidism for the modern Jew, which I still stand by. But then, after I had arrived at my current internal state, the Jewish problem and the work on it was ended as far as I was concerned, precisely at a time when it was becoming palpable in the world in an indescribably horrific way. I, meanwhile, was coming back to "pure" psychology.[6]

The letter reached Jung at a critical point of his life. In February 1944 he had suffered a heart attack with almost fatal consequences, which was followed by another one in November 1946. In the twilight zone between life and death in which Jung found himself in the days after the first heart attack, he experienced a series of visions that had a profound effect on him. And it is fascinating to notice that one of the visions was of a Kabbalistic nature:

> I myself was, so it seemed, in the Pardes Rimmonim, the garden of pomegranates, and the wedding of Tifereth with Malchuth was taking place. Or else I was Rabbi Simon ben Jochai, whose wedding in the afterlife was being celebrated. It was the mystic marriage as it appears in the Cabbalistic

---

5   See Gustav Dreifuss, "Erich Neumanns jüdisches Bewusstsein," in *Kreativität des Unbewussten. Zum 75. Geburtstag von Erich Neumann (1905–1960)*, ed. Dieckmann, C. A. Meier, and H. J. Wilke (Basel: S. Karger, 1980), 67–77.

6   C. G. Jung and Erich Neumann, *Analytical Psychology in Exile: The Correspondence of C. G. Jung and Erich Neumann*, ed. Martin Lienscher (Princeton, NJ: Princeton University Press, 2015), 160.

tradition. I cannot tell you how wonderful it was. I could only
think continually, 'Now this is the garden of pomegranates!
Now this is the marriage of Malchuth with Tifereth!' I do
not know exactly what part I played in it. At bottom it was
I myself: I was the marriage. And my beatitude was that of
a blissful wedding.[7]

As an undated letter from Aniela Jaffé to Rivkah Schärf in the spring
of 1944 demonstrates, Jung had been studying kabbalistic literature
at the time before the heart attack. He thanked Schärf via Jaffé for
providing him with the texts. Schärf in return wrote to Jung on May 22,
1944, referring to a discussion she'd had with Jung about the relation
between Tiphereth, Yesod, and Malkuth, which had taken place before
Jung's illness.

It is as if the intellectual development of the two men had crossed
paths during the long years without contact. Neumann, who had accused
Jung in 1934 of knowing more about ancient Indian philosophy than about
contemporary Jewish culture and religion, had refocused his research
interest from Jewish psychology to questions of ethical behavior and
developmental psychology. For Jung, in contrast, Jewish mysticism had
become increasingly important, and the symbolism of the separation
and reunion of the male and female aspects of God, of Tiphereth and
Malkuth, was not only a feature in his vision of 1944 but also informed
his understanding of the *mysterium coniunctionis*. In a letter Jung wrote
to Neumann on January 5, 1952:

Ouranos and Tethys do not sleep together any more, Kether
and Malchuth are separated, the Shekinah in exile; that is the
reason for the affliction in God. The Mysterium Coniunctionis
is the concern of man. He is the *nymphagōgós* of the heavenly
marriage. How can man distance himself from this event?

7   C. G. Jung, *Memories, Dreams, Reflections*, ed. Aniela Jaffé, trans. Richard and Clara Winston (New York: Pantheon Books, 1962), 294.

He would then be a philosopher, who speaks *about* God, but not *with* him. The former would be easy and would give man false security; the latter is difficult and therefore exceptionally unpopular. Precisely that was my lamented fate; therefore it needed a powerful illness to break through my resistance. I am supposed to be *beneath and not above* everywhere.[8]

The first volume of *Mysterium Coniunctionis*, published in 1955, repeated that argument almost word for word, although Jung corrected the factual errors: Kether was replaced by Tifereth as the spouse of Malkuth; likewise, in a footnote, Oceanos as the spouse of Tethys. The *nymphagōgós*, the bridal guide for a previously married man, became a *paranymphos*, who accompanies the couple that gets married for the first time.[9]

The first major text that Neumann presented to Jung was the result of his shift toward "pure" psychology. The title of this study was *Depth Psychology and a New Ethic*, written during the war in Tel Aviv with, as he wrote to Jung, "Rommel at the door." This was the text he sent Jung in 1945 to reestablish contact. Soon after *Depth Psychology and a New Ethic* Neumann started sending bits and pieces of another manuscript to Jung—draft chapters of an in-depth study of the development of human consciousness on a phylogenetic as well as an ontogenetic level. This text would eventually be published as *The Origins and History of Consciousness* in 1948, shortly after *New Ethic*. With these scholarly texts at hand, Jung started to engage with Neumann on a more intensive theoretical level, which would also change the tone and balance of the correspondence. But the most decisive disturbance of their friendship was the controversy that surrounded the publication of *New Ethic*.

With the help of his friend Gerhard Adler, Neumann visited Switzerland for the first time after the war in 1947. He met Jung again,

---

8   Jung and Neumann, *Analytical Psychology in Exile*, 282–283.
9   C. G. Jung, *Mysterium Coniunctionis* (1955–1956), *CW*, vol. 14 (Princeton, NJ: Princeton University Press, 1963), pars. 18–19.

and at the Eranos conference he was introduced to Olga Fröbe-Kapteyn, who not only invited Neumann to speak on mystical man at the 1948 conference, but also to write an introduction to the first volume of the Eranos picture archive material. The chosen subject was the exhibition on the Great Mother, which had accompanied the 1938 conference on the same subject. As we know today, the introduction to the pictorial catalogue changed it into a substantial book in its own right, illustrated by the images from the picture archive. It finally came out in 1955.

Spring 1948 saw the opening of the C. G. Jung Institute in Zurich, under the nominal presidency of C. G. Jung, but it was effectively run by a curatorium that was presided over by vice president Carl Alfred Meier. When Neumann gave his first Eranos lecture in August of the same year, Jung was absent, but Meier was there, and he left the room, apparently outraged, in the middle of Neumann's lecture.

Another member of the curatorium, Jolande Jacobi, who Neumann would start to single out as his personal antagonist over the years to come, sent Jung a vivid description of Neumann's presentation in a letter dated September 9, 1948:

> I could not follow your advice to engage with Neumann's thoughts, as I did not like his presentation at all. He did precisely what you always rejected, namely to create a "system" from your teaching. Though he warned of "dogmatisation" in his introduction, he did not follow his own warning … By the way, it was quite interesting how easily the women—almost every one of them—were fascinated by him, whereas the men rejected him strongly. It was equally informative how, during his lecture of two hours, he was completely withdrawn and did not notice his audience at all; he was very odd. Of course he is ingeniously talented at formulation, has an abundance of words, and an eloquent and beautiful style, which can be used to express everything magnificently. It seems almost too easy for him. Does this pose a danger for him? I did not

only have to disagree with his schematizing manner, but also
with the content of his deliberations. I did not think that those
"exceeded yours," as you were allegedly quoted as saying,
but remained way *below* yours. Everything that you have
revealed about Christian symbolism and the understanding
of Christianity over the years, is wiped away, if Neumann's
account were to be the *authentic Jungian teaching*. The most
important of your principles, namely that "the damaged,"
"the crippled" is also the chosen one, would collapse. [JA][10]

Jacobi, who had converted from Judaism to Protestantism and finally
to Catholicism, was a close collaborator of Jung during those years and
helped him establish contact with important Catholic clerics such as Père
Bruno de Jésus-Marie, the editor of the Etudes Carmélitaines, who came to
see Jung together with Hans Schnyder von Wartensee in 1946. Indeed Jung
sought out the dialogue with Catholicism after the war, as he described
in a letter to the Dominican priest Viktor White on September 26, 1945:

> I am highly interested in the point of view the church takes with
> reference to my work. I had many discussions with catholic
> priests in this country too and it is on my instigation that catholic
> scholars have been invited to the Eranos lectures of which
> you presumably have heard. We enjoy the collaboration of an
> extremely competent scholar of the patristic literature, Professor
> Hugo Rahner S.J. of Innsbruck University. Quite a number of
> catholic publications have been occupied with my psychology
> in this country too and there are some among them, which are
> really very understanding.[11]

This interest in Christianity during that period can be seen in his letter
exchange with Victor White, or, on the Protestant side, with the recently

---

10 Initials in brackets refer to various collections of unpublished material; see list in bibliography.
11   C. G. Jung and Victor White, *The Jung-White Letters*, ed. Ann Conrad Lammers and Adrian
Cunningham (London: Routledge, 2007), 4–5.

published correspondence with Adolf Keller. These letters also reveal the differences between the psychological and the theological approach. Jacobi's view that sees the Christian ethic in the center of Jung's psychology was a misunderstanding on her behalf. Jung also replied to Jacobi on September 24, 1948, in defense of Neumann:

> I think that Neumann's work is excellent. It is not a dogmatic system, but a structured account, thought through in minute detail. Admittedly he does not take the feelings of his audience into consideration. That is the reason why he does not mention the positive aspect of the damaged. But it is certainly not unknown to him … . His style of presentation must have had a particularly unfortunate effect. But his intellectual achievement is outstanding. You are all a bit spoiled by my anima, which is capable of switching between light and dark—nothing is entirely dark and—thank God— completely light! That is why I am accused of contradictions! With Neumann it is more complex. One needs to think with him, otherwise one is lost. I even recommend a careful reading of his lecture. Neumann comes from his eremitic existence in Tel Aviv, which is unknown to us. The house opposite to his was bombed to the ground and "Israel" is suffering in labour. N. is strongly infected collectively due to his anxious rejection of the outer world. This attitude is responsible for his lack of emotions and thus has to be taken into consideration … . According to my opinion Neumann is a scholar of the first order, and it is up to my students to prove that he does not teach a dogma, but attempts to create a structure. [JA]

Regarding Meier's obstructive behavior at Eranos, Jung suggested that Meier "would fare better to elaborate on the connection between his Asclepius and psychotherapy than to run away from the lecture. He would discover some tricky problems, where groundwork, such as Neumann's, might be more than welcome."[12] Neumann himself referred to this incident in a letter to Meier in the autumn of 1948:

> I was of the opinion that, with the telling of your dream, which seems very clear to me, the complex-laden nature of your reaction to my lecture of which you heard the beginning had become clear to you, and with that, the matter seemed to me to be settled. Now I notice that you evidently believe that you formed a correct picture at that time in a downright anticipatory intuition about its "future" progression. For this well proves that, after you had become acquainted with the lecture for the first time, you had confirmed your "fundamental objections" which came to you before you knew what I had to say. [NP]

The same C. A. Meier, vice president of the Jung Institute, would come to play a decisive role in what unfolded.

The new institute embarked on the ambitious plan of a book series entitled *Studien des C. G. Jung Instituts* [*Studies from the C. G. Jung Institute*], and Neumann was invited to publish his monograph *The Origins and History of Consciousness* as the first title in the series.[13] Meier, whose antagonism toward Neumann had become obvious in Ascona, as vice president, presided over the curatorium and was also responsible for the publication series. His study *Antike Inkubation und moderne Psychotherapie* [*Ancient Incubation and Modern Psychotherapy*] was second in the pipeline of the series of books. Another member of the curatorium was Jolande Jacobi, who did not hold back her criticism of Neumann's book in a letter to Jung on September 9, 1948:

> I have great concerns as to how such an account will look in a volume of more than 800 pages and if such a book at

---

12   Meier's comparison of the ancient divinatory understanding of dream with modern psycho-therapy was finally published as *Ancient Incubation and Modern Psychotherapy*.
13   In a letter from the publisher, Rascher, to Neumann dated July 6, 1948 [RA].

the beginning of our series won't dominate all the others to come? There is also the danger that it will be understood as the "official," approved Jungian teaching and *not* the Neumannian understanding, which in fact it will be. And as Dr. Neumann seemed rather unhappy that his book has not appeared yet, he might, perhaps, be delighted anyway, if his book were to be published outside of the series—it would stand up independently, which would be justified by its size anyway. I have only spoken to him briefly. His interest towards me was only limited to business (i.e., the printing of his book) and that has not prompted me to attempt further conversations. [JA]

In spite of Jacobi's reservations, Jung supported the publication and bestowed upon the book a preface in which he likened the research of Neumann to his own, stating that Neumann followed in the pioneering tracks of Jung.[14]

However, Neumann's first book to be published was *Depth Psychology and a New Ethic*, which caused harsh reactions and criticism in Zurich. In his letter from December 10, 1948, Jung told Neumann about the critical reception of *New Ethic* and the subsequent debate over whether the institute should publish *The Origins and History of Consciousness* in its series at all.[15] Jung assured Neumann, who was taken by surprise by the reaction to his book, of his ongoing support and even emphasized the importance of the cathartic effect of such a controversial text.[16] At the same time, however, Jung warned of the implication that such a controversy could have for the development

---

14   C. G. Jung, "Vorwort zu Neumann *Ursprungsgeschichte des Bewusstseins*," in *GW* 18, no. 2 (1949), 556–557; "Foreword," in Erich Neumann, *The Origins and History of Consciousness*, translated by R. F. C. Hull (Princeton, NJ: Princeton University Press, 1954), xiii–xiv; reprinted in *CW*, vol. 18 (Princeton, NJ: Princeton University Press, 1976).

15   Jung and Neumann, *Analytical Psychology in Exile*, 236–37.

16   A letter from Neumann to Olga Fröbe-Kapteyn from December 25, 1948, showed Neumann's delight with Jung's reaction, which seemed to indicate that Jung would take sides with Neumann: "In the meantime, 'Ethic' has come out; I hope that Rascher has sent you a copy, and, as Jung wrote in his very nice letter, it has already caused a stir. To my greatest surprise, even in the Institute itself" [EA].

of the new institute. In his reply on January 1, 1949, Neumann ignored this warning and criticized the institute for compromising its academic credibility in order to avoid confrontations.[17] He would, Neumann wrote, gladly withdraw his book from the series if he were asked to do so. It was this formulation that gave the curatorium—under Meier's vice presidency and, it needs to be said, under Jung's presidency—the opportunity to wriggle itself out of the obligation toward Neumann:

> Dear colleague, as you have already heard from Jung, in the aftermath of the public and private controversy that was sparked by your *New Ethic*, the institute has discussed the question as to whether it was right to publish the *Origins and History of Consciousness* in the publication series of the institute. After an extensive discussion in the board we came to the conclusion that the young institute should not expose itself too much to hefty public controversies. Hence we prefer, for the time being, to publish texts of a monographic character on detailed questions of complex psychology, which still need a better material and scientific underpinning. It therefore seems also personally right, if your big summarising work is published as a separate publication, and I can understand the decision of the board. I hope that you do not have any difficulties with this decision and assure you that we all await the publication of your book with anticipation. Best wishes, always yours, C. A. Meier.[18]

When Neumann wrote a fuming letter to the president of the institute on February 10, 1949, Jung responded by referring to Neumann's previous offer to withdraw his book from the series.[19]

---

17   Jung and Neumann, *Analytical Psychology in Exile*, 239.
18   Ibid., xlv.
19   Ibid., 243–246.

At the same time *New Ethic* caused the institute to chuck out Neumann's *History and Origins of Consciousness* from its series—and replace it with C. A. Meier's monograph on ancient incubation as the first volume—Kegan Paul expressed an interest in publishing an English translation of Neumann's book. Neumann asked Jung for a preface, which provided Jung with the opportunity to suggest changes to Neumann's book. He sent Neumann his detailed amendments and suggested revisions of the text, which have been published as appendix II of the Jung-Neumann correspondence. This is Jung's most detailed commentary of *New Ethic* and a valuable source for understanding Jung's reservations of and problem with the text. In a letter to Cary Baynes from May 9, 1949, he explained his intentions:

> He [Neumann] wanted me to write a preface to the English edition of it. I have written it but not sent it to him yet. Instead I have sent him a whole list of propositions that he might consider if he wants to have my foreword. His reply was not altogether favourable. He says that he could not write in the way I would, that to him the whole problem is as hot as hell and of immediate urgency. [CFB]

Cary Baynes herself was not at all in favor of Neumann's book. A letter to her by Marie-Jeanne Schmid, Jung's secretary, dated March 15, 1949, shows her as being one of the critical and hostile voices:

> What I would like to write to you about—and how I would wish I could *talk* it over with you!—is the "new star" Dr. Neumann, i.e., his books. What you wrote about his "New Ethic" made me long for your presence here. Discussion about it is running rather high over here, both in the "outer world" and in the "inner circle." We are even going to have a discussion evening about it among the members of the

club.[20] Personally I absolutely agree with you, namely that one wonders whether he knows what he is talking about and—although his big book on the "Origins and History" is better—I also wonder with you whether it "really does all that" namely what C. G. says in his foreword. I wish C. G. had never written it. [CFB]

In a letter to Michael Fordham, dated August 6, 1949, R. F. C. Hull expressed his fear that Neumann's *Depth Psychology and a New Ethic* would pour oil on the flames of those who brought forward accusations against Jung of being a Nazi and that "anything may happen if Neumann's account of the Jungian 'new ethic' is taken at its face value—there may be a hurling of epithets like 'Communist,' 'immoralist,' 'Antichrist' and who knows what!"[MFP]. The same R. F. C. Hull not only translated Jung's *Collected Works*, but also Neumann's *Origins and History*, into English.

Neumann's reaction understandably vacillated between anger and disappointment. The anger was mainly targeted against Meier, Jacobi, Wolff, and others whom he associated with the institute. Toward Jung, in contrast, his feeling could be better described as disappointment. Although he was aware of Jung's role in this affair, he was somehow apologetic toward him. Neumann's letter from February 10, 1949, reflects his ambivalence toward Jung as it is separated into an official part addressed to the president of the institute, who supported the decision of the curatorium, and another part to the friend and esteemed Professor Jung, to whom he calls in a biblical vein, "Philistines be upon thee, Samson!" In a letter to Olga Fröbe-Kapteyn on March 14, 1949, he ventilated his anger, calling Jung's dissociation from the institute's decision ironic [EA]. The entire affair was a shameful disgrace, and he had written to Jung, whose role in all of this he called outrageous. A month later he softened his critique of Jung slightly: "Personally, Jung is still nice to me, sometimes even

---

20 On March 26, 1949, a discussion on Neumann's *Depth Psychology and a New Ethic* took place at the Psychological Club Zurich.

movingly so, but it remains that he is not reliable—an old man" [EA]. Years later Neumann would describe Jung to Aniela Jaffé as an uncertain friend in particular matters.

There is another aspect that comes into play when Neumann reflects upon those incidents, and that is anti-Semitism. Neumann understood the rejection of his new ethic and the refusal to include his book in the series as part of a wider anti-Semitic climate that continued to sweep over Europe: "This is how it was in Nazi Germany, cowardly and opportunistic, but while it was truly dangerous there, it is only business in Z.—and one that is wrongly understood to boot, but this is no consolation" [EA]. In another letter to Fröbe-Kapteyn on May 22, 1949, he is even more explicit about his understanding of the affair:

> Jung's behaviour towards me is extremely moving and he cares in a way that truly affects me. Of course this has to be of higher importance to me than his weakness in individual cases, where, in my opinion, he is also factually wrong at times. Nevertheless, the whole affair is important to me in a tragic way, as it demonstrates to me the emergence of a reactionary Europe, which takes possession of Jung. Catholicism, individualism—well, those are words, but they are also powers, and everything rhymes in such a sad and fitting way with fascism and national-socialism. Because of Jung's carelessness it has already been tremendously difficult so far to separate Jung and his work from the embarrassing, even catastrophic, closeness to it. [EA]

On a number of occasions he mentioned the psychological and physical impact that this affair had upon him.[21] Though he recovered, and his relationship with Zurich improved steadily over the years to come, the most important aftermath of these days was that his relationship with Jung

---

21   In letters to Fröbe-Kapteyn dated December 13 and May 11 (or 14), 1949 [EA].

changed. As the letters reveal, Neumann complained about the fragility of Jung, who would not be able to defend Neumann against the intrigues of the Zurich circles.

On this point Neumann was wrong, as the next chapter of this saga demonstrates. Eventually Neumann was compensated by the institute with an invitation to teach a course on an annual basis. In October 1950 he held a course entitled Zur Psychologie des Weiblichen. Anhand des Märchens Amor und Psyche [On the Psychology of the Feminine: Based on the Fairy Tale "Amor and Psyche"]. Members of the curatorium and the institute used this opportunity to launch another hefty attack against Neumann. In the presence of the students, a fierce discussion among staff members, especially C. A. Meier, broke loose. When Jung heard about this incident, he summoned the main instigators of this attack to Küsnacht. Aniela Jaffé's minutes of this meeting on October 5, 1950, lists the following participants: Marie-Louise von Franz, Emma Jung, and Liliane Frey. C. A. Meier's absence is noted. This is what Jung had to say about the unjustified attacks against Neumann:

> One should not have discussed the problems in public. It is so finely nuanced that it is not possible to sort it out in a discussion. But above all, one can't load these things onto N. in public. One can't load them onto Dr. Meier either. . . . Besides, one must not forget that he has been in Palestine on his own for nine years. When he worked with me back then, many things which you are learning today had not even been uttered. When he left, we did not yet know much that we know today. And besides, we are not dealing with a theory, but a human being. You cannot do this right in the middle of a course. I would like to see the animus in you if you were to be corrected in a lecture. If I had been there, I would have attempted to rectify some things. But I would have said it only once and then shut up. N. is very sensitive, easily gets

> upset. But he is a creative man. And one should not upset
> such people. Leave him alone. [AJP]

The argument brought forward against Neumann can only be partially reconstructed. What becomes clear from the minutes is that von Franz criticized Neumann for interpreting the fairy tale from the female psychological point of view, thereby neglecting the context of the fairy tale, which is given as a dream of the male character of the novel. In her 1970 book *A Psychological Study of the Golden Ass of Apuleius*, she reiterated that argument in support of her view that the novel is about the anima problem of Apuleius and not about the female's process of detachment from the mother.[22]

Through the years there was a partial reconciliation between Neumann and the Swiss Jungian circle. Neumann became a key figure at the annual Eranos conference, which, as he complained in a letter to Jaffé, was shunned by the Zurich circles. Every summer and early autumn he visited Zurich, gave lectures at the club and taught courses at the institute, the patronage of which he also accepted. But the peace was fragile, and rivalries were never far off.

Even in 1959, while teaching a course at the institute in Zurich on child psychology, Neumann and Jacobi would clash with each other. Mario Jacoby, at that time a student at the institute, gave us an account of that confrontation:

> Neumann had the characteristic of radiating great powers of persuasion in support of his ideas—which were new at that time—by using well-polished linguistic expression. Only the ever undaunted Jolande Jacobi, who was also present, dared to contradict him. She was not happy about Neumann's notion of equating the infant's experience of the mother with that of the Self in the Jungian sense . . . . She was—as she said—

---

22 Marie-Louise von Franz, *A Psychological Interpretation of the Golden Ass of Apuleius* (New York: Spring Publications, 1970), 77 n1.

convinced of the fact that the Self is a metaphysical reality which extends into human experience. "This is exactly what the Self is not," interrupted Neumann. With his humour, his clarity of thought and his persuasive clout he could hold his own, even in the face of some training analysts who were present who were all direct students of Jung.[23]

A damning letter from Neumann to Aniela Jaffé 1959, written in the aftermath of this incident and apparently in a state of depression, shows that his general reconciliation with the Zurich Jungians was not successful after all. Here, Neumann explained his wish not to lecture in Zurich any more. The letter is a reply to Jaffé's attempt to emphasize Neumann's importance for Zurich, especially for the institute and the club. She wrote about her impression that the general appreciation that Neumann received by the members would not be reciprocated by him, in a letter dated October 24, 1955:

> Perhaps it is due to past experiences that even today you find yourself in a sort of defensive position in Zurich, and one sometimes gets the impression that you operate according to the principle: "Attack is the best form of defence." That has a remarkably divisive effect on your audience. Two camps immediately form: pro Neumann and contra Neumann—a fact which is then, of course, for the most part ignored and not discussed. [NP]

Calling Jaffé naïve, Neumann set out to strike a balance in his relationship with Zurich over the last decade. There would be no community waiting for him in Zurich or Ascona. This ignorance of the Jungian psychotherapists would have tragic consequences, as Neumann would put his finger on wounds and problems that needed discussion in order for analytical

---

23 Mario Jacoby, "Erich Neumanns Konzept der Urbeziehung im Lichte der neueren Kleink-indforschung," in *Zur Utopie einer neuen Ethik. 100 Jahre Erich Neumann. 130 Jahre C. G. Jung* (Vienna: Mandelbaum Verlag, 2005), 38.

psychology to survive.[24] This is targeted toward Fordham, with whom Neumann would fight another battle and who, years after Neumann's death, wrote a damning account of Neumann's child psychology. Neumann concluded in his letter that he would be prepared to forget the past insults by Jung, Jacobi, Meier, and Frey for the sake of the cause, but his opinion would be sidelined.[25] And his final verdict sounds devastating:

> You know, I put up with some things from C. G. which I am still amazed at today, but at least I know who he is in spite of this and in relation to me. I do not have the feeling that the same is required of me in relation to the Zurichers.[26]

Jung probably would have subscribed to this description of their friendship. His remarks about Neumann in later years show a similar ambivalence. In private Jung would make remarks about Neumann's imbalanced character that lacked the integration of "the feminine creativity," whereas he would always have praise for Neumann and his work in public.[27] But it might be that such contradictions are a necessary prerequisite of a true friendship, at least in Jung's understanding. Jung is reported to have said that he had "only two real friends with whom I can speak about my own difficulties; the one is Erich Neumann and he lives in Israel and the other is Father Victor White in England."[28]

---

24   Neumann to Jaffé, in an undated letter written around late October/early November 1959: "Even more, behind the Eranos work, there is much more inner inspirational experience; the system is, in part, difficult work which seems necessary for me, and whether analytical psychology will survive depends in part, I sometimes fear, on this" [NP].

25   "A lunch with Frau Dr. Frey and Brunner belongs, as kind as they are, in the same category. I have tried hard—for the sake of the cause—to forget the old insults of C. G., Jacobi, Meier and Frey—which does not come easily to someone like me" [ibid.].

26   Ibid.

27   Mircea Eliade, *Journal II (1957–1969)*, trans. Fred H. Johnson Jr. (Chicago: University of Chicago Press, 1989), 41.

28   Reported by F. Elkisch, October 29, 1976; quoted in Adrian Cunningham, "Victor White: A Memoir," in C. G. Jung and Victor White, *The Jung-White Letters*, ed. Ann Conrad Lammers and Adrian Cunningham (London: Routledge, 2007), 334.

Companions on the Way: Consciousness in Conflict

Nancy Swift Furlotti

I have followed the trail of the Jung-Neumann correspondence for more than a decade, suspecting that this long-term friendship must have been deep and meaningful. Now able to read their letters, I was right. Jung described Neumann as one of his closest friends with whom he could share his forming thoughts, accept criticism, criticize back, and remain always respectful and enthusiastic. These two brilliant men, with their substantial age difference, challenged each other, supported each other, and did not mince words with each other—ever. It has been accurately described as a creative relationship, one that deepened and widened the thoughts and understandings of both men. We are the beneficiaries of this interaction, which lasted until the end of their lives.

As I sat quietly to study their correspondence, their thought processes, their interests, I was first struck by the intimacy and genuine caring between the two men. Neumann, the young man, learns from Jung, and one sees his development and deepening of understanding over the years. Jung is patient, supportive, and honest while at the same time challenged to look at his responses to the rise of National Socialism and to learn more about Judaism.

I would like to begin by quoting from the letters to give you a sense of the friendship we are dealing with. These quotes are from later in their lives, when two old men soften and risks are no longer a concern. Though there is a thirty-year age difference, both died within a year of each other, Neumann in November 1960 and Jung in June 1961. Neumann's early death from kidney cancer was tragic. He did not live long enough to shepherd his many creative endeavors properly into the world, and we do not have the benefit of the works he would have undertaken had he lived. His previously unpublished manuscript *Jacob and Esau: On the Collective Symbolism of the Brother Motif* has recently been published, and an extensive work on the roots of Jewish consciousness is forthcoming. His brilliant, unfinished book *The Child* was published posthumously. Much to the displeasure of Michael Fordham, it has survived quite well. Neumann ran into constant sibling rivalry in the Jungian world. From these quotes you can guess why. Jung to Neumann in 1955:

> I would like to sincerely thank you not only that you have taken to the pen for me in such a generous way, but also for that greater thing that you are achieving in your life's work … . Men like you are rare birds whose perspective the world needs.[1]

Neumann to Jung in 1955:

> I constantly consider this interweaving with your work as one of the finest gifts of my life. And I know that even where you see accents differently from the way I do that I am someone who, in your eyes, is taking it forward.[2]

Further, in 1958:

> My link with you is, as you know, not dependent on writing and speaking, nor no longer dependent, I should say, but

1   C. G. Jung and Erich Neumann, *Analytical Psychology in Exile: The Correspondence of C. G. Jung and Erich Neumann*, ed. Martin Liebscher (Princeton, NJ: Princeton University Press, 2015), 310.
2   Ibid., 313.

> meeting with you always brings me a substantial affirmation that cannot be found anywhere else in the world. I hope you understand what I mean. For me, there is only you yourself as a "connecting point" in the center, as far as the task of the work is concerned.[3]

And finally, Jung to Julia Neumann on her husband's death in 1961:

> I was particularly shattered by the unexpected and, for me, sudden death of my friend and companion on the way in whose fate I participated in tranquility and from a distance.[4]

Essential Conflict

We are all quite familiar with Jung and his history, while less so for Neumann. He was born in Berlin January 23, 1905. His close and lifelong friend Gerhard Adler, also a prominent Jungian analyst, ended up moving to England. Neumann went to medical school in Berlin but did not receive his license because of the Nazi racial laws and prohibitions against Jews. He decided to leave Germany for Palestine in 1933, sending his wife, Julia, and son, Micha, along ahead of him. He saw clearly what was emerging in the German collective psyche and the dangers that lay ahead for the Jews. Remaining behind, Neumann requested an appointment with Jung in Zurich and began working with him and Tony Wolff that year, beginning on October 4, 1933, for the duration of seven months. When he departed Zurich in May 1934 for Tel Aviv he was twenty-nine years old.

Interestingly, Jung had visited Palestine in 1933 and found it quite chaotic, perhaps recognizing how difficult it would be for the Jews to carve out their independent state in that land. Jung writes to Neumann in 1938:

---

3   Ibid., 342.
4   Ibid., 354.

> I am right in the thick of it and am following the Palestinian
> question on a daily basis in the newspapers, and think often
> of my acquaintances there who have to live in this chaos.
> When I was in Palestine in 1933, I was unfortunately able
> to see what was coming all too clearly. I also foresaw great
> misfortune for Germany, even quite terrible things, but when
> it then shows up, it still seem unbelievable.[5]

By 1934, toward the end of his stay in Zurich, Neumann sent a letter
to Jung that began with his strong criticism of what Jung wrote in
his 1934 paper, "The State of Psychotherapy Today."[6] This paper is a
criticism of Freud's approach to therapy and reveals how Jung and his
Germanic psyche may have been misunderstood. Jung, in contrast to Freud,
emphasizes the importance of recognizing the subtle, unique differences
between people and criticizes Freud for reducing patients to an infantile
"nothing but" and falling back on the use of technique as opposed to
being "absolutely clear in his own mind that psychological treatment of
the sick is a relationship in which the doctor is involved quite as much
as the patient."[7] Jung maintains that in all neuroses there exist positive
elements that shed light on the health of the individual as well as what is
commonly seen as negative.

In his paper, Jung sternly criticizes Freud and his reductionist
technique:

> Psychoanalysis is evidently a technique behind which the
> human being vanishes, and which always remains the same
> no matter who practices it. Consequently, the psychoanalyst
> needs no self-knowledge and no criticism of his assumptions.
> Apparently the purpose of this training analysis is to make
> him not a human being but a correct applier of technique.[8]

---

5   Ibid., 145.
6   C. G. Jung, "The State of Psychotherapy Today" (1934), in *CW*, vol. 10 (Princeton, NJ: Princeton University Press, 1970), pars. 333–370.
7   Ibid., par. 352.
8   Ibid., par. 350.

As his antipathy builds, Jung suddenly shifts from discussing Freud to speaking in broad, general terms about Jews, comparing them to women who are physically weaker, "they have to aim at the chinks in the armour of their adversary, and thanks to this technique which has been forced on them through the centuries, the Jews themselves are best protected where others are most vulnerable."[9] Is it possible that Jung slipped into a complex here resulting from a wound left over from his relationship with Freud? Did he feel Freud was "protected" while he, Jung, was "vulnerable"?

Jung then continues to discuss the differences between Jews and Germanic peoples. This is where it becomes offensive to Neumann. Jung refers to the emergent movement out of the Germanic/Slavic psyche as having two sides: one that is pathological and the other that is potentially creative, "laboring at the future."[10] It is clear that Jung is quite taken with the potential he sees in the Germanic psyche as he describes its capacity to create new cultural forms, "seeds bursting with energy and capable of mighty expansion."[11] This line of thinking parallels his earlier statements on individuals' neuroses containing both negative and positive seeds, yet with his shift to speaking broadly about cultural groups he seems to have lost his subtle discernment. Jung asserts that the Germanic psyche carries the greatest, youthful potential while Jews as a group carry their shadow between the conscious and unconscious because of their older culture. While Jung reduces Jews to the European, assimilated, culture Jew he was familiar with, like Freud, he warns against using "Jewish categories" on Germanic-Slavic Christendom because, "their creative and intuitive depth of soul—has been explained as a morass of banal infantilism, while my own warning voice has for decades been suspected

---

9   Ibid., par. 353.
10   Ibid., par. 354.
11   Ibid., par. 353.

of anti-Semitism. This suspicion emanated from Freud."[12] One can clearly feel the animosity emanating from his writing. Is it Freud or Jews Jung criticizes, or are they both mixed together, which Neumann suspects?

Of course, Neumann would respond to this line of thinking with great disappointment and dismay, not understanding why this great man was overgeneralizing in an incorrect way and seemingly did not see what he and many others saw so clearly, "that it is also in the Germanic psyche (and in the Slavic one) that a mind-numbing cloud of filth, blood and rottenness is brewing."[13] Could it be that Jung's own complex blinded him? When one is caught in a complex one overgeneralizes, loses one's grounded balance, and gets caught by one side of an archetype.

With the rise of National Socialism out of the Germanic/Slavic psyche Jung saw a germ of an unknown potential catch fire. Steeped in his own feelings around Freudian psychology and having experienced himself as misunderstood and reduced to "nothing but" one might see how he came to give value to the new emerging spark out of the Germanic/Slavic psyche. Neumann takes issue with how Jung too broadly equates National Socialism with the Aryan-Germanic, and how he misunderstands and generalizes Jews. Jung says, "The Jew, who is something of a nomad, has never yet created a cultural form of his own and as far as we can see never will, since all his instincts and talents require a more or less civilized nation to act as host for their development."[14] Neumann took offense at Jung leaning here toward a "race-psychology," believing that all Jews should not be put into the same box with the lack of any in-depth exploration into Jewish culture, past and present. He speaks of the difference between the religious and the assimilated Jew, and the development of Zionism and Hasidism, for example, and makes very clear that "this Jewish renaissance seems to me to be more embryonic,

---

12   Ibid., par. 354.
13   Jung and Neumann, *Analytical Psychology in Exile*, 12.
14   Jung, "The State of Psychotherapy Today," *CW* 10, par. 353.

youthful and full of energy than the Nazi-rigid, brutally organized and stolid, extreme submissiveness of the Aryan revivals."[15]

It is striking how strong this young man is in his convictions and thinking. He catches Jung in a blind spot and challenges him on it. One wonders why Jung did not speak up about his misstatements and deeds at this point. We know Jung was later blacklisted by Hitler. During the war, he worked for Allen Dulles and the United States' Office of Strategic Services, now the CIA, as agent 488 helping to explain the psychology of Hitler. We don't know why communication stopped between Jung and Neumann between 1940 and 1945. In his paper "After the Catastrophe," Jung states:

> Clearly these misgivings came much too late; but even so, it is just conceivable that Hitler himself may have had good intentions at first, and only succumbed to the use of the wrong means, or the misuse of his means, in the course of his development … . But I should like to emphasize above all that it is part and parcel of the pathological liar's make-up to be plausible. Therefore it is no easy matter, even for experienced people, to form an opinion, particularly while the plan is still apparently in the idealistic stage. It is then quite impossible to foresee how things are likely to develop and Mr. Chamberlain's "give-it-a-chance" attitude seems to be the only policy.[16]

Jung had described Hitler as inhuman and must have known that his way was to deceive. Could Jung have been so easily deceived? Did he fall into his own blind spot? Was he too identified with the hopefulness of the Aryan-Germanic psyche, being Germanic himself? Was he blinded

---

15 Jung and Neumann, *Analytical Psychology in Exile*, 14.
16 C. G. Jung, "After the Catastrophe" (1945), in *CW*, vol. 10 (Princeton, NJ: Princeton University Press, 1970) par. 421.

by something with the potential for evil? Evil, the subject of "the finest and deepest of your books," as Neumann describes *Answer to Job*, was a clear preoccupation of Jung and Neumann and a frequent subject in their correspondence.[17] This seems to point to his need to understand the depths of this universal quandary. Gershom Scholem writes in a letter to Aniela Jaffé, in 1963, that Jung acknowledged to Leo Baeck: "Well, I slipped up." Jaffé concludes from this: "probably referring to the Nazis and his expectation that something great might after all emerge."[18]

Jung's Cultural Past

Jung grew up at a time at the end of the nineteenth century when the prevailing mindset was still influenced by both the German Enlightenment (1650–1800) and Romanticism (1815–1848). Jung studied both with great fervor, including the work of Kant, Hegel, Schelling, and Goethe. The difference between them was knowledge versus experience. Kant and Hegel encouraged Jews to give up their mantle of ancient culture, or "cult," and join the universal world of reason through dialectical logic. Schelling, on the other hand, was not a proponent of this extreme thinking. Instead he made it very clear that in contrast to logic, it is, as Mendes-Flohr writes, "by virtue of this mythic imagination that religion grasps the true, transcendent supra-rational nature of the Absolute Spirit" (p. 90). Furthermore, "the universally shared motifs of religious myths and symbols, Schelling argued, point to the universal nature of the human psychic and imaginative sensibility. By grounding religious experience of the Absolute Spirit in universal trans-temporal mythological structures," says Mendes-Flohr, "Schelling in effect challenged the logo-centric supersessionism of the Enlightenment" (p. 90).

---

17   See, for example, Jung and Neumann, *Analytical Psychology in Exile*, 271.
18   A. Jaffé, *From the Life and Work of C. G. Jung* (Einsiedeln, Switzerland: Daimon Verlag, 1989), 100.

Jung quotes Schelling, who coined the term *unconscious*, extensively throughout the *Collected Works* and indeed seems to be a proponent of his views, as seen in his own focus on imagination, experience, and symbolism. Jung railed against the Enlightenment and its focus on reason to the exclusion of all else. Jung's siding with Schelling is a clue to his thinking— pointing clearly to an inclusionary attitude, one that values ancient cultures and what has come before, mythology and all forms of religions, symbols and the nonrational, and individual experience. "Schelling was virtually the only one who did not voice derogatory opinions about Jews and Judaism" (p. 90). It is also interesting to note that Jung's grandfather on his mother's side, Samuel Preiswerk, was an early Proto-Zionist in Basel (see Ulrich Hoerni's contribution to this volume, p. 95-110).

So what then was Jung's blind spot? Was it that he was fascinated by the potential creative contents that can emerge out of the collective unconscious and therefore expressed his thoughts in broad sweeping generalized ways? At times, Neumann as well tended to sweeping generalizations, such as: "One must not forget that the Christian peoples have never deemed the Jews worthy of their conscious interest."[19] At other times, both Jung and Neumann focused on the importance of individual anomalies and propensities, clearly emphasizing the individual experience. What I found stunning in the correspondence, though, was how frequently Jung seemed to remain neutral, standing back and watching the opposite sides of an archetype or conflict play out as they would, rather than forming an opinion on one side or the other.

Jung's comments on Jewish character and Judaism point to a man who seemed in the early 1930s to be either naïve or lacking understanding. Neumann recognized this and took Jung to task for not studying Judaism as he did so many other religions and cultures.

---

19 Jung and Neumann, *Analytical Psychology in Exile*, 45.

Jung was a thinker who struggled with his feeling function, as we can see in the Red Book with his difficult journey into the Spirit of the Depths to find his soul and in relation to those around him. As he says of himself late in life in *Memories, Dreams, Reflections*:

> I have offended many people, for as soon as I saw that they did not understand me that was the end of the matter as far as I was concerned. I had to move on. I had no patience with people— aside from my patients. I had to obey an inner law which was imposed on me and left me no freedom of choice ... . I had to learn painfully that people continued to exist even when they had nothing more to say to me.[20]

He may have been more interested in the broader archetypal stirrings in German culture than German culture's effect on individual human beings. I can understand this interest; while appalled, I am fascinated by the shifting archetypal patterns that produced ISIS, at times overlooking the devastating consequences of individuals caught in the crossfire. Perhaps we would like to hold him to a higher standard than we hold ourselves. But just like everyone on this path, he as well had to struggle with his humanity, his opposites, and his own process of individuation.

Jewish Psychology

In 1937, when in Zurich, Neumann describes experiencing a "rush" of images that left him "now convinced of the authenticity of the phenomena."[21] It seems the reality of the psyche, as the earth spirit and transformed anima, broke through his rational mind, which seems to be confirmed by the images he describes in his dreams and visions around that time.

---

20   C. G. Jung, *Memories, Dreams, Reflections*, ed. Aniela Jaffé, trans. Richard and Clara Winston (New York: Pantheon Books, 1962), 356–357.

21   Jung and Neumann, *Analytical Psychology in Exile*, 131.

Two other important issues discussed in the correspondence are Jewish psychology and evil. Neumann encouraged Jung to study Judaism, specifically the Hasidic movement and Kabbalah. The focus of Neumann's early years was on this topic, and out of it emerged an as yet unpublished book in three or perhaps four parts with the overall title *The Roots of Jewish Consciousness* or *On the Depth Psychology of the Modern Jew.* Part one is *The Problem of Revelation in Jewish Antiquity.* Part two is *The Psychological Meaning of Hasidism,* and the third is *Religious Experience in Depth Analysis.* The first part studies the Jewish historical preconditions while the second studies the recent development of Hasidism as the bridge between the God-principle and the earth-principle, including a deeper understanding of the Shekhinah.

Neumann first framed his discussion of the development of Jewish psychology on the biblical story of Jacob and Esau, the warring brothers. As you remember, Jacob steals the birthright from Esau and therefore is entitled to his father's blessing. Neumann describes Jacob as being introverted and of the nature of the moon while Esau is extraverted and of the sun. The moon-like nature is interior-focused and worships YHWH while the sun nature is outer-focused on the material world, as well as connected to the hairy goat or the devil. The two reconcile in the end, and, as Neumann argues, it reflects the process of individuation, bringing the opposites together and integrating the shadow. Neumann's thinking on this topic, which developed in his correspondence with Jung, crystallized into Neumann's first book—only recently published.

Jung did take up the study of this material as is evident by the presence of books on Kabbalah in his library. According to a letter from Aniela Jaffé to Rivkah Schärf, he thanks her for the texts, although this was not mentioned in his letters to Neumann (p. 29). Nevertheless, in 1944 Jung had an important vision which places him in the garden of the pomegranates with the union of the male and female principles within the Godhead. This makes it clear what an impact the Jewish tradition and the Kabbalah had on his psyche! Jung writes in *Memories, Dreams, Reflections:*

For a time it seemed to me that she [the nurse] was an old Jewish woman, much older than she actually was, and that she was preparing ritual kosher dishes for me. When I looked at her, she seemed to have a blue halo around her head. I myself was, so it seemed, in the Pardes Rimmonim, the garden of pomegranates, and the wedding of Tifereth with Malchuth was taking place. Or else I was Rabbi Simon ben Jochai, whose wedding in the afterlife was being celebrated. It was the mystic marriage as it appears in the Cabbalistic tradition. I cannot tell you how wonderful it was … . At bottom it was I myself: I was the marriage. And my beatitude was that of a blissful wedding.[22]

In a letter dated November 15, 1939, Neumann writes to Jung about a dream he had that refers to the work of the *pardes*.[23] Neumann's discussion in this letter is on his struggle with the central Jewish problem of intuition that is linked to a rootlessness of the Jewish structure. He acknowledges that the symbolism of the Jew is consistent with the European, though it "would have been simpler if a specific symbolism could have been demonstrated." He saw something secular transpiring, pertaining to the individual as "revelation-center and realization-center of the Self." As he says, his "attempt to create the continuity through to the modern Jewish person from the openness to revelation of antiquity via the inner Hasidic revolution is … a new interpretation."[24] His work, then, came to circle "around the Y.H.W.H. earth opposite."[25]

---

22 Jung, *Memories, Dreams, Reflections*, 294.
23 Jung and Neumann, *Analytical Psychology in Exile*, 150. *Pardes* means paradise, orchard, grove, or garden. In the Talmud it refers to the dangers four sages have in entering the garden. One dies, another one loses his mind, the third one becomes a heretic, and the fourth one—Rabbi Akiva—enters and leaves the garden peacefully. *Pardes* serves as an acronym for the four levels of interpreting the Torah, from the concrete to the symbolic. The danger pertains to coming too close to God.
24 Jung and Neumann, *Analytical Psychology in Exile*, 149.
25 Ibid., 151–52.

This reveals the Hasidic influence on his thinking and his intuition of a new interpretation. He writes:

> In Hasidism, the last breakthrough of actual introverted Judaism, all these problems broadly came of age. The redemption of the "sparks" out of matter, for example, is, put psychologically, arguably the taking back of the world into internal space. In this way, everything, every action, every fulfillment of the law can lead to "higher union," to the encounter with Y.H.W.H., and so the structure of the world can be experienced as one that is at the same time "unified" and that is full of Y.H.W.H.[26]

Neumann, in the same letter, continues to say that YHWH is "constantly changing his manifestation, but at the same time he is always the same." And further,

> for me, Y.H.W.H. is not an archetype, but the "God" archetype is only an interchangeable theophany of Y.H.W.H. about which there is nothing more to be said, other than how he appears and what form his "so-called energetic structure" takes, being superior to the appearance itself.[27]

Angelica Löwe describes Neumann's perception of the Jewish exegesis as, "an introduction and initiation into the revelation of eternity in the midst of time" (as revelation is an ongoing process) and compares it to the Christian exegesis which aims at, "progress through time towards eternity" (where revelation comes at the end of time) (p. 396).

This reflects the differences in viewpoints between Judaism and Christianity—but not between Neumann and Jung. Both focus on real-time transformation taking place within the individual. One can gather

---

26   Ibid., 42.
27   Ibid., 49. Neumann does not punctuate the Tetragrammaton in the German original of these letters.

from Neumann's discussion that God for him is very real and beyond the laws of the archetypes. God changes manifestations or takes on different archetypal faces but is not identified with any one. This is similar to Brahma in Hindu theology, a conglomeration of gods making up the one.

For Jung, God in itself is unknowable and beyond the opposites. Psychologically, though, it can be described as the archetype of wholeness, the Self, containing all opposites. Humans perceive the manifestation of the archetype of wholeness as the "God-image." This image takes on different cultural forms. Since the archetype of wholeness contains everything, is there something beyond this? It seems both Jung and Neumann would say yes.

After writing the above monographs on Jewish psychology, Neumann's interests refocused on psychology in general. This may have had to do with the fact that the need in Israel after the war was acute with the arrival of Holocaust survivors and traumatized children who needed real-time care. He, in fact, certified only one Jungian analyst practicing with adults in Israel, Debora Kutzinski, while the rest were certified as child analysts.

After the War

From the end of 1940 to late in 1945 there was no correspondence between Erich Neumann and Jung for reasons that remain unclear. Nevertheless, Neumann remained acutely aware of what was taking place in Europe, and he was very busy with his increasing practice and his writing. Following the years of war in Europe, times were unsettled in Israel. The British mandate came to an end, and there was great uncertainty whether the new state, formed in 1948, would survive the attacks from neighboring countries. In fact, the house next door to the Neumann's was bombed in an incident in which one child died and eighteen were wounded.[28]

---

28 Neumann describes this in a letter to Jung, dated July 12, 1948; Jung and Neumann, *Analytical Psychology in Exile*, 226.

In 1945, Neumann sent Jung his manuscript, *Depth Psychology and the New Ethic,* which renewed their conversations. It is interesting that they did not talk about what went on in Europe during the war years. One can only speculate that sending Jung his book was a way of expressing his thoughts on the horror that took place, without falling into the devastating feeling of it. Both men were thinking types, and inferior feeling gets very messy. It is, nonetheless, present in a very deep way, just difficult to articulate.

Jung's last comments to Neumann in 1940 before their lapse of communication for five years included this: "As you know, we live here in Switzerland on an island with reduced heating. Otherwise there is nothing new to report."[29] There had been no mention of *Kristallnacht* in 1938; this was as evocative as he got. Then in 1945 when they resumed communication Neumann states, "I am writing nothing about the times, nothing about Palestine. My inner dialectic indicated the only possible path for me. At these times, the general human condition moves me and this only. How else could one bear it."[30] Jung added, in his response: "While we are still living on our cultural island as before, everything around us is nothing but destruction, physically as well as morally. To do something reasonable oneself, you have to close your eyes. Germany is indescribably rotten."[31] We know the horrors of this war and the destruction that it left in its wake, and we can only imagine its impact on the individual psyche.

Conflict in Zurich and Discussion of Evil

I begin this next section with a quote from Jung: "I would like to avoid the emergence of some sort of orthodoxy that pushes out other types of

---

29   Jung and Neumann, *Analytical Psychology in Exile*, 158.
30   Ibid., 163.
31   Ibid., 171.

individuality."[32] In 1948 Neumann presented a paper at Eranos and at the newly formed Jung Institute on *The New Ethic* (published in German in 1949), which created a huge stir. It was rejected, vilified, treated as an apostasy, thought to be anti-Christian and to deviate too far from Jung. Jung, of course, after reading it saw this coming and actually said to Neumann beforehand, "I cannot conceal from you my secret pleasure … your writings will be a *petra scandali*, but also the powerful impetus for future developments. For this I am most deeply grateful to you."[33]

Many in the Jungian world were more interested in following Jung, sticking to their own perceived guidelines of what Jungian psychology was all about. Not Neumann; he was an original thinker and for that he was appreciated greatly by Jung. Thus, particularly his lectures evoked strong criticisms by Jolanda Jacobi, C. A. Meier, and Toni Wolff.

The C. G. Jung Institute in Küsnacht was established in 1948 with Jung as its nominal president and C. A. Meier as vice president. Neumann's hope was to publish *The Origins and History of Consciousness*, which was initially selected to be the first institute publication but subsequently rejected by C. A. Meier. Meier and others felt it would dwarf any books that followed. There were myriad criticisms about it, especially that Neumann too neatly formed a system, as if contrary to Jung's theory. The dislike of *The New Ethic* didn't help this situation. Instead of Neumann's book being published first, C. A. Meier published his own, much smaller book, *Healing Dream and Ritual: Ancient Incubation and Modern Psychotherapy*.

Supportive of Neumann's writings, Jung stood up for Neumann and helped him get *The Origins and History of Consciousness* published by Rascher in German and by Kegan Paul in English, instead. What is apparent is that there was a strong sense of sibling rivalry from the Zurich Jungians

---

32   Ibid., 246.
33   Ibid., 237.

against Neumann; he was effectively ostracized from participating there for many years, and he also chose no longer to put himself into such a disagreeable environment. An extremely introverted man, he kept to himself much of the time except for his very active practice. He found himself quite alone in Tel Aviv. He had an early but unpleasant encounter there with Jungian analyst James Kirsch, who had arrived shortly before Neumann but then, not long after Neumann's arrival, left Palestine for London and then went on to Los Angeles, where he was one of the founders of the C. G. Jung Institute. For all his admiration for Zionism, Kirsch ultimately could not tolerate the roughness of the country.

Neumann's communications and periodic visits to Zurich to work with Jung were a lifeline for him. Overall there were sixty-two letters from Neumann to Jung, forty-six from Jung to Neumann. Later, from 1947 on and at the initial recommendation of Jung, Eranos became a supportive intellectual *temenos* for Neumann. His first paper was "Mystical Man," presented in 1948. Because of his well-received participation there, Olga Fröbe-Kapteyn, the founder of Eranos, asked Neumann to write a monograph using the picture archive she had created.[34] This grew into a book, *The Great Mother,* and additional papers that formed the foundation for his other books. Eranos provided Neumann with the broad intellectual environment that he found most satisfying.

Neumann, the ever-sensitive one, did not feel that Jung defended him sufficiently against the criticism. In a later letter to Olga Fröbe-Kapteyn on May 22, 1949, he understood this as a manifestation of the broad sweep of anti-Semitism that infected Europe at that time. In fact, the Analytical Psychology Club of Zurich had a quota to limit the number of Jewish members until it was revoked in 1950, at the insistence of Jung, after Sigmund Hurwitz refused to join because of it. Much later,

---

34   Her picture archive later became ARAS, the Archive for Research in Archetypal Symbolism. It is located at the C. G. Jung Center of New York and is now online at www.aras.org.

Jerome Bernstein asked the president at the time to apologize for this and ran up against anger and resistance, although acquiescing in the end.[35] An apology and atonement were offered in 1993.

Neumann was once again criticized at his lecture on *Amor and Psyche*, and upon hearing about it, Jung gave a group of colleagues from the institute a solid tongue-lashing:

> One should not have discussed the problems in public. It is so finely nuanced that it is not possible to sort it out in a discussion. But above all, one can't load these things onto N. in public. [. . .] Besides, one must not forget that he has been in Palestine on his own for 9 years. When he worked with me back then, many things which you are learning today had not even been uttered. When he left, we did not yet know much that we know today. And besides, we are not dealing with a theory, but a human being. You cannot do this right in the middle of a course. I would like to see the animus in you if you were to be corrected in a lecture. If I had been there, I would have attempted to rectify some things. But I would have said it only once and then shut up. N. is very sensitive, easily gets upset. But he is a creative man. And one should not upset such people. Leave him alone.[36]

One can see how their relationship was challenging to both men, but the final sensibility is expressed unequivocally by Jung when he is reported to have said, "I have a huge correspondence, see innumerable people but have only two real friends with whom I can speak about my own difficulties; the one is Erich Neumann and he lives in Israel and the other is Father Victor White in England."[37]

---

35   Jerome Bernstein, personal communication, 2011.
36   Jung and Neumann, *Analytical Psychology in Exile*, 288, note 518.
37   C. G. Jung and Victor White, *The Jung-White Letters*, ed. Ann Conrad Lammers and Adrian Cunningham (London: Routledge, 2007), 334.

The New Ethic certainly challenged many established notions of the time, and before Jung agreed to write the foreword to the book he gave Neumann a list of points to consider as supplementary suggestions. Jung's position was different from Neumann's, who points out that this has to do with the fact that Jung is an Occidental Christian while Neumann, a Jew, is more of the East.

Even though Neumann's book, *The New Ethic*, ran into severe criticism in Zurich, Jung thought Neumann's thinking was brilliant, and he modified or deleted a portion of his paper "A Psychological View of Conscience," as a result of Neumann's responses to his criticism of *The New Ethic*.[38]

While agreeing with most of *The New Ethic*, Jung begins his discussion of the book by stating that there is a difference in language. He points out that there is no new ethic, that what Neumann is proposing is the same old ethic, more differentiated and with fewer illusions.[39] Jung ends by saying he is unsure what is right as he does not have a clear answer and will have to leave the dilemma to God himself. His position is that evil will befall us and there is really nothing we can do as it is unconscious. He says:

> Evil is and always remains the thing one knows one should not do. Man overestimates himself unfortunately in this respect: he thinks it is within his discretion to intend good or evil. He can persuade himself of this, but in reality he is, in view of the greatness of these opposites, simply too small and too unconscious to be able to choose the one or the other in free will and under all circumstances. It is much more the case that he does or does not do the good that he would like to for overwhelming reasons, and that in the same way, evil just happens to him like misfortune.

---

38   C. G. Jung, "A Psychological View of Conscience" (1958), in *CW*, vol. 10 (Princeton, NJ: Princeton University Press, 1970), pars. 825–857.

39   Jung and Neumann, *Analytical Psychology in Exile*, 329.

Ethics is that which makes it impossible for him to do evil intentionally and encourages him to do good—and indeed often with little success. I.e., he can do good and cannot avoid evil, although his ethic causes him to test the powers of his will in this regard. In reality he is the victim of these powers ... under no circumstances can he absolutely avoid sin, as he also on the other hand may hope to be able to do good. Now, as evil is unavoidable, so one never completely evades sin and it is a fact that one must accept.[40]

Jung frames this in an ethical light: Since we cannot avoid sin, how can we deal with this situation? From a Christian standpoint, one accepts the fact of sin and lives with it, trying to be as good as possible for the Lord and also morally substantial to appear good to others. Earlier in his list of suggested revisions Jung emphasized "that the shadow or the unconscious absolutely cannot be eliminated and subject to consciousness. We can only learn how a grain of corn must behave between a hammer and anvil."[41] This is actually quite a pessimistic point of view.

Neumann received this criticism and responded strongly with impressive conviction. For him, he said, "*The New Ethic* was the attempt to process a series of phantasies that roughly corresponded time-wise with the extermination of the Jews, and in which the problem of evil and justice was being tossed around in me."[42] Then he had a profound vision after which the world looked different:

I seemed to be commissioned to kill the apeman in the profound primal hole. As I approached him, he was hanging, by night, sleeping on the cross above the abyss, but his— crooked—single eye was staring into the depths of this abyss. While it at first seemed that I was supposed to blind him, I all

---

40   Ibid., 327–328.
41   Ibid., 361.
42   Ibid., 331.

of a sudden grasped his "innocence," his dependence on the single eye of the godhead, which was experiencing the depths through him, which was a human eye. Then, very abridged, I sank down opposite this single eye, jumped into the abyss, but was caught by the Godhead, which carried me on the "wings of his heart." After that, this single eye opposite the apeman closed and it opened on my forehead. (Bit difficult to write this, but what should one do.)[43]

Neumann discussed evil in relation to his psyche's clarification in the dream as being something he had to experience—it was not sin but a "necessary action." In his vision, he jumps into the abyss, rather than falling. He is held by something greater in all his actions, both good and bad. Sin becomes irrelevant in relation to this "new divine." A new morality compels one to integrate as much of the unconscious or the opposites that are God as one is able. This includes evil.

Jung remained concerned because of what he recognized as the limited consciousness-forming ability of humans and therefore believed the actual transformation of evil takes place in the unconscious, through the changing symbols in relation to the God-image and the Self.

What Is Consciousness?

This idea leads to an important shift in their discussion about whether God is unconscious or conscious. Jung seems to suggest God is unconscious and needs humans to reveal consciousness. Neumann muses, "If we were the unconscious complexes of God that are endowed with consciousness and the possibility of consciousness, our task of consciousness and integration would also be sacred."[44] Neumann goes further in wondering if humans' relationship to God is similar to all the cells and organisms

---

43   Ibid.
44   Ibid., 344.

that make up the human body. If so, he ponders, do the infinite small experiences of humans add up to absolute knowledge? What about the act of revelation, which Neumann wrote about from a historical Jewish perspective in the 1940s? It seems here that revelation reverses course, and humans, in contrast to common notions, enlighten God. With this possibility, both Jung and Neumann have arrived at similar conclusions.

Just a year and a half before his death, Neumann clarifies his thinking in this discussion on the consciousness of God after reading Jung's chapters in *Memories, Dreams, Reflections,* "Life after Death" and "Late Thoughts." If God incarnates in humans through likeness as an ego-Self, what is significant is that becoming conscious leads to the birth of the new divine. The creator and the Self create new experiences that did not exist beforehand. It is the ego-Self that carries the possibility for consciousness, for incarnation, and for change as it becomes conscious. Neumann refers to this as "the 'actualization of messianism' in individuation."[45] What is most relevant is the development of the individual, the conception of the archetype, and absolute knowledge as a counterpoint to Darwinist notions of haphazard transformations. The way to meaning and consciousness has not been found by accident but through the individual as the "unit of salvation."[46]

Returning to the problem of evil, Neumann proposes that "the light wishes to illuminate, it creates dark bodies with the possibility that they will radiate light."[47] In other words, consciousness can emerge from either light or dark, good or evil. Our life experiences that generate consciousness come from what we would consider creative as well as destructive. This may explain in part why, during the war, Neumann outrageously stated that the sacrifice of millions of Jews could result in a positive outcome for Jewish cultural development.

---

45   Ibid., 345.
46   Ibid., 346.
47   Ibid.

Two statements he made in the correspondence suggest he may have done something contrary to the prevailing morality, and in so doing "sinned" for a greater good, namely, his conscious development.[48] This goes back to the idea that each unique life lived contributes to God's consciousness. The ideas of evil and consciousness keep interweaving in their conversation, pointing to how closely connected they are.

We know that Jung lived according to the deep interior morality of the Self as opposed to the collective moral/ethical code of behavior. Jung, in response to Neumann, reminds him that the idea of the existence of a conscious God is not easily debated, pointing out that creation itself was a random, chaotic act of formless gas organizing itself into a circular order. He includes the creation of archetypes in this process. He explains that order is distinct from meaning and that without humans there is no ability to detect meaning. Through creation, the psychic (inner) and the physical (outer) are both present in the psychoid. Jung said, "It is through the archetype that we come closest to this early, irrepresentable, psychoid stage of conscious development; indeed, the archetype itself gives us direct intimations of it."[49] The psychoid is not psyche or matter alone but the neutral state of both together. Since we cannot conclude that the psyche, which is a higher synthesis, can emerge by chance alone, we need a hypothesis of latent meaning to explain it. Conversely, Jung says, "We do need the synchronistic experiences to be able to justify the hypothesis of a latent meaning that is independent of consciousness."[50] Synchronicity consists of acausal phenomena that can be seen as mere chance until meaning is attributed to them. The individual's own lived

---

48 Neumann's first statement is: "To speak for myself, if I now fully or approximately understand the breaking in of the anima experience into my life (and my marriage) . . ." The second statement is: "I have subsequently had to do 'evil,' for these images are to be fulfilled personally, but I did not experience it as a sin but as a necessary action. That has changed nothing in the suffering I have caused and into which I have fallen, but my feeling experience was different." Jung and Neumann, *Analytical Psychology in Exile*, 92 and 332, respectively.

49 Jung and Neumann, *Analytical Psychology in Exile*, 349–350.

50 Ibid., 350.

experience and awareness of something other is the point of conjunction between meaning and synchronicity.

Finally, Jung moves on to discuss two possibilities for the genesis of consciousness. One is that humans are attributed with a latent ability for reflective consciousness that gives us a reason for being. The second is that latent meaning is attributed to the creator through a conscious plan of creation. If this second one is true, Jung wonders why the creator would bother creating such a plan when the creator already knows the outcome? Why should the creator create a second inferior consciousness alongside its omniscience? He puts it quite bluntly when he imagines "billions of dull little mirrors of which he knows in advance what the picture will be like that they will reflect back."[51] Jung's conclusion from this exercise in logic and from the myth of the *incarnatio* is that God is similar to or the same as humans, in other words, as unconscious. For that reason God felt compelled to become human and offer himself up for sacrifice to humans to become conscious.

Conclusion

This was the end of the substance of Jung and Neumann's conversations. Neumann mentioned becoming ill in his last letter in September 1959 to Jung, and a year later he died, closely followed by Jung's death. They were both pondering the meaning of life and consciousness at the end of their lives, one coming from a Christian starting point and the other Jewish, which seemed to influence their perceptions. At this point in their lives, Jung was a tired old man, while in reading Neumann the reader feels his pressure to make sense of life as death approached prematurely. I hope these two good friends were able to continue this discussion beyond the veil, wherever they are, perhaps with the advantage of the greater consciousness of God at their disposal. I certainly cannot include the

---

51   Ibid.

increasing consciousness of humans, since life as it is playing out seems to dispute this possibility.

Neumann and Kirsch in Tel Aviv: A Case of Sibling Rivalry?

Ann C. Lammers

Now that the Jung-Neumann correspondence is happily available for study, many things have come to light. As editor of the Jung-Kirsch correspondence, I've been asked to comment on the relationship between James Kirsch and Erich Neumann, and their respective relationships with Jung. What strikes one immediately, when reading the letters from 1934 and 1935 in which Kirsch and Neumann mention each other, is the feeling of intense competition between these two Jungian disciples. At first glance, their relationship resembles nothing so much as sibling rivalry. The original impetus for their competition seems to have come from Kirsch; but, as we shall see, Neumann also gave as good as he got.

In May 1934, during one of the most intense exchanges between Kirsch and Jung, Jung asked Kirsch to speak to Neumann, now living in Tel Aviv, about a planned exchange of letters between them on the topic of Jewish culture.[1] As Martin Liebscher comments in his introduction to *Analytical Psychology in Exile*, it must have been a trial to Kirsch to carry this message to Neumann, as he probably thought he himself should have

---

1   C. G. Jung and J. Kirsch, *The Jung-Kirsch Letters: The Correspondence of C. G. Jung and James Kirsch*, ed. Ann Conrad Lammers, trans. U. Egli and Ann Conrad Lammers (London: Routledge, 2011), 45, 47.

been Jung's primary interlocutor on the subject.[2] And indeed, Kirsch's reply expressed his resentment: "In closing, I would like to inform you that Dr. Neumann, who for some time apparently has been living in Tel Aviv, just around the corner from my place, has not yet found an occasion to get in touch with me."[3]

While it was true that Julia Neumann had been living in Tel Aviv for several months when Kirsch wrote these lines, Erich Neumann had arrived there just a few weeks before. One might think that Kirsch, the established professional, now living in Tel Aviv for more than six months, would have reached out to his newly arrived colleague, rather than waiting, peevishly, for Neumann to contact him. But his expectations may have been based on traditional European hierarchy, which dictated that a junior colleague should make the first call.

Let us recall the early professional lives of James Kirsch and Erich Neumann, with the patterns of a sibling relationship in mind. Kirsch was four years older than Neumann. Partly due to the good fortune of being born earlier, he had a professional advantage in having gained his medical license before Hitler's rise to power. He set up his private psychiatric practice in Berlin in 1926, met Jung in early 1929, and began analytic work with him that summer. Neumann, on the other hand, had been deprived of his medical license by National Socialist laws that prevented him from doing an internship. He met Jung in Berlin in late June 1933 and began his analysis and training with him that fall. Thus Kirsch not only held higher status as a licensed psychiatrist, he also had a four-year lead as a Jungian analyst. In addition, Kirsch had received Jung's blessing for two brief lectures he had written about Judaism.[4]

---

2   C. G. Jung and Erich Neumann, *Analytical Psychology in Exile: The Correspondence of C. G. Jung and Erich Neumann*, ed. Martin Liebscher (Princeton, NJ: Princeton University Press, 2015), xxiv.

3   Jung and Kirsch, *The Jung-Kirsch Letters*, 53.

4   J. Kirsch, "Das Problem des modernen Juden" (lecture, Psychological Club, Zurich, October 4, 1930; unpublished typescript, Library of the Psychological Club, Zurich); and "The Jewish Image of the World" ["Das Weltbild des Juden"] (1931), in *The Jung-Kirsch Letters*, 15–16.

These facts were the external basis for Kirsch's claim to authority. An even more important factor may have been his unconscious, lifelong identification with the Self.[5]

In his letter to Jung in June 1934, Kirsch made an odd reproach against Neumann, saying that a year before, Neumann had called himself "the only Jungian analyst in Palestine": "To be ignored in this manner does not really surprise me since—as I mentioned to Fräulein Wolff in Berlin—he was already describing himself in June 1933 as the only Jungian analyst in Palestine."[6] If Neumann used such words in June 1933, he can only have been speculating about the future. At that moment there were no Jungian analysts working in Palestine/Israel. Neither Kirsch nor Neumann had yet left Berlin, though they would each leave for Switzerland in a matter of weeks. In June 1933, Neumann was just planning the intensive work that would, he hoped, make him an analyst. But now, having accused Neumann of shunning him, Kirsch explained such behavior by implying that the younger man was suffering from a nearly delusional inflation. Remember the context: Kirsch had just learned that Jung wanted Neumann (not Kirsch) to exchange letters with him about Judaism. Kirsch's shadow projection, at this moment, suggests his painful insecurity.

In their respective articles published in the Berlin Zionist paper, *Jüdische Rundschau*, both Kirsch and Neumann were attempting to clear Jung's name after his published statements in the December 1933 and February 1934 issues of the *Zentralblatt* had raised troubling questions about his attitudes toward Nazi Germany and the Jews. The intention of both writers was to make Jung once again trustworthy to Jewish readers.

---

5 On this aspect of Kirsch's personal psychology, see the final exchange of letters between Kirsch and Jung (Jung and Kirsch, *The Jung-Kirsch Letters*, 256f and 261f); see also a brief memoir which Kirsch wrote in old age (J. Kirsch, "Reflections at Age Eighty-Four," in *A Modern Jew in Search of a Soul*, ed. J. M. Spiegelman and A. Jacobson [Phoenix, AZ: Falcon Press, 1986], 149f.

6 Jung and Kirsch, *The Jung-Kirsch Letters*, 53.

Kirsch even hoped to restore Jung's book sales in Palestine.[7] But their articles presented discrepant interpretations of Jung and of Judaism. The particulars of the argument between Kirsch and Neumann will occupy us below.

When Neumann's *Rundschau* article appeared, Kirsch was evidently stung. He would have been even more so if he had seen Jung's letter to Neumann in August 1934, in which Jung agreed with Neumann's criticisms.[8] Kirsch defended himself with a brief essay he called "Conclusion [*Schlusswort*], for the Palestinian Public," expanding and clarifying the positions with which Neumann had taken issue.[9] Kirsch's "Conclusion" was not published, but he had the satisfaction of sending it to Jung and presumably also to Neumann.

At this point, in early summer 1934, Eva Kirsch entered the fray, attacking Neumann for being so rude as to publish a critical response to a Jungian colleague. We know about her intervention because Neumann described it to Jung, with understandable concern:

> By the way—something else. Mrs. Kirsch informed me at the end of a detailed conversation about my response, which confirmed my impressions of Dr. Kirsch's essay, that I had gone against the comment of the Jungian analysts by responding in public. I replied that I considered my response to be objectively necessary and important, and that I am not willing to retract factual material out of affiliations unknown to me ... . I'd like to ask you to tell me if I have behaved incorrectly. I do believe I can communicate with Dr. Kirsch within certain limits, but for me he is anything but authoritative, although, as Mrs. Kirsch informed me, in your opinion, he articulated the best thinking on the Jewish

---

7   Ibid., 41.
8   Jung and Neumann, *Analytical Psychology in Exile*, 51.
9   Jung and Kirsch, *The Jung-Kirsch Letters*, 54ff.

problem years ago, and has been authorized to educate Jungian analysts, and his opinion coincides with yours, for example, on the Yahweh complex, the Christ complex, and on collective neurosis. I very much strive for objectivity; I see much in these issues very differently from Dr. Kirsch, and would like to find out for myself whether your opinion deviates so much from mine … . I have considered myself (and still do) to be very attached to you and your work—does this oblige me to a public conformity with your students?[10]

The claims that Eva Kirsch reportedly made for her husband were inflated; but one might argue that they had some historical basis. First, in late 1930 Kirsch had delivered a lecture to the Psychological Club in Zurich, "The Problem of the Modern Jew," which interested the audience so much that he was invited to deliver it a second time.[11] Jung seems to have thought well of it, too, for he requested a copy for himself.[12] Second, preserved in Jung's archive we find another brief lecture by Kirsch, "The Jewish Image of the World," written in early 1931.[13] In it Kirsch refers to Jung's concept of "earth-boundness" (Jung, 1927) but argues, in distinction to Jung, that the roots of Judaism are, and have always been, grounded not in the land but in God.[14] Jung approvingly called this piece "your meaty lecture" and instructed his secretary to keep it for reference.[15] Indeed, this is the first document by Kirsch that Jung seems to have preserved.

Eva Kirsch went wrong, however, in the hierarchical assumption that she apparently shared with her husband. Judging from Neumann's account, she believed that Jung had given final approval to Kirsch's interpretations, awarding his opinions about Judaism a sort of canonical

---

10   Jung and Neumann, *Analytical Psychology in Exile*, 21.
11   Jung and Kirsch, *The Jung-Kirsch Letters*, 10, note 32.
12   Ibid., 17.
13   Ibid., 15f.
14   C. G. Jung, "Die Erdbedingtheit der Psyche," in *Mensch und Erde*, ed. Hermann Keyserling (Darmstadt: Otto Reichl Verlag, 1927).
15   Jung and Kirsch, *The Jung-Kirsch Letters*, 17.

status, after which there could be no further, or competing, revelation. Her position was apparently based on the assumption that there existed a Jewish-Jungian orthodoxy, protected by a circle of believers. Neumann thus asked Jung if there was just one true interpretation of Jung's psychology and one authorized group of interpreters. Jung's reply, on August 12, 1934, gave him the answer: "Above all, be assured that there is no secret society of Jungian disciples—the Word has been freely given to all."[16]

Jung returned to the problem of quasi-religious orthodoxy in his letter of February 19, 1935:

> What you write about Kirsch sounds not unfamiliar to me, unfortunately. I really have the impression that you are seeing this all too correctly. I have such an awkward feeling about both of them that for a long time I could hardly touch the Kirsches' letter[s] from Tel Aviv.[17] It is indeed a very pathetic story. *I can only tell you how glad I am, firstly that I have not started a religion, and secondly that I have not founded a church.*[18]

Although Jung's letters to Neumann show that he was sometimes at wits' end with Kirsch, he held both his Jewish "sons" in a consistently respectful gaze, depriving neither Kirsch nor Neumann of positive regard. His letters to Kirsch never betrayed the exasperation we now know he sometimes felt. For example, referring to the period between November 1933 and February 1934, he confessed to Neumann that "for a long time I could hardly touch the Kirsches' letters from Tel Aviv." And yet, when he did break silence in February 1934, Jung was entirely reassuring toward Kirsch: "There's nothing to be concerned about on my side."[19] And in his next letter to Kirsch (dated

---

16   Jung and Neumann, *Analytical Psychology in Exile*, 51.
17   Martin Liebscher kindly informed me that Jung's original letter has an error here, presumably a typist's mistake: "die Kirsch'schen Brief" (for "Briefe") (personal communication, April 7, 2015). It is clear that Kirsch sent Jung at least one letter from Tel Aviv which Jung did not preserve, and to which his reply was delayed (Jung and Kirsch, *The Jung-Kirsch Letters*, 39).
18   Jung and Neumann, *Analytical Psychology in Exile*, 89; emphasis added.
19   Jung and Kirsch, *The Jung-Kirsch Letters*, 39.

May 26, 1934), he let it be understood that, in his mind, a normal, collegial relationship existed between Kirsch and Neumann and that he was warmly inclined toward both. So he urged, "When you see Dr. Neumann, please greet him from me and remind him that I am waiting to hear from him."[20] Kirsch may not have felt reassured, but he did deliver the message.[21]

Remembering the interpersonal dynamics of Neumann and Kirsch, let us look at the content of their dueling 1934 articles in *Jüdische Rundschau*. Kirsch's essay was published first.[22] When Neumann's followed a few weeks later, he took aggressive aim at several of Kirsch's statements.[23] On first glance, it seems he could have taken a more conciliatory tone. Common ground existed, for example, in the two men's respect for the writings of the prophets, their use of the concept of sin, their dislike of what they saw as Freud's overemphasis on the shadow (what might be called his pathologizing tendency), and their common dependence on certain biblical scholars.[24] With caveats, Neumann might even have seconded Kirsch's statement: "There is a still larger task before us, to rediscover in the soul the living connection with the primal powers."[25] Neumann, like Kirsch, was concerned about the estrangement of individual Jews from any direct personal encounter with the divine.[26]

---

20   Ibid., 47.

21   Jung and Neumann, *Analytical Psychology in Exile*, 19.

22   J. Kirsch, "Die Judenfrage in der Psychotherapie: Einige Bemerkungen zu einem Aufsatz von C. G. Jung," *Jüdische Rundschau,* no. 43 (May 29, 1934), 11; reprinted as: "The Jewish Question in Psychotherapy: Some Remarks on an Essay by C. G. Jung," trans. A. C. Lammers, *Jung Journal: Culture & Psyche* 6, no. 4 (2012): 78–84.

23   Erich Neumann, "Die Judenfrage in der Psychotherapie," *Jüdische Rundschau,* no. 48 (June 15, 1934), 5; reprinted in Jung and Neumann, *Analytical Psychology in Exile*, 355–56.

24   For example, both Kirsch and Neumann cite with approval Friedrich Häussermann's book on Old Testament prophecy, *Wortempfang und Symbol in der alttestamentlichen Prophetie* (1932).

25   Kirsch, "The Jewish Question," 80.

26   For Neumann, this spiritual estrangement was not merely a function of exilic (*Galut*) experience. He traced it to the very foundation of Judaism, the Sinai Event: "Es ist ein fuer die Geschichte des Judentums entscheidendes Phaenomen, dass das Volk als Ganzes nicht in den Sinaischmelzofen einbezogen werden konnte" ["That the people as a whole could not be included in the smelting furnace of Sinai is a decisive phenomenon for Jewish history"] (Erich Neumann, *Ursprungsgeschichte des jüdischen Bewusstseins* [*On the origins and history of Jewish consciousness*], [unpublished typescript, 1934–40], 27, trans. ACL). This theme is central to the first part of Neumann's long, unpublished work, which he worked on in the 1930s. He gave the whole work various titles, including "The Origins and History of Jewish Consciousness" and "The Depth Psychology of the Modern Jew" (see Jung and Neumann, *Analytical Psychology in Exile*, 156).

Instead of embracing their points of agreement, however, Neumann energetically differentiated himself from Kirsch. First, he disputed Kirsch's theory that Freud's psychology had been distorted by experiences of the *"Galut"* (exile). Jewish emphasis on the shadow goes back to the prophets, Neumann argued, "and if one misconstrues this fundamental fact as a trait of Galut psychology, one is not doing Judaism any favors."[27]

Neumann then disagreed with Kirsch on a related point; and here we discover a fundamental opposition between them. Kirsch had distinguished between the "phenotype" of the Galut Jew and the "genotype" of authentic Judaism. Neumann sharply disagreed with this distinction:

> We all belong to "the phenotype of the Jew living in exile from the shekinah," i.e., of the Jew as he is, but we also do not need to take flight into the image of a nonexistent "real" "actual" Jew. It is a false path to emphasize "a special link between the Jew and the eternal source," even if it may once have existed.[28]

In making his distinction between the phenotype (historical particularity) and the genotype (eternal truth) of Judaism, Kirsch had privileged the latter, positing it as an ideal form of what it means to be Jewish. This ideal form, Kirsch insisted, was a desirable alternative to the distorted, exilic psychology of modern Jews, tragically estranged from the presence of God. In contrast to this quasi-Platonic ideal, Neumann's intrinsic existentialism not only privileged "the Jew as he is" but also declared that the "real" or "actual" Jew, Kirsch's supposed genotype, simply did not exist.[29] Here we are looking not at the personal friction of sibling rivals,

---

27 Jung and Neumann, *Analytical Psychology in Exile*, 355.
28 Ibid., 356.
29 My appreciation of Neumann's existentialism began in conversation with Professor Tamar Kron. She has also shared with me a lecture she coauthored with David Wieler, in which they persuasively link Neumann's existentialism to both his European education and his study of Buber's dialogical philosophy. T. Kron and D. Wieler, "Erich Neumann: A Jungian Dialogical Existentialist" (lecture, IAAP Congress, Copenhagen, August 2013; unpublished typescript).

but at a profound dispute between two thinkers, based on irreducible, philosophical commitments.[30]

When Kirsch wrote his "Conclusion," defending his article against Neumann's criticisms, he emphasized his genotype idea in a way that further defined their basic differences. He wrote:

> I am (in contrast with Jung) of the opinion that it is particularly damaging and dangerous for us to destroy the connection with the unconscious as our creative original foundation. I emphasize this connection with the original foundation because *the timeless type of the Jew* has always expressed even the negative on the basis of his connection with the Eternal.[31]

Kirsch's phrase, "the timeless type of the Jew," suggests a quasi-Platonic or essentialist cast of thought, in contrast with Neumann's phenomenology. As we have seen, Neumann insists that there is no alternative to historically shaped, immediate reality. If the exilic Jewish experience is tragic, it is nevertheless the real experience of real people. This is where we must start, Neumann maintains, in the search for psychic healing. In defense of Jung (and in further distinction from Kirsch), Neumann wrote this trenchant comment:

> Jung is not disputing that the Jews of the Bible saw and lived the "greater aspect of the human soul," but his work with the contemporary Jewish person has allowed him to see a clear and fateful tendency to repress this greater aspect, and this is what the issue is today.[32]

From this brief comparison of their writings for the *Jüdische Rundschau* in 1934, I hope it is clear that Neumann and Kirsch were not merely jealous

---

30 It goes beyond the scope of this paper to explore the impact of Kirsch's essentialism and Neumann's existentialism on their understandings of Jung's psychology. One would expect to find important differences, for example, in their respective approaches to archetypal theory.

31 Jung and Kirsch, *The Jung-Kirsch Letters*, 56; emphasis added.

32 Jung and Neumann, *Analytical Psychology in Exile*, 356.

siblings, sparring for Jung's favor. A pattern of personal competition may have been part of what drove them apart during their brief time as neighbors in Tel Aviv. But they also inhabited conflicting philosophical territories, the implications of which could fruitfully be explored in greater depth.

PART II. CULTURAL BACKGROUNDS

German *Kultur* and the Discovery of the Unconscious: The Promise and Discontents of the German-Jewish Experience

Paul Mendes-Flohr

In his memoirs, the late German literary critic Marcel Reich-Ranicki, a survivor of the Warsaw Ghetto, tells that during his internment in that accursed way station to Auschwitz he was invited to join a few others to listen to phonographic recordings on a gramophone that one of them managed to bring into the ghetto. Among the recordings was one by the violinist Yehudi Menuhin, playing the first movement of Mozart's Concerto no. 3 in G Major. The elegant mastery of Menuhin's rendition left Reich-Ranicki "speechless" and, for a fleeting moment, lifted the dark clouds of doom and despair. Years later, after the war, he met Menuhin by chance in of all places Peking. Reich-Ranicki asked Menuhin what he was doing in the Chinese metropolis. He answered briefly: "Playing Beethoven and Brahms with the local orchestra. And what are you doing here?" "I am giving lectures on Goethe and Thomas Mann." Menuhin was silent, but not for long: "Ah well, we're Jews, of course." After a moment he added: "That we travel from country to country, spreading German music and German literature, and interpreting it—that's good and how it should be."[1]

---

1 Marcel Reich-Ranicki, *The Author of Himself: The Life of Marcel Reich-Ranicki* (London: Weidenfeld & Nicolson, 2001), 376.

The Jews' abiding devotion to German culture reaches back to the beginnings of their emancipation in the late eighteenth century. The fact that the most passionate and vocal advocates of liberating the Jews from the confines and indignities of the medieval ghettos were the intellectuals who promoted the Enlightenment and the rule of universal, humanistic values decisively determined the course of German-Jewish history. In their unyielding struggle to open the gates of the ghettos, the votaries of the Enlightenment signaled that their efforts would be greatly enhanced were the Jews to adopt enlightened German culture. This culture was animated by the ethos of what the Germans called *Bildung* or the ongoing, never-ending educational process of self-formation through aesthetic and intellectual refinement. Even before the gates of the ghettos were fully torn down, the Jews rushed to the libraries and bookstores of Germany to devour the writings of educated Europeans and to learn the requisite languages. Concurrently, they eagerly cultivated a knowledge of music, literature, and the arts and filled the theaters and concert halls.

This process was exemplified by Moses Mendelssohn. Born in 1729 in the ghetto of Dessau, the capital of the German principality of Anhalt, he left his parental home at the age of fourteen to study with a renouned Talmudic scholar in Berlin. There the young Mendelssohn was soon drawn to the city's burgeoning centers of the Enlightenment. Parallel to studying rabbinic commentaries on Hebrew scriptures and medieval Jewish philosophy, Mendelssohn surreptitiously learned German—which he had not known prior to his youthful pilgrimage to Berlin—as well as Latin and Greek, English, French, and Italian. He soon befriended Gotthold Ephraim Lessing, one of the leading voices of the German Enlightenment. Under Lessing's tutelage, he too became a preeminent and respected representative of the Enlightenment, eventually to be hailed the "German Socrates"—and being so crowned while still officially a denizen of the ghetto along with his fellow Jews. His grandson Felix Mendelssohn, baptized at the age of six, became one of the most celebrated composers of Germany, and as a conductor and pianist nigh singly served to restore Bach to the musical canon of Europe.

Bildung had two distinct but complementary vectors: a cosmopolitan horizon, embracing all expressions of the human spirit, ancient and contemporary, and an inward individual, introspective focus. This twofold path to Enlightenment is succinctly put forth in a manifesto from 1799, apparently penned by three young students together at a Lutheran seminary, who were destined to play a seminal role in setting the contours of the German culture of *Bildung*, namely, the philosophers Hegel and Schelling and the poet Hölderlin. Disaffected by institutional religion, they decided to leave the seminary in Tübingen before ordination and thereupon pledged to work for the establishment of what Mendelssohn's patron and friend Lessing called an "invisible church" of the spirit. The manifesto reads in part:

> The first idea is naturally the conception of oneself as an absolutely free, self-conscious being ... [The] absolute freedom of all spirits who carry the world of *Geist*—spirit and intellect—within themselves will need not seek either God or immortality outside of themselves.

> Finally the idea that unites all, is the idea of beauty ... . The philosopher must possess just as much aesthetic power as the poet. Those who are bereft of this aesthetic sense are our philosophers of the letter. [In contrast] the philosophy of the spirit is an aesthetic philosophy. One cannot be clever in anything, one cannot even reason cleverly in history— without an aesthetic sense ... Poetry thereby obtains a higher dignity; it becomes again in the end what it was in the beginning—teacher of [the history], of the human race. ...

> At the same time we so often hear that the great multitude should have a sensual religion. Not only the great multitude, but philosophy also needs it. A monotheism of reason and

the heart, a polytheism of the imagination and art—that is what we need!

Towards this end the manifesto speaks of the need to create a "new mythology," a "mythology of reason":

Until we make ideas aesthetic, i.e., mythological, they hold no interest for people at large, and conversely, before mythology is reasonable, the philosopher must be ashamed of it. Thus finally the enlightened and unenlightened must shake hands; mythology must become philosophical, and the masses reasonable, and philosophy must become mythological in order to make philosophy sensual ... . Never again the contemptuous glance, never again the blind trembling of the masses before their wise men and priests.

Only then will the equal development of all powers await us, of the individual as well as of the masses. No power will be suppressed any longer, then general freedom and equality of spirits will reign—A higher spirit sent from heaven must establish this religion among us, it will be the last work of the human race.[2]

This eschatological vision of a universal church of pure spirit refracted through "a monotheism of reason and the heart, and a polytheism of the imagination and of the arts" adumbrated a post-traditional religion that was to embrace all of humanity. Although the Tübingen manifesto was never published in the lifetimes of its signatories, it articulated the fundamental conviction of the German advocates of the Enlightenment that under the overarching rule of Reason, Europe was on the threshold of

---

2 *Mythologie der Vernunft: Hegels "Ältestes Systemprogramm des deutschen Idealismus,"* edited by Christoph Jamme and Helmut Schneider (Frankfurt a.M.: Suhrkamp, 1984). Discovered by Franz Rosenzweig, a doctoral student at the time, who attributed it to Schelling, later scholars debate whether it was written by him or alternately by Hegel and Hölderlin. Whoever actually wrote the unsigned manifesto, one must assume it expressed a vision shared by the three friends.

an age that would overcome the invidious religious and ethnic divisions that lacerate the human family. Unbounded by particularistic doctrinal precepts and practices of traditional religion, the universal religion of the spirit was thus theoretically open to all of humanity. And so it was to be understood by German Jews as they peered over the walls of the ghettos.

Under the tutelage of the likes of Kant and Hegel, *Bildung* became not only a cultural project but also a compelling spiritual, indeed, a profoundly religious project—and one in which Jews were welcome to participate. Ideally, as fostering an all-encompassing spiritual universe, *Bildung* would create a cultural space where Jews and non-Jews would meet, free of the prejudicial constraints of particularistic ethnic and religious affiliations. But the invitation to Jews to embrace the cosmopolitan promise of *Bildung* was, alas, fraught with inconsistencies and a gnawing ambivalence.

No less than Immanuel Kant, the *spiritus rector* of the German Enlightenment and the cosmopolitan ethos of *Bildung*, unabashedly rendered the Jews' admission to German culture and society conditional on their ceasing to be Jews. While acknowledging the Jews to be fellow human beings, he at the same time called upon them to "throw off the garb of [their] ancient cult, which now serves no purpose and even suppresses any true religious attitude." The consequent "euthanasia of Judaism" would enhance the prospects of their emancipation, for it would "quickly call attention to them as an educated and civilized people who are ready for all the rights of citizenship."[3] *Educated* and *civilized* are, of course, loaded terms that bear a bivalent message. On the one hand, they signal that the Jews are perceived to be not "educated" or "civilized," that is, according to the criteria of "enlightened" Europe. On the other hand, these terms intimate that emancipation is conditioned not only on the Jews' adoption of the standards of education and culture of enlightened, that is, bourgeois Europe but also on the jettisoning of their ancestral religious

---

3   Immanuel Kant, "The Conflict of the Faculties," in Immanuel Kant, *Religion and Rational Theology*, trans. Allen W. Wood and George di Giovanni (Cambridge, UK: Cambridge University Press, 1996), 276.

culture. This expectation was given cynical expression by Kant's disciple Johann Gottlieb Fichte, who declared that liberal Europe would only be prepared to accept the Jews if they were to "decapitate" their depraved "Jewish heads" and have them replaced with those of cultivated Germans![4]

Even Mendelssohn's benign patron Lessing deemed traditional Jews as uncouth and "incapable of abstract thought," but he charitably added that this was not an intrinsic, incorrigible condition, for they would grow out of their intellectual and spiritual "immaturity" once they were exposed to the Enlightenment.[5] Until then, as the twentieth-century German-Jewish philosopher Franz Rosenzweig observed, the Christian is to ignore "the Jew in order to tolerate him," and the Jew is to ignore "the Christian in order to allow himself to be tolerated."[6] This strategy of studious indifference is precisely what Lessing recommended in his celebrated didactic play *Nathan the Wise*. A parable of tolerance, this play, which premiered in Berlin in 1783, in effect argues that the difference between the bearers of the three monotheistic faiths—Judaism, Christianity, and Islam—is of no consequence because they are first and foremost human beings. As Nathan, Lessing's wise Jew, rhetorically asks, "Are Christian and Jew sooner Christian and Jew than human beings?" Indeed, as Rosenzweig noted, Nathan is "abstracted" from his Judaism. He is to meet non-Jews solely as fellow human beings, his ancestral patrimony is to fade into the distant background.

All well and fine, but there was a portentous twist to Lessing's message: whereas Judaism was deemed an anachronistic relic of a benighted bygone era, Christianity was said to represent a far higher stage of intellectual and spiritual development and was thus held to be capable

---

4   Johann Gottlieb Fichte, "Beitrag zur Berichtung der Urteile des Publicum über die Franzö-sische Revolution" [1793], in Johann Gottlieb Fichte, *Sämtliche Werke*, ed. J. H. Fichte (Berlin: Verlag von Velt, 1845), 6:145.

5   Gotthold Lessing, "The Education of the Human Race," in *Lessing's Theological Writings*, trans. Henry Chadwick (Stanford, CA: Stanford University Press, 1956), pars. 16, 20.

6   Franz Rosenzweig, "Lessing's Nathan," in Franz Rosenzweig, *Der Mensch und sein Werk. Gesammelte Schriften*, part 3: *Zweistromland. Kleinere Schriften zu Glauben und Denken* (Dor-drecht, Netherlands: Martinus Nijhoff, 1984), 452.

of adapting its teachings and practices to the rational faith envisioned by the Enlightenment. But German intellectuals were soon to discern the limitations of a religious faith purified in the crucible of pure reason. As Hölderlin ironically put it, "Man is a god when he dreams, a beggar when he reflects."[7] Indeed, as the other signatories of the Tübingen manifesto also concluded, reason alone could not plumb the depths of human experience. Accordingly, each would posit a *dialectical logic* whereby the ascendancy of reason is perforce realized in tension with nonrational impulses of human consciousness and imagination. For Hegel, a dialectical logic incrementally resolves the discordant cultural and political contradictions that blight the unfolding drama of history on its path to realizing the unifying reign of the Absolute Spirit (God) and the invisible, post-traditional Church of Pure Spirit. Hegel's classmate Schelling demurred and argued that the triumph of the Absolute Spirit is not tantamount to the ultimate subjugation of all the imponderables of existence to the rule of reason. For Schelling the Absolute Spirit—the primordial "spiritual power" that sustains the ontological ground and promise of a "unified and undivided human race"—lies beyond the reach of reason.[8] The Absolute Spirit is thus comprehended by religious intuition rather than by what Hegel called the dialectical cunning of reason. By dint of a spurious conception of the dialect that rules history, Schelling averred, Hegel regrettably regarded religion as a primitive, inchoate metaphysics that over the course of history is progressively absorbed into the Absolute Spirit's web of rational concepts and purged of its irrational mythic imagery and fantasies. On the contrary, Schelling protested, it is precisely by virtue of its mythic imagination that religion grasps the true, transcendent, suprarational nature of the Absolute Spirit. Thanks to its distinctive mythological— and poetically inflected—vocabulary, religion is able to express man's

---

7   Cited in *Hölderlin: Selected Verse*, with an introduction and prose translations by Michael Hamburger (London: Anvil Press Poetry, 1986), xix.

8   F. W. J. Schelling, *Historical-Critical Introduction to The Philosophy of Mythology*, trans. Mason Richey and Markus Zisselsberger (Albany, NY: State University of New York Press, 2007), ch. 8.

experience of the enduring tension between the rational and irrational, or better, nonrational structure of human existence. Schelling thus sought to examine the myths and the symbolic language of so-called pagan as well as theistic religions in order to arrive at a hermeneutic allowing for the interpretation of religious experience as a universal struggle between the rational and irrational, between conscious and unconscious mental processes evoked by the experiential, intuitive apprehension of the Absolute Spirit. When viewed from the perspective of their myths and symbolism, Schelling concluded, there is an essential continuity between paganism and the purportedly true religion of Christianity. The universally shared motifs of religious myths and symbols, Schelling argued, point to the universal nature of the human psychic and imaginative sensibility. By grounding the religious experience of the Absolute Spirit in universal trans-temporal mythological structures, Schelling in effect challenged the logocentric supersessionism of the Enlightenment. It may, therefore, be said that he recast humanism on a more inclusive basis than the earlier sponsors of the Enlightenment. In this regard, it is apposite to note that in exploring the dialectic of the mythological imagination, Schelling consulted Jews knowledgeable about medieval Kabbalah and its theogonic myth of God's becoming manifest in the world through the ongoing act of creation. It is perhaps not coincidental that among nineteenth-century German philosophers Schelling was virtually the only one who did not voice derogatory opinions about Jews and Judaism.

Schelling, who died in 1854 just shy of his eightieth year, served as a prime inspiration to the existential turn of twentieth-century Christian and Jewish religious thought. He was also a precursor of Jung's Eranos circle in Ascona, Switzerland, in several seminal respects. Not only is he generally considered to be the first to have coined the term *unconscious*, his book of 1842, *The Philosophy of Mythology*, stimulated and laid the foundation for the scholarly study of myth and religious symbols. Schelling's focus on the generic features of religion and religious experience as reflected in paradigmatic myths likewise anticipated what has been characterized as the "religion after religion" of the Eranos circle—the preposition *after* denoting both temporal and spatial location, hence *religion after religion*—religion subsequent to traditional religion of given doctrines and practice, and religion behind institutional religion, that is, the foundational experience of all historical religions. In a *laudatio* marking the eightieth birthday of Jung, Eric Neumann celebrated his teacher's approach to the study of religion as fostering a "universal humanism" which by positing "the essential unity of human nature and human culture ... unites East and West, the very modern and the primitive, science and religion, the collective and the altogether individual."[9]

The scholars who had gathered yearly since 1933 at Casa Gabriella on the shores of Lago Maggiore shared with Jung this post-traditional religious perspective. While affirming the intrinsic integrity of all religious phenomena, they gave preeminent attention to the archetypal symbolism of myth and mystical experience at the root of the religious imagination, and in doing so deemphasized the significance of ritual, law, and doctrine for an understanding of *Homo religiosus*. Henry Corbin, a French scholar of Islamic philosophy and one of the pillars of the post–World War II Eranos conferences, gave voice to this approach in locating the core of Islam in a secret mystical doctrine, a gnosis:

> It should be apparent to everyone why we have associated the concept of gnosis with the look of eyes of fire. Inasmuch as the look of gnosis is a visionary look and not the look of theoretical knowledge, it is wedded to the look of the prophets, spokesmen of the Invisible. To open "the eyes of fire" is to go beyond all false and vain opposition between believing and knowing, between thinking and being, between knowledge and love, between the God of the prophets and the God of

---

9   Erich Neumann, "C. G. Jung: 1955," in Erich Neumann, *Creative Man: Five Essays*, trans. Eugene Rolfe (Princeton, NJ: Princeton University Press, 1979), 255.

the philosophers. The Gnostics of Islam, in agreement with
the Jewish Kabbalists, have particularly insisted on the idea
of a "prophetic philosophy."[10]

And Corbin concludes with an appeal, which echoes the manifesto written
by the erstwhile students at the Lutheran seminary in Tübingen and their
vision of a universal religion of the spirit: "It is a prophetic philosophy
that our world needs."

The Jung-Neumann correspondence constitutes an eloquent endorse-
ment of this vision. It also attests to the *depth* of the friendship that
evolved over three decades between them. To be sure, their epistolary
exchange, as Neumann noted, oscillated between "love and vexation,"
but that is what seems to have rendered their friendship genuine (as is
perhaps the case of all true relationships).[11] In Neumann's assessment
of their friendship, Jung succeeded to "by-pass," as it were, his ego and
to speak "directly to the center of [his] psyche." And thus, Neumann
gratefully underscored, "it was in this way ... that [Jung] gave me, like
a gift from a higher power, the courage to be myself."[12]

Yet, as Angelica Löwe observes in her excellent, recently published
biography of Neumann, the correspondence, alas, attests to the failure
of Neumann to bring Jung to confront the existential and spiritual
reality of the German Jew, torn between a seemingly Sisyphean task of
reconstructing a meaningful post-assimilatory Jewish identity and the
urgency of facing an increasingly virulent anti-Semitism.[13] From the
very beginning of their exchange, initiated by Neumann in September
1933 when he was still a patient of Jung's in Zurich, Neumann sought
to speak to Jung as a Jew and insisted that his teacher and therapist not
ignore the fact that he was a Jew. And at this critical juncture, when

10   Cited in Steven M. Wasserstrom, *Religion after Religion: Gershom Scholem, Mircea Eliade, and Henry Corbin at Eranos* (Princeton, NJ: Princeton University Press, 1999), 31.
11   Neumann, "C. G. Jung: 1955," 255.
12   Ibid., 256.
13   Angelica Löwe, *"Auf Seiten der inneren Stimme ...": Erich Neumann—Leben und Werk* (München: Verlag Karl Alber, 2014), 361–372.

the humanistic culture of the Germany they both cherished was under assault, the twenty-nine-year-old Neumann wrote to his therapist, in a letter dated July 19, 1934: "I have the firm intention not to give you any peace about the Jewish problem."[14] And try as Neumann did to persuade Jung to probe the roots of Nazi anti-Semitism and to acknowledge that he too was beholden to negative stereotypes of Jews and Judaism, Jung consistently fended off his younger colleague's appeal.

On the other hand, Neumann was more successful in appealing to Jung to extend the purview of the study of religious myth and symbols beyond Eastern religions to include Judaism. Although Jung himself did not make an effort, as Neumann had hoped, to examine Jewish, especially Hasidic, mysticism, he apparently prompted Olga Fröbe-Kapteyn, the founding director of Eranos, to extend an invitation to Martin Buber to come to Casa Gabriella and address the society's second conference in the summer of 1934 on "Symbolism and Sacramental Existence in Judaism."[15]

When the Eranos conferences were resumed after the war and the fall of the Third Reich, scholars of Judaism—most prominently the eminent scholar of Kabbalah Gershom Scholem—were regular participants. The German-Jewish dialogue, which Scholem claimed had never truly taken root in prewar Germany, was now firmly an integral dimension of the educated discourse on religion.

---

14   C. G. Jung and Erich Neumann, *Analytical Psychology in Exile: The Correspondence of C. G. Jung and Erich Neumann*, ed. Martin Liebscher (Princeton, NJ: Princeton University Press, 2015), 35.

15   See the unpublished correspondence between Martin Buber and Olga Fröbe-Kapteyn: Martin Buber Archive, Arch. Var. 350, Israel National Library, Jerusalem, "Martin Korrespondenz," Mappe 83 and 221. Martin Buber, "Sinnbildliche und sakramentale Existenz im Judentum," in *Martin Buber Eranos Jahrbuch 1934* (Zürich: Rheinverlag, 1935), 340–367.

Basel, Jung's Cultural Background, and the Proto-Zionism of Samuel Preiswerk

Ulrich Hoerni

A n important subject in the correspondence between Erich Neumann and C. G. Jung is Judaism. In the following pages, I would like to comment on some aspects of the general historical and cultural background pertaining to Jung's side of the discussion. Jung spent the formative years of his childhood and adolescence in Basel, Switzerland, the son of a Swiss Reformed pastor and the grandson of a famous Basel clergyman, Samuel Preiswerk. This upbringing left a mark on him and framed some of his attitudes about religion, both Christian and Jewish. To take a case in point, in 1897 the First Zionist Congress took place in Basel under the presidency of Theodor Herzl (1860–1904). Herzl noted afterward in his diary: "In Basel, I founded the Jewish State."[1] Not far from the venue the medical student C. G. Jung delivered, from 1896 onward, his Zofingia lectures. Decades before that, pastor Samuel Preiswerk (1799–1871), Jung's grandfather, had postulated the return of the Jewish people to Palestine in the journal *Das Morgenland* [*The Orient*], which is why he was later seen as a proto-Zionist. What was the cultural context of Herzl's congress and Preiswerk's journal, and are there traces of it to be found in Jung's work? The cultural background of the city of Basel is,

---

1 Heiko Haumann, ed., *Acht Jahrhunderte Juden in Basel* (Basel: Schwabe Verlag, 2005), 146.

of course, closely intertwined with all of Europe's history. The subject is therefore complex. Although I can offer some insights, the picture will necessarily remain incomplete.

Basel is located where today the borders of Switzerland, France, and Germany meet. One cannot see the snowy mountains with which Switzerland is often associated from Basel. With regard to geography and culture, it has much in common with the nearby French region of Alsace. The lifeline of Basel is the Rhine. It has its source in the Alps, flows westward through Lake Constance, and passes over the Rhine Falls in Schaffhausen. At Basel, it changes course northward and empties, after about 800 kilometers, into the North Sea. For thousands of years, human beings, goods, and ideas have traveled along the Rhine. It has often been used as a border between countries and cultures. The area of today's Basel was already populated in the Bronze Age, in the second century BCE, by a Celtic tribe called the Raurici. The Romans conquered their territory, and under Augustus they founded Colonia Augusta Raurica, a city equipped with all the facilities of Mediterranean cities of the day. There is evidence of a Christian bishop there already in the third century. Germanic tribes from the other side of the Rhine started to attack Roman settlements, and around 400 CE, the fatal turning point, Rome withdrew its soldiers. The Germanic-Alemannic tribes were then able to settle in the unprotected area, and slowly they began to take possession of its civilization. It is this process that Jung referred to when writing in 1918: "As civilized human beings, we have a history reaching back perhaps 1,500 years," and "we Germans still have a genuine barbarian in us."[2] He was aware of the fact that he himself was an offspring not of civilized Romans but of savage intruders.

---

2 C. G. Jung, "The Role of the Unconscious" (1918), in *CW*, vol. 10 (Princeton, NJ: Princeton University Press, 1970), par. 16, 19, respectively. The English translation in the *Collected Works* does not correspond accurately to the original German wording of 1918. "We Germans" does not refer to modern German nationality but to the original German tribe.

It took about four hundred years before a new Western culture, founded by Charlemagne, began to develop. His Frankish state was later divided into three parts: the western regions became the French Kingdom, the eastern regions became the German Empire, later called the Holy Roman Empire of the German Nation (962–1806). The people of Basel and along the Rhine found themselves in the eastern part, at the border between the two cultures. Here several small states, some of them bilingual, would later emerge: Belgium, the Netherlands, Luxembourg, and Switzerland. Basel was located in the German-speaking area, near the language border. In the tenth century, it belonged to the glorious Kingdom of Burgundy. It had a close relationship with its francophone neighbors. In the eleventh century, it fell to the German emperor, who declared it a free imperial city. In the twelfth century, a new bishop's church was built out of red sandstone in the Romanesque style, the Basel Minster. Later, Gothic towers were added, and it is in this form that Jungians know it well because of Jung's famous "Basel Cathedral vision."[3]

After struggles with the bishop and the nobility, the citizens finally gained political power over the city. In the thirteenth century, Basel got a bridge over the Rhine and city walls. In the fourteenth century, the city suffered some setbacks: the plague was raging and part of the city collapsed in an earthquake. The city's history was, by the way, documented in a large chronicle, called "The Red Book."[4] At the beginning of the fifteenth century, Basel was a prospering city republic, but it did not manage to expand its small territory. It was, however, greatly honored in the years 1431 to 1445, when the seventeenth Ecumenical Council took place there in order to bring about the renewal of the Roman Catholic Church. Basel was chosen because of good transportation

---

3   C. G. Jung, *Memories, Dreams, Reflections*, ed. Aniela Jaffé, trans. Richard and Clara Winston (New York: Pantheon Books, 1962), 36ff.

4   Werner Meyer, *Da verfiele Basel überall: Das Basler Erdbeben von 1356* (Basel, Switzerland: Schwabe Verlag, 2006) 91ff.

connections, its position between France and Germany, its political stability, and its suitable range of lodgings. For fourteen years, it was the center of church diplomacy. The council ended without result, but the circumstances proved beneficial: the secretary of the council was elected pope soon afterward and permitted Basel to found a university in 1460. Furthermore, a businessman had built a paper mill to meet the needs of the council, and at the same time, Johannes Gutenberg invented movable printing type in Mainz, a city farther down the Rhine. Soon the first of many Basel printing companies started operating. The university and printing trade initiated the city's promotion to a place of scholarship.

This was also a time of change. On a political level, Basel joined the Swiss Confederation, a union of small rural and urban states, the cantons. The Confederation had no capital or central government, but it had defended itself successfully against Burgundy, the Habsburgs, and even the German emperor. The new alliance strengthened Basel's foreign policy. With regard to religion, it adopted the Reformation in 1529, which had been initiated by Luther in Germany and Zwingli in Switzerland. In a bloodless coup, the bishop of Basel was driven away, and mass, confession, and the veneration and images of saints, as well as church music, were abandoned. Emperor and pope, previously the highest authorities, were replaced by the city council. In the following years, a reformed church in Zwingli's sense was established, introducing a strict morality, and all traces of the former Roman Catholic past were erased. However, there were two exceptions: the famous Basel Carnival and the municipal coat of arms. Both continue to embody Basel's historical identity today. The coat of arms proudly shows the bishop's crook, the symbol of the spiritual ruler who had been driven away. For two years, Jean Calvin stayed in Basel before he became a reformer in Geneva. Calvinists and Zwinglians could come to an understanding of each other, but the relationship to Lutherans was strained because of differing views of the Lord's Supper.

By the time of the Reformation, science and the art of printing had reached a high point, not least thanks to personalities from abroad. In 1516, the scholar Erasmus of Rotterdam, who now lived and taught in Basel, published the New Testament in its original Greek form for the first time. This was followed by works of the Church Fathers and classical authors, among them *Adagia*, an annotated collection of Greek and Latin proverbs. This work contains the story of the oracle that would become Jung's motto: *Vocatus atque non vocatus deus aderit.* In 1525, the city council gave Theophrastus Paracelsus—a complex and controversial personality—the position of city physician. He left Basel in 1528 because of a conflict with the city council, but his vast literary work was published there. Toward the end of the sixteenth century, the doctoral theses of such physicians as Heinrich Khunrath and Michael Maier, who would both become famous alchemists, led to a new upswing. There were also beginnings of scientific work in the modern sense. Basel printers published everything that was of interest for the times. Between 1514 and 1531 the well-known painter Hans Holbein the Younger (1497–1543) lived in Basel where, among other things, he decorated the new town hall with murals.

Not all the cantons of Switzerland had adopted the Reformation. About half of them remained Catholic. With regard to domestic politics, the Confederation was paralyzed. In its foreign policy, it more or less maintained neutrality, which allowed it to emerge from the European wars mostly unscathed. At the Treaty of Westphalia in 1648, Switzerland received its independence from the German Empire, but then it came under the influence of France, which advanced to become Basel's immediate neighbor in the same year. At that time the city lived on crafts, book printing, trade, and banking. In the sixteenth and seventeenth centuries, a new trade, introduced by French Protestant refugees, the Huguenots, brought prosperity: silk ribbon weaving and silk dyeing. At the university, science was making progress. Well known are the mathematicians Bernoulli and Euler. The oligarchic city council, together with the state church, governed all public life in the city and its surrounding rural areas in a restrictive, conservative, and economical way. For the fine arts such as painting, architecture, music, and theater, Basel proved to be less hospitable. Since the Reformation, no new churches or representative municipal buildings had been erected. An exception was the copperplate engravings by the Basel draftsman Matthäus Merian, showing views of European cities, which became famous. The so-called Amerbach-Kabinett with its holdings of works by Hans Holbein, Konrad Witz, Lucas Cranach, and other artists became one of the first municipal art collections of Europe.

In the eighteenth century, opposing intellectual currents reached Basel: from France the Enlightenment, from Germany Pietism. Both rejected the authority of the state church, but they managed, despite attracting the suspicion of the ruling class, to avoid outright repression. Rationalism was now pitted against personal religious experience. Unlike the dogmatically and theologically shaped state church, Pietism advocated an emotional experience with God. The German revivalist brotherhood of the Count von Zinzendorf, called the *Herrnhuter*, won many followers. Supporters of the Enlightenment, on the other hand, demanded the adoption of ideas originating from the French Revolution. Shortly afterward, France made Switzerland a satellite and introduced *liberté, égalité, fraternité*. But the French rule was unpopular because of wars and shortages of supplies. When the Congress of Vienna restored Switzerland in 1814–1815, conservative Basel circles wanted to restrict rights and treat the inhabitants of the rural areas as subjects again. However, after a short civil war, they formed their own canton in 1833.

The city developed a conservative Protestant sense of community. Charitable societies were founded and theologians were trained, more than were needed. In 1815, Pietists founded the Basel Mission Society. From 1827 onward, its representatives successfully took up posts mostly in West Africa and India. Their logistics department later became a large international trading company. While at the beginning of the nineteenth century Basel had about 15,000 inhabitants, this number now increased in parallel with the beginnings of industrialization. From 1844 onward, French, Swiss, and German railway lines met in Basel and turned it into a railway junction. City walls and gates were taken down. In 1858, a silk dye factory was transformed into the first modern chemical works—it was the beginning of the big pharmaceutical industry that continues in Basel to this day. For the growing population, the city had to provide many buildings, among them the Stadt-Casino, a concert hall with superb acoustics which would later be the meeting place for the First Zionist Congress. In 1844, the Hotel Drei Könige ("Three Kings Hotel"), Theodor Herzl's future residence, was built near the mooring of the new steamboat line.

The university's medical faculty, which had descended into unimportance during the eighteenth century, had appointed the German physician Dr. Carl Gustav Jung, professor of anatomy, surgery, and obstetrics, in 1822. He was then twenty-eight years old and had converted from Catholicism to Protestantism shortly before—a wise decision for residence in Basel. Besides carrying out the responsibilities in his own department, he strongly supported the extension of the entire cantonal hospital and suggested setting up a kind of psychotherapeutic clinic.

Next to medicine, the humanities reached a new peak. From 1842 to 1844, Johann Jakob Bachofen was professor of Roman law, but he also wrote about historical subjects, most notably in a work that was to become important to Erich Neumann: *Mother Right: An Investigation of the Religious and Juridical Character of Matriarchy in the Ancient World.* From 1858 to 1893, Jacob Burckhardt gave lectures on the history of culture and art, which eventually were published and are still highly regarded today. And in 1869, the University of Basel appointed a twenty-four-year-old German scholar who had not completed his doctorate yet but would one day become world famous, Friedrich Nietzsche. He was professor of Latin and Greek. Moving between philology and philosophy, he corrected the image of classical antiquity and criticized Christian morality. He left Basel in 1879, suffering from health problems. Two artists from Basel became famous: Arnold Böcklin (1827–1901), best known for his five versions of *Isle of the Dead*, and the poet Carl Spitteler (1845–1924), winner of the Nobel Prize in Literature in 1919.

In 1848, Switzerland created a federal government and, inspired by the United States of America, a constitution that strengthened liberal human rights. But Basel still discriminated against certain groups. For Catholics, as an example, it was de facto still impossible to get citizenship, and citizens of other cantons could not be elected to public office. Only the new Cantonal Constitution of 1875—Jung's year of birth—ended the conservative regime. In a slow process, Basel evolved into a modern city.

For the sake of brevity, I refrain from going into detail on the cultural exchange between Basel and the Orient, the so-called Near East, going back to the time when both regions belonged to the same Roman Empire. There would be much to say about archaeological remains of oriental cults in the Rhine region, such as the cult of Mithras which Jung described; about the significance of the Holy Land and Jerusalem for Christians; about pilgrimages, the interruption of the historical ties between Europe and the East after the expansion of the Islam, the cultural impact of the so-called crusades on Western Europe, the reception of Arabic scholarship and achievements like the Arabic numerals, the printing of the first Latin translation of the Qur'an in Basel in 1542, and finally about the nineteenth-century Basel explorer Johann Ludwig Burckhardt, who was the first modern European to visit and describe the legendary city of Petra in Jordan and the temples of Abu Simbel in Egypt.

The oldest evidence for the presence of Jewish people in the area of Basel is an archaeological find from the Roman era, a ring with the picture of a menorah, its origin unknown. In the time of Charlemagne, Jewish merchants coming from southern France reached the Middle and Lower Rhine. In about 1100 CE, Jewish communities were flourishing there, and later in Alsace as well. The Lower Rhine Valley is, by the way, also the area where some scholars locate the origin of the Yiddish language. In the twelfth century, the first Jewish community in Basel is recorded in a contract with the bishop. It had a small synagogue and about one hundred members. According to several documents, Jews were mostly merchants and moneylenders. The church prohibited Christians to charge interest on loans, while Jews, on the other hand, were excluded from most other trades. In this way they seem to have lived together quite peacefully, until a terrible incident changed that situation dramatically: Christians blamed Jews for the plague epidemic of 1348. As in neighboring cities, the Jews of Basel were brutally murdered unless they managed to flee. After 1360, a second Jewish community dispersed again for unknown reasons. Its members settled in the countryside or emigrated. At the beginning of the fifteenth century, Basel prohibited Jews from settling there.

The sixteenth century brought a paradoxical development. For the Protestant church, the biblical word was the primary source of authority. Hebrew was seen as the language in which God had addressed the prophets. Thus the study of the Hebrew language gained great importance, particularly in the sixteenth and seventeenth centuries. Scholars like Johannes Buxtorf, father and son, immersed themselves in Jewish culture and promoted tolerance. In 1580, an edition of the Talmud was published in Basel. At times, printers hired Jews from Alsace and even from Poland as typesetters and proofreaders. At the same time, Jews were excluded and discriminated against on theological grounds. Only in the nineteenth century was a new Jewish community able to establish itself in Basel. In 1868, a synagogue was built, and in 1872, Jews received for the first time citizenship and in 1875, full civil rights.

As mentioned before, it was not only the Enlightenment that influenced nineteenth-century Basel. Pietists took up an idea that had already found support in England: the conversion of Jews to Christianity. For this, complex theological and political arguments were put forth, such as the idea that to convert Jews and let them return to Palestine would bring about the Second Coming of Christ and the Kingdom of God on earth. Since the missionary society of Basel did not support missionary work among Jews, those in favor of it founded the Verein der Freunde Israels, the Society of the Friends of Israel, in 1830. They sought to collect money, employ missionaries, and offer converts religious and social support. In their view, Jerusalem was the world's spiritual center.

This is the background against which one has to view the biography of Samuel Preiswerk, offspring of an old Basel family. After studying theology, he worked as a pastor in Basel and elsewhere. He was an author of texts for hymns and a professor of the Hebrew language both in Geneva and Basel. He also wrote a grammar of the Hebrew language. It is not surprising that he touched upon many questions concerning Judaism. From 1838 to 1843, he published the above-mentioned journal *Das Morgenland* [*The Orient*], which contained articles on theological and biblical matters as well as on the geography, natural life, and history of the Near East. The idea of the return of the Jewish people to Palestine was reinforced by the decline of the Ottoman Empire and the liberation of Greece in 1833. Preiswerk also conceived of a state in the area of Lebanon, Syria, and Iraq. From 1842 to 1852, he was a member of the executive committee of the Society of the Friends of Israel. Apart from his visionary ideas, he deserves particular credit for his effort to provide accurate information about the then little-known Near East. One of Preiswerk's students was Paul Achilles Jung, who was not only learning Hebrew but also Arabic. He later abandoned his oriental studies, though, in favor of theology. He became Preiswerk's son-in-law and C. G. Jung's father. Samuel Preiswerk died in 1871. It is not least thanks to him that the members of the Society of the Friends of Israel were later called "Christian Zionists."

The most important proponent of the Jewish state, however, was, of course, Theodor Herzl. Born in Hungary in 1860, he belonged to a well-to-do family of so-called assimilated Jews who admired German culture. He went to a Lutheran school in Budapest and studied law in Vienna. He became within a short period of time a German language journalist, writer, and author of nineteen plays. Based on his personal experiences, he began to ponder the question of how anti-Semitism might be eliminated. Hard to believe, but for a short time he even considered advocating the conversion of Jews to Christianity, but he quickly reached the conclusion that Jews, despite assimilation, would never be accepted as full citizens by their countries and that only establishing a Jewish state could bring security to his people. As the Paris correspondent for the Viennese newspaper *Neue Freie Presse*, Herzl reported on the Dreyfus affair, in which a French Jewish army captain was accused of treason—an anti-Semitic intrigue as it turned out later. In 1896 he published his book, *The Jewish State*, a kind of action plan. Many Jews, however, rejected his ideas for various reasons. In order to win more people over to his view, Herzl planned the First Zionist Congress. It should have taken place in Munich in 1897, but this met with the resistance of German rabbis, who forced him to relocate. Following this, he asked his Polish friend David Farbstein (1868–1953), who studied in Zurich and had reviewed Herzl's book, if he could recommend a venue in Switzerland. With its liberal constitution, however, Switzerland and especially Zurich had for all of Europe become a popular place of exile for persecuted political activists, which, especially for the Russian government, rendered the city suspicious. David Farbstein was afraid that Russian delegates would not come to Zurich for fear of reprisals. He therefore suggested Basel as a venue for the congress and informed Herzl about the Jewish community there, as well as a fine Jewish restaurant. As to political activities, he added, Basel was less notorious than Zurich, and the Swiss Jews would not cause any problems. Herzl agreed. For the event, he had the Stadt-Casino and an office at his disposal.

On August 29, 1897, the congress convened with two hundred delegates from fifteen different countries. The head of the Basel city government participated as a guest. The preparations for the congress were supported by three representatives of the Christian Zionists. That their action was not quite without ulterior motive did not seem to have bothered Herzl; on the contrary, he attached great importance to Christian support. The congress ended on August 31 and was deemed a success. The most important result was the "Basel Program" with its central statement: "Zionism aims to establish for the Jewish people a publically and legally assured home in Palestine."[5] The Bible-oriented, Protestant city of Basel offered the Zionists a warm welcome. This was one factor that contributed to further Zionist congresses being held in Basel, which was not quite self-evident after so many years of discrimination.

Theodor Herzl did not live to see the realization of his vision. He died in 1904, only forty-four years old. Whether he was familiar with Preiswerk's writings is not stated in my sources. But in 1912, the journal *Israelitisches Wochenblatt für die Schweiz* [*Israelite Weekly for Switzerland*], published a long positive review of Preiswerk's journal, *Das Morgenland*, entitled "A Basel Precursor of Zionism."

In *Memories, Dreams, Reflections*, Jung describes his youth and student years in Basel. His works contain many explicit and implicit references to Basel. On several Basel characters, such as Paracelsus, the alchemists, the poet Carl Spitteler, and of course Nietzsche, he comments at length.[6] Jung grew up in surroundings shaped by theology, the Old Testament, and Pietism. He was familiar with theology although he never

---

5   Haumann, *Acht Jahrhunderte Juden in Basel*, 261: "Der Zionismus erstrebt für das jüdische Volk die Schaffung einer öffentlich-rechtlich gesicherten Heimstätte in Palästina"; English translation from Wikipedia.org, First Zionist Congress.
6   C. G. Jung, "Paracelsus as a Spiritual Phenomenon" (1942), in *CW*, vol. 13 (Princeton, NJ: Princeton University Press, 1967); "Paracelsus" (1934) and "Paracelsus the Physician" (1942), in *CW*, vol. 15 (Princeton, NJ: Princeton University Press, 1966); *Psychology and Alchemy* (1944), *CW*, vol. 12 (Princeton, NJ: Princeton University Press, 1953); *Psychological Types* (1923), *CW*, vol. 6 (Princeton, NJ: Princeton University Press, 1971), pars. 275ff; and in particular in the seminar on Nietzsche's *Zarathustra*.

studied it formally. In *Psychological Types,* for instance, he discusses the famous disagreement between Luther and Zwingli on the interpretation of the Lord's Supper.[7] While he was not a Pietist himself, his insistence on a living relationship between human beings and God somehow reflects this influence. He remained a member of the Protestant Church, but he rejected superficial religious activities. He could not continue in the specific Basel religiousness. His *Answer to Job* can be seen as a late reaction to that. His way of bringing rational and irrational aspects of the mind into a dynamic balance is reminiscent of the intellectual environment in eighteenth-century Basel. It is probably no coincidence that while the inscription *Vocatus atque non vocatus deus aderit* was carved above his front door, a bust of Voltaire occupied a place of honor in his consulting room.

At the end of 1900, Jung left Basel. It had become too narrow for him, and at times he spoke critically or ironically about it. His colleagues knew about his Basel roots. In 1910 the Zurich minister and psychoanalyst Oskar Pfister wrote a study entitled *The Piety of Count Ludwig von Zinzendorf.*[8] He ascribed the religious fanaticism of this prominent Pietist to perverse eroticism and dedicated the work to Jung. Jung expressed his enthusiasm and would have liked to publish the piece in the psychoanalytic journal of which he was editor, the *Jahrbuch für psychoanalytische und psychopathologische Forschungen.* At Freud's request, however, it was published separately.

Jung did not get to know his grandfather, Preiswerk, personally. Sometimes he referred to the biblical orientation of Preiswerk but not to his proto-Zionist ideas. In a seminar of 1930 he explained:

> in the unconscious of the Protestant one finds a Jew; the worldly
> success of the Protestant comes from the fact that he is a Jew

---

7   Jung, *Psychological Types*, *CW*, vol. 6, pars. 69ff.
8   Isabelle Noth, ed., *Sigmund Freud—Oskar Pfister: Briefwechsel 1909–1939* (Zürich: Theologischer Verlag, 2014), 60ff.

inside. For instance, my great-grandfather [*sic*] on my mother's side was a very pious Protestant, and he believed that the language spoken in Heaven was Hebrew. Therefore he became a Professor of the Hebrew language.[9]

But he also observed the opposite: "In a way it is true, the Jew today is quite christianized, his psychology has taken on an absolutely Christian quality."[10] In Jung's youth, there were only a few Jews in Basel, but as a psychiatrist in Zurich, he got to know many Jewish students and physicians, most noteworthy among them, of course, Sigmund Freud. All of his adult life he maintained important relationships with Jews. He saw a certain similarity between Jewish and Protestant religiosity, comparing the religions as follows: "[the Catholic] has no need to go in search of ... something that would link him with the eternal and the timeless. These are always present and available for him: there, in the Holy of Holies on every altar, dwells the presence of God. It is the Protestant and the Jew who have to seek."[11] Among his clients there were Jews, but he had no intention of making them into Christian converts. Some he even helped to become more aware of their Jewish roots. Jung was interested in the psychology of the native soil, and it was this aspect of Zionism that was of importance to him. Comments about Judaism can be found in many of Jung's works.

His personal course was, however, not directed toward a worldly or heavenly Jerusalem. Like other intellectuals at the turn of the twentieth century, he was looking for new inspiration and insight beyond the classical-antique and biblical traditions, which had been so dominant in the nineteenth century. A slim volume nicely documents this reorientation. Around 1915, Jung began to study the Gnostics. In 1916 he published "Septem Sermones ad Mortuos," "written by Basilides of Alexandria, the

---

9   C. G. Jung, *Visions* (Princeton, NJ: Princeton University Press, 1997), 11. Samuel Preiswerk was Jung's grandfather.

10   C. G. Jung, *Dream Analysis* (Princeton, NJ: Princeton University Press, 1984), 517.

11   C. G. Jung, "The Structure of the Psyche" (1931), in *CW*, vol. 8 (Princeton, NJ: Princeton University Press, 1969), par. 338.

City where the East toucheth the West."[12] The fictitious Basilides stands probably for nothing more than the man from Basel, Jung himself. The first sentence reads: "The dead came back from Jerusalem, where they found not what they sought." It was a step toward the founding of analytical psychology.

---

12   Jung, *Memories, Dreams, Reflections*, 378–390.

The Cultural Psyche: From Ancestral Roots to Postmodern Routes

Erel Shalit

The dialogue between Jung and Neumann is a display of minds and hearts apart, and no less of minds and hearts coming together. While their ideas covered much common ground, their inspiration sprang from different sources. Compassion sometimes seems strikingly absent in their letters, thus the subtle presence of affection is all the more striking. In their correspondence, extending over a quarter of a century, we sense a simultaneous closeness and distance—aloneness and aloofness together with respect and companionship.

While Jung throughout his life remained bound to his home on Swiss soil—"The people who sit in the shell and round its rim are the Swiss, and that is me"—Neumann as a young man broke away from the Germany that no longer could serve as home.[1] Spurred by Zionist yearnings, Neumann turned his back on the Teutonic ground that was to be trampled by marching boots for more than a decade, until the scorched earth collapsed into its own bottomless pit of evil and ruined civilization. Turning east, Neumann went searching for the ancestral terrain in the ancient homeland, where pioneers of the old-new nation already were

---

1   C. G. Jung, *Letters*, vol. 2, ed. Gerhard Adler, trans. R. F. C. Hull (Princeton, NJ: Princeton University Press, 1975), 419.

digging into the harsh Mother Earth, searching for her life-giving wells of water, raising their heads in visionary gaze.[2]

From the day he stepped ashore, Neumann lived at the edge of the land, close to the Mediterranean, with a view through his window toward the world that he had left behind, far across the sea. The ink of his pen always spelled out his thoughts in German, but his soul turned inland, eastward, toward the ancient soil of the Hebrews. It was this so often troubled and bleeding earth that provided the ground and the images for much of Neumann's thinking.

Jung understood and recognized the need for rootedness and the significance of residing on archetypal soil, the need of a cultural home and an autochthonous haven, rather than cultural assimilation and detachment.[3] "I am fully committed to the idea that human existence should be rooted in the earth," he said.[4] Jung criticized the tendency among many modern Jews to assimilate and identify with the surrounding culture, while distancing themselves from the strata of Jewish culture and experience. He wrote to Neumann:

> The "Culture Jews" are always en route to being "non-Jews"; you are completely right, the route does not go from the good to the better, but first downhill to historical actuality. I routinely draw the attention of most of my Jewish patients to the fact that they are self-evidently Jews. I would not do this if I had not so frequently seen Jews who imagined that they were something else. To such as these "being Jewish" is a form of personal insult.[5]

---

2   See E. Shalit, *The Hero and His Shadow: Psychopolitical Aspects of Myth and Reality in Israel,* rev. ed. (Hanford, CA: Fisher King Press, 2012), 36.

3   See Jung's letters 7J and 18J, in C. G. Jung and Erich Neumann, *Analytical Psychology in Exile: The Correspondence of C. G. Jung and Erich Neumann,* ed. Martin Liebscher (Princeton, NJ: Princeton University Press, 2015), 52 and 119, respectively.

4   C. G. Jung, *C. G. Jung Speaking,* ed. William McGuire and R. F. C. Hull (Princeton, NJ: Princeton University Press, 1987), 204.

5   Jung and Neumann, *Analytical Psychology in Exile,* 119. Edgar Feuchtwanger describes the "Jews of Culture," the "Kulturjude," as having an academic, historical, theoretical-philosophical

In this letter from 1935, Jung expresses his critical attitude toward those turning their back on being Jewish. In contrast, he was profoundly interested in and respectful and encouraging of Neumann's endeavor to draw from the ancestral wellspring, from the wisdom of the earth of the motherland, uniting it with the insights of depth psychology. In a certain way, culture does require ground—not the fundamentalism that is tied to the material literalness of earth, but the spirit of the earth that "needs to be tilled," that is, cultivated.

Much has been written about Jung, Jews, and his alleged anti-Semitism. Perhaps as much as he has been accused, he has been defended, not the least by some of his Jewish disciples. Young Neumann relentlessly accused him of romanticizing the pagan awakening of National Socialism, failing to see its shadow of "filth, blood and rottenness."[6] Yet, at the same time, Neumann believed that Jung's psychology "will be crucial in the striving of the Jews to reach their foundation."[7]

There is a distinct complexity both in Jung's attitude toward the Jews and in Neumann's perception of Jung's attitude. While a great many topics are touched on in their correspondence, which lasted until the end of their lives, it is notable that there is actually very little relating to, for instance, *Kristallnacht*, even in the immediate aftermath of the pogrom, not to mention their silence on World War II and the Holocaust when their correspondence resumes barely moments after the catastrophe.

In December 1940, Jung writes: "We live here in Switzerland on an island with reduced heating."[8] In the context of a Europe burning in

---

interest in Judaism, rather than the *experience* of "being Jewish" (*Erlebnis und Geschichte als Kind in Hitlers Deutschland—Ein Leben in England* [Duncker und Humblot, Berlin 2010], 42).

6   Erich Neumann, letter 4N, written while still in Zurich, spring 1934, in Jung and Neumann, *Analytical Psychology in Exile*, 12. While Neumann, as well as others, did see and understand where the wind was blowing, many did not. In retrospect it seems quite astonishing that in 1934, 16,000 Jews who had escaped from Germany the previous year, now *returned* (Robert Rosen, *Saving the Jews: Franklin D. Roosevelt and the Holocaust* [New York: Basic Books, 2007], 26). Trust in and identification with German culture obscured the realization of the deceptive nature of Nazism.

7   Erich Neumann, "Die Judenfrage in der Psychotherapie," letter to the *Jüdische Rundschau*, 48, June 15, 1935, p. 5; in Jung and Neumann, *Analytical Psychology in Exile*, 355.

8   Jung and Neumann, *Analytical Psychology in Exile*, 158.

the ice-cold evil that had begun to spread across the continent, "reduced heating" sounds disquietingly chilly—unless considering that Jung by then had been blacklisted by the Nazis, and for a while the Jung family moved to safety in the mountains.[9]

Neumann resumed the correspondence five years later, on October 1, 1945, shortly after the war ended. In his letter, he refers to his inner difficulties and expresses concern about Jung and his family. He then turns to his inner work and writings. The echo of their silence resonates more disturbingly than the presence of conflict and arguments, but the reason may possibly have been that rather than expressing their feelings to each other, both of them channeled their thinking into profound reflections, such as in *Depth Psychology and a New Ethic* by Neumann and *Answer to Job* by Jung. While Neumann sometimes seems to seek compassion, Jung may have expressed it less in feelings, but rather by supporting his young colleague's independent thinking and writings.

Criticism against Jung, including Neumann's, has targeted his sweeping statements about Jews. In his 1934 paper, "The State of Psychotherapy Today," he discusses the difference between what he terms Jewish and German psychology. While Jewish men are, like women, "physically weaker," Jung also claims that "the Jew, like the cultured Chinese, has a wider area of psychological consciousness than [the Aryan]." He writes that the "Jewish race"

> possesses an unconscious which can be compared with
> the "Aryan" only with reserve. Creative individuals apart,
> the average Jew is far too conscious and differentiated
> to go about pregnant with the tensions of unborn futures.
> The "Aryan" unconscious has a higher potential than the

---

9   Jung's activities on behalf of the OSS are a subject that requires further research. Allen Dulles is reported as saying, "Nobody will probably ever know how much Professor Jung contributed to the Allied Cause during the war" (in Deirdre Bair, *Jung: A Biography* [Boston: Little, Brown, 2003], 493).

> Jewish; that is both the advantage and the disadvantage of
> a youthfulness not yet fully weaned from barbarism.[10]

Besides the categorical nature of such dubious racial speculations, they resonated all too easily with Nazi ideology. Without being apologetic to Jung, Freud, or others, we need to notice that they had a tendency to express sweeping statements and undiscerning projections. It is well known that Freud took advantage of Jung as a Christian to promote psychoanalysis. In a letter to Karl Abraham, in 1908, he speaks about his and Abraham's common intellectual constitution because of their "racial relationship," in contrast to Jung, who as "a Christian and the son of a pastor, can only find his way to me against great inner resistances. His adherence is therefore all the more valuable."[11] Freud ascribes cultural-religious reasons to Jung's presumed resistance and wants to benefit from Jung being part of the surrounding culture that he wants to conquer.

Reaffirming his Jewish identity, Freud writes to Abraham: "On the whole it is easier for us Jews, as we lack the mystical element," while, as David Tacey writes, "according to Freud, Jung's 'mysticism' was due to his Germanic Aryan descent."[12] This reflects the complexity of Freud's attitudes both as regards the nonmystical Jewishness that he adheres to and psychoanalysis presumably being more accessible to what Freud considered "the racial kinship" of the Jews.

Sander Gilman writes:

---

10   C. G. Jung, "The State of Psychotherapy Today" (1934), in *CW*, vol. 10 (Princeton, NJ: Princeton University Press, 1970), par. 353. While Freud agreed that there were "great differences between the Jewish and the Aryan spirit," he also said that "there should not be such a thing as Aryan or Jewish science" (letter to Ferenczi, June 1913, quoted in Ernest Jones, *Life and Work of Sigmund Freud, Vol. 2: The Years of Maturity, 1901–1919* [New York: Basic Books, 1955], 168.) Furthermore, Otto Rank criticized Freud, claiming his "derogatory attitude towards the woman" emanated from a "gigantic projection of the Jew's inferiority complex" (Otto Rank, *Beyond Psychology* [New York: Dover, 1958; originally published in 1941], 286, 288).
11   Jones, *Life and Work of Sigmund Freud*, 53.
12   Sigmund Freud and Karl Abraham, *The Complete Correspondence of Sigmund Freud and Karl Abraham*, ed. Ernst Falzeder (London: Karnac, 2002), 52; David Tacey, *The Jung Reader* (London: Routledge, 2012), 6.

> The biological scientist (and Freud was a biological scientist) and the physician of the nineteenth century absorbed the ideology of race as part of the "truth" of science. It belonged to the "high'" culture of science, and was never completely questioned, even by Jewish scientists, who were seen in this world as being more limited in their mental construction than their Aryan counterparts.[13]

This pseudo-scientific notion of race and racial features was ever present into the early twentieth century—with undeniably devastating consequences. While Freud trusted "the scientific mind," his comparing what he termed the "impossible profession" to "the white-washing of a negro" has little to do with enlightenment and more with the shadow of racism.[14]

As a curiosity we might also mention that James Kirsch left Israel after merely eighteen months, not because of "the land ... but the Jews." He writes to Jung that they do not accept the land and the primitiveness, but attempt to "perpetuate their exile."[15] Seemingly without scrutinizing the contradiction, Kirsch the Zionist leaves while those who presumably perpetuate exile remain.[16] That is, we again find one of those sweeping statements, pertaining more to the psyche's layer of primitivity, projection, and prejudice than to psychological significance and depth. Neumann also expresses disappointment with the new country in disdainful ways, supposedly expecting to find "all his good buddies from Berlin ... but

---

13 Sander Gilman, *Freud, Race, and Gender* (Princeton, NJ: Princeton University Press, 1993), 5.

14 Freud to Otto Rank, in Rank, *Beyond Psychology,* 272.

15 C. G.Jung and J. Kirsch, *The Jung-Kirsch Letters: The Correspondence of C. G. Jung and James Kirsch*, ed. Ann Conrad Lammers (London: Routledge, 2011), 70.

16 In fact, Kirsch gives voice to a great many highly motivated Zionists who have found themselves disappointed with imperfect reality. Cf. the ruminations of the protagonist in my novella: "Rather than groups of pioneers raising their heads in visionary gaze, the land collected hapless losers, miserable outcasts, troubled souls and other homeless misfits who had wandered astray. 'Where lies the truth,' he wondered, 'with the handsome pioneer on the poster, or with the contemptible schnorrer, the despicable beggar?' 'But isn't that the living part of our people?'" (*Requiem: A Tale of Exile and Return* [Hanford, CA: Fisher King Press, 2012], 69).

instead he found a great many Poles, very simple people, artisans, builders, merchants, speculators ... not idealists."[17]

While I do not possess the psychological, historical, or cultural perspective that may be necessary to better understand these indiscriminate proclamations of otherwise brilliant minds, swept away as they seemingly were by the projections that emanate from these primitive layers of the psyche, other than to say that they were human, with flaws and narrow-mindedness like the rest of us, I believe there might be (at least) two additional factors at play: (1) somewhat inflatedly, they too easily seem to have believed that their often profound thoughts and intuitions had universal applicability, thus sometimes failing to discriminate between the gold and the dross; and (2) furthermore, they sometimes used sweeping generalizations and drew vague and indiscriminate conclusions when speculating about the collective psyche.

Regarding the failure to distinguish between essence and nonsense, Jung, in reference to "The State of Psychotherapy Today," eventually told Sigmund Hurwitz: "I have written in my long life many books, and I have also written nonsense. Unfortunately, that was nonsense."[18]

The second point is somewhat more intricate. In *Jacob and Esau: On the Collective Symbolism of the Brother Motif*, Neumann frequently speaks about "the Jew" and claims that "being Jewish is intimately related to being introverted."[19] We only need look around to notice that introversion is not necessarily carved into the character of each individual Jew. We might even say that were Neumann's statement meant to pertain to a trait characteristic of all Jews as individuals forming a collective (the way anti-Semitic and racist projections in general work), this would likely

---

17   Quoted by Micha Neumann in Aviva Lori, "Jung at Heart," *Haaretz*, January 28, 2005.

18   Aryeh Maidenbaum, "Lingering Shadows: A Personal Perspective," in A. Maidenbaum and Stephen A. Martin, eds., *Lingering Shadows: Jungians, Freudians, and Anti-Semitism* (Boston: Shambhala, 1991), 295.

19   Erich Neumann, *Jacob and Esau: On the Collective Symbolism of the Brother Motif*, ed. Erel Shalit (Asheville, NC: Chiron Publications, 2015), 15.

have been an invalid projection of the introverted Neumann himself, possibly based on how "both the extraverted and introverted types tend to consider their psychology to be universally valid and therefore to negate every other standpoint."[20]

When Neumann associates being Jewish with being introverted, I understand him to be implying that structurally introversion is a major, but not necessarily the one and only, dominant in Judaism, grounded in the invisible, "ungraven" God-image—similar to nondepicted Hestia being a goddess of pure interiority. Jacob can then be seen as an archetypal image of a particular cultural attitude, contrasted with his extraverted brother Esau, who serves as his psycho-cultural shadow. In fact, Neumann's positioning Jacob's introversion as prototypical for the Jew might be his way of challenging what he elsewhere describes as the devastating *extraversion* of Judaism.[21]

In his essay "Mind and Earth," originally published in 1927, then republished in 1931, Jung speaks sweepingly about Americans. The essay is scattered with suppositions and intuitive-speculative projections, such as "the inimitable Teddy Roosevelt laugh is found in its primordial form in the American Negro"; or, "the vivacity of the average American, which shows itself … particularly in his extraordinary love of talking—the ceaseless gabble of American papers is an eloquent example of this—is scarcely to be derived from his Germanic forefathers, but is far more like the chattering of a Negro village"; or, "the American presents a strange picture: a European with Negro behaviour and an Indian soul."[22]

But parallel to prejudices and collectivistic simplifications, elsewhere we find Jung expressing thoughts and intuitions about the American cultural psyche, and about trends that we can discern in Western culture,

---

20   Ibid., 46.
21   Jung and Neumann, *Analytical Psychology in Exile*, 140.
22   C. G. Jung, "Mind and Earth" (1931), in *CW*, vol. 10 (Princeton, NJ: Princeton University Press, 1970), pars. 95, 103.

as well as in modern and postmodern society. For example, speaking about America, Jung claimed that it was "so uprooted and divorced from Nature that the 'real, natural man' was in open rebellion" and that "something must be done 'to compensate the earth.'"[23] Even if the New World possibly moves faster and flies higher than the Old World, these are phenomena that accompany unrestrained progress, wherever it takes place.

In fact, categorizing the issue as "American" misses the target—the real issue is when so-called progress and, for instance, technological development are disconnected, when there is a singular and one-sided belief in the rational and scientific mind and in the independence and totality of the ego, without a link to either the earth or the ancestors. Furthermore, Jung speaks about the meaningful and mutual impact of earth and mind. The psyche-in-the-earth, I believe, is quintessential for the understanding of Jung's and Neumann's shared thinking, not least in relation to the Jew, Judaism, and Jewishness.

In "The State of Psychotherapy Today," Jung determines that "the Jew, who is something of a nomad, has never yet created a cultural form of his own and as far as we can see never will, since all his instincts and talents require a more or less civilized nation to act as host for their development."[24] In a letter to Kirsch, Jung claims that this statement is, on the one hand, based on historical data, and on the other hand, he modifies it, for instance, wondering what may develop in the homeland of the Jews.[25] And in a letter to C. E. Benda, Jung distinguishes between

23   From the Richard Evans interviews, quoted in C. G. Jung, *The Earth Has a Soul*, ed. Meredith Sabini (Berkeley, CA: North Atlantic Books, 2008), 9.

24   Jung, "The State of Psychotherapy Today," *CW* 10, par. 353. Freud writes: "In many respects [the Jews] are different from their *hosts* … and where they are admitted, they make valuable contributions to the surrounding civilization" (Sigmund Freud, *Moses and Monotheism* [New York: Vintage, 1955], 115–116). While Freud recognizes a difference between Jews and their host cultures, his empahsis is on their contribution. This can be compared both with Jung's statement and Freud's own regarding "the Negro."

25   Jung, *Letters*, vol. 1, 161.

culture and culture form, pointing out his conviction that "the Jews are a people with a culture."[26]

While we can only remove the thick veil of prejudice and projection by considerable effort, what might we find if we do? I believe that behind Jung's shadow projections we find the following: (1) Jung holds the belief that culture is rooted in the earth; (2) he considers the Jews as nomads, that is, not rooted in the earth; and (3) he generalizes and negativizes the cultural contribution of the Jews, claiming they do not create a cultural form of their own, but require a host nation—the earth of the other—to implement their contributions. Let us look more closely at these three points. First, connecting the earth with nature and instincts is obvious. But earth, ground, and locality hold additional elements of great importance. The spirit, as well, needs to be embodied and contained in order to materialize. It can then emerge from matter, like the grapes spiriting into wine. The relationship between land and language, particularly in the case of Hebrew, illustrates this profoundly. When Hebrew ceased to be a living language, confined primarily to prayer and religious ritual, detached from the land, it stagnated, and its development eventually slowed down. Even among those who knew how to read, and perhaps even write Hebrew, few understood.[27] Only when profanely spoken can its sacred treasures be found. Only when lending itself to desire and dispute, serving both science and society, does it come alive. Only when written and read as modern literature can the ancient scriptures be understood without stagnating into litanies of literalness. When restricted to religious ritual, it dwindles into compulsion and repetition, and its *meaning* goes *unheard* ("to hear" and "meaning" spring from the same root in Hebrew, *shma'*, which is the central prayer in Judaism). However,

---

26 Ibid., 167.
27 In "Sabbath," Oliver Sacks, reflecting on "the seventh day of one's life," writes: "Though I could not understand the Hebrew in the prayer book, I loved its sound and especially hearing the old medieval prayers sung, led by our wonderfully musical hazan." (*New York Times*, August 16, 2015.)

when a language, prominently Hebrew, sprouts up from the life-giving earth, its archetypal roots reawaken. When the language is alive and its spirit is grounded in its archetypal soil, its roots can be impregnated with the life-giving waters. When stifled and unspoken, the root-imagery of the language goes undetected, but when embodied by the soil it can be *rescued* from the *shadows*, and its psychologically meaningful *imagery* can come alive. We may then observe, for instance, that "shadow," "in the image (of God)," and "rescue" stem from the same root, *tzel*. Thus, by tilling the earth, culture is created.

The second point pertains to the claim that Jews are nomads. In their history, Jews have obviously experienced expulsion, been forced to migrate, left out of fear, and sometimes departed in hope for a better future. The external circumstances have to be kept in mind. Host cultures have often been far from welcoming. But we need as well to keep in mind that the origin of the Hebrews, with Abraham, is: "Go from your country, your people and your father's household" (Gen. 12:1). There is a divine command to depart. The very designation, *Hebrew*, implies an archetypally migratory element, meaning "having come from across" (the river). But there is both an origin and a destination—a command to leave "your country" and to go forth to "the land I will show you" (Gen. 12:1) so that departure and wandering are coupled with the arrival in the promised land. The archetypal origin is a polarity, and the implications are complex and multifaceted, but the conclusions we draw, as in Jung's statement, can easily become one-sided and simplistic.

The third point is the most aggravating—and intriguing. The personal rift between Freud and Jung seems to have been intertwined with each of them carrying the other's projected personal and cultural complexes. According to Freud, Jung was resistant to his ideas for religious and cultural reasons. But for the very same reasons, Freud thought, Jung would be better equipped to bring his contribution into the world. For Jung, however, Freud's categories were "Jewish" and not applicable to the culture at large, stated at a time when this suited National-Socialist ideology all too well.[28]

Besides his individual genius, Freud was quite a distinct representative of modern, enlightened German Jewish culture. While he identified himself as a secular and godless Jew, feeling a "racial kinship," he did not know what the essence of his Jewishness was. However, he confidently trusted the scientific mind would one day tell him.[29] We cannot but notice the complexity and the characteristics of Freud's Jewish identity, quite similar to many enlightened German Jews at the time.

German Jewish culture was in many ways an exceptional manifestation of Jewish ethnicity emptying itself of its particularistic culture, with many German Jews seeing themselves as "Germans of Mosaic Faith." Much of modern German Jewry, in fact, identified itself with the center of collective consciousness of Judaism, most prominently the Ten Commandments, brought to the world by Moses. And then, in the course of modern Jewish history, and in his own individual life span, Freud plays out his universalistic fantasy by revising ancestry; in his last work, *Moses and Monotheism*, Freud attempts to turn Moses into an Egyptian and convert him to the Aton religion.[30] Freud turned his back on the dogmatic aspects

---

28 We might note here, as well, Rank's observation, written in the 1930s, that "Freud's whole doctrine of neurosis can be understood as a projection of the Jew's position in our present-day civilization ... Freud could see in civilization only the suffering of the individual and not his positive assertion in creative achievement" (Rank, *Beyond Psychology*, 283–84).

29 "No reader of [the Hebrew version of] this book will find it easy to put himself in the emotional position of an author who is ignorant of the language of holy writ, who is completely estranged from the religion of his fathers—as well as from every other religion—and who cannot take a share in nationalist ideals, but who has yet never repudiated his people—who feels that he is in his essential nature a Jew and who has no desire to alter that nature. If the question were put to him: 'Since you have abandoned all these common characteristics of your country-men, what is there left to you that is Jewish?' he would reply: 'A very great deal, and probably its very essence.' He could not now express that essence clearly in words; but some day, no doubt, it will become accessible to the scientific mind" (Sigmund Freud, preface to the Hebrew translation of *Totem and Taboo*, trans. James Strachey [London: Routledge and Kegan Paul, 1950], xiii). Even though Freud was "ignorant of the language," in *Moses and Monotheism*, he delves (mistakenly, in my opinion) into Hebrew etymology (4).

30 Freud, *Moses and Monotheism*, 27.

of religion, which he considered a "universal obsessional neurosis."[31] Similar to his wish that the unconscious would one day become obsolete, Freud also rejected the shadow side of Judaism—the mystical aspects, in contrast to the strict collective consciousness of formal Judaism.[32] Jewish enlightenment, the so-called Haskala, would dismiss Hasidism and its founder as preoccupied with "magic, exorcism and folk medicine."[33] Thus Freud denies the mystical side of Judaism or, to put it in a cultural rather than religious context, repressed the more soulful side of being Jewish. He identifies Judaism with rabbinical law and religion with rules, rituals, or dogma. Furthermore, just as the essence of his Jewishness would become accessible by means of the scientific mind, Freud was convinced that scientific reason would one day replace faith in God.[34]

Jung then points his finger at the Jew for whom "being Jewish" is a "personal insult." In his critical attitude, he seems to cry out: "Jew, be a Jew!" We hear this clearly in a case reported in *Memories, Dreams, Reflections*, when Jung receives a young Jewish woman for treatment. She is the daughter of a banker, "pretty, chic and highly intelligent," suffering from anxiety neurosis. Jung calls her "a well-adapted, Westernized Jewess, enlightened down to her bones." Since he could not find "a trace of a father complex in her," he asked her about her grandfather:

> For a brief moment she closed her eyes, and I realized at once that here lay the heart of the problem. I therefore asked her to tell me about this grandfather, and learned that he had been a rabbi and had belonged to a Jewish sect. "Do you mean the Chassidim?" I asked. She said yes. I pursued my questioning.

31   Sigmund Freud, "Obsessive Actions and Religious Practices" (1907), in *Standard Edition of the Complete Psychological Works*, vol. 9 (London: Hogarth Press, 1953–1973).
32   "Where id was, there ego shall be" (Sigmund Freud, *New Introductory Lectures on Psychoanalysis*, in *Standard Edition of the Complete Psychological Works*, vol. 22 [London: Hogarth Press, 1953–1973], 80).
33   Moshe Rosman, *Stories That Changed History: The Unique Character of Shivhei Ha-Besht* (Syracuse, NY: Syracuse University Press, 2007), 14.
34   See Sigmund Freud, *The Future of an Illusion* (New York: W. W. Norton, 1975).

"If he was a rabbi, was he by any chance a zaddik?" "Yes," she replied, "it is said that he was a kind of saint and also possessed second sight. But that is all nonsense. There is no such thing!"

With that I had concluded the anamnesis and understood the history of her neurosis. I explained to her, "Now I am going to tell you something that you may not be able to accept. Your grandfather was a zaddik. Your father became an apostate to the Jewish faith. He betrayed the secret and turned his back on God. And you have your neurosis because the fear of God has got into you." That struck her like a bolt of lightning … .

All her conscious activity was directed toward flirtation, clothes, and sex, because she knew nothing else. She knew only the intellect and lived a meaningless life. In reality she was a child of God whose destiny was to fulfil His secret will. I had to awaken mythological and religious ideas in her, for she belonged to the class of human beings of whom spiritual activity is demanded. Thus her life took on meaning, and no trace of the neurosis was left.[35]

Thus, for Jung, "being Jewish" implies quite the opposite of Freud's more rational approach. For Jung, it means to be what you are in accordance with what "destiny prescribes," but clearly not what dogmatic faith commands; rather, re-ligio in the sense of reconnecting with one's ancestral roots.[36]

I find it interesting to note that in the very last letter from Jung to Freud in 1923, a decade after their break, Jung refers a patient of his for continued treatment with Freud. In a note to the letter, Aniela Jaffé writes:

35 C. G. Jung, Memories, Dreams, Reflections, ed. Aniela Jaffé, trans. Richard and Clara Winston (New York: Pantheon Books, 1962, 1965), 138–140.
36 Ibid., 138.

> The case involved a Jew who could not or would not acknowledge his Jewishness. The analysis with Freud did not help him and he turned back to Jung. He then had a dream in which he found himself at an impassable place, beyond which a light shined. At the impass sat an old woman, who said to him: "Only he who is a Jew can get through!" This was the beginning of the cure of his neurosis.[37]

Thus, Jung and Freud speak about entirely different aspects of "being Jewish." While Freud sets up an ego-ideal of Jewishness as rational, enlightened, and free from mysticism, he projects what for him is a shadow aspect onto Jung.

Jung, on the other hand, criticizes the somewhat paradoxical Jewish characteristic of rejecting being Jewish—a view that Neumann tries to modify, rightly claiming that it does not pertain to all Jews. However, that attitude, which Jung observed in Freud, in many psychoanalytic colleagues, and in many of his Jewish patients, contradicted his conviction that culture needs to be rooted. For Jung, being Jewish means to be connected with the inner core and the soulful aspects of Judaism and being rooted in its past. We may in fact say that the earth pertains to being rooted, rooted in one's ancestry, in the spirit of one's cultural psyche. We might add that being rooted, in the earth, in one's culture, in one's life, inevitably makes the shadow surface—which always is painful and disappointing, but when denied, the result may be catastrophic. This is where Jung and Neumann find a common language. Neumann was unmistakably aware of the shadows that lurked in the new-old earth of Israel.

Jung's discovery and Neumann's recognition of the collective layers of the psyche enable a psychological perspective that does not require the

---

37   Letter 359J in Sigmund Freud and C. G. Jung, *The Freud/Jung Letters: The Correspondence between Sigmund Freud and C. G. Jung*, ed. William McGuire, trans. Ralph Manheim and R. F. C. Hull (Princeton, NJ: Princeton University Press, 1974), 553.

reduction of all psychological phenomena to the level of personalization.[38] It is, as well, from this perspective of the collective, objective, archetypal, mythological layer that Jung and Neumann respectively look at and reflect upon society and the era at large, such as man's psyche and future, evil, mass man, rootlessness and meaninglessness, and the process of recollectivization.

I believe both Jung and Neumann in some of their writings were early torchbearers of psycho-ecology—ecology, from the Greek *oikos*, meaning "house, dwelling." That is, ecology is the study of the environment as home. Also, the psyche needs to be at home in the environment, which requires that we let the psyche and the spirit of the environment remain alive, not poisoning it recklessly for the delusions of unimpaired progress.

Being grounded in locality and even in cultural particularism—but not in reactionary xenophobia—were, for both Jung and Neumann, a way to reach out into cultural universalism. While open borders are an antidote to totalitarian regimes with restrictive borders that imprison their populations in fear and persecution, globalization is also greatly unsettling.

The opening up of limitless boundaries, whether physical borders between countries or a boundariless cyberspace, leaves particularly the weaker ego behind, having to struggle with a sense of threat to ego boundaries. The sense of nonlocality and transiency causes in many a sense of being uprooted, disoriented, disconnected, and left with a sense of identity loss. Neumann wrote:

> The global revolution which has seized upon modern man
> and in whose storm center we find ourselves today has led to
> a loss of orientation in the part and in the whole, and daily we

---

38   In *The Origins and History of Consciousness*, Neumann elaborates the significance as well as the limitations of secondary personalization (as in Freudian psychoanalysis); Erich Neumann, *The Origins and History of Consciousness* (Princeton, NJ: Princeton University Press, 1970.)

have new and painful experience of its repercussions in the political life of the collective, as well as in the psychological life of the individual.[39]

Jung wrote, in a letter in 1947, that "collective systems ... have a destructive effect on human relationships ... Totalitarian States ...undermine personal relationships through fear and mistrust, the result being an atomized mass in which the human psyche is completely stifled."[40]

Erich Neumann describes how the detachment from the original group and from the unconscious has, on the one hand, degenerated into overspecialization and, on the other hand "exalt[ed] the mass as a conglomeration of unrelated individuals."[41] The homogenous group making up the tribe, clan, or the village has been exchanged for the mass units of city, office, or factory, says Neumann.[42] This is only more prominent today, when the city and the office have been replaced by the megaunits of social media.

In recollectivization, mass man has taken possession of the person and replaced individual consciousness. As Neumann says, "the individual soul is swallowed back by the Terrible Mother," and as a consequence, the inner voice is being silenced. This happens when, in the transient mass unit, the individual is anonymous and the ego is emptied of all meaning.[43] The collective shadow is most prominent in the disengaged individual. While the negative element, as Neumann says, essentially has "a meaningful place as decomposition and death, as chaos and *prima materia* ... in a fragmented psyche ... it becomes a cancer and a nihilistic danger."[44] Neumann notices that it is the cleavage between ego consciousness and the unconscious that enables our regression to the mass man, and he points out that the mass "is

---

39   Ibid., 438.
40   Jung, *Letters,* vol. 1, 472.
41   Neumann, *The Origins and History of Consciousness*, 436.
42   Ibid.
43   *The Origins and History of Consciousness*, 440, 443–444.
44   Ibid.

the decay of a more complex unit not into a more primitive unit but into a centerless agglomeration."[45]

In a letter to Kirsch, Jung writes: "No one who is a Jew can become a human being without *knowing* that he is a Jew, since this is the basis from which he can reach out towards a higher humanity. This holds good for all nations and races."[46] I believe it is Jung's understanding of the expansiveness of the psyche as not only limited to the mind but also the archetypal dimensions of the psyche and the psyche's rootedness in the world that enabled him, Neumann, and other depth psychologists to see the social and cultural dimensions from a psychological perspective.

By reaching back into the depths and roots of ancestral wisdom, Jung and Neumann were able—and sometimes painfully but humanly less capable—to look out and around and reflect upon the future routes of society and humankind.

---

45   Ibid., 441.
46   Jung, *Letters*, vol. 1, 162.

PART III. TROUBLED TIMES

Hans Fierz and Carl Jung in front of the Dome of the Rock, 1933.
© Jung Family Archive

Carl Jung and Hans Fierz in Palestine and Egypt

Journey from March 13 to April 6, 1933

Andreas Jung

In his lifetime Carl Jung traveled a lot, mostly for professional reasons. Several times he traveled for the purpose of experiencing a part of the world, as for instance with his journeys to New Mexico, to Africa, and, in part, to India. But it happened also that he would decide at a moment's notice to accompany a friend on a business trip, as 1920 to northern Africa or in 1933 to Palestine and Egypt. Only a few documents testify to the journey to Palestine. There are some notes in his works or letters and some anecdotes told by others.

This is the received story of this trip. One evening Jung was invited to a dinner party where he met the husband of Linda Fierz, his devoted disciple, whom he had cured of recurring relapses after the Spanish flu. Hans Eduard Fierz (1882–1953) was professor of chemistry at the ETH, the technical university of Zürich. Jung was exhausted, and Fierz told him that he would be leaving a few days hence for a cruise to Egypt and had booked a first-class cabin with a second bed in it that was not being used. He asked Jung if he would like to join him for this journey. Jung rejected the offer; however, on the actual day and time he turned up at the railway station. Apparently he had changed his mind!

On Monday, March 13, 1933, they left Zurich by train and embarked next day in Genoa on the luxury liner of North German Lloyd named *General von Steuben*. Jung was recovering from a nasty catarrh. He wrote to Emma: "I have already properly recovered!—Till now I have not really done anything but just lazed around. One can relax wonderfully. Only no-one dresses or undresses me, and one can't wheel into the dining room on a deck chair!"[1] During the cruise the two men got to know each other better and became quite good friends. Jung wrote: "Fierz is a pleasant and cheerful travel companion."[2]

Passing by Vesuvius they saw its huge cloud of smoke from afar. On Thursday, March 16, they landed in Messina and traveled by train to Taormina. In Catania, Jung was impressed by an enormous lava stream from Mount Etna, still steaming after six years, and by the fruitful lemon gardens all along the way.

Two days later they reached Athens. Jung disliked the old port of Phalerum, a "heap of mud huts." However, the Parthenon was great, with unmistakable Egyptian and Assyrian influences evident. But the country itself seemed "sucked dry to the bones" and "like an extinct planet."[3]

The next day the ship passed the Bosporus and reached Istanbul. There they visited Hagia Sophia and the Blue Mosque. Next stations were Rhodes, where they walked through the old town, and Cyprus, where Jung rented a car to see some Bronze Age terra-cotta pieces in Nicosia.

On Saturday, March 25, they landed in Haifa and traveled by train to Jerusalem. Behind the fertile plains along the sea appeared the bare Jura limestone of Judea. For two nights they resided in the King David Hotel in Jerusalem. While Jung was "overwhelmed" by the sites on Rhodes, unfortunately the city of Jerusalem left him cold. He felt particularly ashamed of the tastelessness of all the Christian churches! He "was so

---

1   C. G. Jung, unpublished letter to his wife, March 17, 1933.
2   Ibid.
3   C. G. Jung, unpublished letter to his wife, March 20, 1933.

disgusted at the Church of the Nativity in Bethlehem" that he sprained his ankle "in a diabolic manner." As a result, he missed the Church of the Holy Sepulchre. In contrast, Jung thought the Dome of the Rock was "splendid," though claiming that it was built by the Roman emperor Justinian![4]

In spite of his sprained ankle, Jung was able to go down to the Dead Sea the next day, 1,200 meters below Jerusalem and 400 meters below the Mediterranean Sea. The rift valley left an immense impression. Down there the climate was nearly tropical, with banana plantations and even papayas. On March 27, they drove via Jaffa back to Haifa and boarded the *General von Steuben* again.

One day later they reached Port Said, the farthest point of the cruise. At the harbor, they met a fortune-teller, who said to Professor Fierz: "You are a clever man. You are well off, but people think you are much richer than you are. That's always good!" To Jung he said: "Oh ... you are one of the very few great men I have seen; I can't say more." And he added: "For great men and their friends there is no fee"—but he got something, of course![5]

They went on to Cairo and visited the Alabaster Mosque and explored nearby the Pyramids of Giza with their bustle of camels and tourists. Probably by Pullman coach they traveled up the Nile to Luxor to see the enormous Karnak temples.

On Friday, March 31, they embarked again at Port Said. On the way back they landed in Corfu and a last time in Ragusa. Finally on Wednesday, April 5, they reached Venice. Jung intended to meet his wife, Emma, in

---

4   C. G. Jung, unpublished letter to his wife, March 27, 1933. In his Zürich Visions seminar Jung corrected this statement; the church built by Justinian nearby was destroyed in the seventh century and replaced later on by the Al-Aqsa Mosque.

5   Letter to Erich Neumann dated December 19, 1938, in C. G. Jung, *Letters*, ed. Gerhard Adler, trans. R. F. C. Hull (Princeton, NJ: Princeton University Press, 1973), vol. 1, note 1; Heinrich Fierz, "Memory of C. G. Jung," Carl Jung Depth Psychology, July 15, 2014; accessed at http://carljungdepthpsychology. blogspot.ch/2014/07/memory-of-cg-jung-by-henry-k-fierz.html. Hans Fierz's son, Heinrich, mistook Alexandria for Port Said.

Lugano, Switzerland. He reported: "Fierz wants to convince me to give lectures at the Poly—this was the secret motive. The cat came out of the bag in Athens!"[6]

This trip was the beginning of a close relationship between the two men. While still on the steamer, Jung transferred a part of his land in Bollingen to Fierz, and six weeks later Fierz began to build his house in the near neighborhood of Jung's tower. In May, Jung sent his application to the ETH, proposing to start lecturing in autumn. The same month he reported his impressions of the Dome of the Rock in his Zürich Visions seminar, and in June he spoke about the mosques and their relation to the mandala in his Berlin seminar. There he became acquainted with Erich Neumann, and in October the two met a second time—in Jung's library in Küsnacht!

In 1945 Hans Fierz dedicated his new book, *Die Entwicklungsgeschichte der Chemie* [*Development History of Chemistry*], his best work according to his own statement, to Carl Jung, "with Admiration and Friendship"![7]

One final remark: the recent discovery of the steamer's itinerary allows us to rectify some imprecise information in former accounts of this journey. In particular, it was found that the date of one of Jung's letters to his wife was misinterpreted, reading 29 instead of 20, which changed the order of the letters and thus the sequence of the visited ports. Also it has shown that the encounter with the fortune-teller happened in Port Said, not in Alexandria, since there was only one landing in Egypt.

6   C. G. Jung, unpublished letter to his wife, March 20, 1933. The Eidgenössische Technische Hochschule (ETH) Zürich (Swiss Federal Institute of Technology) was founded 1855 under the name Polytechnikum.
7   H. E. Fierz-David, *Die Entwicklungsgeschichte der Chemie* (Basel: Birkhäuser, 1945).

1933—The Year of Jung's Journey to Palestine/Israel and Several Beginnings

Thomas Fischer

Nineteen thirty-three was not only the year Jung got a chance to travel to Palestine/Israel on a cruise in the eastern Mediterranean, it was also a pivotal moment in life that spurred a number of important developments in his later career. Outwardly, Jung at the age of fifty-eight was a well-respected private academic with a thriving analytical practice in his home in Küsnacht near Zurich. He was at the height of his intellectual work, and dedicated followers were flocking to Zurich in seemingly ever greater numbers to attend his private seminars and lectures. In the previous two decades he had established the basis for his own theoretical concepts and was in the midst of teaching his methodology of active imagination to a wider audience in his Visions seminars. Following a rather deprived youth, Jung had started to travel widely after his studies and by the 1920s, he was invited to give lectures all across Europe and the United States. He went on longer trips to northern and eastern Africa, and by the early 1930s, he was turning his attention increasingly to Eastern philosophy and thought, which as a subject was much in vogue with European intellectuals at the time. By that time he had engaged in a wide correspondence with colleagues and followers from literally all over the world, much of it relating to his studies of symbolism and archetypes.

In terms of new writings in 1933, the publication of *Modern Man in Search of a Soul*, a volume of eleven recent essays, added to the popularization of his work in the Anglo-Saxon world to a previously unknown extent. His longtime editor at Princeton University Press, William (Bill) McGuire, spoke of *Modern Man in Search of a Soul* as "a smashing title, saleswise" and "one of the first of Jung's books in English to attract a large popular readership" beyond his own circles.[1]

Jung's popularity at the time is also reflected in his fairly comprehensive lecturing activities during that year. In February Jung, together with his wife, Emma, embarked on a long-planned lecture tour in Germany to Cologne, Essen, and Frankfurt, the latter stop which Jung in a letter to a German friend a few months later called a "fabulous success."[2] In June, he held his well-known Dream seminar in Berlin with Erich Neumann in attendance. Later in the year, Jung also held a smaller seminar in Basel, Switzerland, in the first week of October, before he started teaching regularly on a weekly basis at ETH Zurich (the Swiss Federal Institute of Technology). That was in addition to the previously mentioned privately held Visions seminars which ran throughout the year in three terms on a weekly basis at the Zurich Psychology Club.[3]

---

1 William McGuire, "Firm Affinities: Jung's Relations with Britain and the United States," *Journal of Analytical Psychology* 40, no. 3(1995): 301–326. This was a lecture given March 4, 1994; the quote is from a mimeo (p. 28). The title *Modern Man in Search of a Soul* was never published in German, but some of the essays contained therein were part of the equally popular title *Seelenprobleme der Gegenwart*, published in 1931, and all the other texts, individually published at first, were later included in the German and English versions of *The Collected Works of C. G. Jung*.

2 In Cologne and Essen Jung presented "Über Psychologie," an extended version of a lecture first held in 1931 in Dresden and in 1932 in Zürich (on the occasion of the awarding of the first literary prize ever by the city of Zurich). The lecture was first published in *Neue Schweizer Rundschau* 1, no. 1 (May 1932): 1–28 and no. 2 (June 1932): 98–106. An updated and revised version under the title "Die Bedeutung der Psychologie für die Gegenwart" was also included in *Wirklichkeit der Seele: Anwendungen und Fortschritte der neueren Psychologie* (with contributions by Hugo Rosenthal, Emma Jung, and W. M. Kranefeldt). An English translation of this version is included in *The Collected Works of C. G. Jung* (C. G. Jung, "The Meaning of Psychology for Modern Man" (1934), in *CW*, vol. 10 [Princeton, NJ: Princeton University Press, 1970], pars. 276–332). According to his own account, more than one thousand people had attended the Frankfurt lecture (C. G. Jung in a letter to Vera Curtius dated November 6, 1933, in C.G. Jung Papers Collection, ETH Zurich University Archives, Hs 1056: 2337.

3 Winter term: January 18—March 8; spring term: May 3—June 21; fall term: October 4—December 13, 1933.

Nineteen thirty-three was also the year that the first Eranos conference in Ascona in the south of Switzerland took place, to which Jung contributed "A Study in the Process of Individuation."[4] For the first two decades, the Eranos conferences, initiated by Olga Fröbe-Kapteyn, were pretty much built around Jung's interests and work, and they provided a welcome platform for him to discuss his ideas with respected peers and to launch himself into new subjects, like his recently discovered interest in alchemy and the possibility for a psychological reading of these enigmatic centuries-old texts. The Eranos conferences were significant insofar as they allowed Jung to expand beyond his close circle of students in Zurich to engage in a wider interdisciplinary dialogue with scholars of symbolism, religious studies, philosophy, and natural sciences.

At the same time, Jung continued to stay in touch with his medical colleagues in the Swiss Association of Psychiatry, to which he gave a presentation in October at their yearly meeting in Prangins in the French-speaking part of Switzerland.[5] To round off the year he gave yet another lecture on dreams in December in Lucerne. And that is just a brief overview of the lecturing activities he actually accepted. In addition, he was invited to speak on numerous other occasions in Switzerland and abroad in 1933, which he declined for lack of time due to the heavy workload he was already facing.[6]

Most of the individual lectures he held that year he also turned into written contributions to journals, a task which must have consumed

4   C. G. Jung, "A Study in the Process of Individuation" (1950), in *CW*, vol. 9i (Princeton, NJ: Princeton University Press, 1968).
5   C. G. Jung, "Diskussionsvotum von Dr. Jung (über Halluzination)," lecture at the Swiss Association of Psychiatry, Prangins, Switzerland, October 7–8, 1933; published in *Schweizer. Archiv für Neurologie und Psychologie* 32(2):382. (English translation "On Hallucination" (1933), CW 18, 38).
6   Among the events that he declined were invitations to Holland, Stettin (part of Germany at the time), Paris, and Geneva, along with lecture invitations to the Davoser Kulturgesellschaft in the Swiss Alps, to the Siemens Gesellschaft, and to a group of teachers in Zurich as well as to Protestant priests and doctors in the neighboring town of Winterthur. This nonexhaustive list is based on a perusal of 1933 correspondences in the C. G. Jung Papers Collection at the ETH Zurich University Archives.

yet more of his time. The same goes for a number of book reviews to monthly publications and forewords he was asked to contribute to new monographs by friends and colleagues.[7] Not to forget that he still saw numerous patients on most working days and was reading through piles of letters, requests, and manuscripts that were sent to him for comments.

Outwardly, Jung's life and career was well established and thriving in 1933. On the inside, however, Jung had just resurfaced from his challenging and troubling experience of working through his own inner fantasies and unconscious material, which coincided with his struggle to find an arrangement with his confidant Toni Wolff and his wife Emma. As Jung later recalled, he had been no less than nearly shattered at first by the stream of unconscious material documented in the Black Books, which he then subsequently aesthetically elaborated in the Red Book.

While stressing the importance of his outer life at the time to hold himself together—meaning his medical work with patients, his wife, his family, his home in Küsnacht—he felt that he was no longer capable of continuing his teaching at the University of Zürich.[8] Jung had been lecturing there since becoming the assistant medical director at the university psychiatry hospital, known as the Burghölzli clinic, in 1905. Feeling that he possibly could not talk about the things that were going on inside him in this exposed situation, he withdrew from the university altogether in 1913. By taking that step Jung had quite consciously sacrificed the academic career that had lain ahead of him at the time. He reflects in his memoir about the absolute inner necessity of this decision and his unwavering willingness

7   C. G. Jung, "Bruder Klaus," *Neue Schweizer Revue* 1, no. 4 (August 1933); English translation: "Brother Klaus" (1933), in *CW*, vol. 11 (Princeton, NJ: Princeton University Press, 1969). C. G. Jung, "Geleitwort des Herausgebers," *Zentralblatt für Psychotherapie* 6:3; English translation: "Editorial in *Zentralblatt*, VI" (1933), in *CW*, vol. 10 (Princeton, NJ: Princeton University Press, 1970). C. G. Jung, "Rezension von: G. R. Heyer: Der Organismus der Seele," *Europäische Revue* 9:10; English translation: "Review of Heyer: *Der Organismus der Seele*" (1933), in *CW*, vol. 18 (Princeton, NJ: Princeton University Press, 1976). C. G. Jung, "Foreword to Adler: *Entdeckung der Seele*" (1933), in *CW*, vol. 18 (Princeton, NJ: Princeton University Press, 1976).
8   C. G. Jung, *Memories, Dreams, Reflections*, ed. Aniela Jaffé, trans. Richard and Clara Winston (New York: Pantheon Books, 1962, 1965), 214 and 219 in the 1967 Fontana Press edition.

to take that risk at all personal costs, but he also clearly regretted the fact that during the following two decades he did not receive more academic or public recognition in his hometown of Zurich.

Despite his bravado and seemingly self-assured character, Jung was obviously driven by strong intellectual ambitions ever since his student days and was quite sensitive to criticism. He actually never stopped longing for formal recognition of his intellectual achievements after he had left his teaching position at the University of Zurich. In fact, the twenty years from 1913 to 1933 were characterized as much by personal insecurity as by outward success. Thus it must have given him great personal satisfaction finally to be given the opportunity to teach once again at an academic institution in Zurich.

As a private scholar after 1913, Jung had practically been excluded from the academic discourse within the University of Zurich. Given the faculty's persisting skepticism toward the discipline of psychology, it is not surprising that when he was eventually given an academic teaching position again it was in the neighboring Swiss Federal Institute of Technology (ETH).[9] What psychology in general—and Jung's school in particular—was lacking by way of support at the university obviously existed at the ETH: a network of personal acquaintances among the regular faculty members who had the necessary clout to prompt and support Jung's candidacy.[10]

Once Jung, instigated by Hans Fierz's proposition while on their trip to the eastern Mediterranean, formally submitted his claim for habilitation (postdoctoral lecture qualification) in May 1933, it only took a few weeks

9   The first full chair of psychology at the University of Zurich, originally instigated by Gottlob Friedrich Lipps in 1911, was assigned by the faculty of philosophy to Eberhard Griesebach, a proper philosopher, after Lipps's death in 1931. The faculty of medicine in Zurich at the time was equally reluctant to embrace the field of psychology in its own right. See Andreas Maercker, "Geschichte des Psychologischen Instituts der Universität Zürich" (online paper, June 15, 2007; accessed at http://www.maercker-website.ch/images/data/Gesch_Psych_Instituts_260607.pdf), 6.

10   Angela Graf-Nold, "C. G. Jung's Position at the Eidgenössische Technische Hochschule Zürich (ETH Zurich): The Swiss Federal Institute of Technology, Zurich," *Jung History* 2, no. 2 (Fall 2007): 12–15.

until he received word of the positive decision "to grant Dr. Jung the *venia legendi* (teaching credentials) for eight terms as a private lecturer with the elective course program at ETH in the field of psychology."[11] Jung started lecturing at ETH on October 20, 1933, and continued to do so until summer 1941, when he resigned from his teaching position for health reasons.[12]

Over the course of that period of time spanning nearly a decade, Jung lectured on the whole of his theories, hypotheses, and methods developed so far. As of 1935, when he was given the formal title of a *Titularprofessor* (visiting senior professor), in addition to the weekly lecture Jung also started a regular German seminar series at ETH for a smaller group of people.[13]

The difference between the ETH lectures and his teaching more than twenty years earlier at the University of Zurich was that while the latter had been of a rather clinical character for the education of future medical doctors, the former were now addressed to a broader variety of students. In fact, teaching within the framework of the elective course program of the ETH meant that Jung had to formulate his ideas for a general audience. When the ETH was founded in 1855 in the wake of the creation of Switzerland as a modern nation state in 1848, the idea was not only to build a first-rate academic school for the training of natural scientists and engineers but also to give them an education as citizens in the wider sense, including the fields of economics, literature, philosophy, social science, and cultural studies. It is in this context that Jung's lectures became part of the ETH curriculum.

---

11 Schweizerischer Schulrat, Beschluss vom 24.6.1933. The nomination was based among other things on the positive reviews of Jung's application by ETH professors Fritz Medicus and Eugen Böhler.

12   I owe most of the information regarding Jung's nomination to the ETH in 1933 to the research of Ulrich Hoerni, who has studied related documents in the ETH archives and in Jung's private papers accounting for this story in connection with the preparation of a foreword to an edition of Jung's ETH lecture series, which is currently underway with the Philemon Foundation.

13   The lectures, always held on a Friday evening between 6 and 7 p.m., usually attracted some 250 students during the winter terms and some 150 students during the summer. The seminars were normally held with a participation of about 30 students. While the lectures were open to the public, the seminars were restricted to qualified students.

It may be worth mentioning that Jung was not the first to teach psychology at ETH. Since the 1890s, there had been occasional lectures in psychology, and since 1904 Dr. Arthur Wreschner of the University of Zurich had offered psychology as a regular subject in the elective course program. When Wreschner died in 1932, an opening occurred, at which point Jung's friends from within the ETH faculty probably encouraged him to apply in order to fill this void in the school's curriculum.

While Jung's application letter of 1933 to the authorities examining his submission reads more like a letter of acceptance for an invitation extended to him, there can be no doubt that eventually being granted a formal professorial title from a hometown university meant a great deal to Jung even at this later stage of his career.

The appointment to ETH definitely elevated his academic standing, but the spring of the same year also brought another nomination, which put him in a politically much more challenging position. By May 1933, Hitler and his National Socialist Party had definitely seized power in Germany and were swiftly installing the laws of *Gleichschaltung*, the so-called regime of conformity, for all professional societies throughout the country. Jung got entangled with this development because since 1928 he had been a member of the General Medical Society for Psychotherapy, which was based in Germany. Furthermore, in 1933 he was also the vice president of the organization. When the German president of the society was forced to resign in spring of that year because of the international nature of the organization, the task automatically fell to Jung. Within a few months he was asked by his German colleagues as a "neutral Swiss" to take over the reins as president of the *international* part of the society's membership so as to allow for the establishment of an exclusively national German section, which would then be able to abide by the requirements of *Gleichschaltung*. With the establishment of an international, politically and denominationally neutral, umbrella organization under Jung's presidency—including national chapters in Holland, Sweden, Denmark, Switzerland, and later also Great Britain—it was hoped that the German group, which had the greatest number of members, could be sufficiently counterbalanced and contained.

Jung remained the president of the International General Medical Society for Psychotherapy for the remainder of the decade until war broke out in Europe in 1939 and he resigned. It is in this function that he got involved with professional politics in Nazi Germany in the 1930s, which consequently led to widespread allegations of Nazi sympathies and anti-Semitism on Jung's part. Still today Jung's statements on contemporary cultural and political questions made in that context are widely and controversially discussed.

In fact, Erich Neumann, who came in touch with Jung just around the time when Jung assumed the chairmanship of the General Medical Society for Psychotherapy in Germany, was one of the first to challenge him on this affiliation and on some of his comments made about the distinctive traits of "Jewish psychology." In their exchange of letters, neither of the two men were easily budged, which makes this one of the most interesting and informed discussions on the subject. Based on this exchange, Neumann later became one of Jung's strongest defenders when it came to further public accusations of anti-Semitism and Nazi sympathies.

While already a hotly debated issue at the time, a serious scholarly examination of the subject of Jung and his relationship to National Socialism has taken place again in more recent times, beginning with the seminal study of Geoffrey Cocks on psychotherapy in the Third Reich and the important results of the conferences organized by Aryeh Maidenbaum and Stephen Martin, published under the titles *Lingering Shadows* and *Jung and the Shadow of Anti-Semitism* in the 1990s and early 2000s.[14] Since then a number of studies have appeared adding new research based

---

14 Geoffrey Cocks, *Psychotherapy in the Third Reich: The Göring Institute*, 2nd ed. (London: Transaction Publishers, 1997); A. Maidenbaum and Stephen A. Martin, eds., *Lingering Shadows: Jungians, Freudians, and Anti-Semitism* (Boston: Shambhala, 1991); Aryeh Maidenbaum, ed., *Jung and the Shadow of Anti-Semitism* (Berwick, ME: Nicolas-Hays, 2002).

on the original source material in the C. G. Jung and C. A. Meier papers collections stored at the ETH Zurich University Archives.[15]

Instead of reviewing Jung's activities and decisions during his presidency of the International Medical Society for Psychotherapy between 1933 and 1940 once more, the focus here is on the origins of the society and Jung's initial involvement in the years 1928 to 1933, to clarify the circumstances under which Jung ended up becoming the president of the society throughout the remainder of the decade.

Geoffrey Cocks, in his book *Psychotherapy in the Third Reich,* has written a substantial chapter on that part of the history of the society. We also have at least one interesting contemporary source available in the form of an account of the early years of the Medical Society for Psychotherapy, written in hindsight by Walter Cimbal, who was the secretary of the society in Germany and the main point of contact for Jung to the German group established in 1933. Cimbal was a Hamburg medical doctor, who in his own words had no deep affiliations with any of the existing schools of psychology at the time, but with strong interests in the neuroses of infancy and adolescence and their possible explanation by hereditary factors and depth psychology. It seems that for ideological and opportunistic reasons he was prone to the ideas of National Socialism early on, but later he fell out of favor with some members of the party and was relieved from all functions of the society in 1935.[16]

---

15   Carl Alfred Meier (1905–1995), Swiss psychiatrist and Jungian psychologist, was the first president of the C. G. Jung Institute in Zürich and a successor to Jung as professor of psychology at the ETH Zurich. During Jung's presidency of the International General Medical Society for Psychotherapy in the 1930s, C. A. Meier served as Jung's right hand and the secretary of the society's journal, the *Zentralblatt für Psychotherapy*. His papers, which are integrated into the Jung Papers Collection at the ETH Zurich University Archives, contain the single most important source of material on Jung's professional dealings with Germany during the period of Nazi rule. The Foundation of the Works of C. G. Jung is currently cosponsoring a project providing a detailed introduction and description of the pertinent materials in the Meier collection. The project is carried out by Giovanni Sorge, author of "Psicologia analitica e anni Trenta: Il ruolo di C.G. Jung nella Internazionale Allgemeine Ärztliche Gesellschaft für Psychotherapie, 1933–1939/40" (PhD thesis, University of Zurich, 2010).
16   According to Cocks, Cimbal joined the National Socialist Party in March 1933; Cocks, *Psychotherapy in the Third Reich*, 90–92.

Toward the end of his life Cimbal wrote an account of the early history of the society partly from memory and partly based on some of the records he had kept from the time. There were at least two versions of this report, the first one typed up in 1952, which is presumably lost, and a later one, nineteen pages long, dating from 1956–1957, of which a copy is preserved in Jung's private papers.[17]

According to Cimbal's report, the General Medical Society for Psychotherapy was first founded in 1926 by a number of practitioners and professors from Munich, Germany, and Vienna, Austria, with the aim of establishing psychotherapy as a means to work with patients. The ultimate goal was having psychotherapy recognized by the health insurance system as an acknowledged method of treatment. As Cimbal reminds us, this would have meant no less than an outright revolution in light of the predominant somatic-monistic mindset of university medical schools at the time, which rejected all ideas of psychological influences on the soul and mind as unscientific.

It is no surprise, then, that the initial task of the group was finding an understanding among the different emerging schools of psychology and psychotherapy, which also included psychoanalysis. Much of the discussion at the first meetings in 1926 and 1927 was dedicated to this debate. But more than diverging opinions on the merits of different methods and schools, an underlying conflict soon cropped up along social and political lines. By the time of the 1928 congress, the society had openly split into what Cimbal termed an "Eastern" (meaning a Soviet-socialist)

---

17 Walter Cimbal, "Versuch einer Geschichte der Internationalen und Deutschen allgemeinen ärztlichen Gesellschaften für Psychotherapie—1926 bis 1935" (mimeo, 1956–1957). Cimbal had been prompted in late 1956 by Theodor Winkler, professor at the psychiatric clinic in Tübingen and secretary of the reestablished General Medical Society for Psychotherapy in Germany in the 1950s, to elaborate on his first version of the report. The first, shorter version was written in 1952 and sent to Gottfried Kühnel, MD, who was a member of the German group of the society and of the so-called Göring Institute Berlin in the 1930s. After the war he was the initiator of a meeting that led to the reestablishment of the General Medical Society for Psychotherapy in 1948 under Ernst Kretschmer, who had been president prior to 1933. Kühnel was a student of Kretschmer. See Cocks, *Psychotherapy in the Third Reich*, 184, 338, 359, and 362.

camp and a "Western" (meaning a national conservative) camp, and it was only due to the integrative and mediating personality of then president Karl Robert Sommer, professor of psychiatry at the University of Giessen, that a total failure of the congress could be prevented.

It was at this time that Sommer asked Cimbal (as somewhat of an outsider) to become the executive secretary of the society, and together they organized the next conference program of less politically inflammatory topics around questions of practical psychotherapy and its relationship to neighboring disciplines, striving for the establishment of an "international medical society for psychotherapy and depth psychology" in the future. To achieve the latter, Jung was invited to become a member of the society and was immediately elected vice-chairman of it in 1928, tasked with giving the keynote lecture at the upcoming 1929 congress in Bad Nauheim.

By that time the General Medical Society for Psychotherapy already included a number of members from countries outside the German-speaking parts of Europe (Germany, Austria, Switzerland). These included loosely organized groups and individuals from the Netherlands, Sweden, Hungary, and Czechoslovakia and soon also members from France, Belgium, Poland, and Russia. Already in 1928 Jung was invited to join the society with the aim of making him the future chairman of an international organization spanning a number of national chapters.

Looking again at the broader picture, this must have been an intriguing perspective to Jung, who had left the International Psychoanalytical Association, which he had helped found, after the split with Freud's circle in Vienna and who since then had no institutional stronghold, in particular in the German-speaking parts of Europe. Here obviously was a chance to establish analytical psychology internationally as one of the leading schools of psychotherapy on a level playing field alongside psychoanalysis of Freudian distinction and Adler's individual psychology, as well as other methods such as autogenic training and psychocatharsis. It should be stressed that the General Medical Society for Psychotherapy was not meant to bring domination to one school of thought over another, but rather to build more clout for these coexisting schools to face the bigger common challenge of being denied formal recognition within the established university faculties of medicine and psychiatry.

Professor Sommer resigned from all his functions in the Medical Society for Psychotherapy and retired to a more private life when his wife, who had been seriously ill for a long time, died in 1932. Ernst Kretschmer, one of only two other remaining university professors of psychiatry among the members of the society, took over the presidency, trying to hold the different strains together at the helm of the organization. However, within only a year his efforts suffered a severe blow: the General Medical Society for Psychotherapy had decided to hold its next congress in spring 1933 in Vienna with Freud, Adler, and Jung scheduled to give the three main presentations. According to Cimbal, more than 4,000 invitations had been sent out and about 1,000 persons had registered for participation, when just a few weeks before the event the National Socialist Party prohibited the conference from taking place and forced Kretschmer to resign from his post as president of the society if he did not want to lose his appointment as university professor in Tübingen.[18] While Cimbal's report largely remains silent about the reasons for the forced cancellation of the Vienna congress in 1933, it is only reasonable to assume that with the National Socialists taking over control over all social and professional organizations in Germany, an international congress organized by a German society abroad and including a prominent number of Jewish and Soviet speakers with socialist orientations, as well as all sorts of other "suspect individuals," was out of the realm of what the National Socialist Party was willing to tolerate in the future.

With Kretschmer forced to resign in 1933, Jung as vice president became the new chairman by default. The very existence of the society

---

18   On Kretschmer's resignation see Cocks, *Psychotherapy in the Third Reich*, 101.

was now very much at stake. Jung's German colleagues rightfully feared a total ban of the society under National Socialist rule, and they quickly began to discuss the possibilities remaining for continuing the activities of their organization in some fashion under the prevailing circumstances. Already having prepared for the establishment of a strictly German national group within the society, they elected Matthias Heinrich Göring, a psychiatrist and distant cousin of Reichsmarschall Hermann Göring, the new head of the German branch and tasked Jung with the formal founding of an international umbrella organization comprised of several other additional national groups.[19]

As explained earlier, this move would allow the German group to abide by the rules of the National Socialist regime, while the newly formed *International* Medical Society for Psychotherapy with Jung as a neutral Swiss at the helm would provide a container for the remaining members of different nationalities. This set-up, in turn, would allow the German colleagues to remain in contact with the other members of their former society. As Jews were now forbidden to be members of the executive of any organization in Germany, cofounders Wladimir Eliasberg and Arthur Kronfeld, both former members of the executive committee, resigned in a demonstrative fashion and left the General Medical Society altogether, with most other Jewish members taking the same step in the course of the next few years. Most of them actually emigrated from the country and tried to establish a new life elsewhere. As president of the international society, Jung tried to help Jewish members by instigating a change in the charter of the society in 1933–1934, which allowed for a direct individual membership status not being bound to membership in a national group. This mainly aimed at being able to issue professional credentials for German Jewish colleagues until they were able to emigrate. Interestingly enough, Cimbal, a National Socialist

---

19   On Matthias Heinrich Göring, see Cocks, *Psychotherapy in the Third Reich*, 35f.

Party member himself, was helpful in clearing this formality with the executives of an organization that was still largely dominated by German members.[20]

The years 1933 to 1935 ended up being a critical balancing act for Jung, during which time—and after a number of what one may call initial missteps—he learned to refrain from repeating his earlier comments on the differences between Jewish and Aryan psychology, at least in public. The years 1934 and 1935 were also the last two that the congresses of the International and the General (German) Medical Society for Psychotherapy were held together, after which time it became increasingly impossible for all involved to stick to the illusion of keeping politics out of professional discussions. Jung and his colleagues in the international society now concentrated all the more on building up other national groups—in particular with the addition of a British branch—to counterbalance the German influence. However, the printing of its official publication, the *Zentralblatt für Psychotherapie und ihre Grenzgebiete*, of which Jung had assumed coeditorship, remained in Germany and thus succumbed to obvious (self-)censorship and control by the Nazi affiliates within the German national group.

Whether it was a wise decision on Jung's part to accept the presidency of the General Medical Society for Psychotherapy in 1933 at all in light of the looming situation can be rightly debated. Different arguments have been made for his motivation to do so, ranging from credulity or naïveté on Jung's part to reckless ambition and an outright embrace of anti-Semitic politics. Yet, in light of the above source material, Jung's own explanation that he had felt compelled to help his German colleagues in difficult professional times also has to be taken into account at face value. There is documentary evidence that shows he did actively help his Jewish German colleagues who were preparing for emigration with

---

20   Ann C. Lammers, "C. G. Jung und die Gesellschaft für Psychotherapie," *Jungiana* 18(2014): 69f.

personal letters of recommendation and certificates.[21] As Jung himself later never fully accounted for his decision to take over the presidency, it is ultimately left to the present-day reader to form an opinion based on the firsthand material that has been preserved on the subject.[22] With the publication of the Jung-Neumann correspondence, an excellent source on this aspect of Jung's life has now become available to a wider public, which allows us, among other things, to grasp a better sense of the issues at stake regarding Jung's involvement with professional politics in Germany at the time.

In conclusion, the year 1933, which started with a seemingly innocuous holiday cruise for Jung with his friend Hans Fierz in the eastern Mediterranean, turned out to be a pivotal moment which would leave its imprint on Jung's life in the following decades. The beginnings of the yearly Eranos conferences, Jung's ETH lecture series, as well as his chairmanship of the International General Medical Society for Psychotherapy, which all began in 1933, definitely belong to the more significant developments in the second half of Jung's life and career.

---

21 See Giovanni Sorge, "Jung's Presidency of the International General Medical Society of Psychotherapy: New Insights," *Jung Journal: Culture & Psyche* 6, no. 4 (Fall 2012): 46.

22 Key statements by Jung on professional issues and the situation in Germany in the 1930s have been republished in his "Essays on Contemporary Affairs" (1946), which are included in *CW* 10, *Civilization in Transition*; beyond that, Jung always left it to his students and followers to defend him against accusations in public.

Jungians in Berlin 1931–1945: Between Therapy, Emigration, and Resistance

Jörg Rasche

The Berlin Jung Society 1931

It was a remarkable date when the Berlin Jung Society was founded: December 24, 1931—a cold Christmas Eve in Berlin, thirteen months before Hitler came to power. The elected president was Eva Moritz, who trained with Jung. Among the founding members were Toni Sussmann, Wolfgang Kranefeldt, Adolf Weizsäcker, and, unofficially behind the scenes, Kaethe Buegler. Many of the members or affiliates of the Jung Society emigrated in the following years: Gerhard Adler, Toni Sussmann, Ernst Bernhard, Werner Engel, Heinz Westmann, James Kirsch, Max Zeller, and Erich Neumann. All of them were able to influence, promote, and develop Jungian psychology in other countries and on other continents. Their emigration was a big loss for the young Jungian group in Berlin. But here I want to reflect on the situation of those who did not or could not leave the so-called Third Reich.

We have limited information about the life and work of many of these early colleagues. Some wrote later about their experiences—Geoffrey Cocks, Ann Lammers, Tom Kirsch, to name only a few. Nevertheless the situation of the Jungians who did not emigrate, who stayed in Germany, remains in shadow.

To get a picture of the situation before the Nazis gained political power one should keep in mind that the antidemocratic turmoil in Germany had already begun with World War I. With the retirement of the German emperor in 1918 the patriarchal and militarized society had lost its leader. The young republic had to grapple with enormous social and psychological problems. There were fights between the Communists and National Socialists in the streets, along with poverty, the Spanish flu epidemic, unemployment, incredible monetary inflation, and hundreds of thousands of crippled soldiers begging for support. Many were traumatized by what they had experienced on the battlefields and in the trenches, where gas had been used. And there were psychological effects of the Treaty of Versailles, which was regarded by many as unjust. C. G. Jung observed already in 1918 in many of his German patients that there was a "peculiar state of mind then prevailing in Germany. I could only see signs of depression and a great restlessness, but this did not allay my suspicions … The archetypes I had observed expressed primitivity, violence, and cruelty."[1]

On the other side of this "peculiar state of mind" there was an exploding longing for freedom and experiment, for leaving behind the chains of the authoritarian system. The old world had collapsed, and the contours of a new democratic world began to surface in a chaotic way. In the midst of misery and disorientation came the outbreak of the Roaring Twenties, the arrival of Expressionist art, of new media like the famous film productions of directors such as F. W. Murnau, Fritz Lang, and Ernst Lubitsch, and the Bauhaus school of art and architecture. All of these made Berlin the center of an emerging new world—of what we call modernity. Part of this emerging modernity was psychoanalysis. There were no restrictions on foreign psychotherapists who wished to work in the Germany of the Weimar Republic, and many pioneers of

---

1   C. G. Jung, "The Fight with the Shadow" (1946), in *CW*, vol. 10 (Princeton, NJ: Princeton University Press, 1970), par. 447.

psychoanalysis from other countries came to Berlin. Here the first and most influential Freudian institute was established in 1920, even more important than the one in Vienna. The list of the members of the institute in Berlin reads like a who's who of early psychoanalysis and includes Karl Abraham, Max Eitingon, Melanie Klein, Wilhelm Reich, and so on—everybody was in Berlin. The Jungians were a minority, and after the split between Freud and Jung the Freudians stayed among their own. Other groups like the Adlerians and Jungians were initially marginalized. Some analysands began with a Freudian analysis and later changed to Jung, and some traveled to Zurich for a Jungian training. The foundation of the Berlin Jung Society in 1931 was a step toward establishing a Jungian frame for professional exchange. Jung himself visited the group several times. His seminars became famous.

James Kirsch may have been the first among the Jungians to realize not only the gathering dark clouds but the immediate danger for Jews of the racist Hitler party—and he also recognized the ignorance of most of the German bourgeoisie of the threat that Hitler posed. When Hitler came to power in 1933, democracy had already fallen into ill-repute and had pretty much ceased to exist. I think there were two reasons for this. The first was the bloodletting in World War I, where the most energetic and gifted died first, added to the disorientation and brutalization suffered by many of the soldiers who survived. Most academic, political, and business leaders had been in favor of war and nationalism, claiming that in times of war you have nothing to discuss, only to win. It was the same in England and France, the major difference being that Germany, in the end, lost the war. The second reason why democracy had all but vanished by the time Hitler came to power was the terror waged against all social democratic or liberal thinkers, which increased in the late 1920s. The novelist Robert Musil, author of *Der Mann ohne Eigenschaften* [*The Man Without Qualities*], wrote in his diary that during the Nazi era he had no vision of a Germany without the Nazis because any alternative had disappeared even before 1933.

By then it was too late; the Gestapo, as well as other terrorist members of the National Socialist Party (NSDAP), were protected by the new government.

Psychotherapy was especially important in the Weimar Republic because of the many traumatized soldiers and disoriented people after World War I. In the Berlin Freudian institute, the diagnosis and treatment of these was their major source of work. The founding of the Allgemeine Ärztliche Gesellschaft für Psychotherapy (AÄGP) was to cope with the increasing need for psychotherapy—not only for psychoanalysis. Many schools of psychotherapy emerged in the creative time of the 1920s in Germany, including early body therapies, breathing therapy, Gestalt therapy, chirology, and so on. C. G. Jung was open to all these developments, and psychotherapy became the domain of the Jungian approach. Jung was often in Berlin and gave seminars. He was elected vice president of the psychotherapeutic society, which was supplementary (complementary) to but also in competition with the Freudian psychoanalytical scene. The AÄGP had many Jews among its members. The Freudian International Psychoanalytical Association excluded its German Jewish members in 1934. Kretschmer, the president of the AÄGP, resigned in 1933 after Hitler was elected as Reichskanzler and declared that all professional organizations had to be coordinated (*gleichgeschaltet*) and Jews had to be excluded. As is well known, Jung took over the position, for which he has been criticized. However, I think that Kretschmer was not the honorable man he is often thought of; that same year he became a sponsoring member of the Schutzstaffel, the SS, and signed a public letter of allegiance to Hitler.

The resignation of Kretschmer was not a protest against Nazi politics, as is often said in order to blame Jung. To the contrary, Kretschmer was an opportunist. Jung, a Swiss citizen, took over, as he always stated, out of his sense of responsibility for psychotherapy in Germany and his Jewish colleagues who had become "hot potatoes." Soon he was attacked for this by the Freudians. It may well be that Jung went too far in trying to make an arrangement with the ruling Nazi Party and in using the wrong vocabulary, referring to what was called Jewish psychology. And he may have slipped for a time into the trap of narcissism and his anti-Freud complex. But, for example in his Berlin seminar in 1933, he tried to work as a group psychotherapist for the one hundred disoriented psychotherapists in his audience, and he avoided any political statements which may have interfered with his mission to save psychotherapy in Hitler's state. Perhaps, as Aniela Jaffé and Barbara Hannah said later on, he was too optimistic.

A Circle of Friends

Step by step and train after train most Jewish Jungians left Germany. The few remaining ones tried to manage themselves in difficult conditions. The Analytical Institute had to be transformed into a so-called Reichsinstitut (State Institute for Psychological Research and Psychotherapy), where some continued teaching for a while. The practicing Jewish doctors lost their licenses and had financial troubles. A few Freudian colleagues like Edith Jacobson and John Rittmeister were secretly engaged in the Communist resistance, completely against the directive of Anna Freud, who ordained that analysis and political activity do not go together.

There was one remaining circle that included Jungian analysts. I got most of my information about this group from the late Hildemarie Streich, a Jungian analyst, who gave me documents in the years before her death. Tom and Jean Kirsch visited her during their trip to Berlin in 2008. She was a friend of James Kirsch and his wife Hilde, with Franz Riklin (former president of IAAP) and especially with Adolf Portmann (a biologist who became the leader of Eranos after the death of Olga Fröbe-Kapteyn) and his wife.

The center of the secret circle in Berlin was Hildemarie's father, Alfred Peter (1886–1945). A historian, active in Christian circles, he taught seminars on the Bible. Peter was married to Anna-Barbara (1891–1949), with whom he had five children, and he was close to the Wandervogel, a liberal and romantic youth movement active before the outbreak of World War I.

The story begins in August of 1914 with Dr. Peter participating in an international peace conference in Konstanz only a few days before the outbreak of World War I. On the railway platform, while saying their farewells in those uncertain times, the French, British, and German participants shook hands and founded the International Council for Reconciliation (Internationaler Versöhnungsbund). They had in mind that the murderous war, with its accompanying nationalistic demagogy on all sides, would one day come to an end and that they should begin the preparations for a time of reconciliation. The leading figure of this historical agreement on the German side was Friedrich Siegmund-Schultze (1885–1969), a Protestant priest and famous social activist who also founded the first youth office (*Jugendamt*) in Germany. Peter became one of its first members and worked for the following twenty years as secretary of the association for reconciliation. Siegmund-Schulze was a close friend of his and became a godfather to Peter's daughter Hildemarie. After 1933 the Gestapo arrested him several times, but he survived because of an old letter of commendation, signed by the former Emperor Wilhelm II. He was regarded an important person, and the Nazis brought him to the Swiss border and set him free.

Others of the circle were less fortunate. Another close friend, the Lutheran priest Hermann Stöhr (1898–1940), refused to vow allegiance to Hitler and was sentenced to death in 1940. "Uncle Hermann" was the godfather of Hildemarie's sister Caritas. He often visited the family and enjoyed the music; their mother, Anna-Barbara, played the viola da gamba and Hildemarie and Caritas played the flute. Yet another friend was Harald Poelchau (1903–1972), the chaplain of the Tegel and Plötzensee prisons, who smuggled letters from prisoners and arranged refuge for many Jews and resistance fighters. As chaplain of the prisons, he was the confidant of many resistance fighters, yet he had to assist them on their way to death, either by beheading or by hanging. Poelchau was also a member of the Kreisauer Kreis, an influential secret circle of resistance around Helmuth James Graf von Moltke. The Kreisauer Kreis planned an alternative government to replace Hitler. When Moltke was captured in 1942 by the Gestapo, some surviving members of his circle joined the group around Claus von Stauffenberg, who was involved in the July 20, 1944, plot to kill Hitler. Poelchau was never captured by the Gestapo and survived. In Yad Vashem he is honored as a *Chassid Umot ha-Olam* (חסיד אומות העולם), that is, of the Righteous of the Nations. In the first years of the war, Poelchau had attended lectures at the Reichs Institute and studied psychology with John Rittmeister, who was later executed as a resistance fighter. Poelchau made friends with this "careful and humanly engaged doctor," whom he later visited in prison and finally had to accompany to his execution like so many others. After the war Poelchau underwent analysis to work through his horrible experiences and to recover from the trauma.

Hildemarie Streich told me that everybody in the secret and informal circle that met in the Peter family home had to find their own way of surviving and of inner or outer resistance without giving up hope or faith. When Hermann Stöhr said that he would risk his life by openly standing up against Hitler's demand of an oath of allegiance from every German, the members of the circle tried to convince him that he should remain quiet. But Stöhr said that his faith would not allow this. In times like these, everyone has to make their own choice. Some choose to save "the physical body of the people," and others "have to save its soul." Stöhr felt he could continue his open protest because he had no family who would suffer the consequences of his stance. Others, responsible for their children and spouses, should remain quiet and follow their faith in other ways. Alfred Peter, for example, helped many people by listening to them and by providing shelter for Jews, but he did this secretly so as not to endanger his family and friends. In following this path, he was supported by the chaplain of the Swedish Church, Birger Forell

(1893–1958), another friend of the family whom Hildemarie Streich knew well. The Swedish Church owned a block in Berlin-Wilmersdorf, which had extraterritorial diplomatic status, into which the Germans were not allowed to enter. Forell protected hundreds of Jews under the roof of his church and organized passports for them. When Forell had to return to Sweden in 1942, his successor was surprised by this effort. He said later: "I thought I'd come to a normal church and a community, but I found so many people hidden under the roof of the church!" He continued with Forell's work.

Among the close collaborators and friends were also Jungian analysts Kaethe Bügler and Sigrid zu Eulenburg. Hildemarie often saw both of them visiting her parents and listening to the family concerts. Kaethe Bügler (1898–1977), trained by Jung himself, was classified under the Nuremberg Laws as half Jewish. She survived the Nazi era in Berlin mainly by hiding, where she carried out the few Jungian training analyses that occurred during the war. She was protected by her life partner, Gustav Richard Heyer (1890–1967), who had become a professed Nazi and member of the NSDAP in 1937. Heyer, like Bügler, was also trained by Jung. He was invited to the first Eranos meetings, but when Jung realized that Heyer had become a Nazi, he broke off his relationship with him. After the war, Kaethe Bügler became the analyst of Hildemarie Streich, as well as of Harald Poelchau, the former prison chaplain in Plötzensee.

Sigrid zu Eulenburg, called "Eule" (Owl), was a member of a famous noble family and a close relative of the young Libertas Schulze-Boysen. Eule was a deaconess, belonging to the secular Protestant order of Lutheran nurses, and a practicing Jungian therapist. Her young relative Libertas (1913–1942) grew up in the family castle, Liebenberg, of the Eulenburg clan north of Berlin. In 1933 Libertas was working in the Berlin film business as a representative for the American company Metro-Goldwyn-Mayer, which gave her access to American newspapers. In 1934 she met Harro Schulze-Boysen and married him two years later. Harro was appointed to the Reich Air Transport Ministry and was engaged in rescuing people. He also had contact with the secret service arm of Stalin's Soviet Union. Libertas was upset by the Munich Agreement of 1938, a treaty that turned parts of Czechoslovakia over to the Nazis. In 1942 she began collecting documents about German war crimes in the eastern countries. In September 1942 Harro was arrested by the Gestapo because of a telegraph contact with Russian agents ("Rote Kapelle"). Libertas was mentioned, and was imprisoned as well. A false comrade in the cell was a spy of Roland Freisler, the supreme judge of Hitler's Volksgerichtshof. Libertas was beheaded, together with her husband and eight other resistance fighters on December 24, 1942. Her last words to the executioner were: "Please don't kill me, I am so young!" She was twenty-nine years old.

Hildemarie told me many moving details from these dark years. When Hermann Stöhr was sentenced to death, Poelchau managed to arrange a last little concert for him and others in the prison. So one day in the summer of 1940, Caritas and Hildemarie were smuggled into the prison with their flutes. They were told to keep their eyes on their notes and not to look up at the prisoners. They played their music the best they could, not knowing that their beloved Uncle Hermann was to be executed only a few days later.

To close this dark chapter, I will only mention that Hildemarie's father died from starvation in 1945, and his wife died in 1949. After the war, Hildemarie studied music therapy and became an analysand and trainee of Kaethe Bügler. For supervision she traveled to Gustav Heyer, the former Nazi, who was again living in Bavaria. A dream warned her not to go into any transference with him. In 1946 Bügler tried to establish a Jungian institute in Berlin. Jung, however, told her to join the "others"—the Freudians and neo-Freudians—exactly what Bügler did not want to do after the experience with the mixed Reichsinstitute. Her project ended after a year and a half. Her trainee, Hildemarie, was thrown into the confusion surrounding the foundation of the new joint

Berlin institute. Hildemarie was not accepted as a member of the new institute or of the Deutschen Gesellschaft für Analytische Psychologie (*DGAP*), headed by Hans Dieckmann—fallout resulting from her loyalty to Kaethe Bügler.

Hildemarie's marriage to Rudolf Streich remained childless. Their house concerts were a kind of institution in West Berlin, and after his retirement Rudolf Streich began to build organs himself. He was a fine man who died in 1988. I received one of his beautiful instruments.

In spite of her exclusion from the new Berlin Jung Institute, Hildemarie Streich was a prominent figure in the international scene and in the International Association for Analytical Psychology (IAAP). After 1972 she spoke several times at Eranos, where she met Gerhard Scholem, who had become Gershom Scholem (or Shalom, in Hebrew) when he emigrated to Palestine in 1923, a leading Jewish scholar of mysticism. She also met others, such as Adolf Portmann, at Eranos. The Streich and the Portmann families became close friends. Sometimes Franz Riklin and James and Hilde Kirsch visited her in Berlin to speak about dreams. Her special field was music in dreams. The newly reestablished Berlin C. G. Jung Society made her an honorary member in 2012, one year before her death.

Inner Resistance—The Zohar Studies of Alfred Peter

Among the manuscripts I received from Hildemarie Streich is a dense study called "Sohar-Studien"—studies of the kabbalistic *Zohar*, the *Book of Splendor*. In the years 1937 until his death in 1945, Streich's father, Alfred Peter, translated the book from French into German (he could not read Hebrew well enough). He studied the mystic messages intensively against his own Christian background and wrote four mediations. This was a risky endeavor in those times, and Hildemarie wrote that the family was often deeply concerned when the Gestapo entered and the books and papers had to be hidden quickly. The first of these meditations is about the theocentric point of view: not man and his thinking but God in his revelation is the source of all experience. The second meditation is about the encounter between man and God, and the third is about light and language in the *Zohar*. There Peter also refers to the *Sefer Yetzirah*, the *Book of Creation*. The fourth meditation is about polarity and sexuality in kabbalistic thinking. Peter's studies are in fact a deep reflection about the meaning of his times, about what position a Christian should take during the apocalyptic disaster of the Third Reich. As I have also been told by Hildemarie, he wrote that a Christian conclusion could be: *Ihr seid teuer erkauft—werdet nicht der Menschen Knechte*, "You were bought with a price; do not become slaves of men" (1 Cor. 7:23). Peter also emphasized: find out the source of the messages you hear. There are evil powers in the world that can confuse you about the reality and the meaning of your life.

I can't go into great detail about Peter's meditations here, but I am sure further study would be revealing about how Jung was perceived in Peter's circle. His writings were studied intensively. Also, the Kabbalah was an interesting topic in the secret Jungian discussion of those times. In 1933 Gerhard Adler gave an excellent speech about the Kabbalah at the Psychology Club Zurich. I found a transcript in the papers of Hildemarie Streich. I suppose that he spoke about Kabbalah also at the Berlin Jung Society. And Erich Neumann and James Kirsch also studied and interpreted their Jewish heritage in their own ways in this milieu. In the first of his studies, in 1943, Peter refers to Jung's 1940 paper at Eranos about the Trinity. Peter writes about the trinity of the first three sephirot—Kether, Chochma, and Bina—emphasizing how important the divine pattern of these three emanations or aspects of the divine is. He states that the third sephirah, Bina, is female—with the conclusion that the feminine is not missing in the Trinity of the higher sephirot. Regarding Jung he said: "It seems that Jung doesn't know these pages from the *Zohar* whereas he knows well the pages about Esau."[2]

---

2   Alfred Peter, "Sohar-Studien" (unpublished manuscript, Berlin, 1937–1945), 8 [my translation].

Peter continues:

> At the end of his paper Jung notes that in his studies of
> the deep structure of his patient's soul he never came
> upon the Trinity but always the Quaternity. This in his
> thinking becomes the reason to give up Threefoldness
> as the primary structure of his patients and to include
> Satan. But by this his method becomes metaphysically
> blind and loses all protective means against destructive
> spiritual powers."[3]

This means, as far as I understand Peter, that the integration of the fourth
position in the quaternity is dangerous. Peter argues that Jung's method
becomes blind if he includes evil, Satan, in a quaternion and therefore
loses protection against destructive spiritual powers—a protection which
will only be provided by a trinitarian model.

Jung, as Peter argued, was not well advised to emphasize the
quaternary structure as the basic pattern for wholeness. He continues
that in some therapeutic treatments phenomena of "obsession" can
appear—this is what Jung would call psychic inflation. Obsession can
be a reality—we would say, a social reality too, in a collective psychosis.
Peter concludes:

> When you go through hell, as we do, you can never fight evil;
> you can't take the position of a fighter, you have to take the
> position of a winner, of victory. But this position is possible
> only with the "resurrected Christ" in mind. He is the source
> for inner resistance.[4]

This idea is not so far from Erich Neumann's "actualized messianism,"
as he calls the individuation process and the stabilization of the ego-
Self axis.

---

3 Ibid., 9.
4 Ibid.

This meditation was finished and signed "Trinitatis 1943. Alfred Peter." *Trinitatis* is the Christian day of the Holy Trinity. I imagine Peter, in his fifty-seventh year, having lost his best friend to the Nazis in the fourth year of the war, every day and night threatened by fear and despair, aware of the coming apocalypse, sitting in his dark flat in Hitler's capital meditating on the first three sephirot in Jewish mysticism! Outside in the street were the flags with the *Hakenkreuz*—the swastika—hanging on all the houses, the fatal quaternary symbol of Nazi madness. We know that for C. G. Jung the problem of Three and Four was essential and that the fourth corner stood for the integration of the forgotten, the suppressed, the inferior side, the shadow, and the feminine. I imagine that an integration of the Four, of the shadow, was terribly difficult for those who lived under the Nazis, suffering from suppression, torture, fear, and starvation. It must have felt insane to be told that one has to integrate the shadow, to integrate the soul of the enemy.

This was, as I see it, also the point of Erich Neumann's "new ethic." But Neumann's criticism came from the other side: Jung was, as I read Neumann, not aware enough of his own shadow. Peter's argument is at one end of the spectrum: if the time you have to live in is so horrible, you have no other chance than to trust in God's power and to believe in the resurrection of Christ. This was also the central faith of other eminent Christians during those dark years, such as Dietrich Bonhoeffer, who was sentenced to death in 1942, and Jochen Klepper, who committed suicide with his Jewish wife in 1942 when she was to be deported to Auschwitz. Martin Buber, the Jewish opponent of Jung, stated at the end of his life, that he knew only one revelation of God: the revelation through silence.

I will close here with an open question: dictatorship and totalitarianism, and fundamentalism today, constitute a war against the population and humanity, and during such wars integration of the shadow—this means of the enemy in yourself—is most difficult and painful. Maybe it doesn't make sense. I don't know. The only meaningful action is to make an end to war in general. Today we are in a kind of World War III. Again we feel we have to win and to defeat our own shadow in the soldiers and terrorists on the other side.

PART IV. THE PROBLEM OF EVIL

The Search for a New Ethic: Professional and Clinical Dilemmas

Henry Abramovitch

"Deep psychotherapeutic healing is an ethical act, and ... every ethical act is indirectly therapeutic."

~ Luigi Zoja, *Ethics and Analysis*

"If a man does not judge himself, all things judge him, and all become messengers of God."

~ Rabbi Nachman of Breslau
(in Erich Neumann, *Creative Man: Five Essays*)

Erich Neumann's *Depth Psychology and a New Ethic* was the first notable attempt to formulate the ethical problems raised by the discovery for ['for' or 'of'?] the unconscious. Jung, in his foreword, called Neumann's book "brilliant ... piercing ... challenging and aggressive." He read the book three times in a single fortnight and made dozens of suggestions for a proposed English translation that appeared only after Neumann's death. In a letter dated June 14, 1957, Neumann revealed to Jung that the inspiration for *New Ethic* was a series of fantasies that Neumann had during the Holocaust, which Murray Stein discusses in his chapter (p. 192ff).[1] In those fantasies, Neumann experienced the ethical transformation he described in his first masterpiece. Ethical awareness can be transformed in the space of the imagination. Imagining good and evil is central to our experiences as humans and therapists.[2] We might consider, for instance, what we imagine the worst thing a therapist can do.

As part of confronting the shadow, it is crucial to accept that each person is vulnerable to committing ethical violations.[3] Keeping this in mind, I will review Neumann's ideas concerning the evolution of ethical awareness and then explore the significance of the new ethic for therapists and analysts working today.

The Evolution of Ethical Awareness

Neumann understood the evolution of ethical awareness in terms of three stages. The first stage of "primal unity" parallels the primal unity of mother and infant. In this stage, the group is responsible for every individual, and each individual is viewed as the incarnation of the whole group. What is paramount is loyalty to the group and not right and wrong. Such primal unity provides a profound sense of belonging and solidarity to its members. The whole group shares moral responsibility for every member. Responsibility and its corollary, revenge, are based solely on group identity. As a result, the actual guilty perpetrator need not be punished; punishing anyone in his or her collective will do. Honor killings, suicide bombings, and even mass sporting events reflect the moral

---

1   C. G. Jung and Erich Neumann, *Analytical Psychology in Exile: The Correspondence of C. G. Jung and Erich Neumann*, ed. Martin Liebscher (Princeton, NJ: Princeton University Press, 2015), 331–33.

2   See H. Abramovitch, "Stimulating Ethical Awareness," *Journal of Analytical Psychology* 52: 449–461; H. Abramovitch, "Ethics: A Jewish Perspective," in *Cast the First Stone: The Ethics of Analytical Therapy*, ed. L. Ross and M. Roy (Wilmette, IL: Chiron Publications, 1995); H. Abramovitch, "Erich Neumann and the Search for a New Ethic," *Harvest: International Journal for Jungian Studies* 52(2): 130–47.

3   See Abramovitch, "Stimulating Ethical Awareness"; Anonymous, "The Unfolding and Healing of Analytic Boundary Violations: Personal, Clinical and Cultural Considerations," *Journal of Analytical Psychology* 50, 661–91.

ideology of primal unity. In a milder form, it might explain why *Depth Psychology and a New Ethic* was received so negatively by the Zurich Jungian establishment. The conflict was not about the content of the book, but rather about how Neumann as an outsider challenged solidarity and primal unity of the group.

The Rise of the Old Ethic

Neumann argued that ethics advances to a second stage, which he termed "the old ethic." Such ethical revolutions, he claimed, came exclusively from introverted intuitives, "Great Individuals," such as Socrates or Moses, who experienced a personal revelation from an "inner Voice." Such great individuals acted as a creative center, as a kind of Self to the group. As Neumann wrote to Jung in 1933, "great men have always been called upon to exercise discernment and to stand against the crowd."[4]

The old ethic is familiar from the spiritual teachings of the Ten Commandments, the five Pillars of Islam and the Eightfold Way of the Buddha. Its archetypal image is that of the wise, devout, spiritual hero acting as a person of immense self-control. "Who is the hero?" asks the Hebrew *Sayings of the Fathers*, and the answer is given, "The one who conquers his [evil] impulses" (6:3). It embodies an idealized, absolute, and hence one-sided view of spiritual perfection. This new order does lead to a strengthening of the ego over the tyranny of the unconscious but heightens the conscious/unconscious split. The psyche of the old ethic functions like an absolute monarchy or one-party state because it assumes there is only a single moral perspective. But Jung argued convincingly that ethics is relativistic, depending precisely on one's point of view. Jung wrote: "It is an actual fact that what is good to one appears evil to the other." He went on:

---

4   Jung and Neumann, *Analytical Psychology in Exile*, 12.

> You have only to think of the careworn mother who meddles
> in all her son's doings—from the most selfless solicitude of
> course—but in reality with murderous effect. For the mother
> it is naturally a good thing if the son does not do this and does
> not do that, and for the son it is simply moral and physical
> ruin—so scarcely a good thing.[5]

Psychic life in the old ethic necessarily revolves around repression and suppression. Repression necessarily leads to a dangerous cycle in which shadow elements are projected outward, scapegoated, and then sought to be annihilated. In Neumann's time, Chinese, blacks, and Jews, in turn, became the focus of these shadowy projections. Today, the targets may have changed but the psychic process remains the same.

Suppression, in contrast to repression, is often considered as a mature defense mechanism. Neumann, however, argued that suppression risks leaving the personality flat, with a loss of both creative and animal-like energy. Such unhealthy suppression may be seen in the "soft men" described by Robert Bly in *Iron John,* men who are "good" but lacking in resolve and vitality.[6]

Moral life in the old ethic becomes an endless struggle between our good and bad parts, representing the dual and dueling aspects of the human soul. This dynamic is illustrated in the archetypal theme of the hostile brothers: Cain and Abel, Seth and Osiris, Balder and Loki, Jacob and Esau, and so on, are examples of the endless conflict between opposites. The good person aspires, in the old ethic, to be purely good. In Jungian terms, one might say that the ego overidentifies with the collective values of the society and so denies the shadow. In this process, the ego may lose touch with its own limitations in attempting to become disembodied pure spirit and may become "inhuman." This can be illustrated by a joke: Two women

---

5   C. G. Jung, *Letters*, vol. 1, ed. Gerhard Adler, trans. R. F. C. Hull (Princeton, NJ: Princeton University Press, 1973), 518.
6   Robert Bly, *Iron John: A Book about Men* (Cambridge, MA: Da Capo Press, 2004).

are talking about their husbands. The first says, "My husband is an angel!" The other one replies, "Yes, my husband is not human either!" Neumann showed how easily the idealism of the old ethic leads to atrocities.

The New Ethic

The old ethic has no place for evil, which must be resisted and defeated. In contrast, Neumann argued: "Evil, no matter by what cultural canon it be judged, is a necessary constituent of individuality" and "part of the world to be experienced."[7]

What, then, is the new ethic?

At the core of the new ethic is personal responsibility for the dark side. In this context, Neumann presented a patient's dream in which a hunchback grabs the dreamer by the throat and shouts, "I, too, want a share of your life!"[8] The goal is to grant that dark "hunchbacked" side a share in one's life. Our fascination with profound evil in art and literature, from Raskolnikov to Othello and from serial killers to vampire movies, reflects our own secret desire to know this hidden, evil side. In so doing, the ego must give up its innocence and its simplistic victim psychology.

The key commandment of the new ethic is to become conscious. Becoming conscious leads to psychic expansion. Undoing repression reduces the ever-present danger of murderous projection. Neumann summarized the difference between conscious and unconscious evil as follows:

> The acknowledgment of one's own evil is "good." To be too
> good—that is, to want to transcend the limits of the good,
> which is actually available and possible—is "evil." Evil done
> by anybody in a conscious way (and that always also implies
> full awareness of his own responsibility), evil, in fact, from

---

7   Erich Neumann, *Origins and History of Consciousness* (Princeton, NJ: Princeton University Press, 1970), 352; and Jung and Neumann, *Analytical Psychology in Exile*, 32.
8   Erich Neumann, *Depth Psychology and a New Ethic* (Boston: Shambhala, 1990), 81.

which the agent does not try to escape—is ethically "good." The repression of evil, accompanied, as it invariably is, by an inflationary overvaluation of oneself, is "evil," even when it is the result of a "positive attitude" or a "good will."[9]

In the realm of the new ethics, real evil lies in splitting good from evil; genuine goodness resides in their acceptance in depth. This attitude is expressed in the *Zohar* in connection with Job: "As Job kept evil separate from good and failed to fuse them, he was judged accordingly. First he experienced good, then what was evil, then again good. For man should be cognizant of both good and evil and turn evil itself into good."[10]

To amplify the need to enter this dark underworld, Neumann used a kabbalistic midrash, based on Rabbi Nachman of Bratzlav's rereading of Leviticus 19:18—"Love your neighbor as yourself: I am the Lord." The word *reacha*, usually translated as "your neighbor" or "your fellow," may equally be read as "your evil," *ra'acha*, since Hebrew is written without vowels. Using a standard rabbinic technique, the passage may be reinterpreted to read: "If you love your evil, so too do I, the Lord, love it." Neumann, in this case, was deeply influenced by kabbalistic teachings concerning the origin of evil and the possibility of repair, since "the most holy sparks are to be found at the lowest level," or as he put it in a letter to Jung, "evil" is only a "servant of God."[11] Evil is a necessary part of the individuation process. A secure individual needs to do "evil" against the collective values or conventional cultural canon. The individuated person must betray, and Neumann used biblical examples to drive his point home: Abraham abandoned his father and set out to kill his son, Jacob deceived his father, and Moses committed a premeditated act of murder.

In contrast to the old ethic which seeks to split the spiritual from the material, Neumann felt that the new ethic affirms the earthy and

---

9   Ibid., 114.
10   H. Sperling and M. Simon, *The Zohar* (London: Soncino Press, 1931, 1934), 109.
11   Neumann, *Depth Psychology and a New Ethic*, 126; Jung and Neumann, *Analytical Psychology in Exile*, 65.

the body. Clinically, Neumann understood dreams of flying, or being invisible, as attempts to heal the archetypal split inherent in the old ethic. Flying dreams revealed that the dreamer's ego was "ungrounded," too far removed from earth; being invisible meant that the dreamer's ego was "unbodied," too removed from body with all its embodied symbolism. Trying to fly too high, like Icarus, risks a regressive falling back to the Great Mother Earth in a literal, or symbolic, uroboric suicide.[12]

Neumann believed that depth psychology and the new ethic development would push humanity toward greater consciousness and awareness of our evils. Thus the ecology movement, of which Neumann was a prophetic forerunner, made us acutely aware of the evil done to environment. Feminism made us aware of the brutal and subtle ways women are oppressed. The animal rights movement has sensitized us to the evil done to animals. In each case, a new ethic arose to expand our awareness and extend our empathy into new areas. Future movements, he predicted, will do the same, expanding ethical awareness into areas in which we are currently unconscious and morally insensitive.

Clinical Applications of the New Ethic

Neumann's vision is daring and revolutionary. Jung himself wrote that Neumann's individual ethic makes far heavier demands than the Christian ethic does.[13] It is elitist and yet profoundly democratic, since new ethic remains open to anyone willing to wrestle with his or her shadow, as Jacob had done.

The problem Jungians face concerning the new ethic lies in the paradoxical nature of the individuation process. Individuation, the process of becoming more and more ourselves, requires a necessary distancing from the voices of others and the demands of society, as both

---

12   Erich Neumann, *The Great Mother* (Princeton, NJ: Princeton University Press, 1972), 42.

13   Jung, *Letters*, vol. 1, 518.

Jung and Neumann emphasized. They believed the inner voice, the voice of the Self, will guide and show what is right and wrong.

How can we know whether that inner voice is in service of the Self or merely an ego possessed by the shadow, rationalizing immoral behavior? This is a question that Martin Buber asked. Jung and Buber had a long and ambivalent relationship.[14] Buber spoke at the Psychology Club, Zurich, in 1923 and at Eranos in 1934. After the war, Buber called Jung a Gnostic. Jung, wounded at feeling misunderstood, claimed Buber did not understand psychic reality. Yet Jung wrote that there had never been any personal friction between them.[15] Buber corresponded warmly with Emma Jung and once with Neumann about his monograph on Franz Kafka. Neumann drew often on Buber's versions of Hasidic stories. Buber, in *Eclipse of God*, made a penetrating critique of Jung (and implicitly of Neumann).[16] Buber asked, in the wake of rise of Hitler: When one hears that inner voice, how can one tell whether it is the voice of the Self or the Devil?[17]

The great individual may be a moral innovator, but ethics is never the exclusive property of the individual. It must reflect shared values of the community. Significantly, Neumann, in the introduction to the Spanish edition of *New Ethic*, explained that the new ethic "presupposed a person was 'moral' by the standards of the old ethic."[18]

The challenge is how to apply the new ethic to our professional lives. Let me start by considering how Neumann's stages might apply to an ethical violation.

At the beginning of the chapter, I asked the reader to imagine the worst thing a therapist can do. Now consider, for instance, that a specific

---

14   See H. Abramovitch, "The Influence of Martin Buber's Philosophy of Dialogue on Psychotherapy: Lasting Contribution," in *Dialogue as a Trans-Disciplinary Concept*, ed. P. Mendes-Flohr (Berlin: De Gruyter, 2015).

15   Jung, *Letters*, vol. 2, 101.

16   M. Buber, *Eclipse of God: Studies in the Relation between Religion and Philosophy*, trans. M. Friedman (New York: Harper and Row, 1975).

17   Ibid., 33–34.

18   Neumann, *Depth Psychology and a New Ethic*, 21.

ethical violation is brought as a complaint to a psychoanalytic institute or professional society. How would the complaint be handled? In the stage of primal unity, the institute will attack and discredit the whistleblower. The membership would rally around the perpetrator to fiercely protect the accused, regardless of the whistleblower's innocence or guilt. In the initial stage under the old ethic the accused, if found guilty, would be seen as a traitor of group ideals, scapegoated, and expelled while those who remain inside the group are "good." This splitting into "we are good" and "they are bad" seems natural and satisfying to those caught up in the morality complex of the old ethic. Only in the next stage under the new ethic would the institute seek a deeper understanding of the significance of the complaint and not split the situation into good and bad people, even when the perpetrator has done terrible things.

The group psychology of an ethical complaint may be amplified by a Talmudic exploration of biblical text of Deuteronomy 21:1–9, dealing with the intrusion of evil: "If someone is found slain, lying in a field … and it is not known who the killer was … Then the elders … [who sacrifice an innocent heifer in a virgin valley] shall declare: 'Our hands did not shed this blood, nor did our eyes see it done.'"

In one sense, this is a typical scapegoat ritual. The innocent heifer is sacrificed to purify the guilt of the entire community. The Talmud, however, does not accept this reading of the text based on the splitting of innocence and guilt of the old ethic. Instead it asks:

> Why do elders declare, "Our hands have not shed this blood, neither have our eyes seen it." Can it really enter our minds that the Elders themselves have shed blood! No! The meaning of their statement is to assert that the man found dead did not come to us for help and we dismissed him without supplying him with food; nor we did see him depart and let him go without an escort or warning him of the dangers along the way. (Babylonian Talmud, Sotah 46b)

The Talmud extends the scope of collective responsibility. Elders must ask themselves not whether they actually killed the person but rather: Did we do everything to prevent this tragedy? Only then can the elders, as representatives of the community, declare their hands clean. And so, I argue, we must follow the Talmud in approaching the ethical violations of our colleagues. We must ask ourselves individually and as a collective: Did we really do everything we could to prevent this violation? Did we fail to "accompany" him? Did we fail to warn him of the dangers on the way? What was lacking in our training or the institute's ethical culture that allowed this member to go off the track? Each member would ask themselves: What are the slippery slopes in my own practice? How can we revitalize the moral muscles of the society? Synchronistically, why is this evil happening in our institute now, or what has this evil come to teach us? Neumann wrote that Abraham, who protested against "righteous being slain with the wicked" at Sodom, ended with the recognition of the collective guilt, even of the righteous (Genesis 18:23ff).

However, many ethical dilemmas are private and indeed can never reach the public domain. One such private moral event I grapple with is when an analysand tells the analyst something disturbing about a colleague. When this happens to me, clinically, I struggle to understand the meaning of this disclosure within the therapeutic process, asking, for example, why is my patient telling this to me now, and what are its implications in terms of transference dynamics? But within myself, I may feel shocked, defensive and complicit, even dirtied by the disclosure. Such disclosures remain under the seal of confidentiality and thus are all the more disturbing. Jung understood this kind of dilemma when he wrote: "Ethical decision is concerned with very much more complicated things, namely conflicts of duty, the most diabolical things ever invented and at the same time the loneliest."[19]

---

19   Jung, *Letters*, vol. 1, 520.

Erich Neumann dealt with just such a clinical-ethical situation shortly after he arrived in Israel. Former patients of James Kirsch, who left Palestine at the beginning of 1935, came to see Neumann for analysis and told him disturbing things about their former analyst. On June 27, 1935, Neumann wrote to Jung about his experience:

> At the moment I have to keep quiet anyway as the Kirsch matter unfortunately created much resistance to analytical psychology ... . I am extremely sorry not to be able to discuss with you thoroughly the question of the analysis of analysts, this is my biggest interest, practically and theoretically. There is a lot to be said for the methods of the Freudian school with its training and supervisory analyses although I know that this is more difficult in the case of analytical psychology with its fundamental emphasis on the being of the analyst. Please do not misunderstand me, every analyst makes mistakes and I notice every day how much more difficult, responsible, and important every analysis is, especially here in Palestine. I now have a certain insight into Kirsch's work and I am quite speechless. (About half a dozen patients of his are now with me, those that terminated and others.)

> ...

> (I am fully aware of the unreliability of patient's testimonies. Only consensus makes me more sure.) The worst thing, aside from inflation and curiosity, seems to me his lack of psychological sensitivity that amazes me because he is actually quite a warm human being ... . Perhaps he is extraverted and it comes from that. He "goes on" constantly about a "religious problem" and convinces people they have one and thus he scares them off their center. Precisely for

Palestine this is a disaster because, for the Jews, the central problem is the religious one. It is possessed by the strongest resistance.

…

In my work with you—and this was my particular case—it depended, I believe, not on the personal unconscious but, as you also said, on the breaking open of the perspective onto the Self and the collective unconscious, and this consequently thrust me simultaneously into the world and out of myself. With Miss [Toni] Wolff, the personal unconscious came more into its own, in both good and bad aspects … . the religious problem can be structurally central and the sexual problem secondary, but this must slowly become evident to the patient from the inside through the analysis of dreams, not because he hears it out of my mouth. Only the Self must speak in this language, I must, I fear, be unassuming.

I hope, dear Professor, that it will be clear to you that the Kirsch case is important to me not for his sake.

…

K[irsch] is only secondary in this. Things are going well for me. My wife and son also. There is much work.[20]

There is so much of interest in this letter: the training of analysts (a subject which sadly Neumann did not pursue), differences between Neumann's own analysis with Jung and with Toni Wolff, relation of the sexual to the spiritual. But what I want to focus on is how Erich Neumann dealt

20   Jung and Neumann, *Analytical Psychology in Exile*, 110–13.

with the moral dilemma concerning what he heard about Kirsch from his own patients. True to the new ethic, Neumann does not demonize Kirsch but calls him a warm human being. He uses the experience to examine his own work more deeply, admitting mistakes and clarifying issues in clinical practice, and all for the sake of the work in the spirit of the new ethic. Instead of merely criticizing Kirsch, Neumann examines his own shadow in his own clinical work. "Only the Self must speak … " he concludes and adds with symbolic resonance: "There is much work." Eighty years on, his words maintain enormous vitality.

Neumann's mature response reminded me of an experience of my own. I recall a female patient, herself a mental health professional, who came to me for analysis. Gradually, it emerged that her previous therapist had sexually abused her. It was not full intercourse but it was highly inappropriate. Like many victims of such abuse, she blamed herself and felt unclean, while I felt enraged at this therapist for abusing his power. Caught up in the complex of the old ethic, I wanted him accused, humiliated, and stripped of his license to prevent further harm. But it soon became clear that my patient had no energy to mobilize for any complaint. She said: "I just don't have the strength." I therefore focused on what was right for her, even if it was not right for the collective. After much hard work, the patient eventually came up with a unique solution. She felt that although the therapist had abused her, she was grateful for other good work they had done and decided not to make a complaint but to confront him. She demanded that he never work with female patients ever again. It was a compromise, but I believe it was a compromise of which Neumann would be proud.

Forgetting a Session

Regularity of sessions is a crucial part of the temenos. It has happened to me that I forgot a session with a patient. In two cases, the patient called me, and I rushed over in time to apologize and salvage something for the session. In terms of the old ethic, I felt terrible and culpable, and I worried that I had permanently damaged the therapeutic relationship. I promised the patient and myself that it would never happen again. This is the repression and suppression of the old ethic. The new ethic demands trying to understand not only my own hidden shadowy motives concerning this specific patient but also the unconscious synchronicity of this unethical behavior. Neumann required that we take responsibility for our own "evil" and come to a deeper understanding of why this negative synchronicity occurred; and why now?

Debora Kutzinski, who is Erich Neumann's leading disciple and was my control supervisor, told me a remarkable story about how Neumann handled missed supervision sessions with her.

> I came as usual to him for my session but he was with another patient. "Excuse me. Come again next week," he said. The next week, the same thing happens. He apologized again, and I began to wonder what was going on. I arrive on the third week, and he says, "I have analyzed what has happened and I realized you do not need supervision any longer. Twice I forgot. That means you have finished supervision. You are on your own." I began to beg him. "It is just before your summer holiday, give me one more session. What is your hurry?" He said, "You will be better off without me!" It is a sentence I will never forget. That was Neumann the supervisor, who gave you the freedom to grow."[21]

He had set her free. A few months later, Neumann was dead.

The New Ethic in Israel / Palestine

Times of great despair may bring forth great hope. Let me end with one more story, which illustrates something of the spirit of Neumann's new ethic.

21   H. Abramovitch, "Erich Neumann as My Supervisor: An Interview with Dvora Kutzinski," *Harvest: International Journal for Jungian Studies* 52(2): 172.

During the intifada, I was part of a small group of Israelis and Palestinians, which included Paul Mendes-Flohr, who met regularly in each other's homes in Ramallah and Jerusalem in what we called a "dialogue group." I particularly recall one Palestinian man, much younger than me but who looked much older and had particularly bad teeth. He had served a long prison sentence in an Israeli jail as a member of a so-called Palestinian terrorist organization that had been banned. One day, he told us, while in prison, he was speaking with his jailer about their own children, and suddenly he realized that "for the sake of the children" there must be a stop to the endless cycle of killing. He renounced violence at a time when it was very dangerous for him to do so. We felt like witnesses to a "now moment" of transformation. When the Jews in the group spoke of relatives murdered in the Holocaust, he wept. When we heard stories of life under the occupation, we wept, as, for example, when parents said they preferred their adolescent sons to be in jail because at least they knew they were "safe." No member of the group had personally committed any atrocities, but all were members of collectives who did and seemed trapped in a cycle of violence and counterviolence based on victim psychology. In this special, safe setting we were able to acknowledge the evil that was being done.

Neumann felt strongly that by digesting our own evil, a fragment of the collective evil may be digested as well. He wrote: "But the pre-digestion of evil which one carries out as part of the process of assimilating his shadow makes him, at the same time, an agent for the immunization of the collective ... as he digests his own evil, a fragment of the collective is invariably co-digested at the same time ... decontaminates evil."[22] Instead of scapegoating, one takes on "vicarious suffering." By assuming responsibility, evil itself is decontaminated. Neumann felt we are all partners in the work of repairing the world, *tikkun olam*.

---

22 Neumann, *Depth Psychology and a New Ethic*, 130.

Amichai's Poem as Conclusion

I want to conclude my chapter with an extract of a poem by Yehuda Amichai, Israel's best-loved modern poet.

Wildpeace

not the peace of a ceasefire

nor even the vision of the wolf lying down with the goat

rather

as a heart after excitement

speaking of great weariness ...

Without words. Without

the thud of the heavy rubber stamp, let it be easy

floating above the lazy, white foam.

Rest for wounds

even not long

(The howl of the orphans is passed on from generation

to generation like a relay race; the baton never falls)

let it be

like wildflowers:

suddenly, because the field

must have it: wildpeace.[23]

Like Neumann, Amichai was born in Germany and arrived in Palestine in the 1930s. The poem brings together so many of Neumann's themes,

---

23 Author's translation.

such as the quest of a creative man, the search for a new moral perspective, and the tension between different kinds of peace. In an unexpected act of creation, Amichai invites the reader to encounter the flowering of a new ethic pushing up in the field of the Great Mother, "suddenly, because the field must have it: wildpeace." It was a wildpeace that Neumann would have well understood.

Erich Neumann and C. G. Jung on the Problem of Evil

Murray Stein

The problem of evil is indelibly inscribed into the table of contents of our collective memory, conscious and unconscious, and this chapter was deeply read and commented upon by both C. G. Jung and Erich Neumann. It is a critical topic not only for theologians, philosophical ethicists, artists (of all kinds), criminologists, and cultural historians, but also, and today perhaps most of all, for psychologists because of the question of human motivation to commit evil acts. Perhaps it was due to the excessively cruel times in which they lived that Jung and Neumann focused on this issue in their writings with such laserlike energy. Yet it is also an age-old question that has inspired agonized reflections throughout recorded history: What is evil, whence does it come, and how are we to deal with it? These questions are no less with us today, although our answers tend to be less mythological than in ancient times and more sociological, philosophical, political, or psychological.[1]

For psychology, the problem of evil brings the issue of ethics front and center. Ethics is a product of human consciousness attempting to confront the problem of evil and to contain it by defining it, setting up

---

1   See Curatorium of the CG. Jung Institute, Zurich, EVIL,trans. R. Manheim and H. Nagel (Evanston, IL: Northwestern University Press, 1967).

boundaries for behavior, proposing horizons and perspectives from a variety of cultural settings, and perhaps setting up some specific rules of behavior. The elaboration of ethics is an ongoing human project because times and cultural settings change and evolve, creating new issues to consider. Psychology may be able to contribute some insights into the motivation and the psychic roots of evil as defined by ethical constructs, and it may also offer some suggestions for how to deal with evil on an individual and a social/collective level by considering levels of responsibility for actions deemed to be evil and designing methods of containment, punishment, and conditions of atonement that follow a judgment of evildoing.

A question for us as depth psychologists is: Can ethics be grounded in psychology as we understand it, or is ethics a matter purely of legal considerations, therefore wholly conscious, culturally conditioned, and relative or even arbitrary? Traditionally, ethics has been embedded in mythological and theological foundations and has been seen as derivative from such things as "the will of God, or the gods." In modernity, this does not wash. We no longer live in an age of faith. Yet there is still a need for ethics, and the conviction that evil exists continues to occupy us. So can ethics be rooted in psychological perspectives as it was once rooted in mythological and theological ones? This would be a point for discussion between depth psychology on the one side and theology, philosophy, criminology, and other social sciences, as well as neurobiology, on the other. My attempt at establishing a depth psychological basis for ethics in psychology is presented in *Solar Conscience/Lunar Conscience*, in which I argue for an archetypal ground for an ethical attitude in two types of innate conscience.[2] In other words, I believe that humans are innately ethical creatures, but not only so: they are also innately given to the opposite, to violations of the laws written in their hearts, and when this force takes charge people become possessed by evil. This is the great

---

2 M. Stein, *Solar Conscience/Lunar Conscience* (Wilmette, IL: Chiron Publications, 1993).

theme of Gnosticism and symbolized by the monster god, Yaldabaoth.[3] This is a problem of inherent opposites embedded in the human psyche itself and therefore not resolvable on a rational and purely conscious level, try as we might to master the problem of evil.

From a depth psychological viewpoint, the problem of evil is connected to the perception that it is largely controlled by unconscious factors. With the exception of out-and-out psychopaths, evildoing is something people generally try to avoid, at least to some extent. Most people want to be on the side of the good, or at least seen to be so, not on the side of evil. So the enactment of evil is generally much more subtle and insidious than it is consciously malicious. One may in all good conscience serve evil while consciously intending to do good by obeying an evil law, for instance. Evil operates and may be done in perfect innocence, with good intentions and a sense of civic responsibility. Jesus on the cross, praying "Father, forgive them; for they know not what they do" (Luke 23:34), speaks to this point. Evil's will is carried out unknowingly and with a sense of duty. It is invisible. Evil uses the ego's talents, its will and its powers, to do its malicious work. Ego rationalizes marvelously and indeed infinitely, convinced by its own deceptions and rhetoric. When ego serves evil, whose hand in the matter is kept hidden, even the law, which speaks ostensibly for truth and justice, may itself be used to subvert those very values. The ego is unconsciously complicit in this and puts forward the law to cover the handiwork of evil. This is the problem of evil as seen from the perspective of depth psychology.

Erich Neumann brilliantly describes this psychological problem of consciously identifying with the good and remaining unconscious of the evil within ourselves in his book *Depth Psychology and a New Ethic*. An individual or a community identifies itself wholly with the good and projects evil outward, he writes, and thus remains free from

---

3   M. Stein, *Minding the Self: Jungian Meditations on Contemporary Spirituality* (London: Routledge, 2014), 87.

guilt in consciousness no matter what atrocities might be performed against the perceived "evil other." This is the well-known scapegoat phenomenon.[4] Neumann's solution as described in *Depth Psychology and a New Ethic* is for the individual or the community to become aware of the shadow within, to take it fully into account in decision making and behavior, and to consider all the consequences of subsequent actions for oneself and for others. It is a tall order. Neumann's new ethic takes the normal ethical position of careful and scrupulous obedience to a moral tradition a step further by making evil conscious as an inner factor and not projecting it exclusively onto the malefactor. This would apply to individuals and collectives (corporations, nations, etc.) alike. It says: consider your own shadow—your hidden agenda, your most devious motives, your secret desires and inclinations—before you criticize, attack, or condemn the other. This demands the onerous psychological work of recognizing and accepting one's own shadow as a part of one's selfhood, thereby relativizing naïve claims to purity and virtuous righteousness. Simply being a victim is not good enough to justify retaliatory shadow enactments and revenge. Before claiming the high ground, he says, consider your own shadowy regions. In fact, psychologically considered, there is no high ground without a low ground right beside it.

Jung's analysis of the problem of evil is somewhat different, although on many points in agreement with Neumann's. "One of the toughest roots of all evil is unconsciousness," Jung wrote in 1948, after reading Neumann's *New Ethic* and praising it, "and I could wish that the saying of Jesus, 'Man, if thou knowest what thou doest, thou art blessed, but if thou knowest not, thou art accursed, and a transgressor of the law,' were still in the gospels, even though it has only one authentic source. It might well be the motto for a new morality."[5] Here we see Jung advocating with Neumann for a "new morality" based on the same idea of making the

---

4   Erich Neumann, *Depth Psychology and a New Ethic* (Boston: Shambhala, 1990), 50ff.
5   C. G. Jung, "A Psychological Approach to the Dogma of the Trinity" (1948), in *CW*, vol. 11 (Princeton, NJ: Princeton University Press, 1969), par. 291.

unconscious shadow conscious before acting. Jung, however, is skeptical about the human capacity for sustaining such a level of consciousness; moreover, in *Answer to Job*, his later confrontation with the problem of evil as an archetypal matter, he tells us why even such consciousness of the personal shadow would be insufficient for the absolute solution to the problem of evil. Something more is needed. What would that be?

The background for both Neumann's and Jung's reflections on the problem of evil in the 1930s, '40s, and '50s is the grave situation in Europe. Neumann called it the German "schizophrenic episode"; Jung described it as the collective state of "possession" (*Ergrifenheit*) in Germany by the archaic Germanic god Wotan.[6] It encompassed the catastrophic aftermath of war and the horrors of the Holocaust, the Stalinist atrocities in Russia, and the threat of atomic warfare as the West faced off against the Soviet Union in the Cold War. How to understand this extraordinary rupture in moral consciousness in modern culture and history on a collective level, and how to manage evil on the personal and the collective level—these were the enormous questions that preoccupied them. The proposals they came up with are still highly relevant today, and will be for as long as humans have to struggle with the problem of evil, which means most likely forever or as long as human beings as we know ourselves and our psychology continue to exist.

The problem of evil, as we consider it in psychology, results from the problem of opposites built into our very nature. In the course of personality development, the Self becomes divided. Ego-consciousness necessarily separates itself out from the original wholeness of the personality as given in the primal Self, and it leaves behind in the shadow all the rejected and unacceptable tendencies and everything else that cannot be integrated into this small territory of the psyche that we

---

6   C. G. Jung and Erich Neumann, *Analytical Psychology in Exile: The Correspondence of C. G. Jung and Erich Neumann*, ed. Martin Liebscher (Princeton, NJ: Princeton University Press, 2015), 140; C. G. Jung, "Wotan" (1936), in *CW*, vol. 10 (Princeton, NJ: Princeton University Press, 1970), par. 386.

reference as our personal identity, whether personal or collective. Thus a counter-will takes form in the psychic system: the one side strives in a certain direction, usually toward attachment to others and adaptation to environmental conditions, while the other goes in a very different direction, namely, toward isolation and naked self-assertion. On one side we are family people and decent citizens, on the other egoistic monsters and criminals. Or vice versa. This is why we have a secret alliance with the opposite other and why we collude with the shadow enactments of others, sometimes even cheering them on. The more tension one places on the system by emphasizing the positive features of the conscious side over the negative features of the unconscious shadow, the more the split deepens and creates neurotic conflicts, increasing the strength of defenses such as projection, and exacerbating the differences until the one side is all light and the other all dark. This sets up the condition for enactments where evil uses the personal shadow to do its will, all the while remaining hidden and unconscious to the doer. Neumann's thesis is that this problem can be overcome or at least greatly ameliorated by making the shadow conscious and thereby defusing the power of evil. Jung is not so sure; evil may be beyond human capacities of conscious containment by this means. This was a point of disagreement between them.

In a late letter, dated June 3, 1957, Jung writes to Neumann:

> In relation to the so-called *New Ethic* we are basically quite in agreement, but I prefer to express this delicate problem in a rather different language. It is not really a question of a "new" ethic. Evil is and always remains the thing one knows one should not do. Man overestimates himself unfortunately in this respect: he thinks it is within his discretion to intend good or evil. He can persuade himself of this, but in reality he is, in view of the greatness of these opposites, simply too small and too unconscious to be able to choose the one or the other in free will and under all circumstances. It is much more the case that he does or does not do the good that he

would like to for overwhelming reasons, and that in the same
way, evil just happens to him like misfortune.[7]

Jung thinks that Neumann is overestimating the capacities of human
consciousness in his description of the new ethic. Evil is so large and so
insidious a force that human consciousness is incapable of encompassing
it and escaping its manipulations. We must remember that Jung thought
of evil as an archetypal and collective power and not only a personal
shadow feature of the personality. Evil is a force with a personality
like Satan that is transpersonal and vastly superior to the ego's ability
to know or understand its insidious ways. Always we are tricked by it
into doing that which we would not do, and into not doing that which
we would do. When speaking of the problem of evil, Jung is thinking of
Goethe's Mephistopheles, the Antichrist of Christian theology, Satan in
the Book of Job, and other such archetypal figures and not only or even
primarily of the shadow material that is housed in the complexes of the
personal unconscious. Evil draws on the power of instinct and archetype
and is conceptualized by Jung as an inherent aspect of the Self, as a
kind of autonomous spiritual force, just as goodness is. They are a pair
of opposites resident in the Self: Christ and anti-Christ. For Jung, as he
writes in *Answer to Job*, human consciousness (represented by the figure
of Job) may be an instrument for bringing about a reduction of archetypal
evil by instigating a development in the Self (represented by Yahweh),
but the transformation must be carried out above the ego's head, so to
speak, that is, by the Self in its own progressive unfolding and internal
integration process.[8] The problem of evil is just too big for humans to solve
by means of our frail conscious powers, as important as consciousness
is in instigating evolution in the Self. Thus becoming conscious of the
shadow and taking it into account in our decisions and actions will not

---

7   Jung and Neumann, *Analytical Psychology in Exile*, 327.
8   C. G. Jung, *Answer to Job* (1952), in *CW*, vol. 11 (Princeton, NJ: Princeton University Press, 1969).

place us beyond enactments of evil. Humans will always be vulnerable to the wiles and power of the evil one.

Neumann answers Jung's letter a few days later. In his reply, he tells Jung of an experience in active imagination that lay at the source of his work on ethics and the problem of evil.

> The New Ethic was the attempt to process a series of phantasies that roughly corresponded timewise with the exterminations of the Jews, and in which the problem of evil and justice was being tossed around in me. I am still gnawing away at these images at the end of which, in brief, stands the following. I seemed to be commissioned to kill the apeman in the profound primal hole. As I approached him, he was hanging, by night, sleeping on the cross above the abyss, but his— crooked—single eye was staring into the depths of this abyss. While it at first seemed that I was supposed to blind him, I all of a sudden grasped his "innocence," his dependence on the single *eye of the Godhead*, which was experiencing the depths through him, which was a human eye. Then, very abridged, I sank down in opposite this single eye, jumped into the abyss, but was caught by the Godhead, which carried me on the "wings of his heart." After that, this single eye opposite the apeman closed and it opened on my forehead. (Bit difficult to write this, but what should one do.) Working outward from the attempt to process this happening, I arrived at *The New Ethic*. For me, since then, the world looks different. Your formulations in the letter are also valid for me, but they do not go far enough.[9]

Neumann's moving account of the source of his thinking about the problem of evil and a new ethic, which emerged in a period of maximum

---

9   Jung and Neumann, *Analytical Psychology in Exile*, 331–332, italics added.

threat to the Jewish people, answers Jung on a level that seems to go far beyond his more rational theses in *New Ethic*. I surmise that this letter brought a new level of respect to Jung's already high estimation of his most gifted student, for he wrote back to Neumann that he was changing some paragraphs in a paper he was writing on the problem of conscience at the time.[10] In his account of this active imagination, Neumann reveals his ultimately decisive degree of faith in God. He is supposed to kill the apeman and finds this primitive being (a classic shadow image) staring into the primal hole, an abyss of evil. The apeman itself is innocent, however, as he discovers when he sees it staring down through the eye of the Godhead, which is at the same time a human eye. God is using the eye placed in the primitive apeman to look into the depths (to become conscious of God's own depths). Then the narrator jumps into the abyss himself! This is a remarkable leap of faith, of the type made famous by Kierkegaard, and as with Abraham, about whom Kierkegaard was writing as the great model for the man of faith, there is a divine intervention and he is caught and carried on the "wings of his heart." Neumann says that this experience transformed him and gave him the confidence he needed to find a solution to the problem of evil: "For me, since then, the world looks different."

There is in Neumann's writing a kind of rapturous embrace of evil as though by embracing it he is also embracing God, as though evil is a part of God and this is a path to being near to God's will:

> As I see it, I do not fall, but jump, and I know that the danger exists that I will die, but my prayer goes that "wings of the heart" may hold me. This means that I am, in my action, within and not outside of the Godhead, because it is not about an action of the ego, but about a happening that I must hand myself over to. If the issue of "Job" is relevant, according to which the Godhead wishes to come to consciousness, an

---

10   Ibid., 334.

aspect of its subjectivity is evident, then I have to live with the single eye of the Godhead and also to experience the darkness of the abyss. But then evil is not a sin, but part of the world to be experienced.[11]

The leap is a mystical moment of encounter and realization, and this ultimately leads to complete acceptance of reality as it unfolds before us in history. This is Neumann's solution to the problem of evil. Evil is a part of God, and so paradoxically by participating in history, even if evildoing is part of it, humans are participating in God's will. I believe that when Jung read this he realized that he was dealing with a human being of profound and bold religious imagination and intuitions quite similar to his own.

Jung had been preoccupied with the problem of evil and ethics from very early on in his professional life. In part, this was due to his friendly but quite sharp exchanges with religious professionals like his Zurich friend Adolf Keller, the pastor of St. Peter's Church in Zurich and a founder of the World Council of Churches.[12] Jung was often challenged by his religiously minded colleagues about the ethics of individuation, and he had to formulate a response to this question. It touched upon the question of responsibility, to oneself, to others, and to the social world. Is individuation itself morally defensible? The argument that it is not has been made by some of his critics, such as Martin Buber.

In *Answer to Job*, written in a feverish few months during a mild illness in early 1951, Jung takes up the problem of evil in both a highly personal way but also speaking to and for all of Christendom. He offers a stinging critique of Christianity and its cultural effects in history. Christianity, by one-sidedly supporting and affirming the good ("God is light and in Him there is no darkness") and denying the reality of evil in the pernicious (to Jung) doctrine of evil as *privatio boni* (absence of good) and by relegating

---

11   Ibid., 332.
12   M. Jehle-Wildberger, *C. G. Jung und Adolf Keller* (Zurich: Theologischer Verlag, 2014).

Satan to eternal damnation, in the end splits good and evil even farther apart than they had been heretofore, and this played into the hands of evil, paradoxically. Identifying itself with the good, Christianity projected evil outward (onto the Jews, among others), just as Neumann describes the old ethic in his *New Ethic*, and now, "after the catastrophe" of World War II and the tragic breakdown of moral fabric in the twentieth century, it must answer for its dogmatic choices.

To solve the problem of evil in the Christian theological setup, Jung proposes a further step in the evolution of Christian doctrine and theology— namely, the integration of evil into the Godhead. This would overcome the split and draw evil into a more realistic relationship with the equally archetypal good where dialogue and mutual effects would be possible. This is something already suggested in Neumann's *New Ethic* and strongly advocated in his later letter to Jung in which he describes the origins of his work. Evil must be integrated into the whole. Jung is saying, though, that a process of integration must take place in the pleromatic state, in the Godhead, which could then be reflected in theological dogmas. Dogma does not create the God-image of a religion; it reflects it. Mankind can participate in this only to a degree, perhaps like Job stimulating the development through greater consciousness (through the "eye of the Godhead" in a human frame, as shown in Neumann's active imagination).

Is this possible? At the end of his letter to Neumann in 1957, Jung writes: "I feel myself very uncertain in relation to the question of pessimism and optimism and must leave the solution to fate. The only one who could decide this dilemma, that is dear God himself, has withheld his answer from me so far," and then goes on to quote from *Candide*: "Hopefully you are well *dans ce meilleur des mondes possibles. Tout cela est bien dit, mais il faut cultiver notre jardin.*"[13] As ever, Jung is ironical when speaking of God (Neumann had pointed this out to him already when he first read the

---

13   Jung and Neumann, *Analytical Psychology in Exile*, 329–330.

draft of *Answer to Job*), and so he remained undecided. Unlike Neumann, he was not carried on "the wings of his [i.e., God's] heart."

Will the problem of evil ever be solved? Will good prevail over evil by integrating it into the larger whole? Or will evil prevail by remaining outside the whole and causing endless trouble from this position as outsider to the Godhead? In the end, each of us is left with this question. Neumann seems to cast his ballot on the side of the faithful; Jung seems to remain skeptical, but perhaps hopeful, in a slightly ironic way.

PART V. NEUMANN AND ERANOS
(1948–1960)

Neumann at Eranos

Riccardo Bernardini

Neumann and the Eranos Conferences

The ancient Greek word *Eranos* means "a banquet held thanks to the contributions liberally offered by the table companions." The Eranos conferences were a project of Olga Fröbe-Kapteyn (1881–1962) and came into being at Ascona-Moscia, Switzerland, in 1933, as a "place of encounter for East and West," a "free space for the spirit" where Eastern and Western philosophies could meet. The model was that of annual interdisciplinary gatherings, with traces of the style of some Italian Renaissance circles, the intellectual circles of German Romanticism, and the great salons of the nineteenth century.[1] Eranos brought together some of the most

---

1 For a historical panorama on the Eranos phenomenon, see H. T. Hakl, *Eranos: An Alternative Intellectual History of the Twentieth Century* (Montreal: McGill-Queen's University Press, 2013). For Carl Gustav Jung's involvement in the Eranos project, including a detailed bibliography, see R. Bernardini, *Jung a Eranos: Il progetto della psicologia complessa* (Milan: FrancoAngeli, 2011), and R. Bernardini, G. P. Quaglino, and A. Romano, "Introduction," in C. G. Jung, *The Solar Myths and Opicinus de Canistris: Notes of the Seminar Given at Eranos in 1943*, eds. R. Bernardini, G. P. Quaglino, and A. Romano (Einsiedeln, Switzerland: Daimon, 2015). For a complete list of the *Eranos Yearbooks*, lecturers, and contributions from 1933 to 2014, see the 72nd *Eranos Yearbook* (2013–2014). A view on the present interests, activities, and projects of the Eranos Foundation is proposed in F. Merlini, "Eranos: A Space and a Time for Thought," *Spring: A Journal of Archetype and Culture* 92 (2015): 41–55.

influential scholars of the twentieth century—psychologists, historians of religions, Orientalists, theologians, philosophers, anthropologists, ethnologists, archaeologists, biologists, physicists, art historians, literary critics, musicologists, and historians of esotericism. A myriad of impressive writings bear witness to the influence of the Eranos conferences in Western culture—more than seven hundred articles in over seventy yearbooks.

The conferences, held in the luminous Eranos Hall, lasted about ten days, typically during the second half of August. Each speaker had an entire morning or afternoon for his or her lecture, which normally lasted about three hours. The lectures were often divided into two parts. During the breaks, the attendees could question the lecturers, enjoy a glass of champagne on the beautiful terrace facing the shore and the Alps, or take a quick dip in the lake just above the lecture hall. The evocative nature of the place certainly played a significant role at Eranos. As Laurens van der Post recalled, Carl Gustav Jung considered the Swiss mountains as a bastion, a "magic circle" or mandala, which protected the work at Eranos in the darkest years. In fact, Eranos was the only active international convention center in Europe during the war.[2] In a publication celebrating the first twenty-five years of the conferences, Erich Neumann recalled: "Eranos. Landscape on lake, garden, and house. Inconspicuous and off the beaten track, and yet a navel of the world, a small link in the Golden Chain. As lecturers and as listeners, we always have to be grateful."[3]

At its founding, the activities at Eranos were planned and coordinated by Mrs. Fröbe-Kapteyn herself. For the first twenty years, she was assisted by an Eranos Circle, a small group of scholars "of variable geometry" who were attracted by Jung. These individuals were responsible for suggesting names of potential lecturers. The Eranos conferences wound up becoming the most important interdisciplinary meeting point between Jung and

---

2   O. Fröbe-Kapteyn, "Eranos—A Survey of its history since 1933, of the facts connected with it, a. the Tagungen, b. the Eranos Archive …" (Ascona: unpublished typescript, 1942; Eranos Foundation Archives).
3   Quoted in O. Fröbe-Kapteyn, ed., *25 Jahre Eranos: 1933–1957* (Zurich: Rhein-Verlag, 1957), 20.

many other scholars on the topic of archetypal structures underlying religious phenomena. In the years of Jung's presence in Ascona, the Eranos gatherings were characterized mostly as a meeting and converging of different paths of research that had been conducted independently. Gradually, this encounter became an original and fertile interdisciplinary crossroad, above all for authors such as Erich Neumann, Marie-Louise von Franz, and James Hillman. Jung appeared as a speaker at Eranos for the first time in 1933. Up to and including his last lecture in 1951, he gave a total of fourteen talks, which were regularly published in the Eranos yearbooks and then included in his *Collected Works*, and a seminar, which was only recently brought to publication.[4]

Neumann's encounter with Eranos (in 1947) coincided with a decisive phase in his intellectual life. Neumann would become a much sought-after speaker in Europe, lecturing in Switzerland, Holland, Spain, and eventually also in Germany.[5] Between 1948 and 1960, Neumann lectured at Eranos thirteen times. With the exceptions of *Depth Psychology and a New Ethic* and *The Origins and History of Consciousness*"[6], Neumann developed his scientific work primarily through the Eranos conferences.[7] His Eranos

---

4   C. G. Jung, *The Solar Myths and Opicinus de Canistris: Notes of the Seminar Given at Eranos in 1943*, eds. R. Bernardini, G. P. Quaglino, and A. Romano (Einsiedeln, Switzerland: Daimon Verlag, 2015).

5   In 1952, 1954, and 1956, for example, Neumann lectured at the School voor Wijsbegeerte, an international school of philosophical-esoteric studies in the Dutch town of Amersfoort, which was directed by Jan M. Hondius. Hondius, who translated some of Jung's works into Dutch, was the husband of Ada Hondius, a longstanding friend and confidant of Mrs. Fröbe-Kapteyn. An exchange both of experiences and of lecturers took place between Eranos and the School voor Wijsbegeerte (Hakl, *Eranos*, 137).

6   In *The Origins and History of Consciousness*, Neumann mentions however the "numerous examples of representations [of the *ouroboros*] collected in the Eranos Archive" (E. Neumann, *The Origins and History of Consciousness* (Princeton, NJ: Princeton University Press, 1970), 10, n. 12.)

7   Neumann spoke at Eranos on the following topics: "Der mystische Mensch. Versuch einer psychologischen Interpretation" ["Mystical Man: Towards a Psychological Interpretation," 1948], "Die mythische Welt und der Einzelne" ["The Mythical World and the Individual," 1949], "Zur psychologischen Bedeutung des Ritus" ["On the Psychological Meaning of Rite," 1950], "Kunst und Zeit" ["Art and Time," 1951], "Die Psyche und die Wandlung der Wirklichkeitsebenen. Ein meta-psychologischer Versuch" ["The Psyche and the Transformation of the Reality Planes: A Meta-Psychological Experiment," 1952], "Die Bedeutung des Erdarchetypus für die Neuzeit" ["The Importance of Earth Archetypes for Modern Times," 1953], "Der schöpferische Mensch und die Wandlung" ["The Creative Man and the Transformation," 1954], "Die Erfahrung der Einheitswirklichkeit und die Sympathie der

lectures clearly show the development of his interests and his thought, as Thomas Kirsch notes.[8] In them, we recognize the main topics of his psychological theory. They also represented the first attempt to develop a post-Jungian psychology, according to Antonio Vitolo.[9] Neumann was the first analytical psychologist after Jung to speak at Eranos. Jung, who had been a kind of *spiritus rector* of the symposia, personally invited Neumann to lecture there, with the aim to hear his "experiences in the field of medical psychology."[10] Jung also interceded with the federal immigration authorities in Bern for granting Erich Neumann and his wife, Julie Blumenfeld Neumann, an entry visa into Switzerland in order to allow

---

Dinge" ["The Experience of the Unitary Reality and the Sympathy of Things," 1955], "Der schöpferische Mensch und die 'Große Erfahrung'" ["The Creative Man and the 'Great Experience,'" 1956], "Die Sinnfrage und das Individuum" ["The Question of Meaning and the Individual," 1957], "Frieden als Symbol des Lebens" ["Peace as the Symbol of Life," 1958], "Das Bild des Menschen in Krise und Erneuerung" ["The Image of Man in Crisis and Renewal," 1959], and "Die Psyche als Ort der Gestaltung" ["The Psyche as the Place of Creation," 1960]. A further contribution of his, entitled, "Über den Mond und das matriarchale Bewußtsein" ["About the Moon and the Matriarchal Consciousness," 1950], appeared in a special yearbook, published on the occasion of Jung's seventieth birthday. Neumann's lectures were regularly published in the *Eranos Yearbooks* (*Eranos-Jahrbücher*). His first lectures were also included in a monographic series entitled, *The Encircling of the Center* (*Umkreisung der Mitte*, three volumes, 1953–1954). Some essays were later republished in special Eranos series, such as the *Papers from the Eranos Yearbooks*, edited by Joseph Campbell (in English language, 1954–1968), the *Quaderni di Eranos*, edited by Claudio Risé (in Italian language, 1989–1999), the *Eranos Series*, edited by Rudolf Ritsema and Toshihiko Izutsu (in Japanese language, 1990–1992), and the *Círculo Eranos (Cuadernos de Eranos)*, edited by Andrés Ortiz-Osés (in Spanish language, 1994–2004). Some lectures, translated into English, were also included in four monographic volumes of the prestigious Bollingen Series, entitled, *Art and the Creative Unconscious* (1959), *Creative Man* (1979), *The Place of Creation* (1989), and *The Fear of the Feminine* (1994). Some essays were re-published in two miscellaneous volumes of Eranos lectures, respectively entitled, *Aspects of Life* (*Aspekte des Lebendigen*), edited by Karl Epting and prefaced by Hugo Rahner (1965), and *The Psyche as the Place of Creation* (*Die Psyche als Ort der Gestaltung*), edited by Gerhard M. Walch (1992). Neumann's papers were then included in the five-volume series of Neumann's collected *Eranos Lectures* (*Eranos Vorträge*), edited by Regula Bühlmann (2007–2009), and, more recently, in the volume entitled, *Man and Meaning*, translated into Hebrew from German and edited by Tamar Kron and David Wieler (2013).

8 T. B. Kirsch, *The Jungians: A Comparative and Historical Perspective* (London: Routledge, 2000), 180.

9 A. Vitolo, "The Analytical *Leitmotif* of the Eranos Conferences," *Spring: A Journal of Archetype and Culture* 92 (2015): 109 ff.

10 C. G. Jung and E. Neumann, *Analytical Psychology in Exile: The Correspondence of C. G. Jung and Erich Neumann*, ed. M. Liebscher (Princeton, NJ: Princeton University Press, 2015), 186, 205, and 206.

them to take part in the conferences.[11] Eranos thus represented a real *trait d'union* between Jung and his pupil.[12]

Neumann usually lectured at Eranos as the keynote speaker. He preferred to speak as the first lecturer in order to free himself from the tension connected with the public engagement.[13] Neumann had a large circle of followers, as he always touched on points of central interest. As Ximena de Angulo-Roelli reports, for example, Neumann's 1950 lecture, "On the Psychological Meaning of Rite," was one of the high points of that year's conference. She also regretted that there were not more young people there to benefit from his talk.[14] What made his lectures so interesting was that he always made a connection to present-day spiritual problems and did not simply hold forth in an abstract way about distant cultures, according to Hans Thomas Hakl.[15] As Gerhard Adler and William McGuire point out, Neumann thus became one of the most important figures at Eranos, if not the dominant one.[16] On the occasion of Neumann's death, both Mrs. Fröbe-Kapteyn and the Swiss biologist and zoologist, Adolf Portmann (1897–1982)—who succeeded her in the guidance of Eranos in 1962—published eulogies in the yearbook, acknowledging Neumann as "perhaps the only follower of Jung's to establish his own school of followers."[17] The Jewish mysticism scholar,

---

11   Ibid., 184, 185, and 195. Julie Neumann practiced chiromancy and possessed a large collection of palm prints for purposes of comparison; U. von Mangoldt, *Auf der Schwelle zwischen Gestern und Morgen* (Weilheim: Otto Wilhelm Barth, 1963), 147; Hakl, *Eranos*, 149. After Erich Neumann's death, Julie Neumann continued to correspond with Mrs. Fröbe-Kapteyn, for whom she also did some palm readings in the 1950s.

12   Gilles Quispel relates, in particular, how deeply moved Neumann was by Jung's 1951 Eranos lecture, "On Synchronicity"; quoted in Hakl, *Eranos*, 363, n. 161.

13   A. Vitolo, "Erich Neumann e la prospettiva mitica," in *Psicologia analitica contemporanea*, ed. C. Trombetta (Milan: Bompiani, 1989), 467.

14   X. de Angulo-Roelli, "Eranos 1950. August 21–August 29" (Ascona: typescript, 19509; Eranos Foundation Archives); Hakl, *Eranos*, 150.

15   Ibid.

16   G. Adler, "Erich Neumann: 1905–1960," *Spring* (1961): 6; William McGuire, "Editorial Note," in E. Neumann, *The Place of Creation—Six Essays* (Princeton, NJ: Princeton University Press, 1989), vii.

17   O. Fröbe-Kapteyn, "In memoriam Erich Neumann," *Eranos-Jahrbuch* 29 (1960): 7.

Gershom Scholem also wrote a necrology, published in a Jewish journal, in which he recalled Neumann's important role at Eranos.[18]

Neumann's Eranos lectures were not, however, received with unanimous appreciation, particularly from some members of the Jungian circle in Zurich. In August 1948, for example—as Martin Liebscher reported—Carl Alfred Meier left the lecture hall in the midst of Neumann's speech—an action that Neumann referred to in a letter to Meier as "complex driven."[19] In general, however, Neumann's first Eranos lecture, "Mystical Man" was a great success and earned him effusive praise from Jung. Later, Jung also defended Neumann against the accusation made by Meier and Jolande Jacobi that he was advocating a "new dogmatism," that is, a "system" for Jung's teaching.[20] On the contrary, Jung considered Neumann to be "a scholar of the first order … He does not teach a dogma, but attempts to create a structure."[21] Mrs. Fröbe-Kapteyn was also impressed by Neumann's first talk. The encounter with the numinous, of which Neumann spoke on that occasion, had of course been very familiar to her.[22]

From the 1940s, the formal part of the conference, held in Eranos House (Casa Eranos), was complemented by informal discussions, reserved for a smaller group of lecturers and a few other guests, on the terrace of Gabriella House (Casa Gabriella), the second building that is still owned by the Foundation. Every day during mealtimes, the group gathered around a large green Round Table, under two tall cedar trees, facing Lake Maggiore. A stone sculpture with the Latin inscription, *Genio loci ignoto* ("To the unknown genius of the place"), stood in the

---

18 Gershom Scholem attended the Eranos conferences from 1949 to 1979. In a letter dated April 3, 1948 to Mrs. Fröbe-Kapteyn, Neumann expressed his disappointment that Scholem wouldn't be able to attend the gathering planned for that summer (Jung and Neumann, *Analytical Psychology in Exile*, 173, n. 390). Later, Neumann urged Fröbe-Kapteyn get the money together for Scholem's attendance, which would have been in his opinion "very nice and important" (ibid.).
19 Jung and Neumann, *Analytical Psychology in Exile*, xxxix and 252, n. 472.
20 Ibid.
21 Ibid., xli.
22 Hakl, *Eranos*, 149.

background. The monument, built in 1949, was the idea of Jung and historian of religions Gerardus van der Leeuw. As Jung's secretary and then student, Aniela Jaffé, recalled:

> Conversation between Jung and the other conference speakers took place in a small circle, in pleasant calm, at midday and evenings around the great Round Table in the garden, or in Gabriella House. At the very beginning of Eranos, Jung once appeared for dinner, pointed out the Round Table, and said: "This is the true Eranos!" Jung talked about all the topics he could and the young psychologists participated there with special interest.[23]

Mrs. Fröbe-Kapteyn wrote that these informal discussions—to which Neumann contributed—were almost more important than the lectures themselves and that it was too bad the words were not taken down.

Another particular moment at Eranos was the so-called terrace-wall session (*Mauerchen-Sitzung*), which—as still Aniela Jaffé recollected—took place as follows:

> During the intermission and after the lectures, Jung would perch on the little wall of the terrace, and immediately participants and pupils ... would gather around him like a cluster of grapes. Jung would discuss each lecture psychologically, and every question, however short and simple, received a rich response.[24]

Aniela Jaffé also recalled that the terrace-wall sessions took on a "special nuance" when Neumann was present, for "then—unlike the usual situation, where we only questioned—there arose a true *dialogue*. We listened."[25]

Eranos influenced Neumann's work in a significant way—both on an intellectual level and on a more personal one. While pointing out to Mrs. Fröbe-Kapteyn that she probably was "overestimating [his] role at

---

23 A. Jaffé, "C. G. Jung and the Eranos Conferences," *Spring* (1977): 202.
24 Ibid., 202 f.
25 Ibid.

Eranos," Neumann admitted: "Eranos has become a friendly island for me to which I belong."[26] He also wrote to her:

> You know that it is not by coincidence that I am living in Israel, and to a large extent I belong there ... But another— unconditional and differently conditioned—part of me, which is essentially without a homeland ... was joyfully surprised to find a piece of home ground within Eranos, whose spirit lives in your heart, in the talks at the large Round Table on the terrace by the lake, and in the wide-reaching efforts of many lecturers to grasp the real essence of the Western spirit. Believe me that this joy goes together with a deep sense of gratitude for being blessed, again and again, in every conceivable way, with new gifts from that *mandala*.[27]

Eranos and the "Feminine" Quality of the Place

Parallel with the development of conferences was the creation of an archive—the Eranos Archive for Research in Symbolism—which served as an indispensable iconographic base for important studies, such as Jung's *Psychology and Alchemy*, Mircea Eliade's *The Forge and the Crucible*, and Neumann's *The Origins and Structure of Consciousness* and *The Great Mother—An Analysis of the Archetype*. The Great Mother theme in particular, to which Neumann dedicated one of his main works, played a crucial role in Mrs. Fröbe-Kapteyn's life and, as a consequence, at Eranos. This archetype, we could argue, represented the convergence point between Eranos and Neumann's work. But what was the story of Neumann's encounter with Eranos? It was said that it happened in 1947. Our account however has to begin some years earlier.

---

26 Neumann in a letter to Mrs. Fröbe-Kapteyn, January 20, 1951; quoted in Jung and Neumann, *Analytical Psychology in Exile*, l.
27 Quoted in H. Prokop, "Erich Neumann in Israel," *Psychologie des 20. Jahrhunderts*, 3, 2 (1977): 850; Hakl, *Eranos*, 149.

To start, it could be interesting to know that on one of the two small Brissago Islands in Lake Maggiore, in front to Eranos, a temple to Aphrodite was supposed to have stood in ancient times.[28] Those islands and that temple, as well as the idea of an inner initiation into a realm of the Great Mother, had occupied an important place in Mrs. Fröbe-Kapteyn's inner experiences since 1934, when she began to work with Jung and had some analytical sessions with him.[29]

Moreover, between 1905 and 1911, on the renown "Mountain of Truth" ("Monte Verità"), in the same Ascona where the Eranos conferences took place almost thirty years later, the psychoanalyst, anarchist, and revolutionary Otto Gross (1877–1920) had planned to create a "free university" for the emancipation of human beings, which aimed to change the Western world. For Gross, Ascona represented a utopian matriarchal society, in contrast with the violent, authoritarian, and patriarchal one. In Ascona, Gross tried to renew Astarte's cult through sexual liberation and scientific teaching.[30] The Swiss curator, artist, and art historian, Harald

---

28   G. Mondada, *Le isole di Brissago nel passato e oggi* (Isole di Brissago/Locarno: Amministrazione delle Isole di Brissago/Tipografia Stazione S.A. 1975); Isole di Brissago and Parco Botanico del Cantone Ticino, ed., *1885-1985. Cento anno dall'acquisto delle Isole di Brissago. La Baronessa Antonietta St. Leger. 1950-1985 Trentacinque anni d'apertura al pubblico del Parco botanico del Cantone Ticino* (Isole di Brissago: Isole di Brissago/Parco Botanico del Cantone Ticino, 1985); D. Hasenfratz, *Das Schicksal der Brissago-Inseln—Le Isole di Brissago e la loro storia: Vom Venustempel zum Eukalyptusbaum* (Ascona, Switzerland: Ferien-Journal, 1994); D. Hasenfratz, "Il destino delle Isole di Brissago: dal tempio di Venere all'albero di eucalipto," *Ferien-Journal. Ascona* (1994).
29   Hakl, *Eranos*, 110; Bernardini, *Jung a Eranos*, 83–112; R. Bernardini, "Jung nel giardino di Eranos: il paesaggio dell'analisi," in *L'Ombra del Flâneur: Scritti in onore di Augusto Romano*, ed. F. Vigna (Bergamo, Italy: Moretti&Vitali, 2014); R. Bernardini, "Guest Editor's Introduction," *Spring: A Journal of Archetype and Culture*, special issue, *Eranos—Its Magical Past and Alluring Future: The Spirit of a Wondrous Place* 92 (2015): 9–11.
30   See, for example, E. Hurwitz, "Otto Gross. Dalla psicanalisi al Paradiso," in H. Szeemann, ed., *Monte Verità. Antropologia locale come contributo alla riscoperta di una topografia sacrale moderna* (Locarno/Milan: Armando Dadò/Electa, 1978), 109–118; E. Hurwitz, *Otto Gross, „Paradies"-Sucher zwischen Freud und Jung. Leben und Werk* (Zurich: Suhrkamp, 1979); E. Hurwitz, "Conflitto e verità. La dimensione politica della psicanalisi per Otto Gross," in A. Schwab and C. Lafranchi, ed., *Senso della vita e bagni di sole. Esperimenti di vita e arte al Monte Verità* (Ascona: Fondazione Monte Verità, 2001), 143–155; J. E. Michaels, *Anarchy and Eros—Otto Gross' Impact on German Expressionist Writers—Leonhard Frank, Franz Jung, Johannes R. Becher, Karl Otten, Curth Corrinth, Walter Hasenclever, Oskar Maria Graf; Franz Kafka, Franz Werfel, Max Brod, Raoul Hausmann and Berlin Dada* (New York, NY: Peter Lang, 1983); J. E. Michaels, "Otto Gross und das Konzept des Matriarchats," in G. Heuer, ed., *2. Internationaler Otto Gross Kongress. Bürghölzli, Zürich 2000* (Marburg an der Lahn: Lit-

Szeemann (1933–2005) was aware of the maternal quality of the place and titled his 1978 exhibition on the history of the Mountain of Truth, "Monte Verità—The Breasts of Truth."[31]

A few kilometers away from Monte Verità, the Eranos Center was founded in 1930. Mrs. Fröbe-Kapteyn was convinced that only a woman could guide Eranos. She wrote: "Generally we are used to consider an organizing and managerial activity as a male activity. However, it seems to me that it is specifically feminine. The forming and procreative force is always feminine, even if it deals with the creative activity of a man."[32] Adolf Portmann also pointed out that "the plan for these meetings matured in a woman's spirit."[33] In her view, the collegial work at Eranos, always risky, was anchored in a "spiritual earth"—the Earth archetype about which Neumann spoke in his 1953 Eranos lecture. In the physical place where the Eranos play was staged, Mrs. Fröbe-Kapteyn sensed some mysterious, "feminine, maternal qualities."[34] In December 1959, she had a dream, which she reported as follows:

> I am to be initiated into a kind of modern Order by a woman. I seem to have passed into a certain degree shown by a straight line in a diagram of four grades. Then I stand before the door of a high priest, which again reminds me of the Templars.[35]

eratur Wissenschaft.de, 2002), 105–115; M. Green, *The von Richthofen Sisters—The Triumphant and the Tragic Mode of Love. Else and Frieda von Richthofen, Otto Gross, Max Weber, and D. H. Lawrence, in the Years 1870–1970* (New York, NY: Basic, 1974); M. Green, *Mountain of Truth—The Counterculture Begins. Ascona 1900–1920* (Hanover, NH/London: University Press of New England, 1986); M. Green, *Prophets of a New Age—The Politics of Hope from the Eighteenth through the Twenty-first Centuries* (New York, NY: Charles Scribner's Sons, 1992); M. Green, *Otto Gross, Freudian Psychoanalyst, 1877–1920* (Literature and Ideas. Lewiston, NY: Edwin Mellen, 1999); M. Green, "Una Nuova Era. New Age e nuovi "Centri di vita" dal 1890 al 1920," in Schwab and Lafranchi, *Senso della vita e bagni di sole*, 207–222; and M. Lo Russo, *Otto Gross: Psiche, Eros, Utopia* (Rome: Editori Riuniti University Press, 2011).

31 Szeemann, *Monte Verità: Antropologia locale come contributo alla riscoperta di una topografia sacrale moderna.*

32 O. Fröbe-Kapteyn, "Eranos Vortrag" (Ascona: unpublished typescript, 1939; Eranos Foundation Archives), 5.

33 A. Portmann, "Vom Sinn und Autrag der Eranos Tagungen," *Eranos-Jahrbuch* 30 (1961): 7.

34 O. Fröbe-Kapteyn, "Vorwort," *Eranos-Jahrbuch* 23 (1954): 6.

35 O. Fröbe-Kapteyn, "Dream" (Ascona: unpublished typescript, December 21, 1959; Eranos

In one of his last letters to her, Jung wrote that her problem was a father complex, that is, an overvaluation of the masculine. For this reason, Jung continued, an initiation into a female order would have been helpful both for her and for Eranos.[36]

Mrs. Fröbe-Kapteyn always felt herself split between her role as spiritual mother of her cultural enterprise, Eranos, and her duties as natural mother toward her daughter, Bettina Gertrude.[37] She also confessed to being aware of her connection with the Eranos lecturers as a relationship between mother and sons.[38] This was probably the reason for her difficulties in accepting female scholars among the Eranos lecturers. It is said that she was annoyed when the lecturers came to Ascona with their wives. During the 1938 conference, dedicated to the Great Mother, she got into an argument with the archaeologist, Vera Christina Chute Collum. From that moment and until her death, female scholars were tacitly excluded from the Eranos platform.[39] Mrs. Fröbe-Kapteyn was ironically and affectionately nicknamed by some of the Eranos scholars close to her as "Mother Fröbe," "*Domina* Fröbe," "Revered Mother" (Rudolf Otto), "Adored *Ur*-mother" (Henirich Zimmer), and "Mother Olga" (Rudolf Ritsema). Considered to be a "priestess of a new religion" (Mircea Eliade), she herself once spoke of Gabriella House as a temple of Aphrodite. Even someone with as skeptical a mind as Gershom Scholem could recall, after three decades of participation at the conferences:

> When we, Adolf Portmann, Erich Neumann, Henry Corbin,
> Ernst Benz, Mircea Eliade, Karl Kerényi, and many others—
> scholars of religion, psychologists, philosophers, physicists,

---

Foundation Archives).

36   C. G. Jung, letter to O. Fröbe-Kapteyn, January 14, 1960, unpublished (© Foundation of the Works of C. G. Jung, Zurich); quoted in Bernardini, *Jung a Eranos*, 88.

37   C. G. Jung, letter to O. Fröbe-Kapteyn, August 20, 1945, in C. G. Jung, *Letters* (Princeton, NJ: Princeton University Press, 1973); Bernardini, *Jung a Eranos*, 87–89.

38   O. Fröbe-Kapteyn, letter to H. Corbin, November 1, 1951; quoted in R. Bernardini, "La corrispondenza Carl Gustav Jung–Henry Corbin," *Historia Religionum* 5 (2013): 97; and O. Fröbe-Kapteyn, letter to C. G. Jung, March 11, 1960, unpublished (Eranos Foundation Archives); quoted in Bernardini, *Jung a Eranos*, 87.

39   William McGuire, *Bollingen: An Adventure in Collecting the Past* (Princeton, NJ: Princeton University Press, 1982), 27.

and biologists—were trying to play our part in Eranos, the figure of Olga Fröbe was crucial—she whom we always referred to among ourselves as "the Great Mother." Olga Fröbe was an unforgettable figure for anyone who came here regularly or for any length of time. I have never been a great Jungian . . . but I have to say that Mrs. Fröbe was the living image of what in Jungian psychology is called the Anima and the Animus.[40]

In the first edition of *The Great Mother*, Neumann wrote her this dedication: "That for you, dear Olga, the 'Great Mother' belongs to you in a special way, we both know. In old friendship and gratitude, your, Erich Neumann."

In 1934, Mrs. Fröbe-Kapteyn began to plan an archive in which "the phenomena of the Unconscious (the Collective Unconscious according to C. G. Jung), in its various forms of written descriptions, phantasies, or drawings, can be studied, compared, interpreted, ordered, or classified by competent workers in this fields of psychology."[41] In 1935, she undertook a picture research project at the request of Jung, who needed visual materials for his studies on alchemy and the theory of archetypes. At that time, she didn't know anything about alchemy, as she recalled, but she accepted the job without hesitation nevertheless. In order to collect archetypal images as a complement to Jung's theoretical treatises on alchemy,[42] she began traveling, normally during the winter season, to European and American libraries such as the British Museum and the Warburg Institute in London, the Bibliothèque Nationale de France and the Bibliothèque de l'Arsenal in Paris, the Biblioteca Apostolica Vaticana in Rome, the Stadtbibliothek in Munich, the Zentralbibliothek in Zurich, and the Archaeological Museum in Athens, as well as to other libraries

---

40   G. Scholem, "Identifizierung und Distanz: ein Rückblick," *Eranos-Jahrbuch* 48 (1979): 463.
41   O. Fröbe-Kapteyn, "Eranos Archive" (Ascona: unpublished typescript, 1934; Eranos Foundation Archives); O. Fröbe-Kapteyn, "Eranos—A Survey," 7.
42   Ibid.

and archives in Stuttgart, Oxford, Crete, Berlin, Bonn, Trier, and New York. Between 1935 and 1938, she did this research exclusively on behalf of Jung.[43]

The iconographical researches that she did between 1938 and 1941 were funded by Mary Elizabeth Conover Mellon (1904–1946) and Paul Mellon (1907–1999). For more than twenty years, they were—personally and later through the Bollingen Foundation, which was founded at Eranos in the early 1940s—the main sponsors of Eranos.[44] Unfortunately, Mary Mellon died too young. Mrs. Fröbe-Kapteyn wrote that her relationship with Jung and with Mary Mellon were the strongest ones of all her life.[45] When Mrs. Fröbe-Kapteyn experienced a great delusion connected with the interruption of the relationships between Eranos and the Bollingen Foundation during the war, Jung wrote to her: "As far as your 'bleeding heart' feeling is concerned, perhaps you have not fully realized the extent to which you have adopted Mrs. Mellon as your daughter and the person to continue Eranos. You have been severely disappointed, which weighs all the more heavily in so far as you were totally identified with Eranos—indeed to a dangerous degree. One should not hang one's heart on anything, for it belongs to the Self; everything else is transient."[46]

Together with organizing the conferences, iconographical research thus became Mrs. Fröbe-Kapteyn's main enterprise for about ten years. She was thus able to obtain a large number of photographic reproductions of symbolical representations derived from Eastern and Western iconographic traditions—alchemy, folklore, mythology, and religions,

---

43 O. Fröbe-Kapteyn, "Erster / Zweiter / Dritter / Vierter / Funfter / Sechster / Siebenter Abend / Kommentar" (Ascona: unpublished typescript, 1957–1958[?]; Eranos Foundation Archives), 14.

44 McGuire, *Bollingen*; P. Mellon with J. Baskett, *Reflections in a Silver Spoon—A Memoir* (New York, NY: William Morrow and Company, Inc., 1992); W. Schoenl, *C.G. Jung—His Friendships with Mary Mellon and J. B. Priestley* (Wilmette, IL: Chiron, 1998).

45 O. Fröbe-Kapteyn, "Vision" (Ascona: unpublished typescript, July 3, 1947; Eranos Foundation Archives), 2.

46 C. G. Jung, letter to O. Fröbe-Kapteyn dated January 17, 1943, unpublished (© Foundation of the Works of C. G. Jung, Zurich); quoted in Hakl, *Eranos*, 210, ft. 47.

as well as contemporary archetypal representations—and catalogue them on the basis of their archetypal themes. The Eranos Archive for Research in Symbolism, which began being consulted by several scholars after 1941, grew eventually to about 3,500 images.[47] Originally, Mrs. Fröbe-Kapteyn planned to build an Eranos Studio in an apartment just above the Eranos Hall for storing the pictures,[48] but because she had to rent out that space she continued to store the photographs at Gabriella House, where she lived.[49] As an extension of and to further develop the Eranos Archive, she also wanted to create an Eranos Institute for Research into Religious Symbolism. This would have operated through conferences, seminars, and specialized publications, with the addition at some later date of a summer school for the study of symbolism and for specific training in that field.[50] On the occasion of the 1941 conference, the outline for this institute was presented to Jung. He fully approved the project, saying that it was exactly what was needed. It would be the first research institution of its kind.[51]

In 1937, Mrs. Fröbe-Kapteyn wrote to Jung about her intention to collect images of the Great Mother archetype for the Eranos Archive. At the British Museum in London, she had in fact found "surprising things"—amazing representations on this subject from Crete, Cyprus,

---

47 O. Fröbe-Kapteyn, letter to L. Ettlinger dated July 9, 1954. In a previous letter to Paul Fejos dated September 5, 1949, she wrote of about 3,000 images. Jessie A. Fraser, who later catalogued the images of the Eranos Archive for the Bollingen Foundation, estimated there were about 4,000 images (J. A. Fraser, "ARAS: Archive for Research in Archetypal Symbolism," *Spring* [1964]: 61); the same number is reported by Mircea Eliade (M. Eliade, "Eranos," *Nimbus* 2 [1954]: 58). Hans Bänziger wrote instead of about 6,000 images (H. Bänziger, "Das Eranos-Archiv, *Du* 15, 4 [1955]: 62).
48 O. Fröbe-Kapteyn, "Eranos Archive" (Ascona: unpublished typescript, 1941; Eranos Foundation Archives).
49 O. Fröbe-Kapteyn, "Eranos Archive for Research in Symbolism" (Ascona: unpublished typescript, 1947[?]; Eranos Foundation Archives); McGuire, *Bollingen*, 29.
50 O. Fröbe-Kapteyn, "Eranos Institute for Research into Religious Symbolism" (Ascona: unpublished typescript, 1941; Eranos Foundation Archives).
51 O. Fröbe-Kapteyn, "Eranos Institute for Research into Religious Symbolism (Archetypal Images)" (Ascona: unpublished typescript, 1947; Eranos Foundation Archives).

Asia Minor, and other places.[52] In January 1938, while engaged in research of images on the Great Mother, she had an intense inner experience, which she described as a "descent into Hell." These visions had revealed to her the "maternal aspect of Hell" in the form of a cave covered by black breasts from which milk flowed. Later, between September and November 1938, she spent a period of time in Athens, Crete, and then in Rome. Before moving on to Berlin, she wrote to Mary Mellon: "I feel as if I were going into the unknown, because this cruise into the territory of the *Magna Mater*, where all her cults were alive, is a different thing from getting her images from the northern museums. I am going to collect every archetypal representation I can find."[53] She also reported to Mary Mellon that in Crete she had "the greatest experience" of her life.[54] She wrote the same to Cary Baynes, to whom she explained that some psychosomatic symptoms she had suffered from during her trip were connected with her identification with the Great Mother. While looking for archaeological traces of that mythologem, she had become completely "inflated" by it. In Knossos Palace, where a serpent-god was worshiped, she saw herself as an "island of ancient traditions." This trip into the realm of the Great Mother was so intense and destabilizing that she had to ask for Jung's help—as she often did in those years. She wrote to him that she wasn't able to free herself from the "mythological net" in which she was trapped.[55]

It is not surprising, therefore, that on April 16–19, 1938, the annual August conference was preceded by an intensive seminar given by Ernesto Buonaiuti (1881–1946), a historian of Christianity, on the theme, "The Cult of the Mother-Goddess in Mediterranean Religiosity" ("Il culto della Dea Mater nella religiosità mediterranea").[56] The Eranos conference planned for

52 O. Fröbe-Kapteyn, letter to C. G. Jung dated December 3, 1937, unpublished (Eranos Foundation Archives); quoted in Bernardini, *Jung a Eranos*, 268.
53 Quoted in McGuire, *Bollingen*, 29–30.
54 Ibid.
55 O. Fröbe-Kapteyn, letter to C. G. Jung, November 16, 1938, unpublished (Eranos Foundation Archives); quoted in Bernardini, *Jung a Eranos*, 296.
56 Every morning, Buonaiuti lectured on the following topics: "Divinità femminili della Pre-

that summer had the title, "Form and Cult of the 'Great Mother'" ("Gestalt und Kultur der „Grossen Mutter"").[57] Mrs. Fröbe-Kapteyn reported that "this handling of the many various cults of the Mother-Goddess proved the intimate relationship of this great archetype with the psychology of every individual present. The reaction in the audience was extremely strong, and every speaker was gripped by the subject."[58]

On the occasion of the 1938 conference, Mrs. Fröbe-Kapteyn also set up an exhibition of the Eranos Archive, dedicated to the Great Mother.[59]

---

istoria" ["Female Divinities in Prehistory"], "Divinità femminili dell'Oriente Antico" ["Female Divinities in Ancient East"], "Divinità femminili nella terra di Canaan e nella religiosità Israelitica in Palestina e fuori dalla Palestina" ["Female Divinities in Canaan and in Jewish Religiosity in Palestine and outside Palestine"], "Divinità femminili nella Grecia Antica" ["Female Divinities in Ancient Greece"], "Divinità femminili nelle Religioni di Mistero" ["Female Divinities in Mystery Religions"], and "Maria Vergine e Madre nella tradizione del Cristianesimo" ["Virgin and Mother Mary in Christian Tradition"]. Afternoons were reserved for group discussions. Two evenings featured a further lecture on the topic, "Origine, storia e condanna dei Templari" ["Origins, History, and Sentence of the Templars"], and a reading of Euripides's *Bacchae*.

57 The invited scholars were Jean Przyluski, Orientalist at the Collège de France in Paris, who lectured on "Les origines et l'évolution du culte de la Déesse Mère" ["The Origins and Evolution of the Mother-Goddess Cult"] and on "La Déesse Mère comme trait d'union entre les divinités locales et le Dieu universel" ["The Mother-Goddess as a Trait d'Union between the Local Divinities and the Universal God"]; Charles Picard, director of the Institut d'Art in Paris and of the École Française d'Athènes, who lectured on "L'Ephésia d'Anatolie" ["The Ephesia of Anatolie"] and "La Déesse Mère de la Crète à Eleusis" ["The Mother-Goddess from Crete to Eleusis"]; Assyriologist and archaeologist Charles Virolleaud, president of the Société Asiatique and fellow of the Académie des Inscriptions et Belles-Lettres in Paris, who lectured on "Ishtar, Isis et Astarté: La Grande Déesse en Babylonie, Egypte et Phénicie" ["Ishtar, Isis, and Astarte: The Great Goddess in Babylon, Egypt, and Phoenicia"] and "Ishtar, Isis et Astarté" ["Ishtar, Isis, and Astarte"]; Louis Massignon, president of the Institut des Hautes Études Iraniennes of Paris-Sorbonne University, who lectured on "Le culte gnostique de Fatima dans l'Islam Shî'ite" ["The Gnostic Cult of Fatima in Shî'ite Islam"]; Indologist Heinrich Zimmer, professor in Heidelberg, who lectured on "Die Indische Weltmutter" ["The Indian World Mother"]; archaeologist Vera Christina Chute Collum, who lectured on "The Creative Mother-Goddess of the Celtic-Speaking Countries"; historian of Christianity Ernesto Buonaiuti, who lectured on "Maria Santa Immacolata nella tradizione mistica e ascetica del Cristianesimo" ["Holy Immaculate Mary in the Christian Mystical and Ascetical Tradition"] and "Die Heilige Maria in der christlichen Überlieferung" ["Holy Mary in Christian Tradition"]; and psychiatrist Gustav-Richard Heyer, who lectured on "Die Große Mutter im Seelenleben des heutigen Menschen" ["The Great Mother in Today Man's Psychological Existence"]. Jung came to Ascona directly from Oxford and held a lecture on "Der psychologische Aspekt der Grossen Mutter" ["The Psychological Aspects of the Great Mother"]. Emma Jung-Rauschenbach provided an English summary of her husband's lecture for those who didn't understand German (E. Thayer, "Eranos and Ascona" [unpublished typescript; Kristine Mann Library Archives]).

58 O. Fröbe-Kapteyn, "Eranos—A Survey," 4.

59 Mrs. Fröbe-Kapteyn set up a series of exhibitions of the Eranos archive between 1935 and 1940. The first one, in 1935, included a series of psychological drawings belonging to the Eranos collection. After the 1938 exhibition on the Great Mother, a third exhibition was set up in 1939

Some of the artworks were lent by Baron Eduard von der Heydt (1882–1964), the owner of the Hotel Monte Verità, where he regularly hosted several lecturers and participants to the Eranos conferences.[60] Hildegard Nagel (1886–1985), a member of the Analytical Psychology Club of New York who attended the meetings as a listener, was deeply impressed by this thematic collection. She proposed to Mrs. Fröbe-Kapteyn that the same exhibition be set up at the New York Analytical Psychology Club. In October 1939, with a grant of 1,000 Swiss francs provided by Mary and Paul Mellon, Mrs. Fröbe-Kapteyn and Cary Baynes traveled to New York on the SS Count of Savoy. The exhibition, "The Great Mother", which included three hundred images, represented the debut of Eranos in the United States.[61] In this way, Mrs. Fröbe-Kapteyn noted, "Eranos first appeared in America in its pictorial aspect."[62] On October 27, 1939, for the exhibition's opening, Mrs. Fröbe-Kapteyn gave a lecture entitled, "The Psychological Background of Eranos."[63] The American experience made her think about a possible continuation of Eranos in the United States in case Switzerland were occupied by Nazi Germany.[64] Funded by the New York Analytical Psychology Club, the exhibition was then moved to Paris, most likely to the local Analytical Psychology Club there. A further exhibition was planned at the Analytical Psychology Club in London, with

on the topic of rebirth, and a fourth in 1940 on the symbols of early Christianity (J. C. Reid, Jung, My Mother and I: The Analytic Diaries of Catharine Rush Cabot [Einsiedeln, Switzerland: Daimon, 2001], 291).

60 Baron von der Heydt, Emperor Wilhelm II's banker, was an important collector of primitive, Oriental, and contemporary art. He had converted the beautiful park at Monte Verità, which he had acquired in 1926, into a botanic garden where he placed exotic plants, Chinese birdcages, and sculptures inspired by Far Eastern art and the Great Mother (M. Folini and L. Zaza-Sciolli, "La collezione Barone Eduard von der Heydt al Monte Verità," in Dal Seicento olandese alle avanguardie del primo Novecento: La collezione Eduard von der Heydt al Monte Verità, ed. M. Khan-Rossi [Zurich: Museo Cantonale d'Arte/Pro Litteris, 1996]. An Indian statue was donated to Mrs. Fröbe-Kapteyn and placed in the Eranos garden, where it remains to this day.

61 H. Nagel, ed., Eranos Archive: Images of the Great Mother Throughout the Ages (New York, NY: Analytical Psychology Club, 1938); H. Nagel, ed., The Eranos Conference 1938: Papers of the Analytical Psychology Club of New York (New York, NY: Analytical Psychology Club, 1939).

62 O. Fröbe-Kapteyn, "Eranos—A Survey," 7.

63 O. Fröbe-Kapteyn, "The Psychological Background of Eranos" [1939], Spring: A Journal of Archetype and Culture 92 (2015): 31–38.

64 Hakl, Eranos, 121.

an explanatory lecture by Violet de Laszlo, but the customs expenses and difficulties were so great that the plan was abandoned.[65] As it turns out, the Eranos collection of photographs on the Great Mother had a destiny that Mrs. Fröbe-Kapteyn couldn't imagine at that time.

Neumann and the Making of "The Great Mother"

In 1933–1934, after leaving Germany for Switzerland with his wife, Julie, and his oldest son, Micha, Erich Neumann underwent analysis with Jung in Zurich for about eight months. He then went on to Palestine and established an analytical practice in Tel Aviv. He did not return to Europe until 1947. That summer, he traveled to Ascona to visit his boyhood friend, Gerhard Adler (1904–1989), and to spend a vacation there.[66] Adler, who was also Jewish and born in Berlin, was used to renting a house in Ascona during the summer holidays for his family. On this occasion, Adler introduced Neumann to Mrs. Fröbe-Kapteyn and to a member of the Bollingen Foundation, John David (Jack) Barrett Jr. (1903–1981), at that time editor of the Bollingen Series.[67]

Mrs. Fröbe-Kapteyn showed Neumann the Eranos Lecture Hall, the garden, and the Archive. Julie Neumann recollected that her husband was deeply impressed by the Eranos collection. In 1950, recalling his first encounter with Eranos, Neumann wrote to Mrs. Fröbe-Kapteyn: "When I came back to Europe in 1947 for the first time after the World War and having being away for eleven years, I was sure that, after all that had happened to me, Europe would seem alien and disturbing. There was one place, however, where I found my initial foothold—a ground for myself, my way of life, my work—and that was in the Eranos Archive,

65 O. Fröbe-Kapteyn, "Eranos—A Survey," 8.
66 Already in 1945, Adler wrote to Jung suggesting that he invite Neumann to Eranos, believing that Neumann could "deliver something valuable and original" (G. Adler, letter to C. G. Jung, December 12, 1945; quoted in Jung and Neumann, *Analytical Psychology in Exile*, xxxvii).
67 P. Mellon, W. McGuire, K. Coburn, and J. Campbell, *To Celebrate the Life of Jack Barrett: 1903–1981* (New York, NY: Bollingen Foundation/ Pierpont Morgan Library, 1981), 5.

whose world of images had enchanted and seized me … . For some years now I have been coming to Switzerland and to Europe, but strangely enough—or is it in fact so strange?—in truth, it is always to Ascona and to Eranos that I come."[68]

Erich and Julie Neumann attended the 1947 Eranos conference as listeners. The conference topic was "The Human Being" ("Der Mensch"). Neumann thus had a chance to discuss his ideas with the other prominent scholars who spoke at Eranos that August, namely, biologist Adolf Portmann; philologist and scholar of mythology Károly Kerényi; physician and physicist Friedrich Dessauer; theologians Hugo Rahner, Karl Ludwig Schmidt, and Victor White; scholar of Gnosticism Gilles Quispel—who was invited by Jung to speak on Valentinus, after the discovery of Nag Hammâdi gnostic manuscripts (1945); scholar of Islam Louis Massignon; and German rabbi Leo Baeck, a leading figure in German Jewry, who had miraculously survived the Teresienstadt concentration camp. Among the listeners, there was also the philosopher and Hebraist, Martin Buber. Neumann also had the opportunity to establish a link with the group of Jung's pupils who came regularly from Zurich to Ascona to attend the gatherings there.[69]

The enthusiasm that Neumann showed for the Eranos Archive deeply touched Mrs. Fröbe-Kapteyn. In early October 1947, before leaving for New York for her iconographical research, she visited Jung in Zurich. On that occasion, Jung advised her to invite Neumann to lecture at the 1948 Eranos conference. She then told Jung about her project to publish a series of iconographical books (*Eranos-Bilderbücher*) of the Eranos Archive and asked him to write a preface for the first volume. Jung replied that Neumann would be the most appropriate person to write such a preface because the volume, which would include images of the Great Mother,

---

68   Quoted in O. Fröbe-Kapteyn, "*In memoriam* Erich Neumann," 7.
69   Jung and Neumann, *Analytical Psychology in Exile*, xxxvii.

went well with the book Neumann was working on at that time.[70] Jung also advised her to ask the Bollingen Foundation to fund Neumann's travel to Ascona and to grant him a subsidy so he could write a work on the subject.[71]

Mrs. Fröbe-Kapteyn was already positively moved by the encounter with Neumann in 1947. Upon receiving Jung's advice, she was persuaded that Neumann was the most appropriate person for editing the first publication of the Eranos Archive, which would be on the Great Mother.

---

70 In December 1947, Neumann wrote to Jung: "It is very important to me to first complete the *Psychology of the Feminine* as a completion of the *Origins History* in which the deviations from the masculine stages in the psychology of consciousness will be portrayed." (E. Neumann, letter to C. G. Jung dated December 17, 1947, in Jung and Neumann, *Analytical Psychology in Exile*, 210). As Liebscher notes, although Neumann didn't write a specific monograph on the psychology of the feminine, he used the title, *Zur Psychologie des Weiblichen*, for the second volume of the series of his collected essays, *Umkreisung der Mitte* (see Jung and Neumann, *Analytical Psychology in Exile*, 210, n. 424).

71 O. Fröbe-Kapteyn, letter to C. G. Jung dated April 24, 1948, unpublished (Eranos Foundation Archives); quoted in Bernardini, *Jung a Eranos*, 284. The *Eranos-Bilderbuch* on the Great Mother that Mrs. Fröbe-Kapteyn was thinking about in 1947 is different from the one that she planned on the same subject nine years before. When Mary and Paul Mellon first visited Eranos in 1938, in fact, they discussed with Mrs. Fröbe-Kapteyn the project of publishing a miscellaneous "Eranos volume" for presenting Eranos to the American public. The table of contents, prepared by Cary Baynes in January 1939, included writings by C. G. Jung, Heinrich Zimmer, Jakob Wilhelm Hauer, Caroline Augusta Foley Rhys-Davids, Paul Masson-Oursel, Henri-Charles Puech, Andreas Speiser, Ernesto Buonaiuti, Erwin Rousselle, and Jean Przyluski. Cary Baynes was put in charge of the project. The Mellons granted a sum for that volume, for which the New York publisher, Farrar and Rinehart, showed an interest. Mrs. Fröbe-Kapteyn asked Jung to write an introduction (O. Fröbe-Kapteyn, letters to C. G. Jung dated March 31, 1939, and April 15, 1939, unpublished [Eranos Foundation Archives]; quoted in Bernardini, *Jung a Eranos*, 296–297). On May 15, 1939, Jung wrote the introduction, in which he also mentioned the "archive of iconographic material, collected by Mrs. Fröbe-Kapteyn, [which] is available during the conference, illustrating the subjects treated" (C. G. Jung, "Introduction to the American Eranos Volume," *Spring*; reprinted *Spring: A Journal of Archetype and Culture* 92 [2015]: 58). However, with the dissolution of the first Bollingen Foundation (1942), the project of the Eranos American volume stalled. No trace can be found of Mrs. Fröbe-Kapteyn's foreword. The English typescripts of the lectures were donated to Yale University Press and were never published. Ximena de Angulo-Roelli gave copies of the translations to the Analytical Psychology Club of New York as well. They were later rediscovered and given to the Kristine Mann Library (William McGuire, "Jung and Eranos in America," *Spring* [1984]: 51–59; D. Bair, *Jung: A Biography* [Boston, MA: Little, Brown, 2003], 472ff). When the Bollingen Foundation was reconstituted (officially, in 1945), the editorial project of an American Eranos volume was replaced by a wider editorial series—the Papers from the Eranos Yearbooks (1954–1968)—under the supervision of Joseph Campbell. Jung's introduction (with some annotations by Mrs. Fröbe-Kapteyn) was rediscovered by William McGuire at Eranos in 1976 and therefore was not included in Jung's *Collected Works*.

Already seven years earlier, while planning to put together a research staff for working on the Eranos picture collection, she had thought about a "staff of research workers … each of whom would undertake that branch of research for which he or she has proved himself or herself fitted. These should if possible have a knowledge of psychology and Jung's teaching on the archetypes, as well as a clear idea of the nature and form of the Archetypes or Primeval Images."[72] Neumann, of course, fully met the requirements.

On October 15, 1947, from the New York Barbizon Plaza Hotel, Mrs. Fröbe-Kapteyn wrote to Jung's secretary, Marie-Jeanne Schmid, asking for Neumann's address in Tel Aviv. On October 30, 1947, she wrote to Neumann inviting him "to speak on 'Mystical Man' from the perspective of psychology. Jung considered that this theme would appeal to you and we would be delighted if you would accept this invitation. Travel expenses should be covered by Bollingen; a fellowship should be offered … . Even before the war, the Bollingen Foundation planned to publish a series of publications from the Eranos picture archive. They will each consist of around 100 images in large format with a foreword. All images of each volume must relate to a single archetype or primitive image. I have proposed that we commence with the archetype of the Great Mother."[73] Neumann replied to her on November 7, 1947. Although surprised by her invitation, he accepted enthusiastically both to lecture at the 1948 Eranos conference on "Mystical Man" and to study the images of the Great Mother in the Eranos Archive. On November 22, 1947, Mrs. Fröbe-Kapteyn, who was still in New York, informed Jung about Neumann's positive answer to both their proposals. On December 17, 1947, Neumann wrote to Jung letting him know that he had "received the invitation to speak at the Eranos conference on the 'Mystic' and to write

---

72   O. Fröbe-Kapteyn, "Eranos Archive" (Ascona: unpublished typescript, 1941; Eranos Foundation Archives).
73   Quoted in Jung and Neumann, *Analytical Psychology in Exile*, 210, n. 423.

the introduction to the Great Mother publication of the Eranos Archives. Mrs. Fröbe-Kapteyn has been corresponding with me about this up till now and I have now received the papers from America to apply for a Bollingen fellowship."[74]

In early 1948, Mrs. Fröbe-Kapteyn wrote to the Bollingen Foundation asking them to fund Neumann's round trip to Ascona and his stay in Switzerland for about six to eight weeks, except for the week of the conference, which would have been charged to Eranos. She also asked them to grant Neumann a long-term subsidy.[75] Neumann needed three letters of recommendation, one of which should be written by Jung.[76] In any case, Mrs. Fröbe-Kapteyn had already spoken with Paul Mellon, who was agreeable to the funding of Neumann's research.[77] On January 8, 1948, Jung wrote the reference for Neumann's application for a scholarship from the Bollingen Foundation.[78]

On April 5, 1948, Donald D. Shepard, trustee and vice-president of the Bollingen Foundation, wrote to Neumann with regard to his application

> for a grant in aid or fellowship to assist you in the carrying out of a project consisting of research in the Eranos Archive, maintained by the Eranos Foundation at Ascona, and the preparation, upon the basis of the archive material, of an extensive introduction or separate volume designed to accompany a contemplated illustrated volume designed, *The Great Mother.* This proposed work ... will deal with the archetype known as 'The Great Mother,' which plays

74 Ibid., 209.
75 O. Fröbe-Kapteyn, letter to C. G. Jung dated April 24, 1948, unpublished (Eranos Foundation Archives); quoted in Bernardini, *Jung a Eranos,* 284.
76 The other two letters were written by Gerhard Adler and Toni Wolff. See E. Neumann, letter to C. G. Jung dated December 17, 1947, in Jung and Neumann, *Analytical Psychology in Exile,* 211 and n. 426.
77 O. Fröbe-Kapteyn, letter to C. G. Jung dated November 22, 1947, unpublished (Eranos Foundation Archives); quoted in Bernardini, *Jung a Eranos,* 285.
78 Jung and Neumann, *Analytical Psychology in Exile,* 214.

an important role in the psychological theories of Professor C. G. Jung and other analytical psychologists, and which is extensively documented in the Eranos Archive. The Trustees have given careful consideration to your application and I am pleased to be able to advise you that they have decided to offer you a grant in aid or fellowship on the following terms and conditions: The fellowship is for the sum of $1,100.00. This sum shall be payable only if you reach Ascona, Switzerland, as planned, during 1948 … The purpose of this fellowship is to enable you to carry out the project referred to above … When the aforementioned proposed Work is completed, you will present a copy of the manuscript thereof to Bollingen Foundation, and Bollingen Foundation will have, for a period of one year following the presentation of such copy of the manuscript to it, an option to publish or arrange for the publication of such work in the English language.[79]

From that year on, Neumann was listed among the Recipients of Fellowships and Grant-in-Aid of the Bollingen Foundation, "for the preparation of *The Great Mother* and other archetypal studies."[80] Neumann was, however, unsatisfied by Bollingen's offer, which he considered to be

an unsubtle disgrace but at the very least incomprehensible, if one rules out obvious reasons. The comprehensive and precisely defined offer of a total of $1,100 covers little more than the travel and Swiss residential expenses, i.e., I am supposed to cover myself the preparations for the book that must be written, for which I will lose about 2 months

---

79   D. D. Shepard, letter to E. Neumann dated April 5, 1948, unpublished (Eranos Foundation Archives).
80   Bollingen Foundation, *A Report of Its Activities from January 1, 1966, through December 31, 1967* (New York, NY: Bollingen Foundation, 1968), 80.

work, and my family must hopefully also continue to live during this time. Therefore, I am supposed to write the Introduction Book to the 100 images for nothing ... under these circumstances, I will turn this "Fellowship" down and will write my *Psychology of the Feminine* instead. Mrs. Fröbe-Kapteyn wrote to me exceptionally confidently and seemed to have accepted that such an award would be offered to me as an intermediary award for the preparatory work, and that the fellowship would follow for the writing of the book. That would have made sense. She wrote that normally a sum of around $150 per month for three years would be granted, and compared with that, this total award that has been granted me is particularly grotesque.[81]

Thanks to Bollingen's "strongly improved proposal," it was finally possible for Neumann regularly to attend the Eranos conferences and to spend considerable time studying the pictures in the Eranos Archive.[82] He recalled the beginning of his editorial enterprise with these words:

Some years ago, Professor C. G. Jung and Mrs. Olga Fröbe-Kapteyn suggested that I write an introduction to the first publication of material from the Eranos Archive for Research in Symbolism in Ascona, Switzerland—a volume devoted to the manifestations, in art and culture, of the Great Mother archetype. In founding the Eranos Archive, Mrs. Fröbe has taken the lead of an important task of tracking down, collecting, and arranging examples of archetypal material that has found its creative expression in art.[83]

---

81   Jung and Neumann, *Analytical Psychology in Exile*, 222–223. On March 24, 1948, Mrs. Fröbe-Kapteyn wrote to Neumann for letting Neumann know that the Bollingen Foundation has asked her to organize the reimbursement (ibid., 223, n. 439).
82   Ibid., 226.
83   Erich Neumann, *The Great Mother* (Princeton, NJ: Princeton University Press, 1981), vii.

Neumann soon found that something different from a simple introduction was taking shape in his mind. From the original intention to write an introductory text for the Eranos Archive, the fascination exerted by the pictures led in fact to a much wider-reaching project:

> I am deeply grateful [Neumann continued] not only for the original suggestion but also for Mrs. Fröbe's generous consent to my enlargement of her original plan. For it soon became clear that the work was undergoing a transformation in my hands, and that for me the written text, an exposition of the Archetypal Feminine, was assuming paramount importance. The reproductions from the Eranos Archive had become illustrations to this text. These represent perhaps half the pictorial material of the present volume, having been supplemented by many more examples. Yet it should not be thought that the pictures merely provided the first spark of inspiration; throughout my work on this book they held the center of my interest and determined the whole content and rhythm of my thinking. In this sense the book, even in its present form, may be regarded wholly as a presentation of the Eranos Archive.[84]

One is reminded of Jung's idea that "the creative process, in so far as we are able to follow it at all, consists in an unconscious animation of the archetype, and in a development and shaping of this image till the work is completed."[85]

The manuscript was completed in 1951, and in 1955, the book was published as the forty-seventh volume of the Bollingen Series under the title, *The Great Mother: An Analysis of the Archetype*. Neumann's

---

84 Ibid., vii.
85 C. G. Jung, "On the Relation of Analytical Psychology to Poetry" (1922), in *CW*, vol. 15 (Princeton, NJ: Princeton University Press, 1966), par. 130.

fundamental study of the manifestations of the archetypal feminine through the millennia represented the first and only publication from the Eranos Archive, although Joseph Campbell's *The Hero with a Thousand Faces* (1949) is along similar lines.[86] In the course of his writing, Neumann supplemented the original illustrations belonging to the Eranos collection with many more.[87]

At the Bollingen Foundation, there was a clear sense that Neumann was the most original and creative of Jung's followers and, in Adler's words, "the only one who seemed destined to build on Jung's work and to continue it."[88] The Bollingen Foundation published more of his books in the series than any other Jungian author except Jung himself.[89] *The Archetypal World of Henry Moore*, an application of the theories of analytical psychology to the art of the English sculptor Henry Moore (1898–1986), was included among the "Fifty Books of the Year," selected annually by the American Institute of Graphic Arts for excellence in

---

86 McGuire, *Bollingen: An Adventure in Collecting*, 135.

87 In the list of plates, Neumann clarifies that "while about half of the plates were originally chosen from the pictures in the Eranos Archive, many have been replaced by technically more satisfactory photographs obtained from museums, professional photographers, etc … Where original Eranos Archive pictures have been reproduced, the actual photographic source is given if known" (Neumann, *The Great Mother*, xv). On the basis of a list kept at the Warburg Institute, which was probably compiled by Mrs. Fröbe-Kapteyn herself, the pictures belonging to the Eranos archives that were included among the two hundred and fifty illustrations in *The Great Mother* are the following ones: 1*a* and *b*, 3–5, 8, 10–11, 12*a* and *b*, 13, 15, 16, 21, 24, 29, 31*a* and *b*, 33*a*, 34, 37, 40, 44, 46–49, 55*b*, 56–62, 64–67, 69, 70, 74, 79–81, 85, 87, 88, 104, 109–116, 118–127, 129, 131*a*, 133, 134, 136–140, 142–148, 151–153, 155, 156, 158, 159*a*, 161–163. *The Great Mother* in the Eranos Collection of Jungian Archetypes at the Warburg Institute, which still keeps the original classification made up by Mrs.Fröbe-Kapteyn, includes the following sections: *Gorgo, Anna Selbdritt, The Annunciation, Christian, Etruscan, Italian, Cretan, Greek, Prehistoric, Primitive, Babylonian, Phoenician, Cypriot, The Spindle, Sarcophagus Symbolism, Miscellaneous, Greek, the Kore, Egypt, Mexico, India, Tibet, China, Bali,* and *Mater Ecclesia.*

88 Quoted in McGuire, *Bollingen*, 135.

89 Ibid. Among the "Publications Resulting from Research and Writing Done with the Aid of Bollingen Foundation Fellowships and Grants-in-Aid," we find Neumann's *The Origins and History of Consciousness* (Bollingen Series 42, 1954), *The Great Mother: An Analysis of the Archetype* (47, 1955), *Amor and Psyche: The Psychic Development of the Feminine* (54, 1956), *The Archetypal World of Henry Moore* (59, 1959), *Art and the Creative Unconscious* (61, 1959), *Creative Man: Five Essays* (61:2, 1979), *The Place of Creation* (61:3, 1989), and *The Fear of the Feminine and Other Essays on Feminine Psychology* (61:4, 1994).

design and manufacture.[90] In 1964, Julie Neumann was also listed among the recipients "for editing the papers of the late Erich Neumann."[91]

Neumann and Olga Fröbe-Kapteyn

In 1949, thanks to Jack Barrett's interest, the Bollingen Foundation purchased a duplicate of the Eranos Archive.[92] In 1951, also thanks to Barrett, arrangements were made with Jessie A. Fraser, manager of the Kristine Mann Library and librarian of the New York Analytical Psychology Club, to undertake a project of editing, cataloguing, and expanding the Eranos collection. Under her direction, a unique system of subject headings was devised. The enlarged collection was named Archive for Research in Archetypal Symbolism (ARAS). From that moment on, the histories of the two collections—the Eranos Archive and ARAS—proceeded independently.[93] In 1954, Mrs. Fröbe-Kapteyn donated the original Eranos collection to the Warburg Institute in London, where this extraordinary material is still preserved.[94]

---

90   Bollingen Foundation, *Twentieth Anniversary Report of Its Activities from December 14, 1945, through December 31, 1965* (New York, NY: Bollingen Foundation, 1967), 9.

91   Ibid., 80.

92   Bollingen Foundation, *A Report of Its Activities from January 1, 1968, through December 31, 1969* (New York, NY: Bollingen Foundation, 1970), 22.

93   Bollingen Foundation, *Twentieth Anniversary Report of its Activities from December 14, 1945, through December 31, 1965*, 82; Bollingen Foundation, *A Report of Its Activities from January 1, 1968, through December 31, 1969*, 22; J. A. Fraser, "Foreword," in J. A. Fraser, ed., *The Bollingen Catalogue and Indexes to the Eranos Archive* (New York, NY: privately printed, 1958), i–ii; J. A. Fraser, "ARAS"; J. A. Fraser, "Report on the Archive for Research in Archetypal Symbolism," *Quadrant* 6 (1970), 21–24; J. A. Fraser, "Archive for Research in Archetypal Symbolism of the C. G. Jung Foundation (ARAS)," in B. B. Wolman, ed., *International Encyclopedia of Psychiatry, Psychology, Psychoanalysis and Neurology*, Vol. 2 (Indiana, PA: Aesculapius, 1977); D. Lee James, "The Archive for Research in Archetypal Symbolism," *Visual Resources* 1, 1 (1980): 10–11; McGuire, *Bollingen*, pp. 144 and 276; J. L. Henderson, "Introduction," in B. Moon, ed., *An Encyclopedia of Archetypal Symbolism. The Archive for Research in Archetypal Symbolism*, Vol. 1 (Boston, MA/London: Shambala Publications, Inc., 1991), vii–x; T. Gronning, P. Sohl, and T. Singer, "ARAS: Archetypal Symbolism and Images," *Visual Resources* 23, 3 (2007): 245–267; and Bernardini, *Jung a Eranos*, 343–353.

94   In the same year, after the August conference, Mrs. Fröbe-Kapteyn traveled with Erich and

Mrs. Fröbe-Kapteyn believed that with the donation of the archive her life's work was completed. In the spring of 1955, at which time she was seventy-four years old—she wrote in fact about her decision

> to let all Eranos activities close down finally at my death. Rather than think of Eranos as continuing in a different way, possibly not at all in agreement with my own way of working, I should prefer to leave it as a completed cultural enterprise ... The remaining problem is that of Casa Eranos, Casa Gabriella, and the surrounding grounds, and the question as to what these should be used for after my death ... Looking back on the 25 years in which Eranos took shape and developed into the international meeting place of today for scholars of special types and special achievements, I would regret it most deeply if the houses and grounds were to pass into the hands of a casual buyer. The spirit of the place demands that it should be reserved for work belonging to the pattern of which Eranos was and remains a part ... I suggest [to the Bollingen Foundation] that after my death, the *estate be offered as a loan* to *Dr. Erich Neumann* for the duration of his life, so as to enable him to carry on his work in Europe from a permanent residence. As he has not the means of keeping up the estate or of paying the taxes, I further suggest that, in addition to the Fellowship he already receives, for his psychological research and the writing of his books, he receives a Life Grant to cover the expenses of living on the Eranos estate. This solution would give him the opportunity of continuing his creative work, based on C. G. Jung's psychology, but reaching forward into fields as yet unexplored by psychology. I need not

---

Julie Neumann to the Netherlands and then to England (E. Neumann, letter to O. Fröbe-Kapteyn dated May 27, 1954, quoted in Jung and Neumann, *Analytical Psychology in Exile*, 187 and 308; and L. Ettlinger, letter to O. Fröbe-Kapteyn, November 22, 1954, unpublished; quoted in Bernardini, *Jung a Eranos*, 347).

stress the fact that he is obviously the next psychologist of great importance in the sequence Freud-Jung, and that he too is a pioneer, as I know that the Bollingen Foundation realizes this … Dr. Neumann would be able to give seminars or lectures in the Eranos [Lecture] Hall, and in this way the estate would remain in the service of psychology for the duration of its next stage. This would seem to me to be a creative extension of the work done by Eranos. Not a copy of Eranos but a new detail of the pattern in which C. G. Jung's work, Eranos, and the Bollingen Foundation are united, and which represents a part of the general cultural pattern of our time and of the time ahead.[95]

This plan was never realized. Neumann gave what proved to be his final lecture at Eranos, "The Psyche as the Place of Creation," in August 1960, four months before he died at the age of fifty-five. Neumann's sudden death was a true shock for Mrs. Fröbe-Kapteyn. A few months later, she wrote to Barrett: "Looking back, it has become clear to me that in the last twelve years Eranos has developed against the background of Neumann's vision of the *inner man*. His creative work in those years was all for Eranos and when one looks at his creation it seems to be a finished and round whole."[96] In August 1961, the Eranos Foundation was reestablished, as bequeathed by the estate of Mrs. Fröbe-Kapteyn, who named Adolf Portmann to be its first president.[97]

---

95   O. Fröbe-Kapteyn, [untitled] (Ascona: unpublished typescript, May 20, 1955; Eranos Foundation Archives), 1 ff.

96   O. Fröbe-Kapteyn, letter to J. Barrett dated November 12, 1960 (Eranos Foundation Archives); quoted in Hakl, *Eranos*, 150; O. Fröbe-Kapteyn, "Der Uebergang von einem Standpunkt in einem neuen (*I Ging*)" (Ascona: unpublished typescript, 1961; Eranos Foundation Archives). The conferences held between 1947 and 1962, starting from a general theme, "The Human Being" (*Der Mensch*, 1947–1948), featured topics such as "The Human Being and Rite," "The Human Being and Time," "The Human Being and Earth," "The Human Being and Transformation," and "The Human Being and Meaning."

97   The first Eranos Foundation lasted from 1943 to 1955. Adolf Portmann was professor of biology and zoology at Basel University and later rector of the same athenaeum. The other members of the council were Tadeus Reichstein, professor at the Institute of Organic Chemistry at the University of Basel and a 1950 Nobel Prize winner in physiology and medicine, along with

Besides the significant role played in the development of the cultural enterprise of Eranos, Neumann also was for a long time an intimate confidant of Mrs. Fröbe-Kapteyn. Due to their close relationship, he was among the few people who were able to recognize the "much more inner inspirational experience" which stood behind the Eranos work.[98] Mrs. Fröbe-Kapteyn's correspondence with Neumann testifies to a long-standing and intimate rapport, even though it probably never took the shape of a formal analysis. She often discussed with Neumann issues regarding Eranos, her personal problems, and in some cases her differences with Jung.[99]

Here is just a brief example of the nourishment that, on a personal level, Mrs. Fröbe-Kapteyn experienced through her relationship with Neumann. Between 1946 and 1950, she was struggling to emancipate herself from her identification with the Eranos Archive—the "House of Images," as she referred to it in one of her experiences of active imagination.[100] Before her decision to donate the picture collection, she experienced a series of "visions" that led her to understand that she needed to let the archive go, "like a son that is of age and going out into the world." After a good deal of psychological work, she was able to admit:

> The Archive is not my possession, although it is the result of my work, although I have set it in the world. Being a collection of or representing all the archetypes of the collective unconscious, it is far more powerful and loaded with energy than I, and it is quite beyond me to control it. Giving it up, letting it go, detaching completely from it, is

Edward Calvin Kendall and Philip Showalter Hench, for the discovery of cortisone; Hans Conrad Bänziger, a psychiatrist in Zurich; and Walter Keller-Staub, a lawyer in Zurich. The second Eranos Foundation, which was founded in August 1961, still exists.

98   Jung and Neumann, *Analytical Psychology in Exile*, liii.

99   The Erich Neumann-Olga Fröbe-Kapteyn correspondence is now being jointly studied by the Eranos Foundation and Erich Neumann's heirs.

100   Bernardini, *Jung a Eranos*, 337.

perhaps the greatest of my bitternesses ... I possess nothing,
not even my work.[101]

As she later recalled, Mrs. Fröbe-Kapteyn had been particularly impressed
by the final words of Neumann's 1950 Eranos lecture: "The creative world
of the numinous," he stated, "reveals itself in the inner, psychic realm, and
its sacred executor is the individual 'I' to which this numinosity appears.
This means, however, that the person's life loses its individual character
and becomes a symbolic life."[102] Like Jung, Neumann saw psychological
development as a dialectical process between the individual and the
archetypal world of the collective unconscious. In order to reach the
central symbol of the Self, the ego has to gain the necessary degrees of
freedom from the unconscious. Through identification with the collective
dimension, "the limited individual loses contact with his own limitations
and becomes inhuman."[103] However, the ego has to receive from the
unconscious the energy that it requires in order to carry through this
arduous and ongoing process of "centroversion." We may believe that
Mrs. Fröbe-Kapteyn was aided in realizing the need to detach herself
from her dearest work, the Eranos Archive, by Neumann's words. In
October 1950, two months after Neumann's Eranos lecture, she wrote in
her diaries: "I have lived an archetypal or mythological life. Now I am
becoming human, having, I suppose, freed myself from the archetypal
world. *This is a kind of Rebirth.*"[104]

---

101   O. Fröbe-Kapteyn, [untitled] (Ascona: unpublished typescript, May 15, 1949; Eranos
Foundation Archives), 1 f.; quoted in Bernardini, *Jung a Eranos*, 345.
102   E. Neumann, "Zur psychologischen Bedeutung des Ritus," *Eranos-Jahrbuch* 19 (1950): 120.
103   E. Shalit, *The Hero and His Shadow: Psychopolitical Aspects of Myth and Reality in Israel*,
rev. ed. (Hanford, CA: Fisher King Press, 2012), 9.
104   O. Fröbe-Kapteyn, [untitled] (Ascona: unpublished typescript, October 17, 1950; Eranos
Foundation Archives); quoted in Bernardini, *Jung a Eranos*, 346.

Fig. 1

Erich Neumann and Julie Blumenfeld Neumann in the Eranos garden in the late 1940s or early 1950s. Credit: Ph. M. Fellerer (Eranos Foundation Archives; courtesy of Rali Loewenthal-Neumann).

Fig. 2

From left: The scholar of Jewish mysticism, Gershom Scholem, Julie Neumann, Erich Neumann, Carl Gustav Jung, historian of religions Mircea Eliade, John David "Jack" Barrett Jr., and Vaun Gillmor of the Bollingen Foundation at the Eranos Round Table in August 1950. Credit: Ph. M. Fellerer (Eranos Foundation Archives).

Fig. 3
Erich Neumann,
Carl Gustav Jung,
and Mircea Eliade
at the Eranos Round
Table in August
1950. Credit: Ph. M.
Fellerer (Eranos
Foundation Archives).

Fig. 4
The Eranos Round
Table in August 1951.
Screenshot from
Ximena de Angulo-
Roelli and Willy
Roelli, Eranos 1951
(Eranos Foundation
Archives).

Fig. 5
Erich Neumann at
Eranos in August 1951,
when he delivered
the lecture "Art and
Time." Screenshot from
Ximena de Angulo-
Roelli and Willy Roelli,
Eranos 1951 (Eranos
Foundation Archives).

FIG. 6
ERICH NEUMANN AND SINOLOGIST
HELLMUT WILHELM AT ERANOS IN
1951. CREDIT: PH. M. FELLERER
(ERANOS FOUNDATION ARCHIVES).

FIG. 7
ERICH NEUMANN ON THE TERRACE
WALL OF CASA ERANOS IN THE 1950S.
CREDIT: PH. M. FELLERER (ERANOS
FOUNDATION ARCHIVES).

FIG. 8
ERICH NEUMANN AT ERANOS IN THE
1950S. CREDIT: PH. M. FELLERER
(ERANOS FOUNDATION ARCHIVES).

FIG. 9
ERICH NEUMANN AT THE STONE
ROUND TABLES ON THE TERRACE OF
CASA GABRIELLA IN AUGUST 1953.
CREDIT: PH. M. FELLERER (ERANOS
FOUNDATION ARCHIVES).

FIG. 11
ERICH NEUMANN AND SCHOLAR OF GNOSIS GILLES QUISPEL ON THE TERRACE OF
CASA GABRIELLA AT ERANOS IN THE LATE 1950S. CREDIT: PH. T. GIDAL (?)
(ERANOS FOUNDATION ARCHIVES).

FIG. 12
ERICH NEUMANN LECTURING AT ERANOS ON "PEACE AS THE SYMBOL OF LIFE" IN AUGUST 1958. CREDIT: PH. T. GIDAL (ERANOS FOUNDATION ARCHIVES; COURTESY RALI LOEWENTHAL-NEUMANN).

FIG. 13
ERICH NEUMANN IN THE ERANOS LECTURE HALL IN AUGUST 1958. CREDIT: PH. T. GIDAL (ERANOS FOUNDATION ARCHIVES; COURTESY OF RALI LOEWENTHAL-NEUMANN).

FIG. 14
OLGA FRÖBE-KAPTEYN AND ERICH NEUMANN AT THE ERANOS ROUND TABLE
IN THE LATE 1950s. CREDIT: PH. T. GIDAL (ERANOS FOUNDATION ARCHIVES;
COURTESY RALI LOEWENTHAL-NEUMANN).

FIG. 15
FROM LEFT: OLGA FRÖBE-KAPTEYN (SEEN FROM BEHIND), ERICH NEUMANN,
GERSHOM SCHOLEM, RUDOLF RITSEMA (SEEN FROM BEHIND), AND BIOLOGIST ADOLF
PORTMANN IN THE LIVING ROOM OF CASA GABRIELLA AT ERANOS IN THE LATE
1950s. CREDIT: PH. T. GIDAL (ERANOS FOUNDATION ARCHIVES; COURTESY RALI
LOEWENTHAL-NEUMANN).

A Letter from Julie Neumann to Olga Fröbe-Kapteyn

[Translated from the German by Mark Kyburz.]

Dear, dear Olga!

You're the first to whom I write. It hurts still so awfully that I can hardly write. But I feel not only this side of pain but also gratitude and peace, and that is what I want to write to you about.

The gratitude has much to do with you. Erich took nothing for granted. Time and again, he stressed how good things were, that Eranos existed, and that he had an active part in it. Summer 1947 is so clearly in my mind, when Erich stood in your "archive," completely fascinated by the images of the Great Mother, when you came in in your special way and said that we should stay for lunch. I first refused, as we were expected somewhere else, but then Bänziger whispered to me that "we" should accept, because to be invited by you so spontaneously was a great honor. From this lunch on we belonged to the circle, and you and Eranos became a piece of spiritual home. Then, in 1948, Erich held his first Eranos lecture. He went alone, because the State of Israel had just been founded. As it still was somewhat dangerous in the country, I stayed with the children.

And Erich returned happily from Eranos, not only from the conference, but also from the human atmosphere.

Then began a new era. Eranos, after Eranos, before Eranos, and I could always take part and see how your suggestion of the topic for the coming year enthralled Erich and kept him busy until he began writing.

This year the meeting was particularly exhilarating, partly because one could see you more often at the lectures; already the beginning had been so beautiful and apart from the lectures the friendly, human atmosphere was so agreeable, at least for Erich and me, and we experienced the firm protective circle around you with you as its center.

Olga, please, let me still be part of Eranos, even if I cannot come this year. Write me or make others write in your place, because I *must* know how you are and how Eranos is going. You and Erich, you had the most essential thing in common: to be guided from deep within, without any compromise. And therefore there is also peace in me, because I have the feeling that Erich has accomplished his mission, that his life has been meaningful. Again and again he told me, "Why *must I always* write about the "last things," why can't I simply do case discussions, as so many others do and also require from me. But it bores me, and I *must* write this way, even if it surpasses me." Eranos was the forum where he could speak about these last things. I know now, as he had to die so early, why he had to write all this, and also why with such intensity.

Erich was sick for 3 weeks only. He had *no* pain, but only grew weaker and weaker. Until the end he didn't think that he would die. The doctors knew only *after* his death that he had kidney cancer. Everything was untypical of cancer; they thought it was a serious kidney illness and gave us hope. I am grateful that he didn't suffer, that they didn't detect it, because one couldn't have done anything. He passed away softly on Saturday, November 5 at 11:20 p.m. I was with him.

In love

P.S. I was so happy to hear your voice, but I couldn't understand everything, so do let me know how you are keeping. Rahli is back. She needs to return to Zurich again at the end of December for exams and she will call you. She will definitely be returning to Israel and to me at the end of January.

Julie Neumann   Tel-Aviv, 24.11.60
                                       Gordonstr.1

Liebe, liebe Olga!

        Du bist die Erste, der ich schreibe. Es schmerzt noch so
rasend, so dass ich kaum schreiben kann, aber es ist nicht nur
diese Seite des Schmerzes in mir, sondern auch Dankbarkeit und
Friede,und davon will ich Dir schreiben.

        Die Dankbarkeit hat viel mit Dir zu tun. Erich nahm nichts
als Selbstverständliches hin. Immer wieder betonte er, wie gut
wir es doch hätten, dass es Eranos gibt und er daran gestaltend
Teil habe. Sommer 1947 ist noch so deutlich vor mir, wie Erich
in Deinem "Archiv" stand, vollkommen fasziniert von den Bildern
der Grossen Mutter, dann kamst Du in Deiner eigenen Art dazu und
sagtest, wir sollten zum Mittagessen bleiben. Ich lehnte erst
ab, da wir woanders erwartet wurden, doch da flüsterte mir Bänziger zu,"wir" sollten annehmen, denn so spontan von Dir einge-
laden zu werden sei eine groose Ehre, und von diesem Mittagessen
an gehörten wir dazu, und Du und Eranos wurden ein Stuck geistige
Heimat. Dann 1948 hielt Erich seinen ersten Eranos-Vortrag, er fu
alleine, denn es war gerade der Staat Israel gegründet, und da es
noch etwas gefährlich im Lande war, blieb ich bei den Kindern.
Und Erich kehrte begluckt von Eranos zurück, nicht nur von der Tagung, sondern auch von der menschlichen Atmosphäre.

        Danach begann eine neue Zeitrechnung. Eranos, nach Eranos,
vor Eranos, und immer durfte ich mit dabei sein und erleben, wie
Deine Themengebung schon für das kommende Jahr Erich nicht los
liess und er bis zum Zeitpunkt des Schreibens damit beschäftigt wa

Dieses Jahr war die Tagung besonders begluckend, z.Teil weil Du selber mehr in den Vorträgen zu sehen warst, schon der Beginn war so schön und abgesehen von den Vorträgen war, jedenfalls fur Erich und mich, die freundschaftlich-menschliche Atmosphäre so wohltuend, und wir erlebten den festen Kreis mit Dir als Mittelpunkt, der sich auch schutzend um Dich schloss.

Olga, bitte, lass mich weiter Teil haben an Eranos, auch fall ich in diesem Jahr nicht kommen kann. Schreibe mir, oder lass andere fur Dich schreiben, denn ich <u>muss</u> wissen, wie es Dir geht und wie Eranos läuft. Du und Erich, Ihr hattet das Wesentlichste gemeinsam, das ganz von Innen her dirigiert werden, ohne Kompromisse. Und darum ist auch Frieden in mir, weil ich das Gefuhl habe, Erich hat seinen Auftrag erfullt, sein Leben war sinnvoll. Immer und immer wieder sagte er mir, "warum <u>muss ich immer</u> uber die "letzten Dinge" schreiben, warum kann ich nicht Fall-Besprechungen machen, wie so Viele es tun und es auch von mir verlangen. Aber mich langweilt es, und ich <u>muss</u> so schreiben, und wenn es uber mich hinausgeht", und Eranos war das Forum, wo er uber diese letzten Din sprechen konnte. Ich weiss jetzt, da er so fruh sterben musste, warum er es schreiben musste und auch warum in dieser Intensität.

Erich war nur 3 Wochen krank. Er hatte <u>keinerlei</u> Schmerzen, er wurde nur immer schwächer und schwächer. Bis zum Schluss dachte er nicht an den Tod. Die Aerzte wussten erst <u>nach</u> seinem Tod, dass er einen Nierenkrebs hatte. Alles war untypisch fur Krebs, sie dachten an eine schwere Nierenerkrankung und gaben uns Hoffnung. Ich bin dankbar, dass er nicht gelitten hat, dass man es nicht

erkannt hat, denn man hätte doch nichts tun können. Er ist
ganz sanft am Sonnabend d. 5.11. um 11.20 nachts eingeschlafen.
Ich war bei ihm.

                    In Liebe

PS. Ich war so glucklich, Deine Stimme zu hören, doch konnte ich
nicht alles verstehen, also lass mich wissen, wie es Dir geht.
Ich habe kein Telefon, aber im Haus ist Telefon:
Dr.Feilchenfeld, Tel-Aviv, Gordonstr.1, Tel.:25925.
Rahli ist zuruckgekommen, sie muss Ende Dezember noch einmal nach
Zurich zuruckfahren fur Prufungen und sie wird Dich anrufen.
Ende Januar kommt sie dann endgultig nach Israel und zu mir zuruck.

PART VI. ON THE ARTS

The Great Mother in Israeli Art

Gideon Ofrat

The second diagram in Erich Neumann's *The Great Mother* depicts a vessel, a big jar that connects the darkness, the night, the underworld—the unconscious—with heaven through a structure of the archetypal feminine—the mother. Here, the level of the womb equals that of the grave, turning the woman-jar into an urn, whereas her mouth connects and leads through her breath up to the moon. The inside of the vessel, wrote Neumann, is unknown, though "something is 'born' out of it."[1] No less, the archetypal feminine vessel protects and nourishes, but may also swallow, that is, devour. Thus, "the lowest level of this belly zone is the underworld … To this world belong not only the subterranean darkness as hell and night but also such symbols as chasm, cave, abyss, valley, depths."[2] Because "just as the Great Mother can be terrible as well as good, so the Archetypal Feminine is not only a giver and protector of life but, as container, also holds fast and takes back; she is the goddess of life and death at once."[3]

The following essay is a journey through the Great Mothers of Israeli art, avoiding some embarrassing cases of ultranationalistic expressions,

---

1 Erich Neumann, *The Great Mother* (Princeton, NJ: Princeton University Press, 1981), 39.
2 Ibid., 44.
3 Ibid., 45.

such as a 1948 painting by Mané-Katz (a Jewish painter who worked both in Paris and Haifa), representing the Great National Mother, a monumental figure with huge breasts, nourishing her dead children, victims of 1948 War of Independence.

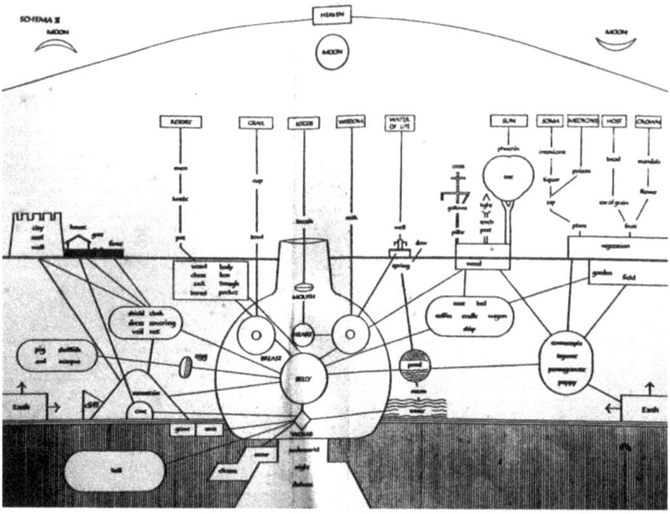

Fig. 1. Erich Neumann, *The Great Mother*

Let me begin with a short reminder from the sphere of Israeli poetry. Already in Hebrew poetry of the mid-1920s, the pioneers' era, the land was repeatedly depicted in mythological terms as both Mother Earth—the one that gives birth and life—and as a deadly mother who demands the sacrifice of her sons, the pioneers. In Avraham Shlonsky's 1925 *Gilboa*, a radical case of oedipal complex characterizes the relationship between the son and his Mother Earth: "And thus my bare foot convulsively moves with joy on the warm clods of Tamuz summer / like the naughty younger child playing on his mother's knees." This is the dead mother, the dry soil of the hot summer with whom the son wishes to erotically unite: "Mummy! Mummy! Tickle me! / grow unto me your wild nails / so that my flesh will be profaned by your clods and fertility." The pioneer-son, almost a necrophilia case, wishes to suck his dead mother's breast: "Here I fell upside down and my thirsty lips sucked your tits' nipples."[4]

The same year, 1925, another great Hebrew poet of the pioneering era, Uri Zvi Greenberg, confirmed one more "necrophilia case" of oedipal unity, this time an engagement ceremony between the son and his dead Mother Earth. In *A Great Fear and a Moon*, Greenberg described Zion's soil as a woman carrying a fetus in her womb. This is a decaying rotten mother, whose rot infects the son as well. Life and death, fertility and decay, giving birth and drinking the son's blood—such is the duality of the land (*motherland* in Hebrew is "Moledet," meaning "one who gives birth"). Only by satisfying the mythological earth with human sacrifice will rain come down to fertilize the soil, infusing it with new life.

Turning from Hebrew poetry to Israeli art, let us begin with Igael Tumarkin's *Jars-woman*, a large ceramic work, the exact date of which is unknown, probably circa 2000. This huge figure, a super-multi-container, the ultimate pregnancy, is the vessel for life water or deadly blood: without a head (that is, without intellect and consciousness), she is the symbolic bodily essence of life and death. This is characteristic of Tumarkin's artistic development. In his *Take Me under Your Wings*, a welded steel sculpture from 1964–65, the protecting mother (originally an indirect figure from Chaim Nahman Bialik's 1905 poem of that title) is also the one from the womb of whom rifles are aimed at the viewer, the artist himself before all others. Tumarkin had a love-hate relationship with his mother, Bertha, as expressed for instance in his sculpture *Von der dicken Berta zur roten Rosa* [*From Fat Bertha to Red Rosa*], a most aggressive direct attack against a big, two-dimensional woman figure painted in red, "Fat Bertha" being both a World War I cannon and the artist's mother's name.[5]

4   The author's translation.
5   G. Ofrat, "Tumarkin: The Father, the Son and the Spirit of Sculpture," in Bikurei omanut [Hebrew] (Tel Aviv: Hakibutz Hameuchad, 2005), 430–447.

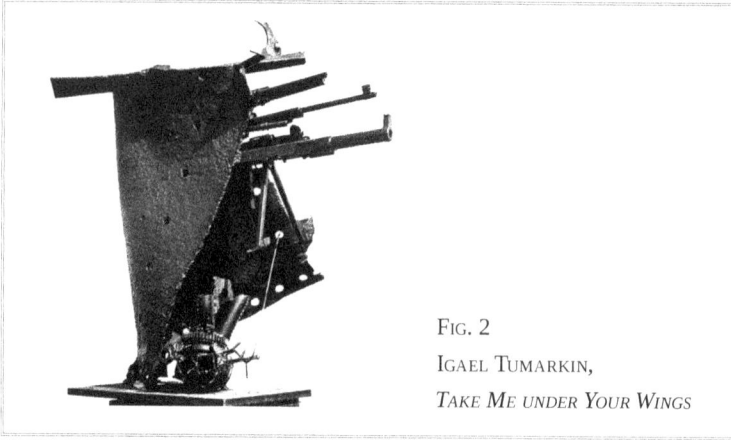

FIG. 2
IGAEL TUMARKIN,
TAKE ME UNDER YOUR WINGS

Accordingly, an examination of Tumarkin's characterization of women in his art will prove how dangerous and cruel such figures are, as much as being the object of the artist's aggression. His counterattacks against the feminine can be seen in such works as *Madonna of the Butchers* (1968–69) or *Lilith* (1968), naked women with mannequin bodies torn apart and organs cut off. At the same time, what would prove Neumann's claim more than Tumarkin's 1994 *Isis*—a personal rearrangement of the original Egyptian mythological mother goddess, to the head of which Tumarkin added a chicken corpse, symbolizing the nourishing/victimizing archetypal Mother. Isis, according to Erich Neumann, is the symbolic culmination of the Great Mother, combining the Good Mother, the Terrible Mother, and the anima.

No less, the mythological figure of Astarte, also central to Neumann's thesis, can be detected in Israeli art in several works, among them Avishay Ayal's magical painting *Astra* [*Astarte*, 1987], a mysterious idol figure who appears in a hot field next to a blue goat (*tragos*/tragedy), or Linda Bar-On's post-Babylonian quilt of Astarte. Indeed, archaic Middle Eastern myths have long nourished the imagery of Israeli art in its long search for self-identity.

Israeli art, already from its "archaic" Zionist roots, has consistently represented a Great Mother that symbolizes the national mythic protection, also known as the Shekhinah, or Bat-Zion (the daughter of Zion). We encountered that heavenly Mother already with the early Zionist congresses, such as in Salomon Roukhomovsky's postcard from around 1903, which shows a womanly figure hovering and leading the people, holding the national flag, or—still in the same year—in Emil Ranzenhofer's depiction of the earthly erotic feminine figure, a fertility goddess, erupting from earth, soon to be impregnated by the omnipotent Jewish pioneer. Often, this national mythic Mother would be identified with Rachel, the biblical matriarch who leads her sons back from the diaspora to the Promised Land, as in David Polus's statue at Kibbutz Ramat Rachel—*Thy Children Shall Come Again to Their Own Border* (1954; Jeremiah 31:17 KJV). Indeed, in that early Zionist era, the Great Mother was still a purely savior figure, the summit of goodness and classical beauty.

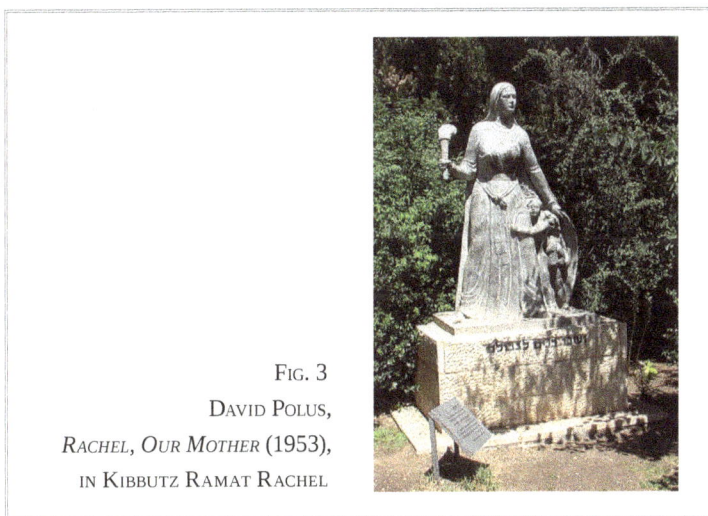

Fig. 3
DAVID POLUS,
RACHEL, OUR MOTHER (1953),
IN KIBBUTZ RAMAT RACHEL

But already in the early 1920s, at the height of the Third Aliyah (the Jewish immigration to Palestine, 1919–1923), the Great Mother began showing her twofold character. By now, the ultimate feminine adopted an Arab appearance, an expression of the Zionist idealization of the Orient and the local inhabitants during the 1920s. Reuven Rubin's 1923 painting depicts an enormous round Arab woman sitting barefoot on the ground, holding a flowerpot close to her belly—a symbol of new life. But do not miss the nearby Arab tombstone: death is associated with the figure no less than life. However, Rubin's Arab woman is more a counterforce to death than its conveyor. Still, something about her confirms the Great Round, to use Neumann's concept of the woman as the universe and the primordial darkness.[6]

Fig. 4
Reuven Rubin,
Arab woman

One thing is for sure: Rubin's Arab woman is an extension of the earth, where flowers are planted and the dead are buried. In Rubin's 1923 *Arab Woman with a Mortar*, the pestle in the monumental woman's hand is almost a phallic object near the womb area (which parallels the vessel).

The Earth Woman is indeed a well-known image in Israeli art, a double visual expression of Eros and Thanatos, as in Ori Reisman's *Mountain-Woman* (1975–79) or Michael Gross's "Woman-Hills" from the 1960s Likewise, we find the paintings of Eliahu Gat, such as *Landscape with a Woman*, and Moshe Hoffman portraying the feminine traits of monumental

---

6   Neumann, The Great Mother, 211–239.

landscapes. All load the barren local nature with pregnancy, all express both personal and collective oedipal unconsciousness of the erotic character of the Mother Land.

Soon enough, the symbolic feminine became a goddess in Israeli art: associating womanly figures with ancient Middle Eastern archaeology, more and more Israeli artists—either through a dialogue with Canaanism or due to personal cultural vision—combined the twofold idea of the vessel with that of the woman-goddess.[7] While Shoshana Heiman's wood sculpture *A Girl* (1946) reminds us of a South Pacific fertility idol, Ruth Zarfati's ceramic vase (1950s) is already an archaic goddess-vessel, the ritualistic and authoritarian presence of which is as strong as Pinchas Abramovitz's intimidating archaic-like ceramic vessel from the early 1960s. Even more convincing is Israel Hadany's wood sculpture (also a semivessel, 1999) of Tiamat, the Babylonian goddess, the same Great Mother who was considered by Erich Neumann as the primordial dark power of the chaos of water.[8]

FIG. 5

ISRAEL HADANY, TIAMAT

But archaic motherly goddesses were soon connected in Israeli art with death. Jacob Steinhardt, for example, not only associated Eve, the mother of all mothers, with the snake (woodcut, 1953) but went on to associate the headless woman with ruins (woodcut, 1962). Other Israeli artists connected mothers with death due to heavy personal residues of the Holocaust. In 1963 Mordecai Ardon, whose family was exterminated in the camps, painted *Eve*—a naked feminine archaeological figure.

---

7 Canaanism was a local cultural movement attempting to reconnect Israeli culture with ancient Mesopotamian-Egyptian roots.

8 Neumann, The Great Mother, 213–215.

The Calculitic ritualistic object was transformed into a heavenly image, immersed in the blue sky under a threatening, bloody moon eclipse.[9] The open mouth of the primordial Mother—Eve—signifies death or at least a painful cry, which might recall another primordial Great Mother—Sarah. Ardon's work from 1947, Sarah weeping over the dead corpse of her sacrificed son, Isaac, is another elegiac expression of the artist mourning the victims of the Shoah. Ardon's 1965 *Venus from Beersheba* (1965) represents a Calculitic find (4500–3500 BC), indeed from Beersheba, a pregnant ceramic figurine with no head and a hole in the belly—a dead mother, lying under a turbulent sky, unable to assist her little children in the shape of young birds.

FIG. 6
MORDECAI ARDON,
VENUS OF BEERSHEBA (1962).
© ORA ARDON. PHOTO BY
AVRAHAM HAY.

The Great Mother of the Shoah victims continued to haunt some Israeli artists during the early 1960s, following the trial of Adolf Eichmann. In 1961 Naftali Bezem, who lost his parents at Auschwitz, painted his elegiac *Pièta*, depicting once again an enormous headless mother, the quintessence of whom are her breasts, holding her dead

---

9 The Calculitic is the period of stone and copper. In the area of the Land of Israel, it pertains to 4500–3500 BCE.

son on her knees. No doubt, this is not yet Neumann's Terrible Mother, the dark monster, but rather a Jewish post-Shoah interpretation of the Christian tragic image of the loving, mourning mother. Still, the growing association between the figure of the archetypal Mother and death cannot be ignored, especially—as in another *Pièta* by Bezem, from 1963, where the dead son is physically connected with the expiatory rooster, thus symbolizing the son's sacrifice. Compare this with Erez Israeli's 2006 video *Pièta*, where the allegedly dead artist-son is being mourned by his mother, who picks feathers from all over his naked body, as if he were the expiatory rooster, a victim of his mother's sacrificing act.

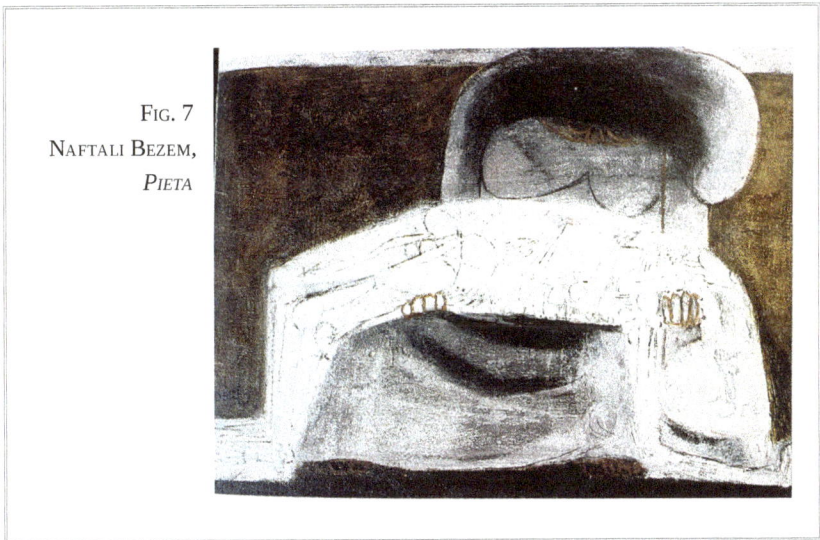

FIG. 7
NAFTALI BEZEM,
PIETA

Let me emphasize that the Shoah Great Mothers of Israeli art are obviously not the devouring Mothers. They are still the goddesses of fertility and protection, even in their state of helplessness. Bezem's Flora goddess, a painting from 1982, is dominated by a monumental pregnant Jewish woman, possibly an orthodox Jewish settler, one more woman-mountain but this time a flourishing mountain. This woman celebrates the alliance between fertility and the land's soil in the tradition of early Zionist poetry and art.

Another painter, Avraham Ofek, had been incessantly treating the mother figure in his paintings since the 1960s. Starting in 1962 with a red, authoritarian demigoddess, who played the role of a mother in his paintings of that year, later to reappear as a monumental fertility figure holding a bowl of fish, symbol of abundance, Ofek went on to endless works where the figure of a cow—the ultimate milk provider—functioned as the man's mate. The cow, also remembered as Hathor, the ancient Egyptian goddess who personified the principles of feminine love and motherhood (but also the one who encompasses the underworld and the watery abyss), was Ofek's complementary image for many years, a constant symbol of protection and fertility (to be transformed in 1978 into *Red Cow*—the biblical animal, the ashes of which supposedly purify the tribe). However, between 1982 and 1986 the cow turned into biblical Sarah, who mourns her son (in the shape of a ram's horns) and whose body stems from the altar, being herself the sacrifice if not the ram (as can be seen in her lifted arms in the shape of horns). Adopting this mother image from northern Bulgarian archaic cave paintings, Ofek endowed his feminine figure with the mysterious prehistoric ritualistic contents of La Dama della Grotta, as the image was coined. Thus, the image of the woman with the upraised arms, as Neumann noted in his book, conveys a religious-magical significance that is connected to caves as well.[10]

Things changed in Israeli art in the late 1960s and early 1970s, with the rise of a new generation of enfants terribles, young angry Sabras—that is, Israelis who were revolting against sacred cows and thus did not hesitate to launch a fierce attack also against the Great Mother. By now, Uri Lifshitz had painted his violent series called *The Schizophrenics*, in which a monstrous, monumental beast-woman threatens to devour the surrounding devastated and distorted human creatures. In Lifshitz's

---

10   Ibid., 114.

painting *The Black Widow* (1967), Eros and Thanatos ("Black Widow" referring also to the deadly spider) are united in yet another monstrous, grotesque figure sitting on a throne. In his *Woman and Mirror* (1968) a parallel black creature reveals her horrible face in the reflection. Remembering Tumarkin's Terrible Women of his 1968 sculptures, we begin to grasp the wider Israeli scope of the phenomenon. Indeed, younger Israeli artists joined the trend by filling their canvases with horrible, grotesque, ugly and enormous naked women, whose open mouths (expecting prey)

Fig. 8
Avraham Ofek, Sara

complemented their big breasts and their fat belly-womb, such as Yair Garbuz's 1972 figures or Michael Druks's 1969 aggressive femmes fatales reminiscent of Willem de Kooning.

At times, fertility and death combined to represent the artist's self. Bianca Eshel Gershuni's ceramic and mixed-media vessels from 1999 also function as the self-grave of the artist, whose faded face can be detected at the bottom of the sculpture together with the self-mourning words: "and it might be that the dead ones are not but loners who wish to think of the living ones." Self-burial is present as well in Gideon Gechtman's gigantic fiberglass urns from 1989: the "pregnant" containers speak of the artist's death (as did all his works from the 1970s on), while provoking the authenticity of unconscious speech through the ironic (conscious) painted imitation of the urn's marble.

Between 1993 and 1994, ceramic artist Lidia Zavatsky created her huge jars, the poisonous materials of which eventually caused the artist's death, containers that were at once ashes' urns and flowerpots, –that is, death and life vessels. Nowhere has such a duality been more explicit than in Menashe Kadishman's sculptural series *Birth* from the early 1990s. Kadishman's steel cutouts represented a monstrous mother, another spider if you will, at the moment of giving birth, the very moment when the future victim-son comes to the world and is destined to be another sacrificed Isaac in future Israeli wars. Thus, Kadishman's *Pièta* (1990) shows a mother lifting the corpse of her son, as if carrying a sacrifice.

FIG. 9

MENASHE KADISHMAN, SCULPTURE OF A WOMAN GIVING BIRTH

But if in Kadishman's works we still perceive a deep sense of tragedy and sorrow over the mother's loss, in Michal Na'aman's works from 1976 the sacrificed baby maintains a metaphysical and theological curse. Na'aman's collage painting *Jehovah über Alles* cannot but recall the German hymn "Deutschland über Alles," thus loading our visual experience with the sense of ultimate evil. Na'aman's heretical words (as the vocal expression of God's private name is forbidden) are spread over a kind of altar (a restructured moonlike circle), at the top of which a photograph is glued. The origin of this is Ira Levin's novel, *Rosemary's Baby* (1967), where a baby is sacrificed by a satanic sect in New York City. A death sentence awaits for the newborn son. One could rightly protest that Satan here is not necessarily feminine, while also pointing out the sun image in the background of the photo, the archetypal symbol of the masculine. But what would such a protesting spectator say in response to Larry Abramson's painting *Lilith* (2000), this time featuring Luna, the moon, a symbol of the feminine? Lilith, as we know, is the mythic mother of the devils. Or in Abramson's words:

> The moon is associated with womankind and the night, with Lilith, with night seed. . . . According to the homiletic tales the semen spilt to the ground impregnates Lilith, who procreates demons and monstrous hybrids. I began with eyes and ended up with large moon. The sense of wasted paintings is tantamount to wasted sperm, I found myself in a cyclic world of life and death.[11]

The more we follow the artistic path of the Israeli Great Mother, the more we are inclined to affirm the double aspect of this archetype in the local art, because alongside its duality of the Good Mother and the Terrible Mother, we repeatedly encounter a more frequent duality of the birth-giving mother and the grieving mother or the dying mother.

---

11   Larry Abramson, Eventus Nocturnus (Haifa: Haifa Museum of Art, 2001), 107.

Here life and death apply to the Great Mother without turning her into a deadly one. Should one therefore speak of a unique Israeli or Jewish, or perhaps a Christian version of the Great Mother archetype, a version that is unable to part from the eternally good "Yiddishe Mame" or Madonna?

Accordingly, let us glance at Aliza Auerbach's photography project titled *Lena* (1998): Lena is Aliza's mother, who passed away at the age of 93. Shortly beforehand, Aliza took a series of photographs of her mother close up, some of them to the degree of abstract fragments. These were blown up and combined with large photographs of newborn babies at the very moment of their exit from the womb, next to a third group of large photographs—always in black and white—of cave openings. Aliza Auerbach did not know of Erich Neumann's theory of the Great Mother, but by way of her intuition she touched, in her *Lena* series, upon her mother in association with life (giving birth), death, and cave—Neumann's explicit symbol of the womb, as specified in his above-mentioned diagram.[12]

So, are life and death a twofold face of the beloved and adored Jewish mother, or are they the twofold face of the archetypal Good and Terrible Mother? Eventually, the ancient Hebrew cultural sources may prove Erich Neumann's victory by calling our attention to the characterization of the daughter of Zion in the book of Ezekiel (which can be visually illustrated by Adva Drori's 2013 installation, where she appeared as the blood-red daughter of the brown and bloody Earth).

Baby Zion, so we read in the Bible, grew up to become a pretty young woman: "Thy breasts are fashioned and thine hair is grown whereas thou wast naked and bare" (Ezekiel 16:7). Then God took her to be his wife: "Now when I passed by thee, and looked upon thee, behold, thy time was the time of love, and I spread my skirt over thee, and covered thy nakedness: yes, I sware unto thee, and entered into a covenant with thee, saith the Lord God, and thou becamest mine" (Ezekiel 16:8). But, alas,

---

12   Aliza Auerbach (1940–2016) was the author's wife.

now came the time of the young queen's prostituting: long verses tell us of the loose character of the daughter of Zion, who happily collects lovers all around: "Thou ... made thy beauty to be abhorred, and has opened thy feet to every one that passed by, and multiplied thy whoredoms" (Ezekiel 16:25).

Moreover, a dramatic shift in the daughter of Zion's unstable character reveals her Lilith face, when her wild and uncontrolled sex drives are substituted by a satanic devouring behavior: the queen, who is by now a mother, slaughters her sons and daughters, sacrificing them to pagan gods: "thou hast taken thy sons and thy daughters, whom thou hast borne unto me, and these hast thou sacrificed unto them to be devoured" (Ezekiel 16:20).

Indeed a most Terrible Mother, our ancient primordial Mother.

Thousands of years later, in 2005, there came a young leading Israeli artist, Sigalit Landau, who—in her one-woman show at Tel Aviv Museum, The Endless Solution—projected a video work showing herself floating naked in the Dead Sea in the middle of an enormous spiral of watermelons. The unavoidable association to the womb was integrated with the "wounded" watermelons that infused the environmental image with "blood," which together with the deadliness of the Dead Sea did not leave much room for Good Motherhood.

Yet, one must admit: contemporary Israeli art of the present millennium rarely allows the archetype of the Great Mother to appear, either as good or terrible. Indeed, seldom is the Great Mother to be found in Israeli art of the last twenty or thirty years. What could be the reason for this? Has the Great Mother been substituted in Israeli culture and art by the Great Father, the terrible binding father, as so often (following local wars) being depicted in Israeli works of art on the topic of "the binding of Isaac"? I am not sure I can answer this question, which might have to do, among other things, with a possibly different psyche of the new young generation, not only in Israel. I shall therefore leave the answer to the Jungian scholars, and to another book.

Jung, Neumann, and Art

Christian Gaillard

Translated from the French by Anita Conrade

The theme, or question, we are about to discuss, is not at all simple: Jung, Neumann, and art. The question is not at all simple because, as I hope to show, it challenges us to examine certain essential characteristics of the psychology and work of both Jung and Neumann.

We shall proceed in three or four steps.

First of all, I must speak of a wicked misunderstanding—a misunderstanding or misinterpretation we hear repeatedly in our institutes, our publications, even in our congresses. It concerns Jung's relationship to the modern and contemporary arts. Then, we will be looking at some of the works that moved Jung and Neumann, along with their approaches to them. Of course, we will also consider some pages from the Red Book and certain drawings by Neumann.

Finally, I would like for us to consider a recent, very unexpected event, which was unknown to Jung and Neumann: the public showing of Jung's Red Book at the last biennale of contemporary art in Venice.

Jung and Modern and Contemporary Art

I spoke of a misunderstanding or confusion on this subject. What misunderstanding? What is the source of the confusion? The subject is the widespread belief that Jung was definitely and radically opposed to modern and contemporary art. Where does this belief, so widespread it is almost dogmatic, arise?[1] It is based primarily and quite notably on a reading of his correspondence. But let me immediately specify that this means his general correspondence and not the letters he exchanged with Freud, Father White, James Kirsch, Bernhard, or Pauli, or Neumann (in which the two men rarely discuss art, oddly enough).

In Jung's Correspondence

In Jung's general correspondence, and in certain interviews, it is true that on more than one occasion Jung expressed objections to and often even his rejection of contemporary art—especially, let us note, between 1938 and 1955.[2] In 1940, he wrote to H. G. Baynes: "I loathe the new style, the new Art, the new Musik, Literature, Politics, and above all the new Man. It's the old beast that has not changed since the troglodytes."[3] Replying to Esther Harding, who wanted to introduce him to the poetry of T. S. Eliot, in 1947, he says: "I am only prejudiced against all forms of modern art. It is mostly morbid and evil on top of that."[4] In 1952, he told British art critic J. P. Hodin: "I cannot occupy myself with modern art any more. It is too awful. That is why I do not want to know more

---

1   As a first counterpoint to this position, and to introduce the analysis that follows, consider the photograph of Jung published by Aniela Jaffé in *C. G. Jung: Bild und Wort* (Olten und Freiburg in Breisgau: Walter Verlag, 1978, 144–145), and later reproduced in many other places. We see Jung in his library, immersed in his studies. The photograph dates from 1960, and as we shall see, the date is a useful detail. On the wall facing him, to the right of the photograph, one can see a painting by the French surrealist Yves Tanguy, who later lived in the United States. Jung had written about Tanguy at some length in 1958, in "Ein moderner Mythus" (C. G. Jung, "Flying Saucers: A Modern Myth of Things Seen in the Sky" [1958], in *CW*, vol. 10 [Princeton, NJ: Princeton University Press, 1970]).
2   T. v. d. Berk, *Jung on Art: The Autonomy of the Creative Drive* (London: Routledge, 2012), 105. Concerning these dates, it is interesting to read the seventh lecture from Jung's 1925 seminar in Zurich; C. G. Jung, *Analytical Psychology: Notes of the Seminar Given in 1925 by Carl Gustav Jung* (Princeton, NJ: Princeton University Press, 1989).
3   Letter dated August 12, 1940; C. G. Jung, *Letters*, vol. 1, *1906–1950*, ed. Gerhard Adler (Princeton, NJ: Princeton University Press, 1973), 286.
4   Letter dated June 8, 1947; ibid., 469.

about it."[5] In these letters, and in others, it is clear that Jung rejects and condemns modern art. Case closed.

But in Other Writings

First, let us recall the two important essays Jung wrote on artistic creation, in 1922 and 1930.[6] In these writings, he makes a clear distinction between works he describes as "psychological," which express the personal preoccupations of the individual artist who made them, and as "visionary," works which, by contrast, open perspectives that come from afar, from the farthest reaches of ourselves, and direct our gaze well beyond the horizons of the individual.

Suzan Rowland asserts that these writings are the core of Jung's positions on art.[7] Her position is justifiable, obviously, if only because Jung thereby clearly dismisses any "psychobiography." There are indeed three major orientations for research into the psychoanalysis of art: the analysis of a work, analysis of the creative process, and psychobiography—the last of which claims to interpret the meaning of a work of art through the analysis of the life of the artist since his or her earliest childhood and, if possible, from the cradle.[8] Freud's 1910 essay *Leonardo da Vinci and a Memory of His Childhood* is the founding work in psychobiography.[9] I shall say more about this later, when we begin to compare the views of Neumann with those of Jung.

---

5   Letter dated June 7, 1952; C. G. Jung, *C. G. Jung Speaking*, ed. William McGuire and R. F. C. Hull (Princeton, NJ: Princeton University Press, 1987), 221.
6   In 1922, under the German title "Ueber die Beziehungen der Analytische Psychologie zum dichterischen Kunstwerk"; in English, "On the Relation of Analytical Psychology to Poetic Art" (1923), in *CW*, vol. 15 (Princeton, NJ: Princeton University Press, 1966); and in 1930, "Psychologie und Dicthung"; in English, "Psychology and Literature" (1933), in *CW*, vol. 15 (Princeton, NJ: Princeton University Press, 1966).
7   S. Rowland, *C. G. Jung and Literary Theory: The Challenge from Fiction* (Basingstoke: Macmillan Press, 1999); *Jung as a Writer* (London: Routledge, 2005); *Psyche and the Arts: Jungian Approaches to Music, Architecture, Literature, Painting, and Film* (London: Routledge, 2008).
8   C. Gaillard, "Psychanalyse à l'Ecole?" in *La Mémoire de l'Art*, ed. J. Gatard and P. Tilman (Paris: Sgraffite, 1984).
9   S. Freud, *Leonardo da Vinci and a Memory of His Childhood* (New York: Norton, 1989).

Jung clearly eschews psychobiography, even in his earliest major writings on art. However, the essays from 1922 and 1930 are still fairly rudimentary. He had yet to make his strongest and most original statements about the arts.

A Serious Debate

It so happened that in the mid-1920s, and then more directly in 1932, Jung discovered *Ulysses* by James Joyce.[10] This strange, unexpected book left Jung feeling profoundly disconcerted. More than that, irritated, offended, and shocked. About the novel, he claims that it obeys so little of the genre's model, does nothing to address the reader who nevertheless takes it up with kind intentions. It turns away from the reader, frigidly, and without mercy.[11] Jung is unhappy. He defends himself with the arms most directly available to him, those of the psychopathologist. This piece of literature, would it not be the work of a schizophrenic? he wonders.

He would like to believe it. But he is forced to observe that, unlike the writing usually produced by schizophrenics, *Ulysses* is not monotonous, repetitive, and shallow. Quite the opposite. The book is lively. It is constantly driven forward, and as the reader proceeds he encounters events and unexpected incidents that are often a delight. And so we see Jung's writing encountering that of Joyce and gradually become freer and more lively. As if the writing were "rejoicing."[12]

And what does Jung delight in when he reads *Ulysses*? He delights in the fact that the book is an antidote, a necessary purge. But what is the poison that requires an antidote? Why is a purge necessary? It is excessive sentiment. We are trapped in sentimentality. He writes: "There is a good

---

10   Sonu Shamdasani has researched and found the edition that Jung had in his library and has published a reproduction of the book's cover in his excellent biography of Jung; Sonu Shamdasani, *C. G. Jung: A Biography in Books* (New York: Norton, 2012), 146.

11   C. G. Jung, "'Ulysses': A Monologue" (1934), in *CW*, vol. 15 (Princeton, NJ: Princeton University Press, 1966), par. 167.

12   It is especially interesting to observe how Jung's voice as a writer changes over the course of his lifetime and work. His expression is transformed, particularly when he speaks of art. We shall see that a similar observation can be made in the case of Neumann.

deal of evidence to show that we actually are involved in a sentimentality hoax of gigantic proportions. Think of the lamentable role of popular sentiment in wartime! Think of our so-called humanitarianism!"[13] He is writing in 1932—at the very moment when, in Germany, terrible events were brewing, even more terrible than anything Europe and the world had ever experienced. In fact, Jung's conclusion is so trenchant it is almost Joycean. "Sentimentality," he writes, "is the superstructure erected upon brutality."[14]

And he does not stop there. As he continues to read Joyce, he begins to lash out at our inherited cultural ideals, the ones we often cherish the most: "Ideals are not beacons on mountain peaks," he writes, "but taskmasters and gaolers, a sort of metaphysical police originally thought up on Sinai by the tyrannical demagogue Moses and thereafter foisted upon mankind by a clever ruse."[15] That is a thought of surprising violence, expressed in writing! It is positively obstreperous. And truly shocking. How can we approach an understanding of it?

Jung does not say here if he was thinking of the prophet Moses as he is presented in the Bible, or of Michelangelo's *Moses*, who mobilized Freud so powerfully. But the fact is that Moses is quite present here, rather abruptly, and associated with a ruthless condemnation—that of "a clever ruse foisted upon mankind"! This is increasingly impressive. Let us try to understand. Let us read the text more closely.

As Jung goes on reading Joyce, he writes: "In its destruction of the criteria of beauty and meaning that have held till today, *Ulysses* accomplishes wonders. It insults all our conventional feelings, it brutally disappoints our expectations of sense and content, it thumbs its nose at

---

13   Jung, "'Ulysses,'" *CW* 15, par. 184.
14   Ibid.
15   Jung writes: *"von dem tyrannischen Hordenführer Moses"* (ibid., par. 182). Elsewhere I have studied the conditions surrounding the apparition of this Moses figure and its effect on the dynamics of Jung's text; C. Gaillard, "Ulysse et Moïse. Première Partie," *Cahiers de Psychologie de l'Art et de la Culture* 3 (1978): 39–62; C. Gaillard, "Ulysse et Moïse. Deuxième Partie," *Cahiers de Psychologie de l'Art et de la Culture* 5 (1979): 31–66; C. Gaillard, "Jung, Picasso et le Bleu," *Revue de Psychologie Analytique* 1, no. 1 (2013): 33–75.

all synthesis."[16] Now, not only our ideals, but even our expectations of beauty and meaning are being challenged. Jung, reading Joyce, does not mince words, to say the least. He adds: "Even though the evil and destructive elements predominate, they are far more valuable than the 'good' that has come down to us from the past and proves in reality to be a ruthless tyrant, an illusory system of prejudices that robs life of its richness, emasculates it, and enforces a moral compulsion which in the end is unendurable."[17] And, just in case we were slow to understand, he specifies: "Everything abusive we can say about *Ulysses* bears witness to its peculiar quality, for our abuse springs from the resentment of the unmodern man who does not wish to see what the gods have graciously veiled from sight," for "it is only modern man who has succeeded in creating an art in reverse, a backside of art that makes no attempt to be ingratiating, that tells us just where we get off, speaking with the same rebellious contrariness that had made itself disturbingly felt in those precursors of the moderns (not forgetting Hölderlin) who had already started to topple the old ideals."[18]

Undeniably, this approach to and appreciation of modernity is strong and vigorous. Quite the opposite of what we read in some of the letters cited above. And, regarding modern works of art, Jung states that it is quite natural for them to arouse fierce, stubborn resistance in us. He writes: "They are drastic purgatives whose full effect would be dissipated if they did not meet with an equally strong and obstinate resistance. They are a kind of psychological specific which is of use only where the hardest and toughest material must be dealt with."[19]

It is increasingly evident that Jung, in this text, is deeply convinced that modern art is "a psychological specific," a "drastic purgative," the effects of which are violent, unquestionably, but necessary. And he comes

16   Jung, "'Ulysses,'" *CW* 15, par. 177.
17   Ibid., par. 182.
18   Ibid., pars. 177–178.
19   Ibid., par. 179.

to conclude that a world is close to disappearing. It is fighting for its survival, but actually that world has already died—and a new one has been born. Jung writes, in German: *"Eine Welt verging und ward neu"* ["A world has passed away and is made new."][20]

Thus, Jung is on Joyce's side. Initially, he resists. A serious debate is necessary beforehand, but in the end, he acquiesces, with relief and enthusiasm. He sees Joyce's work of radical deconstruction for what it is. In the end, he is not only convinced, but positively delighted about it. Laughing with delight.[21]

Indeed, this essay by Jung ends with a sort of gleefulness, with a rousing "Yes!" like the last pages of Joyce's *Ulysses*. In Joyce, the "yes" belongs to Molly Bloom, who says, as you remember, "yes, I will, Yes." In Jung's text, the "yes" is his acquiescence to the transformation that is underway, the transformation of a world.

On the Artist and Art

Reading "'Ulysses': A Monologue," we see that Jung does not grant much importance to the artist as an individual. In fact, he ignores it. The writer's life and personal experience do not matter at all to him.[22] Yet he might have

---

20 Ibid., par. 202.

21 On the subject of laughter: I have always been surprised at the terrible seriousness and confinement in which I often see Joyce scholars—especially French ones. Personally, I often laugh when reading *Ulysses*. It is true that I had an old-fashioned classical education, learning Latin, Greek, and philosophy. In fact, it was a very Aristotelian-Thomistic training—something that I believe I have in common with Joyce and Jung. Jung, as we know, knew how to laugh, sometimes loudly; hence, in particular, his familiarity with the figure of the trickster. See C. Gaillard, "Transcendance et croyance en psychanalyse jungienne à la lumière du *Livre Rouge*," *Cahiers Jungiens de Psychanalyse* 134 (2011): 61–91.

22 This particular disposition, which is his own and carries his vision far—often, very far—is one of his great strengths, apparently. However, farsightedness is not without disadvantages. It may also be a serious weakness. Indeed, sometimes Jung lacks a clear vision of what is going on very close to him, under his nose. That was the case, notably in the 1930s, during the rise of the Nazi Party in Germany. Hence the debate he had on this subject with Neumann. In an essay entitled "Le regard presbyte de C. G. Jung" ["C. G. Jung's Case of Presbyopia"], I mentioned this subject in relation to the range of his vision and his long-term analyses, as well as the problem he sometimes had with seeing the events and persons closest to him, when he was not especially careful of where he trod; C. Gaillard, "Le regard presbyte de C. G. Jung," *Cahiers Jungiens de*

taken a deeper interest in James Joyce.[23] Jung had some reasons to wonder about the subject. More than likely, he had at least heard of Joyce's struggle with his patron, Edith McCormick, who was also generous with Jungian circles. And we know that in 1934, two years after the publication of his essay on *Ulysses*, Joyce asked him to treat his daughter, Lucia. For Jung, this was undoubtedly another opportunity to wonder about the personality of the author of *Ulysses*. Lucia's therapy was somewhat successful, apparently, even if Jung did not really believe that she was cured.[24] His attention was actually directed elsewhere. Taking James Joyce as the subject of a sort of "wild psychoanalysis" does not tempt Jung in the least, not in this text or in any of the other writing he did on the arts.[25]

What lessons can be drawn from the encounter, so surprising for many people, between Jung and *Ulysses*, Joyce's work? I see three. The first lesson is that when Jung is discovering this novel, his attention and analysis are attuned to a scale quite other than that of the individual. He has no taste for psychobiography. Art is more important to him than artists—art and the transformations of a culture.[26] The second lesson is that, for him, the transformations he observes on the scale of a culture are not smooth. They run into resistance that is sometimes fierce and obstinate. The third lesson, and the third characteristic of Jung's approach to art, especially concerning modern and contemporary art and the

Psychanalyse 82 (1995). Here, let us add that the archetypal image and idea of Wotan were what enabled him to write a 1936 essay that, along with being visionary, denounced with great precision the mobilizations of German crowds at the time; C. G. Jung, "Wotan" (1936), in *CW*, vol. 10 (Princeton, NJ: Princeton University Press, 1970).

23   For some idea of Joyce's appearance at the time, see J. Paris, *Joyce par lui-même* (Paris: Seuil, 1957).

24   For the encounters and relationship between Jung and Joyce, particularly the letter Jung wrote to Joyce after the publication of his essay on *Ulysses* and Joyce's reactions to the essay, see R. Ellmann, *James Joyce* (New York: Oxford University Press, 1959); D. Bair, *Jung: A Biography* (Boston: Little, Brown, 2003), chap. 27.

25   The term "wild psychoanalysis" (in German, "*wilde Psychoanalyse*") was suggested by Freud in 1910. It is now part of the vocabulary of most schools of psychoanalysis. See the entry for this term in J. Laplanche and J. B. Pontalis, *The Language of Psychoanalysis* (London: Hogarth Press, 1973).

26   I feel the same way, I must say. Unless, of course, an artist is consulting me or when I can accompany an artist in some other way in his or her creation—an opportunity I sometimes have.

transformations they feed and feed upon, is that he must struggle to accept them. But in the end, he does.

One Hell of a Nekyia

That same year, 1932, shortly after Jung closed his Red Book and shortly before he immersed himself in the exciting study of alchemists' iconography and writings, the Zurich Kunsthaus organized the world's first great Picasso retrospective.[27] Jung went to the show, and what he saw affected him deeply. He wrote about the experience in an article commissioned by the *Neue Zürcher Zeitung*.[28] What does he find most striking about what he saw there, particularly regarding *La Vie*, one of the works by Picasso then being exhibited at the Kunsthaus?

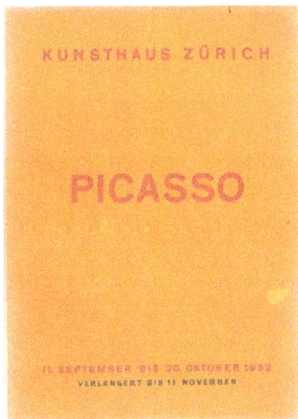

Fig. 1

COVER OF THE CATALOGUE OF THE 1932 PICASSO EXHIBITION AT THE KUNSTHAUS IN ZURICH.

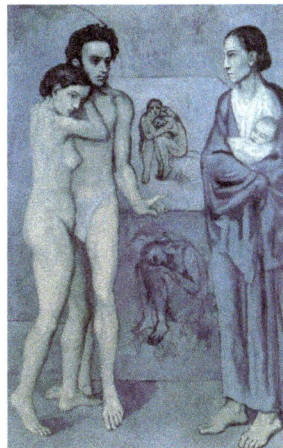

Fig. 2

PICASSO, *LA VIE* (1903). SOURCE: CATALOGUE OF THE 1932 PICASSO EXHIBITION IN ZURICH, TAFEL III.

27   This is the cover of the exhibition catalogue. I owe the document to Murray Stein, who found the catalogue God knows where in Zurich, and sent it to me. With gratitude, I publish it here as an homage to his inquiring mind.

28   C. G. Jung, "Picasso" (1934), in *CW*, vol. 15 (Princeton, NJ: Princeton University Press, 1966).

He observes that the predominant hue in this scene and many others is blue. He notes a shade of blue called midnight blue. Night is looming, a night that is strangely reminiscent of the *Duat*, the underworld of the ancient Egyptians, Jung remarks. Jung associates the paintings with a descent into hell: a *nekyia*, like the ones described by Homer, Goethe, and Nietzsche.

Where does this lead us? he wonders. Is there just as much reason to worry as with Joyce's journey, or perhaps even more? Jung's observation and reflection continue. As he proceeds, he becomes increasingly tense: perplexed and, to be frank, rather alarmed. The figures that appear successively in the works of this painter alarm him. There is a young prostitute; men and women who are stricken with something—illness, or perhaps alcoholism. A rather desperate world. And Jung is despairing along with them. Next, he notes, there are scenes of terrible savagery, battles, cannibalism. Terribly archaic visions. At last, the tragic figure of the Harlequin emerges with the scattered diamonds of his fool's costume in scraps. The characters are more and more fragmented, made of bits and pieces that are falling apart. Now Jung is frightened.

Will he examine the life of the artist to understand if it contains a clue? Not once. He does not say a word about it. Just as he did with Joyce's *Ulysses*, he ignores the individual who created the art. Instead, Jung follows Picasso through the artist's paintings, as if he were analyzing a series of dreams, or as if he were analyzing a series of illuminations in an alchemist's manuscript. This is his strength: to focus his attention on a process that is underway.

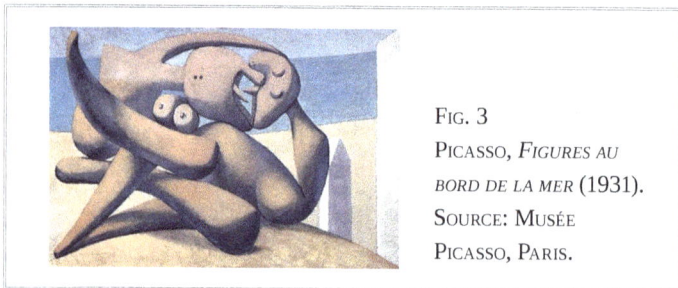

Fig. 3

PICASSO, *FIGURES AU BORD DE LA MER* (1931). SOURCE: MUSÉE PICASSO, PARIS.

This singular strength never ceases to amaze me—because his analytical method anticipates an approach that would be developed much later, thirty years later, by Anton Ehrenzweig in Britain in his book entitled *The Hidden Order of Art* and in France by Didier Anzieu in his writings on the creative process.[29]

In Jung's essay on Picasso, we find the main features of Jung's approach to the arts which we pointed out above in relation to his discussion of *Ulysses*. Here they are sharper. Now Jung speaks quite explicitly in terms of a process that is underway, a work in progress, or at least in process—but with one key difference, it is important to note, when we compare Jung's approach to those of Ehrenzweig and Anzieu: in this essay on Picasso, the point is not to analyze the successive steps or phases that lead up to the creation of a single work of art, painting, sculpture, or poem, but to observe the process at play in the long term, from one year to the next, from one decade to the next, on the scale of an artist's life work—Picasso's, in this case.

What Jung sees of Picasso's life work in 1932 is not reassuring. That's an understatement. Jung is alarmed, as I said. True, he is alarmed for Picasso's sake, just as he was for Nietzsche's. The tragic fate of the latter haunts him, and he is especially anxious about what will follow in Picasso's work. He writes: "This inner adventure is a hazardous affair and can lead at any moment to a standstill or to a catastrophic bursting asunder of the conjoined opposites."[30]

Let us recall that Jung's text on Picasso dates from 1932. Where did Picasso's work go after that year? Jung had no way of knowing. But we do today.

---

29 A. Ehrenzweig, *The Hidden Order of Art* (London: Weidenfeld and Nicholson, 1967); D. Anzieu, *Le Corps de l'Art* (Paris: Gallimard, 1981).
30 Jung, "Picasso," *CW* 15, par. 214.

Picasso after 1932

After 1932, the work and the painter were sorely tried. Jung's fears, concerns, and worries were justified. After 1932, Picasso traversed a crisis in his work, a cruel dry spell of creativity. He painted much less, and the paintings he did make were not colorful. He dove into the blacks and grays of printmaking and into nearly infernal scenes of elemental, bestial combats, in which horses and bulls rip each other apart even more violently than in a bullfighting arena. In a series of prints from 1935, the central figure has a bull's head and a man's body. It looks as though this Minotaur is trying to get out of a labyrinth, or a cave, and we see a hand trying to hold him back, or catch him. Even more strikingly, the Minotaur is walking toward a girl, almost a child, who is holding a bouquet in one hand and a candle in the other, lighting the scene.[31]

Then, in 1936, came *Guernica*, a masterpiece that has marked the contemporary arts. It is a masterpiece, but so gray and black. And it has been burst asunder violently. The scene cries out in pain and terror. The artist is indeed giving us a disaster to look at, to experience. A violent, desperate disaster. Picasso went quite far and quite low into the depths, into the most monstrous, primitive hells, the most fragmented and chaotic; in the depths where the forces of destruction are liable

FIG. 4

PICASSO, *MINOTAURE ET JUMENT DEVANT UNE GROTTE FACE À UNE JEUNE FILLE AU VOILE* (1936). MUSÉE PICASSO, PARIS.
(P. 12, AFTER THE SUB-TITLE)

---

31   We owe to Brigitte Baer, author of the *Catalogue Raisonné of Picasso's Prints*, an excellent study of the prints he made between 1900 and 1942; B. Baer, *Picasso: Gravures 1900–1942* (Paris: RMN, 1996), illus. 59–66. I discussed this in my essay "Jung, Picasso et le Bleu," 42–43.

to win out over the most elementary forms; a place where all form may disintegrate. It is the place where Nietzsche lost himself.

Only after 1939 did life again triumph in Picasso's work, recovering and regaining its momentum from a distant source we might describe as Dionysian, which we can see in the print titled "Woman with Tambourine." In 1946, he painted an even more delightfully Dionysian country scene, which can be viewed at the Picasso Museum in Antibes. The title of this painting is *La Joie de vivre* [*The Joy of Living*]. Obviously, Jung could not have known about this scene in 1934. However, it so happens that in the essay he wrote that year on Picasso he noted that he had rarely seen a clinical case that, after a return to the most elemental forms—he describes them as "neolithic," that is, not far from our life in the caves—had not leapt into the dynamic of a Dionysian world.[32]

I do not wish to say that Jung foresaw everything. Of course not. But I did want to show that with this essay on Picasso the features of his approach to the arts— especially the contemporary arts, all that we noticed when we reread his text on Joyce—were confirmed and reaffirmed. Whether the subject is Joyce or Picasso,

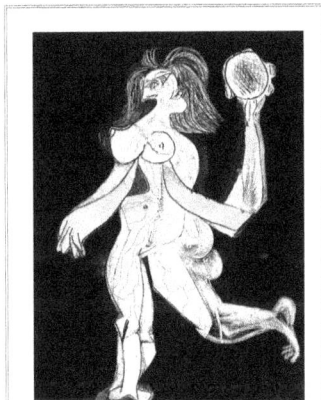

FIG. 5

PICASSO, *LA FEMME AU TAMBOURIN, OU LA GRANDE MÉNADE* (1939). SOURCE: MUSÉE PICASSO, PARIS.

Jung clearly thinks in terms of process, and of long-term processes that are painful to experience. Faced with them, one has good reason to be alarmed and to resist.

Jung shows that the transformations that can be observed at that time may lead, or lead us again, to regions of ourselves and regions in

---

32   Jung, "Picasso," *CW* 15, par. 212.

the history of humanity that we believed we had left behind long ago. Such journeys can be troubling, and Jung himself embarked on them not without some ambivalence and conflict.

Moreover, it is clear now—his essay on Joyce also hints at it—that Jung is thinking in terms of regression. A regression that goes all the way back to the most elementary forms and forces, which are so primitive, so archaic, that they are almost formless. But at the same time, he looks forward: toward what is going to happen in a prospective way. This is an idea that bears coming back to.

Making One's Way—or, Ulysses, Moses, and Voltaire

We can now come to the question that has actually been in the air since we began this reflection on Jung's relationship to the arts. How can we explain the discrepancy between what Jung wrote in his letters, at least in some of his letters, and what he says in these essays on Joyce and Picasso?

In my opinion, it is because Jung was assuredly a "great man," a "great individual," as defined by Neumann: a seeker, a finder, an incredibly creative thinker. And despite being a great man, in some ways he also fit into his social background. We know of his beautiful residence in Küsnacht, and the classical photographs of his consulting room and office, with the medieval-style stained-glass windows behind him.[33]

Jung was a man of culture, a lively participant in the culture of his circles, and he had his own tastes when it came to art. But he was also a seeker—a creative, passionate seeker. As such, he knew how to detach himself, how to step out of his cultural background and away from his own masters, to make his way as an individual, to blaze his own trail in search of his own points of view.

---

33   G. Wehr, *An Illustrated Biography of C. G. Jung* (Boston: Shambhala, 1989), 110.

In the first edition of *Wandlungen und Symbole der Libido* [*Symbols of Transformation*] Jung wrote this dedication to Freud: *"Dem Lehrer und Meister, zu Füssen gelegt von einem ungehorsam aber dankbarem Schüler"* ["To my master and instructor, a book that I lay at his feet as a disobedient but grateful pupil"]. What a beautiful dedication: "disobedient" but "grateful."

Freud was especially fond of the portrait of him taken by his children in 1906. When Jung asked him for a photograph of himself, this is the one Freud chose. Since our topic is the arts, it can be interesting to compare this photograph with a work of art, glimpsed earlier in Jung's writing on Joyce, that especially impressed Freud: Michelangelo's Moses in Rome, which Freud would have viewed at the church of San Pietro in Vincoli.[34] Clearly, Ulysses is not Moses. No more than Jung is Freud, or could make himself a Freudian.

This was true of Jung even as a child. Recall Guido Reni's *David*, a scene that fascinated Jung as a boy. in which David is defeating Goliath.

Fig. 6

Freud in 1906.

Fig. 7

Michelangelo, Moses,
San Pietro in Vincoli, Roma.

---

34 Freud wrote at length about the circumstances surrounding his visit to San Pietro in Vincoli, and impact of this work upon him; see S. Freud, *The Moses of Michelangelo* (London: Hogarth Press, 1955); see also Gaillard, "Ulysse et Moïse. Première Partie"; Gaillard, "Ulysse et Moïse. Deuxième Partie."

A copy of this work by Guido Reni was prominently displayed at the vicarage at Kleinhüningen. It is one of the first works of art that amazed and awed young Carl Gustav. The original hangs in the Louvre in Paris. Apparently, Jung definitely is and always has been on young David's side. He is on the side of one whole part of modern and contemporary arts—the youngsters who attack gigantic old powers and values that are taken for granted. Almost fearlessly, they attack and destroy the old order that must be overthrown. David—the young David of the Bible, and the

FIG. 8

GUIDO RENI, DAVID AVEC LA TÊTE DE GOLIATH. SOURCE: MUSÉE DU LOUVRE, PARIS.

David of Guido Reni—and Ulysses, both Homer's Ulysses and Joyce's, as well as Joyce himself, are cousins.

If the gap between some of Jung's letters and his astonishingly perceptive and enlightening writings on the arts of today is so wide, especially in 1934, it is because in these letters he is expressing opinions that were fairly common in his social circles. However, even when he was very young, and later in his essays and writings as a scholar and in his ventures as a researcher, he goes beyond the most fondly cherished values and certainties of his social class, and beyond his own values and certainties as a man of this class. He then makes great strides with the strength of an intuition that fearlessly detaches itself from established powers and the opinions generally taken for granted and marches on to other worlds.

Hence this other question on the same subject: How is it that so many of our colleagues misunderstand these important essays that Jung wrote on Joyce and Picasso?[35] I shall risk a hypothesis: it could very well be

---

35   Not all of them, of course. Some know how to appreciate Jung's groundbreaking analyses: I have already mentioned Suzan Rowland. John Hill, perhaps because he is Irish, knows how

that the belief that Jung radically objected to and rejected any expression of the modern and contemporary arts is due to the fact that we ourselves, at least many of us, have some trouble overcoming our ordinary tastes, the tastes we owe to our education, our background, and our everyday routines, to become conscious of what is at stake in the arts of today and acquire a taste for them—which will bring us to say a few words on the exhibition of the Red Book at the last Biennale of contemporary art in Venice, an event so unexpected for most of us.

Moreover, and perhaps more radically, there is some chance that we have trouble experiencing the real tension that often opposes what we have learned from the cultures, and especially the religions, that preceded us and the modernists' sometimes harsh criticisms of them.

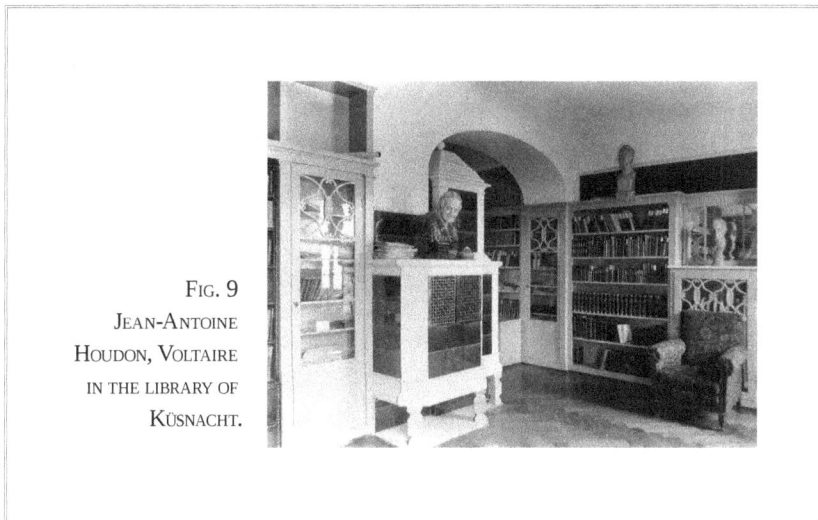

FIG. 9
JEAN-ANTOINE
HOUDON, VOLTAIRE
IN THE LIBRARY OF
KÜSNACHT.

to read Joyce the way Jung did; see J. Hill, "The Venom Destiny: Reflections on the Jung/Joyce Encounter," *Spring Journal* 79 (2008). Tern van den Berg, to whom we owe an excellent recent book on Jung's writings on art, was cited earlier (see note 2). Sylvester Wojtkowsky demonstrated his appreciation in the paper he offered at the first conference on Art and Psyche in New York in 2012—which means I am not in bad company.

Neumann and Jung: Their Experiences of the Arts and Their Ways of Thinking

To approach Neumann's relationship with the arts, we shall begin not in 1925 or 1932, but in 1510 or 1515. Why? Because that is when Leonardo da Vinci painted *The Virgin and Child with Saint Anne*. Neumann devoted one of his most important essays on the arts to this work. It is a well thought out text that leads Neumann to discuss what is known of Leonardo, his life, his works of art, and his amazing work as an inventor and researcher. The essay is well documented, with lively, pertinent quotes from the various writers who have studied Leonardo's works.[36]

Fig. 10
LEONARDO DA VINCI, *LA VIERGE ET L'ENFANT AVEC SAINTE ANNE*. SOURCE: MUSÉE DU LOUVRE, PARIS.

Neumann is writing about Leonardo da Vinci after Freud. And he grants considerable attention and importance to a childhood memory that Leonardo reported, a memory that aroused Freud's interest. The source is Leonardo's *Notebooks*. He writes that one day, when he was a baby, a bird flew down to his cradle and put its tail in his mouth. Neumann writes at

---

36 Neumann's essay on Leonardo dates from 1954. It was revised and augmented in 1959. Neumann cites Vasari, Herzfeld, Burkhart, Wölflin, Pater, Merejkowski, and many other art historians and critics who preceded him, including Otto, Spengler, Kenenyi, and Jung, of course.

length about this memory—or fantasy—lingering over what Leonardo's life would have been like as a young child, between his mother, Catarina, and his stepmother, Dona Albiera. When we read this, we may wonder if Neumann is going to follow in Freud's footsteps and write the same sort of psychobiography.

But Neumann is also writing after Jung. Jung greeted Freud's book on Leonardo in 1910 with enthusiasm! With such great enthusiasm that he even wrote Freud, "[Your] Leonardo is marvelous." He adds that this book is doubtless the first of Freud's writings with which he feels in perfect harmony.[37] Looking back on it today, this harmony seems strange. It leaves us dreaming. And it also leaves Jung dreaming, as if he saw Leonardo's work through what Freud says about it, through what Freud glimpsed yet sensing something that was beyond what he could say about it.[38] Therefore Jung saw with an eye other than Freud's, from another point of view.

Which point of view? Unfortunately, Jung did not develop his own analysis of this work. He wrote about it very briefly and only later, in 1932 and in 1943.[39] It is true, Jung then wrote, that little Leonardo really did have two mothers: his biological mother and his stepmother. This fact is undoubtedly important. However, Jung wrote, it is not essential. According to Jung, what was essential was that Leonardo's *Saint Anne* belongs to a fairly widespread category of themes, and its significance goes well beyond the biographical. It is an example of the iconographic and mythological theme of the two mothers, or dual mother—seen also in an earlier medieval representation, *Ste Anne Selbdritt*, a work from the collection at the Augustiner Museum in Freibourg im Breisgau.[40] Jung evokes and convokes the theme of the two mothers to

---

37   Letter 198, dated June 17, 1910; S. Freud and C. G. Jung, *The Freud-Jung Letters* (Princeton, NJ: Princeton University Press).

38   Jung does note the feeling explicitly, and rather dreamily, in fact, as the letter goes on.

39   C. G. Jung, "Sigmund Freud in His Historical Setting" (1934), in *CW*, vol. 15 (Princeton, NJ: Princeton University Press, 1966), pars. 54–57.

40   See also C. Gaillard, *Le Musée Imaginaire de C. G. Jung* (Paris: Stock, 1998), 184. This theme, something Freud glimpsed but never really focused on, is termed by German art historians that of *Anna Selbdritt,* and in Italian (Anna) *Metterza.* Writing in 1943, Jung cites Benvenuto Cellini, in particular, on this subject.

emphasize the distance between his analysis and Freud's psychobiographical approach. But he does not say how his attention to the theme of the dual mother can help us understand the meaning of Leonardo's work.

How will Neumann make his way between the two approaches, the one Freud developed and the one Jung outlines? In fact, Neumann opens a third path between Freud and Jung. He provides a fairly detailed review of Freud's comments about Leonardo's childhood, and he corrects them in light of what has since been learned about Leonardo's life. Nevertheless, he refrains from psychobiography. He resists the urge to reduce his explanation of the work through the analysis of the life of the artist.

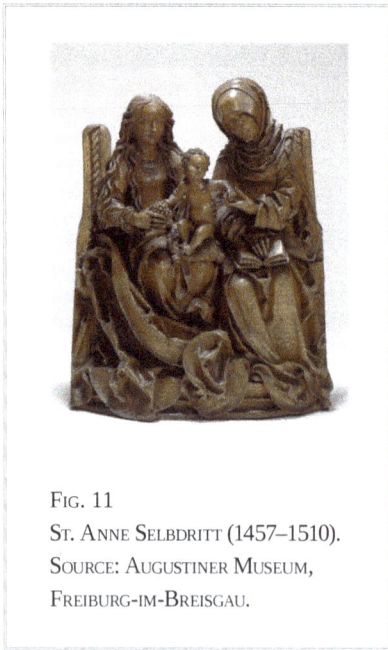

Fig. 11
St. Anne Selbdritt (1457–1510).
Source: Augustiner Museum,
Freiburg-im-Breisgau.

Neumann approaches this work by Leonardo by integrating his thinking into what he wrote a few years earlier on the feminine.[41] I would qualify the "third way" suggested by Neumann between Freud and Jung as *typological*. Neumann sets up a typology. But he does not do so the same way Jung did in *Psychological Types*.

Neumann sets up a typology by integrating what can be known about Leonardo's unique life into what can be observed, more generally, in the life and works of those he calls great men or great individuals. Clearly, Leonardo was one of those geniuses. Moreover, Neumann expands his analysis to an outline of the transformations underway in Leonardo's time, the Renaissance. Lastly, Neumann's approach goes beyond typology

---

41   E. Neumann, *The Fear of the Feminine and Other Essays on Feminine Psychology* (Princeton, NJ: Princeton University Press, 1994).

to archetypology, when he shows how the archetype of the Mother is presented in this painting, and in particular how the typical theme of the relations between mother and daughter is described on canvas—and in a moment, we shall see how he studies the variations of the theme of the mother in another, more recent work, the sculpture of Henry Moore.

Neumann's essay on Leonardo is extremely rich, innovative, and dense. In fact, his writing is so dense that at times it becomes rather heavy—in contrast to the style of his other writings on the arts, for example, his essay on Chagall.[42] Nevertheless, the progression of his thought through the eighty some pages of his essay on Leonardo da Vinci occasionally quickens and grows lively when he is guided by his intuition. Intuition enables his ideas to flow more freely in the best pages of the essay.[43] For example, when he makes the remark, almost in passing, that the double head we see in Leonardo's *Saint Anne* might belong to a single body rather than to two different figures.[44] It is disturbing. Neumann notices it, and he says so. This is his intuition. But he does not linger on it.

Intuition comes from afar at the same time as it directs our gaze and shows the path. Sometimes it takes over, and sometimes it operates in the interstices of thinking, doing its best to pull some strings, but from afar. I like Neumann's intuition, and I follow him when intuition leads him, because that is when he surprises and precedes me. I am less fond, sometimes, I must say, of the way he thinks. Indeed, his thinking often remains too firmly dual, dualist, or we might even say bipolar. Immediately after he mentions his intuitive perception of a single body with two women's heads, he feels obliged to bring dualism into the discussion again, contrasting an earthly maternal, on the one hand, with

---

42 E. Neumann, *Creative Man: Five Essays*, trans. Eugene Rolfe (Princeton, NJ: Princeton University Press, 1979).

43 I understand this tension between intuition and thought. It is an uncomfortable experience when, as you are writing, you see the cumbersome demands of thinking overwhelm the original strength and liveliness of intuition so insistently that you are liable to lose or stifle the intuition.

44 E. Neumann, *Art and the Creative Unconscious* (Princeton, NJ: Princeton University Press, 1959).

a spiritual paternal, on the other. He goes on to struggle in vain with this type of dualist opposition or dichotomy. The bipolarity of his thinking, in my opinion, limits his approach to the arts—to our contemporary arts, in particular, but also to this work painted in the early sixteenth century.

Let me intervene here in this debate between Freud, Jung, and Neumann and about what is offered by the arts. I have a suggestion to make, for us all. I suggest we engage in an exercise that is very simple but not really easy. It consists of forgetting all that we know, all that we have learned from Freud, Jung, Neumann, and art historians about this painting. In fact, let's put aside what we know from the Bible about the story of Saint Anne, the Virgin Mary, and this child. Let us simply be awed. Physically and emotionally, by the emotions and feelings that arise.

Letting Oneself Be Awed

Earlier, I mentioned the benefits of speaking and also thinking in images. Now we shall take a step further and try to think—and especially feel—beneath an image. Beneath this scene of *The Virgin and Child with Saint Anne*. Beneath representation itself. What is there, in the space beneath representation? Perceptions, impressions, and, indeed, emotions. If you really forget all that you already know about this painting, about this scene, don't you see, as I do, a strange and disturbing pyramid of a body with two heads? It is hard to sort out who the various arms and legs belong to. Meanwhile, at the bottom of the pyramid of living flesh, three feet emerge from a tangle of clothing and hang there, as if suspended.

This disturbing, multiple image is even more obvious in the charcoal sketch known as the "Burlington House Cartoon," made prior to the painting of *The Virgin and Child with Saint Anne* that hangs in the Louvre.[45] Here, the extra arms and legs are even more obvious. One

---

45 "Burlington House Cartoon," in A. Green, *Révélations de l'inachèvement: A propos du carton de Londres de Léonard de Vinci* (Paris: Flammarion, 1992), 16.

wonders which ambiguous, indistinct, polymorphic body is holding the child leaning to the right. It is awe-inspiring, indeed. Gripping, disturbing, troubling perhaps. Puzzling, in any case.

Let us continue to be open to emotion, allowing the work to live its own life. We can forget useless discussions. It is good for a work of art to begin by shutting us up, by shutting up our theories and our old debates.

Let's forget the old discussion about the bird—vulture or kite—who flew all the way to Leonardo's cradle when he was an infant and put its tail into the baby's mouth. Freud focused on that. And Neumann returned to it, at length.[46]

On the cover of *Un Souvenir d'Enfance de Léonard de Vinci*, as published by Gallimard in France, we see the vulture (or kite) that is the subject of so much speculation.[47] It takes up far too much room in our discussion, and especially in our perception of the work. The strength of Leonardo's painting, once we cast off this interpretation that is excessively proud and joyful about

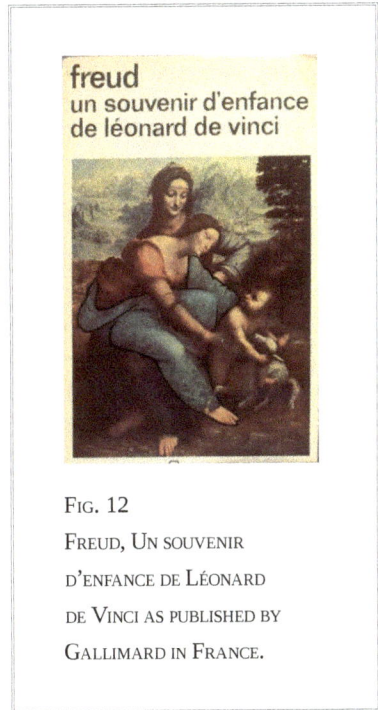

FIG. 12

FREUD, UN SOUVENIR D'ENFANCE DE LÉONARD DE VINCI AS PUBLISHED BY GALLIMARD IN FRANCE.

its own discovery, is the ability of the work to summon up a presence, a presence I would qualify as ambiguous, polymorphic, and hard to sort out. It is uncanny and blurry because it comes from so far away, from beyond our ability to make it out. It is terribly archaic, but at the

---

46 To conclude, oddly enough, that Freud was right.
47 In Green, *Révélations de l'inachèvement* (on the cover).

same time as we see a familiar sight, that of a mother with her child, a mother watching over or holding back her child, while the child plays with an animal, an uncooperative lamb.[48]

Neumann, in his approach to this and other works by da Vinci, takes steps in this direction, exploring this ambiguity and polyvalence. He is well able to see, and show, for example, the more than troubling ambiguity of Leonardo's Saint John the Baptist, when he tells us that actually, Saint John the Baptist might very well also be a Bacchus.[49] Neumann is well aware of it, and considers the hermaphroditic character of the god. And on the basis of such an ambiguity—of gender, of sex—he broaches the more radical subject of the figure of the *uroboros*, reminding us how it merges the masculine and feminine into a single circle, making sexual differentiation really difficult.

But why on Earth does he waste so much time on a discussion of the poor Freudian story of the vulture or kite, instead of seeing the play of shapes in the painting in the Louvre?[50] It might be that his approach to the painting coalesces and structures itself around a sort of explanatory key, around the idea of the Terrible Mother. It is a good idea, of course, and it is essential, in case we are tempted to place too much faith in the Good Mother, the All-Good Mother. But as an approach to the work of art, it fails. It freezes, becomes rigid, staring at its own archetypal knowledge. This knowledge does indeed provide a sort of explanation, and some reassurance: we feel better when we can say the subject is a certain recognizable archetype, an archetype scholars have studied and can identify.

---

48 This approach to a work is not unrelated to a classical clinical term in French, *"attention flottante"*; in German, *"gleichschwebende Aufmerksamkeit"*; and in English, *"evenly balanced or poised attention"* (Laplanche and Pontalis, *The Language of Psychoanalysis*, 43). The difference is that here this approach aims to allow an emotion to be experienced, an emotion that is offered by the work, but that we usually ignore or repress.

49 Neumann, *Art and the Creative Unconscious*, 70–73.

50 It is true that many researchers got caught in the same trap, which contributed to keeping the question alive for so long, practically until today.

Leonardo's painting protests. It protests by showing us the complexity and confusion intrinsic to the experience of a fundamental reality—this more than disturbing reality we described as ambiguous, polymorphic, polyvalent, confusing, which rises from the so troubling predawn undifferentiated—primordial, original, powerfully archaic, and yet always present: a reality we would rather forget or ignore, or at least reduce to something that is already known.

In his book on Leonardo, Neumann takes a bold approach to the artist's work. But then he seems to back off, as if, finally, he would prefer to reassure himself, or us, by resorting to an archetype that is too well established, too explanatory, too firm, and too closed. Because even though he ventures far when he allows himself to be guided by intuition, he returns, too rapidly, in my opinion, to a dualist way of thinking.

So Neumann's thinking resumes. It wants to take over again, conceptually. But his first perception persists and resists, and his intuition moves forward, steadily. It is especially visible in the book he devoted to another set of works by a single artist, those of the sculptor Henry Moore.

The Insistence of a Theme
and Going beneath Representation

In Neumann's *The Archetypal World of Henry Moore*, the debate comes alive again. Notably, it is aroused by a recurring, insistent theme in Henry Moore's work, that of the reclining woman, as depicted in Moore's sculpture of that title. This theme, this presence, prompts Neumann to speak of the feminine/maternal, of course. We are not too surprised: Saint Anne is not far away. In passing, we can note that Neumann chose an artist whose work is almost monothematical—quite the opposite of Picasso, who interested Jung so much.[51] Neumann examines the work

---

51 Likewise, on the world of Chagall, to whom Neumann devoted another of his major essays on art, we can say that it is presented as a set of variations on the same theme—in this case, that of the memory and dream of Russia, with the animals, houses, and peasants that animate the land.

closely. He works seriously. And soon he notices that Moore's work developed in successive phases. Neumann observes the evolution and transformation of forms in Moore's sculpture.[52]

How can we understand what is happening here? Neumann uses the term *abstraction*. I must say, I found that rather astonishing, because what I see is quite the opposite of abstraction. I see a highly organic, touchable reality, a reality that is obviously alive. So why does Neumann speak of abstraction? Because for him, abstraction leads to the essential, all the way to the feminine itself, to the archetype of the Mother.

Fig. 13
Henry Moore,
Reclining Woman
(1979). Source:
Botanical Garden,
New York.

Fig. 14
Henry Moore,
Reclining
Woman (1939).

52   *Reclining Woman* (1933), in E. Neumann, *The Archetypal World of Henry Moore* (1961) (Princeton, NJ: Princeton University Press, 1985), fig. 10.

Neumann looks for the archetype, and he finds the archetype in the series of sculptures all titled *Reclining Woman* that Moore created between 1935 and 1939.[53] Instead of observing the regressive movement to forms that are deformed, true, but especially primitive, elementary, so elementary that a body becomes organic, actually—a sort of nearly undifferentiated organ, so undifferentiated and so natural that the body really becomes stone, or wood, but living stone or wood, almost natural. This presence is really very physical. Like a physical and organic reality that is still forming until it comes to life and develops almost beneath any truly recognizable form.

Neumann is still observing. The work becomes more dramatic in *Mother and Child* (1951).[54] In this depiction of a mother and child, attachment becomes a threat. An attack, even. Breastfeeding becomes cannibalism. How will Neumann react? He clearly sees the powerful, wild, lonely, and transcendent presence in certain works by Moore and cites them in his book, especially those exhibited in Scottish landscapes.[55] What's more, he sees the figures, of which there were two, doubling sometimes. They become a single creature with two heads![56] How can we fail to recognize the same phenomenon, the two heads on the same body, that makes Leonardo's *The Virgin and Child with Saint Anne* so gripping,

Fig. 15
Henry Moore, Mother and Child (1951).

---

53   Ibid., figs. 18, 27, and 50.
54   Ibid., fig. 91.
55   For example, *Two Seated Figures*; ibid., fig. 90.
56   Ibid., fig. 74 or 75.

so disturbing it is almost frightening? Neumann has studied this painting by Leonardo at length. Will he pick up the clue, take the hint, and really venture forward with his thinking? Will he face the archaic that stands there so powerfully, imposing, primitive, raw? Not really.

In fact, I think Neumann needed to reassure himself. And Moore reassures him in the rest of his work. Moore himself will not linger too long with this regression, with such a risk of regression. In the sculptures that followed this one, Moore did indeed return to his more classical reclining women. It must be said that these sculptures, which were better behaved, made him successful, especially after 1959, which is when Neumann's essay appeared. But it is also important to note that, unfortunately, from then on, his creativity seemed to stagnate. He was acclaimed as an artist, one of the great artists of modern times, but there was very little renewal in what he did.

This book by Neumann on Henry Moore is useful, it is important. But I must admit I am disappointed. Neumann conducted a thorough investigation. In my opinion, he crossed paths with one of the main issues of art, yesterday and today—the ability to regress, and the potential for progress produced by regression. If this book by Neumann on Moore disappoints me, it is because of what I know of Jung, who himself took the risk of regression very early and who truly committed to it. Of course, Jung, too, resisted it. As I mentioned earlier, he harrumphed about modern and contemporary art at the dining room table. But in private, in the secrecy of his library and office, he engaged in the struggle he had started in 1912 and 1913 when he personally experienced a radical regression, with the commitment to writing and painting his Red Book.

It is a pleasure to celebrate the beautiful pages of the Red Book. But we cannot ignore the agony it contains.[57] What we see here is not a successful graphic endeavor, a beautiful idea, or anything ideal or

---

57 Published as C. G. Jung, *The Red Book*, ed. S. Shamdasani (New York: Norton, 2009), illustration no. 122.

pleasing. Instead, it is a gripping expression of a terrifying experience. It shows a confrontation—with a creature that is totally unidentifiable. It may not even be human. There is no way to avoid seeing that in its way this painting depicts a nearly unbearable horror. And if one does not see it—or does not want to see it, and especially experience it—read what Jung writes about it. Jung speaks of *shadows, Hell, Good Friday, the Sun eaten by the dragon, the struggle against the snake, doubt, despair, the shadow of God, and the death of the hero Siegfried.*

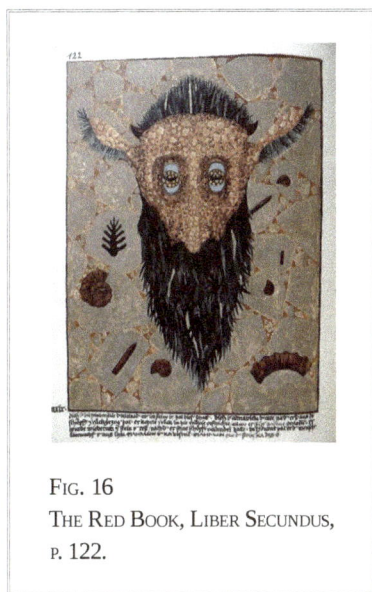

FIG. 16
THE RED BOOK, LIBER SECUNDUS,
P. 122.

Jung knew how to recognize this terrifying experience in others—in other adventures and experiments—in those of the alchemists, especially. On this subject, Jung speaks of *"nigredo."* And he speaks of *"Zerstükelung,"* of "fragmentation."[58] He knows what it is, for having lived it. Having been through this horror, Jung understands the terrible desolation of Christ, the Crucifixion at the heart of Christianity. In a letter to Father Victor White, he speaks of dark night, abandonment, distress.[59] And, on the basis of his personal experience, he could recognize many of the expressions of contemporary artists. And yet Jung also experienced happiness, the joys of art and company. He knew how to express them, too, in his painting.

---

58 See his analyses of transference and his research on the iconography of the alchemists, particularly in C. G. Jung, "The Psychology of the Transference" (1946), in *CW*, vol. 16 (Princeton, NJ: Princeton University Press, 1966), pars. 397–398; and C. G. Jung, *Mysterium Coniunctionis* (1955–1956), *CW*, vol. 14 (Princeton, NJ: Princeton University Press, 1963), pars. 158–159.
59 Letter to White, dated November 24, 1953; C. G. Jung and Victor White, *The Jung-White Letters*, ed. Ann Conrad Lammers and Adrian Cunningham (London: Routledge, 2007); Gaillard, *Le Musée Imaginaire de C. G. Jung*, 168.

How would Jung integrate the experience of the worst horror with the experience of happiness, found or created? In two ways. I've already mentioned the first way: Jung thinks in terms of process. And beginning in 1919, he writes of the individuation process. The second way is epistemological and is based on his experience of the Red Book. Jung produced very curious concepts that have no equivalent in any other tradition of the psychoanalytical movement.[60] Here, I am thinking of Jung's way of expressing, representing, and conceiving the anima or animus, the shadow, and the Self.

I have suggested we speak in terms of imaging thinking.[61] Imaging thinking is a type of thinking that allows itself to draw upon symbolic life, that knows how to be channeled by images. Imaging thinking is a sensitive, sensorial, and often even sensual thinking. This thinking is alive.[62] This type of thinking says more than what it tells us, more than what can be understood intellectually. It is a form of thinking that takes shape the way a sculpture or painting does. The way art is formed. Jung's closest, most lively, and most radical relationship with art is his thinking, the thinking he created. And imaging thinking, this quite Jungian way of thinking, requires that we have a serious sense of transcendence.[63]

Transcendence and Immersion

Indeed, as we know, and as Jung knows, art defies belief.[64] Art, and symbolic life, can never be more than approaches: the best possible expression, at a certain time, of what could not be expressed or experienced in a better way. But art is an experience of transcendence.

---

60   With the exception of D. W. Winnicott or Melanie Klein—but differently in each case

61   C. Gaillard, "The Egg, the Vessels and the Words: From Izdubar to Answer to Job, for an Imaging Thinking," *Journal of Analytical Psychology* 57, no. 3 (2012).

62   As a result, it cannot really be controlled, and that is uncomfortable—especially when it must be taught.

63   Gaillard, "Transcendance et croyance."

64   It is of course important to specify here that a distinction has to be made between belief and faith.

Above all, transcendence is an experience.[65] The experience of disproportion. The little man we see here is kneeling in front of something bigger and stronger than he. Dangerously stronger. Moreover, it is well beyond human proportions—and almost unrepresentable. One may have to grapple with the most violent natural forces, the most irrepressible ones.

Here, the same little man is facing, as best he can, what is presented.[66] He holds himself as best he can. Recall the scene or dream that opens Jung's *Answer to Job*, after he visited the *Diwan-i-Kaas*, at Fatehpur Sikri.[67] Jung might have seen it when he traveled to India and again in the dream that committed him to writing *Answer to Job*, which is Jung's most prospective work. It is the one where he expresses with the most boldness his vision of the history from the most distant sources of our culture to the future times. It is

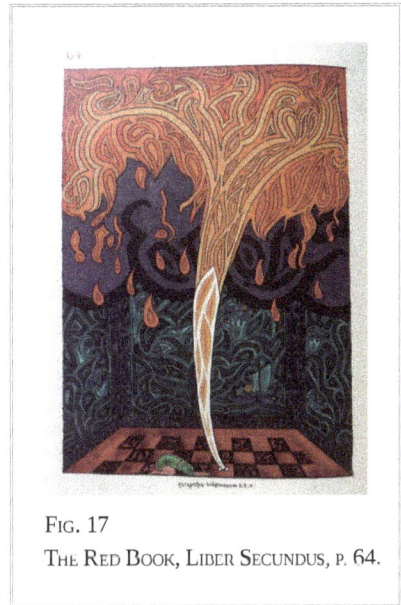

Fig. 17
THE RED BOOK, LIBER SECUNDUS, p. 64.

a prospective book. It shows the way. It is the book in which Jung most precisely states his place and purpose in the past, present, and future of our collective history.

But our abilities to actually regress are at stake. Regression, as we have seen, leads us to the obscure sources of becoming. This journey is not painless. Jung knew it, for having lived it. Neumann also knew what regression is and the risks to which it exposes the individual. I do not know the context of his drawings, particularly the relationship that may

---

65   Jung, *The Red Book*, illustration no. 64.
66   Jung, *The Red Book*, illustration no. 36.
67   The *Diwan-i-Kaas* is the Hall of Private Audiences, in the Red Fort of Delhi, India.

exist between them and his written work. But I observe that the theme of immersion often recurs in his drawings. This theme of immersion is expressed in two different versions in Neumann's drawings: that of drowning, and that of baptism.

The theme of immersion and the risk of drowning also occur in Jung. Doubtless, like me, you are thinking of the well-known story of Jung's visit to Ravenna, in 1931 or 1932. As you may recall, he visited the Orthodox Baptistery in Ravenna in the company of a female acquaintance.[68] He had already been to Ravenna with the same lady in 1912–1913. And, during their second visit, some twenty years later, they both observed and discussed at length a mosaic that represented a dangerous drowning scene: Saint Peter "sinking into the waters." On this subject, Jung speaks of real mortal danger.[69] This baptistery does not actually contain a mosaic representing such a scene. It was a visionary experience that Jung shared with the lady who was at his side. Jung's imagination was truly active. In fact, he knew how to activate it himself, when necessary. The lady probably knew how, too. Jung does not take the time to say what this scene,

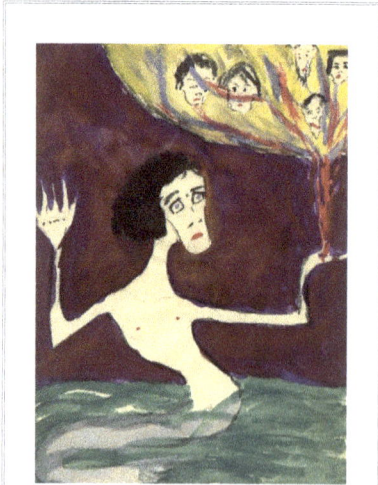

FIG. 18
PAINTING BY ERICH NEUMANN.
COURTESY OF MICHA NEUMANN AND
RALI LOEWENTHAL-NEUMANN.

with its obvious drama, was telling or trying to tell him, and the lady with him. But here, in Ravenna, in 1931 or 1932, a work of art spoke to him, just as it would later at Fatehpur Sikri. It showed him what he would have to say, or what he would have to say to himself.

---

68   C. G. Jung, *Memories, Dreams, Reflections*, ed. Aniela Jaffé, trans. Richard and Clara Winston (New York: Pantheon Books, 1962, 1965), 284–288.
69   Ibid., 286.

A moment ago, I mentioned imaging thinking. Here, the question that arises is clearly the one of this very Jungian exercise that Jung called *active imagination*. One's imagination activates itself, or is activated, because it is an excellent medium we have for conversing, for admitting what we haven't said so far.[70] Art can invite us to do this.

As for Neumann, like Jung, he could fear the dangers of submersion. But he also knew how to greet and celebrate the delights—albeit slightly melancholy—of art, and of Chagall's art, in particular. Neumann writes "there is no above and below" in Chagall's paintings.[71] He speaks of an "earthly, real world of the soul" and of the union of Jewish and Christian, in a world that also knows of the "pagan vitality of the animals."[72]

I wish Neumann and Jung could have discussed their opinions on Leonardo's *Saint Anne*, on Moses, on Picasso, on Joyce, on Henry Moore. Unfortunately, those subjects are practically absent from their correspondence. It's up to us, today, to compare and discuss their approaches. A very recent event is an opportunity for us to do this.

A Postmodern Event in Venice

Why Venice? Because the last Biennale of Contemporary Art in that city was the site of an unexpected, unforeseen event: Jung's Red Book was exhibited at the entrance to the Biennale, as an introduction to a show of contemporary art. The decision to exhibit it there was made by the curator of the 58th Biennale, a somewhat extraordinary and philosophical curator,

---

70   Here it is also important to speak of the Jungian practice of amplification; see A. Samuels, B. Shorter, and F. Plaut, *A Critical Dictionary of Jungian Analysis* (London: Routledge and Kegan Paul, 1987). Amplification, evidently, explains nothing—but unfolds *(ex-plicare)*, thereby enabling us to consider *(betrachten)* and absorb the impact of what is presenting itself to us, and confront it *(sich ausseinandersetzen)*. Gaillard, *Le Musée Imaginaire de C. G. Jung*; E. G. Humbert, *C. G. Jung: The Fundamentals of Theory and Practice* (Wilmette, IL: Chiron, 1987).

71   See Chagall's *The Green Eye*, in Neumann, *Art and the Creative Unconscious*, 138 and plate 7.

72   For Neumann, Chagall's painting, with its sense of colors and dream, replies to Picasso's. It is an answer to the disaster of *Guernica* (ibid., 147). In his essay on Chagall, Neumann also speaks of the fire on Mount Sinai, as well as the fate of the Jews in the modern world. The essay was first published in 1954; ibid., 138, 142, 143.

Massimiliano Gioni. He had the boldness and the authority required to allow Jung's Red Book to set the tone for the event.

I would love to take you for a stroll through the galleries of the Central and National Pavilions of this Biennale.[73] But, of course, we cannot do such a thing here and now. So, instead, I have chosen three moments from the Biennale's catalogue. The first, *Bodhisattva no. 1* (1998), is an expression of inner experience made by a Chinese woman of today, a practitioner of Qigong.[74] Her name is Guo Fenyi. She might have said, "I draw to know." The Jung of the Red Book could have said the same thing. But what I especially see in her drawings is an homage to Neumann: they enable us to perceive something of the ego-self axis that Neumann was able to experience and bring to our attention.

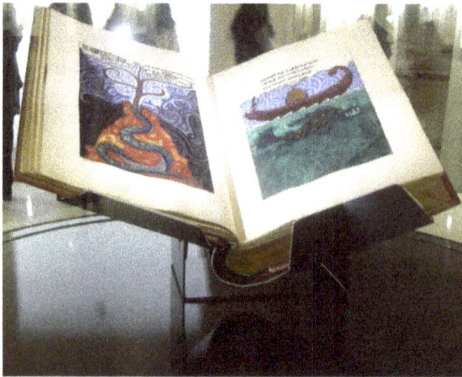

Fig. 19
THE RED BOOK AS EXHIBITED AT THE
ENTRY OF THE VENICE BIENNALE.
PHOTO BY ALIX GAILLARD-DERMIGNY (AGD).

73 See the double volume of the catalogue M. Gioni, *La Biennale di Venezia: Il Palazzo Enciclopedico* [*The Encyclopedic Palace*] (Venice: La Fondazione La Biennale, 2013).
74 Ibid., 1:104.

In the second moment I think we can learn something from observing. This is the performance that British-born artist Tino Sehgal presented at the Biennale.[75] The movements of the figures are very slow and almost ritualistic. Two or three people, dressed in ordinary clothing, are in the middle of the gallery, half sitting or almost stretched out on the floor with their eyes half closed. They move very slowly, as if in slow motion, as if they had just barely emerged, or were in the process of emerging, from slumber or even paralysis. One of the people utters a stream of curious sounds, inarticulate syllables, barely audible, while another receives the message. It is a message of awakening, so the person gradually begins to move, very slowly, as if emerging: a consciousness is awakening, with the slide backward, regression, still in the picture, and the perspective of a gaze that looks forward and is prospective. The movement is prospective. A process is underway, a process that is trying itself out, between regression and becoming.

Fig. 20
Tino Sehgal,
A performance in
Venice. Photo by agd.

---

75   Ibid., 1:34. Since the 1960s and 70s, the world of contemporary art has understood perfor-mance as a public art event consisting of motions, acts, and scenes that take place, leaving no trace of themselves other than films or photographs of the event. These documents are used to give the people who were unable to see or attend the performance some idea of what happened. In fact, Tino Sehgal, who defines his performances very strictly, never arranges for such videos to be made. He has recently presented pieces at the Tate Modern in London and the Palais de Tokyo in Paris.

I am convinced that Jung would have liked this performance, this movement, this experience of emergence. One of the essential characteristics of Jung's advancement in psychoanalysis is his conviction and demonstration that consciousness is a relatively recent and fairly fragile event in biological history, and in each one of us.

The third stop on this quick visit to the Biennale is a piece by the Belgian artist Berlinde de Bruyckere, titled *Kreupelhout* [*Cripplewood*], exhibited in the Belgian Pavilion—quite close to the gallery where Jung's Red Book is shown.[76] It is a sort of giant corpse, made of interwoven stumps and sticks, that are bandaged and bleeding in places. Imagine it, this giant, stretched out on the floor: dead, and the emotional impact of it. In fact, it is ten or twelve meters long and taller than a human being, more than two meters tall. It lies there, in half darkness, as if it had emerged from a cavity in the wall—from a cave, or a tomb. We don't really know where it comes from. Colossal proportions and silence prevail. The dead giant, barely emerged from the darkness, from the shadows, from the night—reminding us, and itself, apparently, of Mantegna's *Christ*, or the one by Philippe de Champaigne, or the one by Dürer in which the limbs in the coffin are almost crushed by the cover of the tomb. The original of the Dürer is in Basel.

Consider the De Bruyckere piece again. This tormented body plunges us into the roots of the darkest hurt. We may fear that it is irreparable, unending torture. This is a work, a body, that really makes us take Christianity seriously: the cross and the tomb—death, without the knowledge that a resurrection will finally occur. It is an amazing deconstruction. That arouses intense emotion. Where one can perceive, feel, and experience the consciousness of a heritage, the sense of history, and the creative progress that comes from the far-off times of our culture, played out again today, over and over, with the risk and the strength of regression. This art knows what it owes to the past, that it is part of a

---

76   Ibid., 2:20–21.

heritage, but it is today's contemporary creation. I see it as an homage to Jung. And, with Neumann, I would say it is truly ethical.

I suggest to you that we end with Jung's Red Book, on one of the two pages to which the Red Book was opened at this Biennale of contemporary art. The monster is still very much there, below. But the boat sticks to its course.[77]

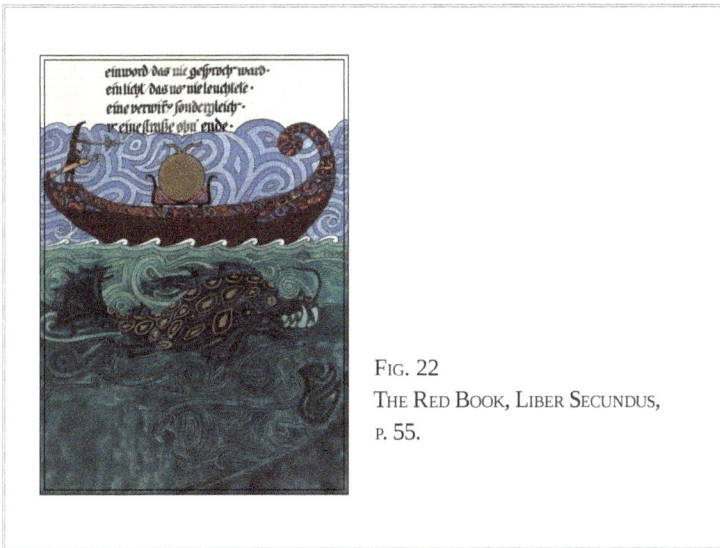

Fig. 22
The Red Book, Liber Secundus,
p. 55.

The journey continues.

---

77   Jung, *The Red Book*, illustration no. 55. It is Day 2, in the *Liber Secundus*. The text says: *One word that was never spoken / One light that was never lit up / An unparallel confusion / And a road without end.*

The Magic Flute

Tom Kelly

E rich Neumann's masterful article on *The Magic Flute*, first published in German in 1953 in *Zur Psychologie* and then translated into English and published in *Quadrant* in 1978, is an in-depth interpretation of this opera as a symbolic expression of the psychological process of growth and transformation. Neumann's grasp and understanding of the archetypal dynamics in this opera are of such impressive depth and breadth that his article can leave one with the impression that nothing more can be added, that everything about *The Magic Flute* has already been said.

To be quite honest, this reaction is no different from the one I have had after reading any of Erich Neumann's publications. Erich Neumann's gift, his genius, is his capacity to present a massive wealth of information, innovative thoughts, and creative ideas in a highly structured format, yet all the while in a very humane and sensitive manner that is easily accessible and understandable. From very early on in my training, Erich Neumann has been an inner guide for me and his publications a compass offering direction, clarification, and understanding, material for thought, sometimes provocative and often challenging, but always insightful and nourishing to the intellect but especially to the soul. I have enjoyed a very special and unique relationship with my inner Erich Neumann for a good many years, and it is with great humility that I offer a few thoughts on an opera that clearly carried a significance and importance for Erich Neumann, as well as for me and a great many people.

The Magic Flute was composed by Mozart and first performed on September 30, 1791, a few months before his untimely death on December 5 of that same year, at the young age of thirty-five. The story was based on a novel, *Sethos*, written in 1731 by a French abbot, Abbé Jean Terrasson, about the initiation of an Egyptian prince. Though the libretto of the opera is officially attributed to Emanuel Schikaneder, it seems likely that Mozart and a number of his friends, many of whom like Mozart were Masons, had a role in putting together what at times might seem like a rather confusing story with a plot that is anything but linear. *The Magic Flute* is a fairy tale put to music and, as with all fairy tales, it depicts a psychological process. As Erich Neumann states in his article: "Fairy tale motifs are motifs of the collective unconscious; they are common to all humanity and are found in remarkable unity of agreement in the most divergent peoples and cultures."[1]

Ingmar Bergman in his 1975 film version of *The Magic Flute* captured the universal aspect of this fairy tale beautifully in the overture. Focusing our attention on the pensive and concentrated expressions on the faces of people in the audience from different cultures, Bergman informs us that the story we are about to see and hear is one that speaks a universal language. Indeed, this was the case with *The Magic Flute*. From the very first performance, it had a strong impact on the audience. Barely fourteen months after the premier, in November 1792, the opera celebrated its one hundredth performance. Today, two and a quarter centuries later, *The Magic Flute* remains the third most frequently performed opera. Clearly, its appeal and the message it carries has not diminished.

---

1 Erich Neumann, "The Magic Flute," *Quadrant* 2 (1978): 6.

The story begins with a young prince, Tamino, who is lost in the forest and finds himself pursued and threatened by a huge serpent (in Bergman's film, the threat comes from a dragon). We are told that Tamino has a bow but no arrows and is therefore ill equipped to deal with the danger confronting him. He falls asleep when three veiled women, the attendants of the Queen of the Night, arrive and intervene to kill the serpent with their spears. When Tamino awakens, he finds himself in the company of Papageno, a young man dressed in green and wearing feathers. He is a bird catcher who serves the Queen of the Night. Tamino assumes Papageno has slain the serpent/dragon, and though he had nothing to do with what happened, Papageno takes credit for this heroic accomplishment. The three veiled women return and punish Papageno for having lied by putting a padlock on his mouth so that he is no longer able to talk, eat, or drink, an extremely severe punishment for him because these are his favorite activities. They then present Tamino with a picture of Pamina, the Queen of the Night's daughter, who, we are told, was abducted by an evil man called Sarastro. Seeing that Tamino is smitten by the beauty of Pamina and that he has fallen in love with this image, the Queen of the Night arrives and, in an aria that is among the most beautiful and the most difficult to sing, tells Tamino about her suffering and helplessness as she watched the evil Sarastro abduct her daughter. She then informs him that she has chosen him to rescue her daughter. If he is successful in accomplishing this heroic task, Pamina will be his forever.

The opening lines of any fairy tale inform us about the psychological problem the story will address. The opening scene of *The Magic Flute* would lead us to believe that this story is a rather classic depiction of masculine development wherein the young man needs to learn to defend himself and to separate from the primeval instinctual forces of the unconscious that threaten to devour him. In face of this threat, he is powerless; he does not have the psychological tools required to deal with this situation. Paradoxically, it is through the intervention of the attendants of the Queen of the Night that the threat is repelled and a task is set in place for the young man to accomplish. This task is meant to help him develop the qualities that are either not present or underdeveloped at this point. Psychologically, we can understand this, at least in part, as the need for the young man to develop a more clearly defined and more stable ego identity, a developmental task which belongs to the first half of life. As her name suggests, the Queen of the Night reigns over the night, the dark, the less visible, and thus is symbolic of the unconscious. As a queen, she represents the highest feminine authority and is therefore a representation of the Mother archetype. It is the mother who sets the stage for the development of the young masculine figure by giving him the task of liberating her daughter.

In contrast to Tamino, Papageno is quite pleased with his lot in life, in service to the Queen of the Night. His only complaint is that he is lonely and without a woman. He is a lighthearted, easy-go-lucky fellow who likes to eat and drink and not overly exert himself. He has no interest in participating in the adventure of rescuing Pamina from the malevolent Sarastro. Papageno is a delightful representation of the shadow of the more heroic Tamino. He is not a dark shadow but rather represents an antihero, or perhaps a reluctant hero, model of masculine development.

The violent abduction of Pamina from the Queen of the Night by Sarastro echoes and therefore connects us to the mythic abduction of Kore by Hades and the painful longing of Demeter for her lost daughter. As Erich Neumann tells us, "the structure of the libretto was originally based on the fairy-tale situation of the struggle between the good fairy and the wicked magician."[2] At this point in the story, for Tamino, the quest to retrieve and liberate Pamina can be seen as reflective of his need to connect with and liberate his inner feminine, the anima. While this is true, we shall see later that the introduction of a dynamic recalling the myth of Kore and Demeter alerts us to the fact that the story we are

---

2   Ibid., 5.

dealing with here is much more complex. It is the first indication that this story is not solely about masculine development but one that addresses and encompasses feminine development as well.

Tamino is guided to a grove in front of Sarastro's temple and is faced with three doors. The door on the left is the Temple of Nature, the door on the right is the Temple of Reason. When Tamino tries each of these, he is rebuffed and told to go away. The door in the middle is the Temple of Wisdom, and it is here that he is allowed to enter. I highlight this to show one of the many subtle details in this opera that give it the depth that makes it so appealing. Here the viewers are told that wisdom is the product of and what unites nature and reason.

In the Temple of Wisdom, Tamino meets a priest who informs him that Sarastro is not the evil villain described by the Queen of the Night and that he should not believe everything he is told. The priest describes Sarastro as a great leader and a man of truth and of wisdom. Tamino finds himself totally confused, full of doubt and no longer certain who to believe, what to do, which way to go. He is not even certain whether Pamina is still alive. In alchemical terms, he is in the *nigredo*, disoriented, in doubt and despair. All previous points of reference no longer hold true. In this liminal space and moment of darkness Tamino, confused and no longer certain about anything, turns inward for direction; he prays and asks, "Oh eternal night, when will you end?" The cryptic answer he is given is: "Soon, soon, youth, or never!" In response to his question about Pamina, Tamino is told she is still alive. This news relieves Tamino and rekindles the sense of hope. For the first time in the opera, he plays his flute. Thanks to its magic, as for Orpheus with his lyre, his sorrow is turned to joy and the animals around him are tamed.

This period of darkness marks a significant shift in Tamino and can be compared to the initial stage of initiation rites, that of separation from the mother and from the community. In contrast to the opening scene where the forest represented danger, something has begun to change. Thanks to the connection he has been able to establish with himself via the flute, his inner animals, his instincts, are no longer threatening but rather are reassuring and empathically attuned to him. Psychologically, we are witnessing here the beginning of what Erich Neumann would refer to as the establishment of a functional ego-self axis.

The story then gently shifts its focus to Pamina, who is asleep in a garden when Monostatos approaches and attempts to kiss her. Just at that moment, the Queen of the Night arrives. Pamina awakens and is initially overjoyed to see her mother. However, the Queen of the Night is angry and, in an aria that recapitulates the one we have heard, reveals her dark and menacing side. This is the point in the story where the feminine development comes into focus.

Pamina is torn between her love for and desire to be reunited with her mother and the price she must pay for this. One way or the other, she must betray either Sarastro or her mother. The price for betraying the mother is excessively high: rejection, abandonment, disowned for eternity. This also brings into focus the shadow of the Queen of the Night and the dark side of the Great Mother, the controlling and devouring Mother. Neumann surmises that "it was probably Mozart himself who transformed this basic concept (of the good fairy and the evil magician) by reversing the polarity of the male and female background figures. The fairy became the Queen of the Night—presenting the principle of evil—and the wicked magician became the priest of light . . . thus leading to a multilevel Mystery drama."[3] It is precisely this multilevel drama that adds such depth to this fairy tale.

This story tells us that, in order to make her own way in life, a woman must separate from the mother and that this can feel like a terrible betrayal. Individuation demands that we make choices. To pull away and to separate requires the capacity to recognize and own one's shadow. In this instance, Pamina is called on to make a choice, in other words, to own her shadow: her capacity to betray and to accept the resultant

---

3   Ibid., 5–6.

feelings of rejection and abandonment. This can only happen through the strengthening of the ego, which, as with physical muscles, is the result of a lot of painful exercise and trial and error. The trials that Tamino and Pamina have to go through in the last part of this opera are meant to do just that: to strengthen their capacity to remain separate, to contain, and then to connect to the other.

This rather brief and cursory overview of *The Magic Flute* would be incomplete without mention of the crucial role of the father, represented by Sarastro, for both masculine and feminine development. In this story, we see how it is important for the father to pull the daughter away from the mother in order to create sufficient distance to help her develop her own feminine identity separate from that of the mother. Many fathers today feel unprepared for this task and fear this function. Subsequently, when a father's young daughter enters adolescence and begins to develop physically, he becomes frightened, distances himself from his daughter, and leaves her entirely in the care of her mother. This is a great loss for the daughter, who needs her father to be present as a representation of the otherness that he represents. In our story, Pamina only gradually recognizes the important role of Sarastro in making it possible for her to establish a relationship with Tamino.

The tasks that Sarastro and his followers set for Tamino reflect the vital role of the father in the development of a young man's masculine identity. These tasks force Tamino to differentiate himself from the mother and initiate him into the world of the fathers, a function that initiation ceremonies in traditional cultures served from the earliest of times. Initiation helps the young man transition from childhood or adolescence to adulthood and includes trials that confront the initiate with a symbolic death. This symbolic death is meant to mark the death of his former child or adolescent status and the birth of his new status as an adult and full member of community. A youth such as Tamino, under the dominance of the mother, needs the help of the father to enter into the world of adulthood. The trials set out for Tamino represent the tasks meant to build up his ego capacity to withstand separation, to contain the fear of death, and to have a more solid sense of his own identity.

In his first trial, Tamino must remain silent as he is confronted with frightening and then seductive images from the anima. This trial is meant to teach him to recognize anima manifestations and to resist being taken in by them, to contain them. In the second trial, Tamino must continue to remain silent but is allowed to play his flute. The sound of the flute leads Pamina to him. But because he cannot speak with her, she takes this to mean he no longer loves her. In addition to abandonment by mother, she is now convinced she has been abandoned by Tamino. This sends her into a profound crisis and suicidal despair. There is nothing left to live for. This is now Pamina's *nigredo.* She has sacrificed everything in order to follow her heart and now fears she has lost everything. The dagger meant to kill Sarastro now threatens to become the instrument she will use to kill herself. Only thanks to the intervention of the three children who represent Hermes-like messengers, does Pamina realize she has misinterpreted Tamino's silence and that he still loves her.

As Tamino prepares to undertake the third trial, Pamina calls from afar and joins him. Freed from the obligation of remaining silent, Tamino can now speak with her and express his love. Each having experienced *nigredo* and emerged from it, they can now unite, a form of *coniunctio,* to face the third trial together.

This third trial, described as having to face the four elements, is one of purification and of confronting their fear of death. It is symbolic of the trials they will face as individuals and as a couple: the fire of heated passions and the many opportunities to lose one's way in the heat of emotion or sexuality, as well as learning to navigate the murky waters of emotional needs and demands. In these trials, Tamino closes his eyes and lets the flute guide them. Pamina keeps her eyes open and guides them through the twisted path of fire and water, confronting the opposites. Here, it is the feminine that must lead, while the masculine connects to deeper inner levels that also guide, thanks to the flute. There is a mutuality where, though separate, they are also together, each contributing to the other on both inner and outer levels.

There is a parallel development of Papageno in the story who, in contrast to Tamino, represents the reluctant hero. Though he is content to stay in service to the Queen of the Night and is not very successful at any of the trials, he nevertheless has an experience of *nigredo* and meets an anima figure that corresponds to what he has been longing for. At the end of the opera we see Papageno with Papagena, both dressed in similar garb, happily surrounded by a large family of little Papagenos and Papagenas. Though Eric Neumann presents this as a development on a lower level, I prefer to see Papageno as a reminder that individuation is truly a very unique and individual process for each person. There is no right way, there is only one's own way to accomplish this lifelong task.

In the final scene, the sun rises and announces a fresh new world and the dawn of a new era. The coming together of Tamino and Pamina in a new way, the *coniunctio*, has led to a renewal symbolized by a new day. In the mythic trajectory of the night sea journey, the sun has conquered the darkness of the night once again.

One of Erich Neumann's major contributions to the field of analytical psychology has been the notion of the ego-self axis. In his book *The Child*, he describes the development of this axis from the moment of birth through infancy.[4] The process he outlines is both deeply personal but also very archetypal. While this fairy-tale-cum-opera clearly espouses the virtues linked with the emergent values of the Enlightenment at the time it was composed, on a deeper level it portrays the arduous developmental process of establishing a functional ego-self axis. Both protagonists, Tamino and Pamina, must leave the world of the mother and confront the fears of abandonment and isolation in order to find their own truth. The crucial role of the shadow in coming to one's truth in this process is highlighted by the figures of Papageno, as Tamino's happy-go-lucky

---

4   Erich Neumann, *The Child*, trans. R. Manheim (Boston: Shambhala, 1990).

and simplistic shadow, of Monostatos as the lustful, trickster shadow compensating for Sarastro's virtuousness, and of the shadow of the Queen of the Night in her ruthless drive for power. The various trials each protagonist has to endure highlight the idea that alignment of the ego-self axis is a process entailing detachment and suffering and requiring containment, time, and space for reflection and introspection, in order to be able to listen to one's inner compass and to learn to differentiate between what one has been taught, what one has learned, and what one needs to learn anew.

The image of the last trial where Tamino closes his eyes and plays the flute while Pamina guides him through the challenges of the four elements is a wonderful image for the new alignment along the ego-self axis that has been established and also a fitting image for what the new order, the *coniunctio*, at the end of the story represents.

Erich Neumann's article on *The Magic Flute* was written a number of years before his untimely death, and it seems very likely that this opera with its rich array of archetypal images provided him with guiding images that contributed to the formulation of his ideas on the development of the ego-self axis.

A Brief Comment on Neumann and His Essay "On Mozart's *Magic Flute*"

Debora Kutzinski

I was asked to add some remarks to Tom Kelly's lecture on Neumann and *The Magic Flute.*

Erich Neumann's interpretation of Mozart's *The Magic Flute* is entirely archetypal, going from the matriarchal stage to patriarchy and to a *coniunctio*, seeing the feminine as equal, and sometimes leading the masculine aspects.

The first part emanates from the mythologem of Demeter and Kore. Kore, the only daughter of the Queen of the Night, is abducted by an evil sorcerer. The queen sends a young prince to bring her back. She provides him with a companion, the magic flute, and three boys—the guiding principle—to show him the way. She is the figure who causes the movement and development of the entire story.

The genius of Mozart creates a complete change and transformation: the evil sorcerer turns out to be the high priest of the temple of Isis, who with the wholly male brotherhood abducted the daughter of the queen for the sake of her education and development. The temple is the Temple of Wisdom, wherein Tamino and Pamina ask to be initiated into the brotherhood.

Two centuries before the teachings of Jung and Neumann, Mozart's unconscious already showed the way of Western culture and the emergence of the feminine aspect of the soul.

For Neumann, the Queen of the Night, that is, the Great Mother, is the dominant figure in the opera. In his essay "On Mozart's 'Magic Flute,'" Neumann writes that artists are the Great Mother's most beloved children.[1] Erich was surely one of them. If you read his essay on *The Magic Flute, Amor and Psyche*, his work about da Vinci, Georg Trakl, and Henry Moore, you cannot avoid hearing the artist, no less than the psychologist.

I would like to bring up something that is less known about Neumann, an interpretation of part of *The Trial* by Frantz Kafka. I am personally very close to Kafka, not only because I think he is one of the greatest writers, but also because I lived in his apartment in the Old Town of Prague, behind the famous clock, as a child. The Nazis did not allow it to be known that this was Kafka's apartment, but after the war it turned out that this was the place where Kafka lived. It is now a museum.

Neumann's interpretation of a chapter of *The Trial*, "Before the Law," was not incidental. I think it brings out the essence of his personality.

The story is well known. There is a simple man from the countryside who arrives before the Gate of the Law. The gate is open. He bows down and sees inside the light of a fire and wants to enter. But in front of the gate stands a guard. The guard doesn't see the fire because he stands with his back to the inside of the law and says, "Not yet."

Neumann's interpretation is that the guard is the representative of the collective cultural attitude, the culture in which Kafka lived in Prague.

---

1   "Those beloved of the Feminine, the Queen of the Night, are the poets and the singers, the musicians of the heart, who not only bring the silence of the feminine darkness to the light of rational recognition and illumination but also let it resound and make music." Erich Neumann, "On Mozart's 'Magic Flute,'" in *The Fear of the Feminine and Other Essays on Feminine Psychology (1950–1959)* (Princeton, NJ: Princeton University Press, 1994), 164.

So the man sits down and waits—days, weeks, months, years. From time to time he asks, "Can I enter?" Every time, the guard responds, "Not yet."

At the end of his life, when his eyes are already closing, he asks the guard, "Tell me, all the time I was sitting here waiting. Nobody entered. For whom was this gate open?" The guard says, "For you. And now I am going to close it."

This is the central and most important part of *The Trial*, because it explains why Josef K., the protagonist, was executed in the end.

Neumann's interpretation is religious. The law is the law of God. The gate is open for everyone. There is only one thing: you have to shove aside your collective being and enter individually. The gate is open.

I think Neumann arrived at this gate early in his youth. He bowed down and he saw the light, he saw the fire. He shoved the guard aside and entered. He stayed there, I believe, until the end of his life. Inside, he could be himself. He could live his Self, and he could be together with his inner Godhead. I believe we are the beneficiaries of this. In my opinion, his last Eranos lectures were his greatest work, especially "The Psyche as the Place of Creation." It is difficult to read. In this essay he went very far. He went further than Jung. Sometimes I ask myself a painful question: Could it be that he paid for this with his life, dying so early, at age fifty-five? Did he come too close to the Great Mother? And she, as the goddess of death, loved him not wisely, but loved him too well, and took him away into her arms.

He died on November 5, 1960. The pity of it!

Three days after his death, I saw him, walking slowly in a shoulder-high golden field. The wind was playing in his hair. A colleague and friend of mine, Michal, who also died early, sat beside me. I pushed her and exclaimed, "Michal! Michal! Quickly, have a look, he is alive, he is alive! He just walks now in other fields."

PART VII. CLINICAL CONTRIBUTIONS

Erich Neumann's Concept of *Distress-Ego*

Rina Porat

Erich Neumann's last work, his unfinished book *The Child*, was published in English in 1973—thirteen years after his death. Although this book is considered the least coherent of all his writings, it offers significant contributions both to the theory of child development and to clinical practice that deepen our understanding of psychopathology, especially the disorders rooted in the primary stage of life.

Carola Meier-Seethaler published an article in 1983 that appreciatively presented Neumann's contribution to the psychopathology of child development. Yet, Neumann has not gained the acknowledgment his writings on this topic deserve. In my clinical work both with adults and children, I have come to appreciate and value Neumann's developmental perspective, including his rich symbolic and archetypal perceptions. It has proven helpful to follow and accompany my patients' individual processes and unique journeys.

In this paper I chose to present a small but important part of Neumann's theory on child development, focusing on the primal mother-child relationship and the development of a *distress-ego*, as the result of a disturbed primal relationship.

The Mother-Child Primal Relationship

As in his other theories of development, outlined in *The Origins and History of Consciousness* and "The Stages of Woman's Development," Neumann, in *The Child*, emphasizes the archetypal roots of child development. Whereas other developmental disciplines in psychology concentrate primarily on external, environmental factors, such as the consequences of early mother deprivation or absence on the child's development, Neumann adopts a Jungian perspective that focuses on internal psychic factors. He investigates disorders in the relationship to the mother who is present, focusing on unconscious, archetypal factors and illustrating their strong impact on the course of development.

The basic assumptions of analytical psychology as regards human development are that the unconscious and the Self predate consciousness and the ego. In the beginning the world is mythological, and reality is archetypal. Neumann writes, "The archetypal structural elements of the psyche are psychic organs upon whose functioning the well-being of the individual depends and whose injury has disastrous consequences."[1]

Neumann begins his theory of the child's development from this deepest layer of the psyche, the archetypal layer of the collective unconscious. He says, "The mother dominates the early development of the human individual just as the matriarchal world, in which the unconscious is paramount and ego-consciousness is still undeveloped, dominates the psychology of primitive cultures."[2] This sentence portrays an early stage of being in which there exists a relationship of dominance and dependency. The archetypal mother, or matriarchal consciousness, dominates a new born individual and an early collective, both in a dependent embryonic stage.

---

1   Erich Neumann, *The Origins and History of Consciousness* (Princeton, NJ: Princeton University Press, 1970), xv.
2   Erich Neumann, *The Child*, trans. R. Manheim (Boston: Shambhala, 1990), 7.

Neumann chooses the Uroboros, the round, tail-eating snake, as the "container" to symbolize the maternal womb. By labeling the initial stage of development "the Uroboric stage," Neumann describes a unitary state of being in which the individual (the child), the collective (humanity), and consciousness (the ego) are contained and embraced by the Great Mother, by nature, and by the oceanic unconscious.

Based on Adolf Portmann's approach and observations, Neumann adopts the notion that what characterizes human development, from the very beginning, is a unique dependency without which the infant can't survive. Comparing the human baby to other newborn creatures in nature reflects the infant's initial lower level of maturity and its stronger needs for containment and protection for a longer period of time. According to Portmann, the human embryo, in addition to the nine months it spends in the womb, needs another year to attain a similar degree of maturity.[3] In this postnatal embryonic phase the child is still contained within its mother though its body is already born. Neumann says: "In mythological terms, the ego is still contained in the Uroboros, and the environing mother is, for the embryo, containing vessel and world in one."[4]

Neumann describes the mother-child relationship in this phase by applying concepts like *a primary unity, dual union, living in an archetypally determined unitary reality.* In other words, the primal relationship in the first stage is a specific and unique archetypal situation in which "a not yet individualized being" (the baby) in the pre-ego phase is joined with an "archetypally functioning being" (the mother) in a unified field. The mother, in this Uroboric pre-ego stage, is everything for the child; she is the "inside," the "outside," the other, and the Self. This state of being in a *participation mystique* with the mother is perceived as the Garden of Eden, a perfect world, with no tension and filled with Eros. For the

---

3   A. Portmann, *Animals Are Social Beings* (New York: Viking Press, 1961).
4   Neumann, *The Child*, 12.

child this experience has a strong impact on its future development (progressive influence), and it is always the source of eternal nostalgia (regressive influence).

It is vitally necessary and helpful to the normal development of the child that the unconsciously directed behavior of the personal mother coincides with the Mother archetype. In other words, the personal mother will adopt the archetypal roles of the Great Good Mother which contains, nourishes, and protects the child both physically and psychically. Experiencing this ongoing care within a safe and tender shelter provides the child with a feeling of confidence in an orderly world, as well as relatedness to it. Neumann calls this order in the matriarchal stage an *Eros-order*, whereas the later order in the patriarchal stage is based on the Logos principle. In "The Moon and Matriarchal Consciousness," Neumann refers to the Eros character of the matriarchal consciousness as wisdom of the unconscious and the instincts of life, of creativity, of relatedness and love.[5]

One of Neumann's most important theoretical contributions is highlighting the dependency of the development of the ego-Self axis on the primal relationship. The primal relationship can either build or damage the child's relations with the most essential aspects of life: relation with the body, with the Self and the unconscious, relation with the other, and with the world. In Neumann's words: "The primal relationship is the ontogenetic basis for being-in-one's-own-body, being-with-one Self, being-together, and being-in-the-world."[6]

In the Uroboric stage, the mother functions as externalized Self that regulates almost at once any physical and psychic disturbances, thereby restoring the well-being and harmony of the baby. Existence in a maternal order at this stage does not mean that the world is seen only in the image

---

5 In E. Neumann, *The Fear of the Feminine and Other Essays on Feminine Psychology (1950–1959)* (Princeton, NJ: Princeton University Press, 1994), 81–118.
6 Neumann, *The Child*, 26.

of the Great Good Mother. The Great Mother contains life and death, day and night; "but the day rises from the darkness of night and this great matriarchal power is always trustworthy."[7] The Great Mother maintains the eternal cycle in an indestructible order.

The child in the primal relationship can feel pain, anxiety, or hunger, but these and other negative feelings are balanced by the good aspect of the maternal, so that despite these unpleasant experiences the child does not lose the feeling of shelter and security.

Normal child development, guaranteed by a secure primal relationship, culminates in the formation of a positive integral ego, which emerges out of the mother-child union. This is an important step in the development of the child that marks the beginning of separation from the mythic mother-child union and their unitary reality. The ego becomes more autonomous and active and starts to assimilate negative experiences. This gradually becomes the ego pole of the Self-ego axis, the Self being the ground to which the psyche is rooted. The development of the integral ego begins in the Uroboric phase of the primal relationship, but it is only in the second matriarchal phase, still dominated by the Mother archetype, that it achieves a more central position.

To sum up: normal development leads to automorphism, to a formation of a stable ego-Self axis, to sociability, to an integral ego, and to adaptation to the environment. This development, according to Neumann, is based on and guided by a relationship of love and confidence and not forced by a negative withdrawal of love.

Disturbances of the Primal Relationship

In turning to primal relationship disturbances, there is a great diversity of deviations from the archetypal constellation that can result in various disorders and symptoms. In this paper, I present what Neumann termed *distress-ego*.

---

7   Ibid., 55.

Where the primal relationship is disturbed, the predominance of negative experiences risks to flood the ego, dissolve it, or give it a negative charge. Neumann calls the ego of a child who has had a negative primal relationship a distress-ego, because its experiences of the world, the Thou, and the Self are characterized by distress and doom. According to Neumann, "the distress-ego is prematurely thrown back on itself; it is awakened too soon and *driven* to independence by the situation of anxiety, hunger and distress."[8]

A normal developmental process takes place in a protected and loving container where the child can rely confidently on the Good Mother and her care. In a disturbed primal relationship, being thrown out of the archetypal, safe container into cold reality, the child is prematurely forced to subsist on its own unequipped resources. It is left feeling unloved, empty, helpless, and anxious. In this state the terrible Negative Mother, "the witch," is constellated. According to Neumann, a central symptom of a disturbed primal relationship is the primal feeling of guilt. The child does not blame anyone. In the early pre-ego phase, the child's misfortune is solely absorbed into its own guilt. The experience is that "not being loved" is identical with being bad, abnormal, and cursed. Neumann says: "A child expelled from the primal relationship is expelled from the natural order of the world and comes to doubt the justification for its existence."[9] A negative situation without a safe container, without love, where no integral ego has been developed, in which the ego-Self axis has not been formed or has remained unstable, might lead to egoless apathy or to a reduction of the child's ego.

However, as Neumann emphasizes, negative development in the earliest and crucial phase of the primal mother-child relationship is by no means always identical with failure or guilt on part of the personal

---

8 Ibid., 77.
9 Ibid., 87.

mother. A disturbed primal relationship may be the consequence not only because of the mother's insufficient emotional attachment or rejection of her child, but whenever the child loses its mother, the foundation of its existence. Such a loss can be constellated by psychic inadequacy in the mother-child relationship or by her physical absence through death, sickness, or separation. In addition, the child can experience overwhelmingly negative life events, which may have nothing to do with the personal mother and for which she cannot be held responsible. For example, in the instance of prolonged trauma caused by continuous war events, in which reality and the world have become dangerous, both mothers and their children may develop distress-egos.

An anamnesis should therefore include both personal and collective, as well as conscious and unconscious archetypal factors. Neumann says that diagnosis of a damaged primal relationship and of a hungry, forsaken, lonely, and despairing child is never a sufficient basis for a prognosis. Although prognosis for treatment of early childhood disturbances is not considered promising, it is necessary to consider the extent of the damage, the time of its onset, its duration, and the way in which it has been compensated or harmed by the environment. Neumann suggests a different direction of therapy in these difficult cases. He reminds us that a child lives naturally in a symbolic world of mythological apperception. Hence, "a compensatory experience of the Good Mother as impersonal archetype of nature, or as tree, garden, forest, home or sky, is perfectly possible."[10] Any symbol of the Great Mother can embrace a child in need of help.

Sandplay Therapy

Sandplay therapy is an excellent tool that seems to fit the spirit of Neumann's suggestion for treating children. For adults, it can reopen a door to the "forgotten" symbolic world. Sandplay therapy, as developed

---

10 Ibid., 80.

by the Swiss Jungian Dora Kalff, is a preverbal and nonverbal technique reaching the unconscious depths of the psyche for the purpose of healing, growth, and personality development.[11] The roots of sandplay can be found in the symbolic play of childhood. It is an activity in which a shallow tray of sand (dry or wet) and a collection of miniature figures are used by patients, adults as well as children, to play out inner images, traumas, or fantasies. According to Jung, the psyche has an autonomous disposition to heal itself and to grow toward fullness.[12] Sandplay is a natural addition to his other techniques of active imagination. Jung talks about the importance of "living the symbolic life," an attitude considered indispensable for giving meaning and orientation. He said that only the symbolic life can satisfy the needs of the soul. Jung believed in the power of imagination and said: "Image and meaning are identical: and as the first takes shape, so the latter becomes clear."[13] The symbolic images and myths as the "primordial" language of the psyche are particularly necessary when working with injured and traumatized people. Ursula Wirtz claims that as the inner world of a traumatized person suffers from fragmentation, the imagination and fantasy are of utmost importance to heal the splits and integrate painful experiences. She writes: "Traumatic experiences attack the connection between body and mind, spirit and instinct, with the result that symbolic meaning-making function is severely impaired and individuals lose sense of animation, playfulness, and imagination."[14]

Through symbolic play, sandplay therapy can stimulate and revive the imaginative function in the wounded psyche of traumatized individuals. Given a free and protected therapeutic space, imagination is given full reign. Even forbidden, ugly, or frightening images can be expressed and transformed.

---

11 D. M. Kalff, *Sandplay: A Psychotherapeutic Approach to the Psyche* (Boston: Sigo Press, 1980).
12 C. G. Jung, "On the Nature of the Psyche" (1954), in *CW*, vol. 8 (Princeton, NJ: Princeton University Press, 1969).
13 Ibid., par. 402.
14 U. Wirtz, "The Symbolic Dimension in Trauma Therapy," *Spring: A Journal of Archetype and Culture* 82 (2009): 33.

Sandplay Images of Distress Ego Caused by Prolonged Trauma

The clinical examples presented here are not individual case studies, but sandplay scenes created by different children within their therapeutic processes, individually or in group settings. The sandplay images reflect common symbolic themes of children suffering from distress-ego due to a shared collective reality of prolonged trauma.

Prolonged trauma develops where people experience continuous stress, threat, violence, and recurring traumatic events over a period measured in years. Israel is a country in a chronic state of warlike events for more than sixty-five years, with intermittent periods of cease-fire, but not yet a real peace with surrounding neighbors. War events, especially where the front is very close to civilian communities, create extreme tension, anxiety, and serious psychological problems. Everyone on both sides of the conflict is affected, if not directly wounded and traumatized.

Living in Israel and working as a Jungian analyst and a sandplay therapist for many years, I have in the last decade become more involved with trauma, both treating patients and training therapists who live and work (like myself) in the southern part of Israel, which has become the region most impacted by Israeli-Palestinian conflicts and war. In addition, the Israel Sandplay Therapists Association (ISTA), following an initiative of mine, has developed a project in which volunteer therapists work with children living in one of the most severely missile-stricken places in Israel—the town of Sderot, less than a mile from Gaza.

For fifteen years, on an almost daily basis, Sderot has been targeted by missiles and mortars from Gaza. The citizens are exposed to sirens and code red alerts booming over loudspeakers, giving them 15–30 seconds to find safety in a bomb shelter. The entire population of about 25,000 people has suffered injury, loss, and psychological damage. Widespread trauma makes everyday life an emotional and economic hardship.

Many children have been referred to therapy, suffering severe symptoms that at face value are related to prolonged trauma: anxiety, attention disorder, bed wetting, lack of impulse control, withdrawal, and depression, as well as psychotic episodes. Almost all the children with whom we have worked, and their parents, were born in Sderot. There are many broken families, single mothers raising their children alone, and children living with grandparents in difficult physical conditions. Unemployment is high, and many are unable to work because of physical and psychiatric illness. Parents, especially mothers, tend to seek educational and psychological help primarily for their children, much less for themselves.

Yet, despite this reality, common to many of the long-term residents of Sderot and their children is a collective attitude or persona that conveys a complete lack of fear. They live in Sderot, refusing to leave their homes, and when interviewed, they deny any connection between their children's problems and symptoms and the anxiety caused by the bombings. It has become increasingly clear that the children we have worked with suffer from different degrees of distress-ego, as do most of their mothers. Most children were born into the reality of war. The mothers themselves have grown up in this unsafe reality and have been unable to supply a safe maternal container to their children. Archetypally speaking, on both the collective and the personal level, the egos of mothers and children were awakened too early and have been thrown into an unsafe reality, creating in them the need to build inner resources for survival.

Examples

The first two images were done by a man in his late forties. These are the only examples of sandplay by an adult; the others were created by children. I present these two scenes for two reasons: first, to illustrate that at any age human beings share a common archetypal ground from which the symbolic themes emerge and images, as their "messengers," are manifested. Second, for this person this was his first experience as an adult to play like a child and build in the sand. While words could not overcome the psychic barrier of the unconscious, the spontaneous images, involuntary unconscious products of the psyche, started a new dialogue, touching and expressing his early wounds and his distress-ego.

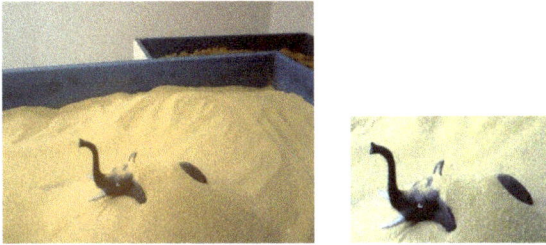

Fig. 1
TRYING TO BURY THE PAST. PHOTOS BY RINA PORAT

He created a scene (figure 1) in which a large elephant is almost entirely buried in the sand. He said: "I want to bury my past. It haunts me." This image and his association reflect his ongoing struggle to bury the past. However, closer observation of the image reveals that the elephant is not fully buried. The elephant, also known for its long memory, is still alive.

His second scene (figure 2) presents a baby with his mouth open and his eyes closed. He said: "This baby seems large, but he is empty inside." The man opened up the story of his life, revealing how he had been forced to grow up and take care of his family from the time he was nine years old, when his father had died. He struggled to survive while most of his life feeling empty and deeply depressed. He developed a distress-ego, and the baby, his primary childhood self, was buried for many years.

FIG. 2
THE SILENT SHOUT
OF A DISTRESS-EGO

The remaining images were created by different children, between eight and ten years old, victims of prolonged trauma and suffering from distress-ego. Some sandplay images illustrate some central motifs that reappear in many therapeutic processes, from the initial state of suffering through the emergence of new energies of healing and transformation.

The following types of scenes (figures 3–5), often created at the onset of therapy, portray terrifying attacks on humans and on the universe by archetypal forces or by natural disaster, such as earthquakes, floods, and tsunami. The attacks end up in total destruction, chaos, and annihilation. This motif reflects a state of anxiety, helplessness, and hopelessness where the inner psychic world and the external reality are perceived as unsafe and dangerous places. The images are of chaos, floods, and being devoured by the unconscious. The next two scenes (figures 6–7) present the beginning of getting help. There are survivors who rescue other people and animals.

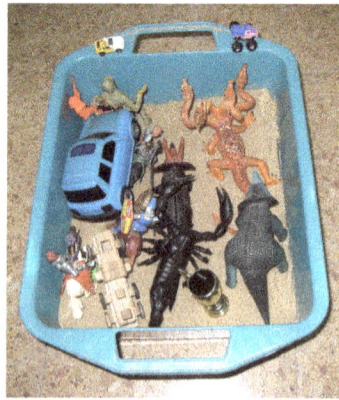

FIG. 3
ARCHETYPAL ATTACK ON THE WORLD

The theme of an abandoned baby or lost child appears in many dreams or sandplay images created both by adults (as in figure 2) and by children (as in figure 8). A baby or a child usually symbolizes the inner child, both the actual and the archetypal child. In the case of a distress-ego, the child is forsaken or neglected, its needs are ignored, its suffering is unheard, and all the gifts of the archetypal divine child are buried deep in the unconscious.

Fig. 4
Chaos and floods

Fig. 5
Being devoured by the unconscious

FIG. 6
GETTING HELP

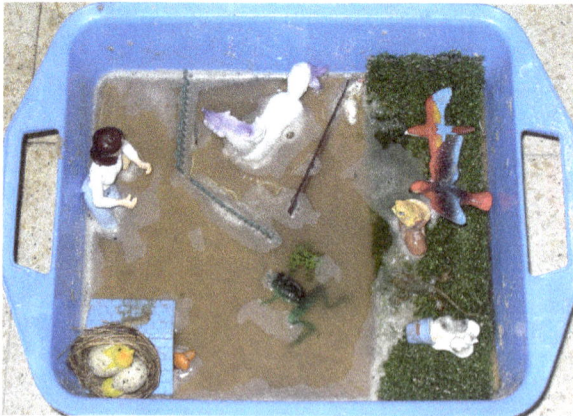

FIG. 7
RESCUE

The motif of rescuing the abandoned child (figure 9) reveals how sometimes a miracle happens; where one part of nature fails (the human mother), another part of nature brings rescue and redemption.

The next image (figure 10) was created by a girl who said: "Many times I wanted to build a hospital … Now I did it … This is a hospital built deep in the earth like an atomic shelter … It is the most protected place in the world … there are also guards around." This hospital, where treatment is given and healing takes place, is a secure and safe container. This place is indestructible both from nature's disasters and from external aggressive life events. It seems that this is a place where deep wounds can be cured.

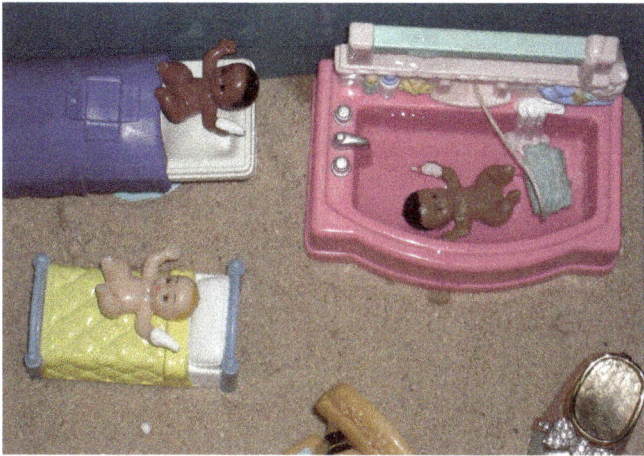

FIG. 8

BABIES LEFT ALONE WITH NO PROTECTION

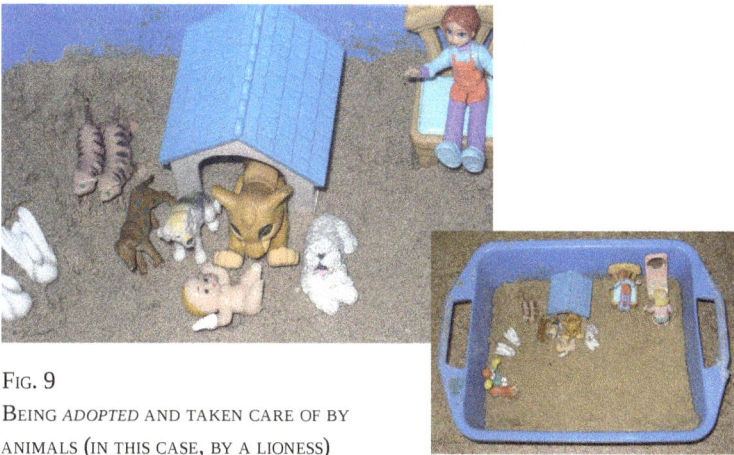

FIG. 9

BEING *ADOPTED* AND TAKEN CARE OF BY ANIMALS (IN THIS CASE, BY A LIONESS)

FIG. 10
THE MOST PROTECTED
HOSPITAL IN THE WORLD

The last images—symbolic manifestations of peaceful nature, of primary Self, and of Eros, as compensatory healing experiences for the distress-ego (figures 11–13)—can be seen as manifestations of the Self that depict a healthier and more solid ego-Self axis that has overcome deep wounding.

FIG. 11
THE
UROBORIC
GARDEN
OF EDEN
(PRIMARY
SELF)

FIG. 12

FINDING TREASURES

FIG. 13

THE HEART RESTORING EROS

In Conclusion

Neumann's unique and original mythological-archetypal perspective to development is of great value for understanding the primary stage of the mother-child relationship that takes place in an archetypally determined unitary reality. For the normal development of the child to take place, the maternal vessel has to provide both physical and psychical nourishment and protection in a loving embrace. This state of matriarchal Eros-order establishes in the child feelings of confidence in the continuous motherly care. Normal development leads to automorphism, to a formation of a stable ego-Self axis, and to an integral ego.

In cases where the primal relationship has been disturbed, the child, who has prematurely been thrown out of the archetypal container into cold and unsafe reality, develops a distress-ego. The child has lost the foundation of its existence and is left feeling unloved, guilty, empty, helpless, unstable, and anxious.

According to Meier-Seethaler, clinical attempts to treat young children suffering from distress-ego have largely been unsuccessful.[15] Neumann suggested a different direction for therapy. On the assumption that the mother-child relationship is archetypally constellated, he believed that an archetypal approach is needed for therapy. While he was looking for compensatory experiences or images of the Great Good Mother, sandplay therapy offers a technique of free imagination and symbolic play that reaches the preverbal layers of the psyche. The primordial language of the psyche, the language of images and symbols, is the original and natural language when we deal with the archetypal, primary mother-child relationship. As has been briefly illustrated, it seems, as well, necessary for the treatment and the healing of victims of prolonged trauma and distress-ego.

---

15   Carola Meier-Seethaler, "*The Child*, Erich Neumann's Contribution to the Psychopathology of Child Development," *Journal of Analytical Psychology* 27 (1982): 357–379.

Can You Hear My Voice?

Batya Brosh Palmoni

O ne of the central questions in understanding the female subject is related to the possibility of giving women a unique, authentic voice. How can women's voice find its place in a society where men, to this day, are privileged? Therefore the question, Can you hear my voice? is relevant to the entire issue of understanding the feminine.

To pose a question is to try to bring something that is unconscious into consciousness. By using Neumann's understanding and writing on women, I will focus on the situation of women and the feminine.

In Jung's writing about the feminine, we find the absence of a realistic autonomous woman.[1] When Jung wrote about contemporary women, he seems to have been writing mainly about his own anima, experienced in projection, loathed and loved. He did not write about the real other, the embodied woman.

Let us imagine the encounter between an experienced woman, the biblical Naomi, and a young woman, Ruth, who was walking toward Naomi on her way back from the granary. "Who art thou, my daughter?" Naomi asked. And Ruth replied, "Are you speaking to me? What's happened to you? What a strange question to ask."[2] These two questions

---

1   C. G. Jung, *Aspects of the Feminine* (London: Routledge, 2008).
2   Here I paraphrase the biblical story of Naomi and Ruth.

represent central issues in any psychoanalysis. While the analyst strives to understand the patient, the patient may question the analyst's ability to truly understand and help.

Ultimately, the particular accomplishments and the personality of each woman, which cannot be reduced to the common denominator of a group or a gender, have not only become possible but have also been proudly proclaimed. It is because I am myself, and specifically myself, that I, as the analyst, am able to ask the question, Who are you? How can we help a woman find her singularity? How can we help women work toward unique, innovative creations and leave their mark on the human condition? How is it possible to preserve each woman's uniqueness within the diversity of the group? Neumann guides us in helping the mature woman discover her authentic self and voice.

Countless theories, articles, and research papers have been written about the feminine subject; here I will discuss the notable contribution of Erich Neumann to understanding the unique psychology of woman. This is not only a discussion about women: Neumann helps us observe, listen, identify, and understand the roots and the unique character of the woman's voice. It is important to remember that psychological knowledge was largely born by means of the twisting and turning of women in therapy.

We focus here on the correspondence between Neumann and Jung. In reading the letters, we discover a wealth of issues that occupied the two during the period of their acquaintance. Undoubtedly, women played an important role in the lives of both these men, and their work involved encounters with many women. There is a great difference between the women who surrounded Jung and those with whom Neumann was associated during his life in Israel. However, both men had a powerful attraction for women.

I was briefly acquainted with Erich Neumann's wife, Julia. I went to her twice for a hand test, and I was greatly surprised by the house on

Gordon Street with its huge library. Julia's hand tests and the conversations that followed were a turning point in my life. I had been in analysis for many years with Debora Kutzinski, one of Erich Neumann's first students, and after that I continued analysis with Ella Amitzur. Although these two women differed greatly from one another, both were Neumannites in spirit and soul.

Erich Neumann wrote extensively about the feminine. I will refer to three concepts that are central to understanding the feminine, which represent his unique perspective. The concepts I will discuss are dynamic, developmental, and spiritual, but they do not encompass the entirety of his writings and work about women.

As a point of departure: in all his work, Neumann referred to the feminine aspects of the psyche and the matriarchal layers as a *psychological* finding, not a sociological base. As the cultural researcher Camille Paglia wrote, he did not long for the days of matriarchy in the style of the soap opera.[3] It is important to emphasize this distinction. According to Paglia, Neumann cited and praised Bachofen's pioneering work in prehistory but was careful to note that the latter's idea of matriarchy (as Neumann explains in *The Great Mother*) must be understood psychologically rather than sociologically, and Neumann held that the matriarchal stage refers to a structural layer and not to any historical epoch.

The first concept I would like to discuss is taken from Neumann's *The Great Mother.* In this book, he thoroughly analyzed and presented a comprehensive study of the archetype of the Great Mother. Neumann stressed the dual element of the nature of the Great Mother, which led him to understand the two main facets of the feminine, or as he put it, the two characters of the feminine: the basic elementary character and the varying, transformative character.

---

3   C. Paglia, "Erich Neumann: Theorist of the Great Mother," *Arion* 13(6): 9–10.

The feminine elementary character can be likened to the Great Round, which tends to hold fast to everything that springs from it, and everything born of it belongs to it and remains subject to it. The elementary character is a great container. The transformative character of the feminine, on the other hand, is the expression of a dynamic element, a drive toward motion and change. The two characters interpenetrate and combine with one another in many ways. Both belong to a dynamic understanding of the feminine personality.

These concepts of the elementary and the transformative character allow us a dynamic understanding of the feminine personality. These two different characters are essential to understanding women, and their meaning is completely different from that ascribed to an archetype, which has a positive and a negative pole. The elementary and the transformative are intertwined. Sometimes they appear together, providing a fascinating perspective, in my view, on women's distress, pain, and dreams.

I would like to emphasize another concept, which is not specifically associated with women but ties all the elements together: the concept that Neumann calls "the unitary reality."[4] Neumann coined this term in order to conceptualize the reality that exists constantly in the collective unconscious. In the unitary reality, the polarization between object and subject, between external and internal, between psyche and world does not yet exist. The world and the psyche are experienced as a unity, the way the small child and the mystic, as well as the creative person experience it. This contrasts with the polar reality that is familiar to ego consciousness, which divides and separates. In his Eranos lecture on man and meaning, Neumann broadened the concept of unitary reality, claiming that it exists not only in the archetypal field but also in all planes of reality, including the plane of consciousness.[5] Thus he did not see paradoxical phenomena as projections but rather as experiences of unitary reality.

---

4   Erich Neumann, *The Child*, trans. R. Manheim (Boston: Shambhala, 1990), 11–12.
5   Erich Neumann, "Man and Meaning," in *The Place of Creation* (Princeton, NJ: Princeton University Press, 1989), 203–263.

Neumann suggests four stages in the psychological development of women.[6] From my perspective as a therapist, the most interesting is the final stage of women's development. In this last stage, the woman, in her process of individuation, seeks her feminine self. After submitting to the father, devoting herself to man, and encountering the animus, she sets out on a quest for her feminine self. This is the last and most important stage in the journey. Importantly, Neumann comments that the entire problem of femininity lies in the last two stages: the woman will either devote herself and remain related only to patriarchal culture and maleness, or she will set out on her own independent journey.

Anyone who is engaged in therapy with women knows that this is a critical stage in female development, both for understanding the woman and regarding her potential for change and development. The possibility of these stages materializing is associated with the triumph over symbiosis with the masculine. The dreams that I present below demonstrate this experience, the process of liberation and the search for every woman's authentic voice or uniqueness.

In the context of Neumann, it is interesting to consider two important female psychoanalysts, who have had a strong voice in understanding and creating a central theory regarding the feminine subject. They are Julia Kristeva and Luce Irigaray.

Julia Kristeva assumed that before entering the symbolic stage, the child, whether a boy or a girl, must give up the previous stage, which she called semiotic, that is, the preverbal stage that precedes the symbolic stage.[7] According to Kristeva, the authentic maternal discourse is beyond signification; it is lost when the subject first begins to speak. Kristeva perceived the creative maternal element, which she called the semiotic, as

6   Erich Neumann, *The Fear of the Feminine and Other Essays on Feminine Psychology (1950–1959)* (Princeton, NJ: Princeton University Press, 1994), 3–63.

7   J. Kristeva, *Desire in Language: A Semiotic Approach to Literature and Art* (New York: Columbia University Press, 1980).

an unconscious subversive dynamic that challenges paternal signification, or the symbolic order. She claimed that the infant's entry into the social-linguistic contract of the group entails the sacrifice of the maternal body. Thus, a form of original communication with the mother is given up, and it remains subliminally active throughout life. Kristeva saw artists, such as poets and painters, as having the potential to bridge the split between maternal and paternal.

I would like to emphasize that according to my understanding of Neumann's article on the psychological stages of women's development, he not only saw a possibility of giving up the maternal, as Kristeva argues, but saw woman's development as different from that of man: she remains connected to the feminine territory and later, after she discovers her masculine aspects, integrates the two elements in her psyche to become unique and authentic and sets out on her own independent path.

Irigaray's central concept, the imaginary, suggests that the masculine imaginary dominates our culture. She writes that we must uncover the feminine imaginary and bring it into the language. The masculine imaginary has reduced us to silence. The imaginary is the domain of prelinguistic specular identification.[8]

Again, what I see and understand is Neumann's fascinating approach, which does not direct us to look back and redeem what was repressed, as Kristeva and Irigaray do, but holds that following a process of dedication and submission to the masculine, the woman must continue to move forward toward her feminine self.

Each of the dreams presented below was related to me by a different woman who was in treatment with me. In each case, I begin by presenting the dream as the woman told it to me, followed by my commentary.

---

8   L. Irigaray, *Ce sexe qui n'en est pas un*, trans. D. Lieber (Tel-Aviv: Resling, 2003).

Dream 1: A Strange Sight

> Students of mine are in a field next to the place where I lived in the past. I'm standing in the background. Suddenly, an animal rapidly flies toward us from the sky. I see that it's a porcupine. It dives toward prey on the land, rummages, and extracts a large rabbit.
>
> The porcupine becomes a human body, with only the head remaining that of a porcupine.
>
> It grabs the rabbit in its hands and places it on the ground but then puts it on its back, with its four legs moving. I begin to approach with other people, and then I see that the man-porcupine has evaporated.
>
> I felt tremendous excitement.

This dream was dreamt by a patient who was about fifty years old and in an ongoing existential crisis. She awoke from the dream very excited.

There is one strong, clear image—the transformation of the porcupine. It begins its journey as an animal coming down from the sky and slowly becomes human—a person with the head of a porcupine. The entire scene takes place in front of the dreamer, who experiences an incredibly exciting sight. Besides the role of the porcupine as an ancient image of the womb, turning what it represents in the dreamer's psyche into emotional content is the very purpose of the therapeutic process.[9] In other words, an unfamiliar content can become understood and humanized. This is a moment of birth of the transformative character, which in the marvelous language of the dream also redeems the elementary character represented

---

9   See M. A. Gimbutas, *The Language of the Goddess: Unearthing the Hidden Symbols of Western Civilization* (New York: HarperCollins, 1989), 256.

by the rabbit. In this dream, there is a discovery of two characteristics of the female, the porcupine as transformative and the rabbit as elementary, instinctual fertility.

This is also the moment when it is possible to look at the relationship between these two elements of the dreamer and complete the pictures of life that are spread out before us. This is the moment when we hold the porcupine that becomes a person, the rabbit, and the entire emotional event is an experience of the unitary reality that occurs in the ego consciousness of the dreamer. The dreamer attributes to the porcupine the way in which she gives birth to her thoughts, her thinking function, while she sees the rabbit, which runs around and gives birth to several offspring at the same time, as representing her emotional function. This is also reminiscent of Kristeva and the semiotic; the entire image is free of words and does not belong to the symbolic system of reason and order, but is semiotic.

Irigaray's concept of feminine imagination applies here as well. However, in my view, Neumann's concept of unitary reality offers the broadest possibility for therapy. What happens here is the coexistence and existential interdependence of the human, the porcupine, and the rabbit. This is the moment when the elementary and transformative are partners in the experience of a single, whole unitary reality. The powerful emotions in the dream belong to the experience of an encounter with the religious self. That which seems to be eternally separate returns and becomes attached.

Dream 2

> There is a sacrificial offering of victims in a large hall, resembling a central temple hall. The victim is a blonde girl, ten years old with glasses and pigtails. There is a search for more volunteers, but no one volunteers. In the end, I volunteer.

> *There is a large audience standing around observing the sacrificial victims. I too am standing around, waiting; I do not know what to do or why I agreed to participate. I look over at the young girl. A nurse comes over and injects her with an anesthetic. A struggle begins from within me. I tell myself "I'm not hanging around here anymore." I decide to leave. I move to the next room, watch a ceremony of women my own age, members of a kibbutz. They are dancing in their work clothes. Their movements are those of a very sensual, seductive Middle Eastern dance. The women create two rows and lead me out of the room.*

This dream has many meanings. It contains a tremendous pain of women and actually constitutes a sort of document of all that is taken from us by the culture in which we live. However, more than anything else, one can see here the image what Neumann refers to in the stages of women's development; the feminine redemption does not lie in devoting oneself to the animus but in the effort to free oneself from everything that has bound us until now. And the path to release from the patriarchal temple is the new feminine path, the one that leads the woman to an encounter with her feminine self.

Above all, she refuses to be a victim. If this is not possible, she will not be able to do anything. She must rescind her offer to volunteer and remember that she is not hopeless. The image of leaving the temple expresses the struggle against a central principle of our culture, a culture based upon victimization—a culture that more than anything else sacrifices our natural rhythms, the tempo of our bodies. The dreamer was raised and lives on a kibbutz, that is, a collective, ideology-minded society. The center of the kibbutz is the dining room, where they conduct the ideological and social life of this collective community. From this central place emerges a new, independent woman. Her departure is based upon strength and empowerment—busy women and working. Nevertheless, these are pathbreaking women who prepare the way out. They are expanding the boundaries of their lives, refusing to be victims any longer. Only when they begin to nurture their imaginative and daring aspirations for themselves will they be able to dream the dreams that are free of chains.

This dream bears the strength of a myth surrounding death and rebirth. A mother's loss of her daughter, a daughter's loss of her mother— that is the core of the feminine tragedy. This tragedy is expressed in the myth of Demeter and Persephone. The true significance of the mysterious ritual lies in the renewed combination of death and birth, at a time when it seems that the patriarchal rift has sentenced them to eternal separation. However, the birth in the dream has yet to occur. The transition from being speechless to verbalization is accompanied by an empowering experience and greater self-esteem.

Dream 3

> This is a woman's journey through a Nordic landscape. The journey is long and exhausting. It is cold. We arrive at a large castle. The objective of the journey is to be with women at the time of birth. It is morning. I awaken, look out the window, and see a strong flow of water entirely covering the road to the castle. All around there are green hills and strongly flowing water. Until a birth occurs, we will not be able to leave the castle. I understand the time has come; it is time to give birth. The castle is high. From the upper level, I am able to see the other levels below, full of beds. The entire group remains; no one continues on. There is a tremendous sense of joy and excitement.

From within a neglected and abandoned home of the initial dream, we have reached this point. What was born? The newborn is a new feminine consciousness that is attempting to rescue itself from the patriarchal prison, its imprisonment in the language, outlook, and expectations of the male world. However, the castle is closed not only to women; it is closed to both men and women. Only through communication and partnership during the same journey will a new consciousness be made possible. The birth of the divine child and the birth of all the developments that we find portrayed in this dream are now experienced as an encounter of the woman's ego and her feminine self as Neumann described it.

Dream 4

> I am touring the Golan Heights with my family. We come to
> a grove of oak trees. Our trip is a guided tour and the guide
> is an elderly gentleman, one of the founders of the kibbutz.
> We come to a bare spot in the forest and look up at the sky.
> I see a flock of storks far off in the horizon, approaching
> us. As they approach, I begin to understand that their flight
> represents symbols or letters. As they draw closer, the birds
> become herons and create the shape of a Star of David, with
> its sides moving in a constant right-left spiraling motion. As
> I look more carefully, I can see that the formation is made of
> the letters of "Hear O Israel." I am amazed! Our guide has
> a pair of old, large and heavy binoculars, with glass lenses.
> As I look through them, the entire vision disappears. I feel a
> sense of disappointment; that I missed something.

This is a dream of revelation, such as described by Erich Neumann in his essay on mystical man.[10] When a woman enters the depths of her

---

10   Erich Neumann, "Mystical man," in *The Mystic Vision: Papers from the Eranos Yearbooks*, ed. J. Campbell, 375–415 (Princeton, NJ: Princeton University Press, 1968).

unconscious in order to meet her non-ego, the search may lead her to a revelation, which stimulates her religious aspects. Observing the vision through a man's binoculars conceals the vision. However, the image has already risen, it has already been called up from the unconscious, it has already changed the accumulative state of consciousness. "Hear O Israel" is the Jewish faith in a nutshell. It is a most profound statement about loving and believing in God. The dream creates a moment of intimate union of the ego and self with the surrounding world, experienced as absolute certainty of safety. Meaning of life is here reconnected with the unitary reality, and the split between the ego and the self is repaired. The world is rebuilt, so we can feel at one with the other, as well as with the numinous.

Every step in life is a lengthy process of change. However, this process does not progress at a constant rate. Throughout life there are many different milestones; some are quite close to one another, while others are far apart and the journey between them is exhausting and difficult. These milestones are also the ceremonies that help us declare that this part of the path is complete, that it is time to move on. Between one milestone and another, life is regenerated. This process cannot occur in a vacuum. As Erich Neumann wrote, individuation cannot occur in a vacuum, individuals develop within their group. This fact also entails a moral commitment that forces the woman to create herself. The images that arose in these dreams show the psyche moving in the direction of a new integration and understanding of the feminine.

Dream 5

> *I enter a very narrow corridor that is lined with shelves made of thin pieces of wood. There are different dishes on the shelves. Old women are sitting on the floor under the shelves, working as they crouch. They are making pottery and their heads are covered with scarves. They sit hunched over. From*

there the corridor leads into a larger room—and in the room
there are shelves covered with curtains; something covered
with cloth is standing on the floor, in the center. I think these
are dishes, too. I leave the room to a sort of large patio,
where there is an olive tree, and I see a bright, blinding light.
And then I see a mountain, and I understand that the light is
coming out of the mountain, and I see women walking up the
mountain, and I tell myself in the dream: I love God so much.

All the women in the dreams that I have presented were in the process of individuation and in the second half of their lives. In this last dream there are, of course, many feminine symbols—pots, and the making of pots. I will not address these subjects here but rather comment on Neumann. Among other things, my understanding of this dream includes components of the elementary character that envelops the dream from all sides in the birth canal in which she walks. But this covering also holds the ability to see the light coming from the mountain and draw the woman in the birth canal to the spiritual experience of an inner love of God, a love so strong that it occurs in this dream. Here we find a description of the strength of women concealed in the unconscious that reaches far beyond those areas that we usually consider in a woman's development.

In addition to the stages of development of men that he discussed extensively in his book, *The Origins and History of Consciousness*, Neumann discussed the stages unique to the psyche of woman. Different theories of women and femininity very quickly lose their value due to the rapid changes in our culture. However, as I have attempted to show, despite the many years that have passed since, Neumann's writings on the subject remain remarkably relevant. As Paglia noted, his work may be a door leading to cooperation between the academic feminist movement and analytic psychology.

In closing, I would like to add something personal: Ruth the Moabite—the symbol and essence of biblical hospitality—was expected to convert in religion and language, to adopt a new people, nation, and homeland. It is important that women in therapy discover their own unique personal language, that they remain loyal to who they are. Alienation is essential to the process of analysis, in which we need to reinvent a personal private language with each patient, a flexible language that is not grounded in any one, singular meaning, a language that responds to the experience and style and personality of each and every individual patient. As I see it, this is particularly true with regard to female patients.

Neve Tzeelim:
A Field of Creation and Development

Rivka Lahav

It is a challenge to tell the story of Neve Tzeelim, which was a very innovative, creative, and dynamic treatment center that thrived for more than forty years on Jungian and Neumannian principles. It was designed, built, and conceptually directed by the head psychologist Marion Baderian, a Jungian analyst who was taught and inspired by Erich Neumann. While Neve Tzeelim continues as a treatment center, the Jungian principles have receded into the background.

Every part and detail in the place was planned with much consideration, and at the same time, things were always changing and the place was constantly altered and renewed. I will try to describe bits and pieces of the place, and hopefully some notion of it and its affinity to Erich Neumann's writings will come through.

In Hebrew Neve Tzeelim means "an oasis of acacia trees." The acacia tree is widespread in dry areas, in the desert, where water is rare. It traditionally symbolizes endurance of the soul and immortality. Neve Tzeelim operated as a place to provide children with emotional difficulties an opportunity to grow and develop in a rich enabling environment. Neve Tzeelim was referred to as the *maon*, which in Hebrew is a special word for "home." As the maon developed and changed, a special language emerged to describe its features. These words were saturated with meaning. Even for Hebrew speakers it takes a while to learn the meaning of the names given to places and activities in the maon. Naturally, it is difficult to translate them into another language.

Some Basic Facts about the Maon

This educational-therapeutic boarding school was established in 1953 by a group of educators and psychologists, some of whom had a Jungian orientation. From 1960 until 2003, the maon was directed by Marion Baderian, the head psychologist, who developed it and introduced many innovations. From 2003 on, the orientation of the maon has leaned more toward social psychology. Here I will focus on the years before 2003. The maon was intended for children with serious emotional problems and average or high intelligence. For some of the children, it was an alternative to hospitalization or postpsychiatric hospital treatment. Originally established for children from kibbutzim, it was later opened to all children in need and could house seventy-five children and adolescents, age ten to eighteen. For most of them it was a boarding school, but some local children came during the day, from 8:00 a.m. to 4:00 p.m.

The working staff in the maon belonged to three groups: the teachers, who had special education training; the therapists, mainly clinical psychologists and social workers; and the counselors. The entire staff worked collaboratively, sharing information, ideas, and creating a support system for the children. Marion Baderian was continuously informed about everything that went on in the maon and consulted on all the work conducted there.

The Maon's Basic Assumptions

Erich Neumann and Marion Baderian both left Germany and came to Israel because of the rise of Nazism. This cultural background is significant in Neumann's writing and was likewise significant in the way the maon was built and functioned. A great emphasis was put on creating a field of unitary reality in which the children's outer world and their inner worlds correspond with each other.

The maon was created according to these basic assumptions:

» Every area in a child's life is an opportunity for an educational-therapeutic growth process.

» The educational-therapeutic process is happening everywhere in the maon and at every hour, day and night.

» Every place in the maon is meaningfully designed, so the child is always in a meaningful and relating field.

» The aim of the maon is to help the child to develop a functioning ego and an autonomous stance, while relating to his or her inner and outer surroundings.

» The developing ego grows in a field that relates to various surroundings: inner surroundings—cognitive position, interests, health, and behavior; close surroundings—nuclear family, peer group, educators, and therapists; and circumference surrounding—the broad community, social-cultural environment, and natural surroundings.

The Structure and Dynamics of the Maon

The maon was organized in the form of different centers. Some of the centers were physical places with designated functions, and some were conceptual centers, not allocated to a single specific location. The centers had some common characterizations: an entrance room, in which the child planned its work at the center, and a main room, divided into work stations. Each center had a symbol, and the symbols, as did everything in the maon, evolved with time. Things changed as concepts developed and altered. Another characteristic of each center was the guide book, which described in detail the different activities and subjects that the center dealt with. In each center there was a record book in which every activity, and the way the activity was done by each child, was registered. For example, did the child work alone, with others, or in a group? Did the child study and learn on his or her own, taught by others, or teaching someone else? Was the child watching, being directed, or directing others? and so on. For some of the centers, their function and characteristics included the following.

A Center for the Reception of New Children (Merkaz Klita). The symbol of the New Children Reception Center was a tree. The root of the tree related to basic features describing each child, such as age, height, preferences, habits, likes and dislikes. The trunk of the tree related to the field which was to enable the child's ego to evolve. The branches of the tree related to other centers in the maon, waiting to be explored by the child when ready to embark on a journey of development.

The symbol of the tree relates to what Neumann would refer to as the ego-self axis and centroversion. The time of entering the maon was considered the "uroboric" stage, in which the child received special, individual care and treatment, both day and night. After a while, when getting used to the place, the child was free to go on and explore other areas. He or she was sent out from this first center on missions to learn about the other new centers.

A Center for the Study of Literature (Merkaz Bilush VeSipur). The symbol for the Center of Language and Literature was a dragon. It symbolizes the basic primitive foundation from which language arises. It deals with the mythological stories that are at the basis of every culture.

A Creative Center (Merkaz Yetzira). The symbol for the Center for Creativity for painting, music, and movement was of hands molding clay. It represents creative work with different materials, for example, wood, metal, fabric, papier-mâché, ceramics, and leather. The creative work in this center was for artistic purposes, as well as for helping to build and keep up the maon.

A Center for Learning Mathematical Principles (Merkaz Hashov Hashev). The emblem was here the owl of Athena.

A Center for Studying English (Merkaz Anglit), which was considered to be "an embassy to the wide world." The symbol was here a key that opens a gate to a castle.

A Workshop Center (Rahavat Itzuv), in which the children performed manual work and contributed to the building, maintenance, and safety of the maon. There were also centers pertaining to gardening, cooking, and physical activities.

One of the main important centers was the Home Center (Betili), which dealt with the children's living space: each room's design was tailored to the specific needs of each child. What took place with the child at the Home Center was meaningful, day and night. This meaningfulness of the day and night can be seen in the drawing of the Egyptian myth of the course of the sun. The maon's emphasis on meaningful activities of the day and the meaningful experience of the night was also evident in the prominence given to dreams in the therapeutic work.

Additional important centers evolved with time. The Center of Relationship (Merkaz Hityachasut) dealt with the social life in the maon, with the relationship of every child with itself, and the relationship between the child and his or her peers. At this center the children planned their day and checked the realization of the plans.

The Yard was also a center (Merkaz Hachatzer), in which many activities took place. One very important activity was Karoz Hayemama— the proclamation of the day and the night, like a town crier—directing the children to their relevant activities for the next twenty-four hours in all respective centers.

Another center was the Mentoring Center, Merkaz Honchut. Each child in the maon had a mentor who was responsible for knowing what and how the child was doing at every moment of the day and night. The other adults who worked in the maon shared all relevant information about the child with the assigned mentor. It was like a web of information. To allow this flow of information among the different workers, information about each child was conveyed both verbally and through an organized system of written reports. Thus each child who entered the maon had a personal mentor, who was aware of his or her habits, likes and dislikes, and was involved in guiding and consulting the child. As the child learned his or her way around the maon, the personal guide became less involved, and the older children were mentored as a group.

Finally, the coordination of the work of all the centers took place in the Center of Centers (Merkaz Hamerkazim). The children participated regularly in the centers' activities. Every one of the centers was managed by a center manager (Merakez Hamerkaz), a teacher or a counselor in the maon. All in all, it was a very busy place.

Life Challenges

The maon's structure came to serve the children's emotional development while dealing with the externally based challenges, such as the country at war, changes in the kibbutz's status, and other difficulties. The maon used symbolic understanding to comprehend and provide creative responses to these challenges. Myths and symbols were a big part of the maon. The children lived among, and constantly related to, concepts from mythology.

For example, there were children who were restless and needed to be constantly in movement. The maon's newspaper was created for them, to allow them to employ their need to get information. The newspaper was called *Haratz—The Messenger*—after the myth of Pheidippides, the Greek messenger who ran to Athens to bring the news of the Persians defeated in the battle of Marathon.

FIG. 1
NEVE TZELIM—AN IMAGE OF UNITARY REALITY

FIG. 2
THE YARD CENTER

Fig. 3
A GLIMPSE AT
THE MAON

Fig. 4
A GLIMPSE AT
THE MAON

Fig. 5
A ROOM IN THE MAON

Fig. 6

Symbols of the various centers

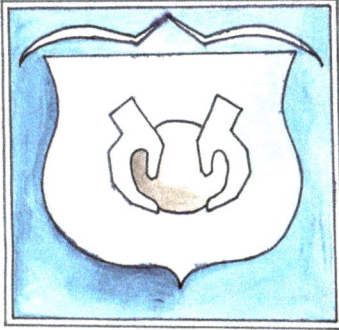

FIG. 7
THE PROSPECT OF ACCEPTANCE CENTER

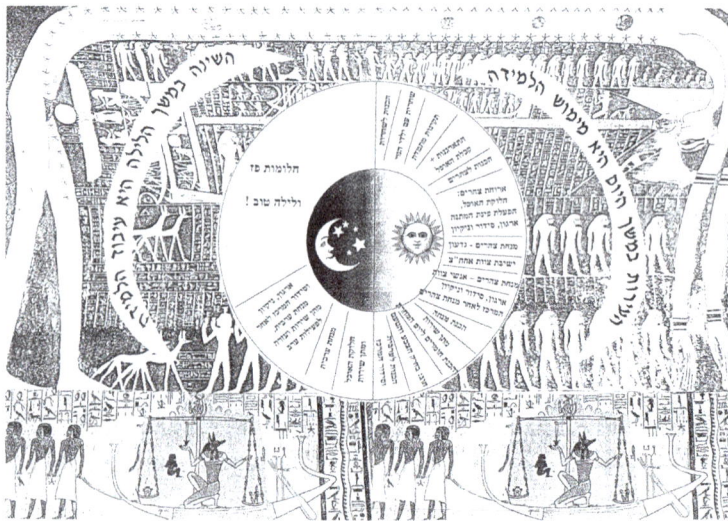

FIG. 8
THE PROSPECT OF HOME CENTER

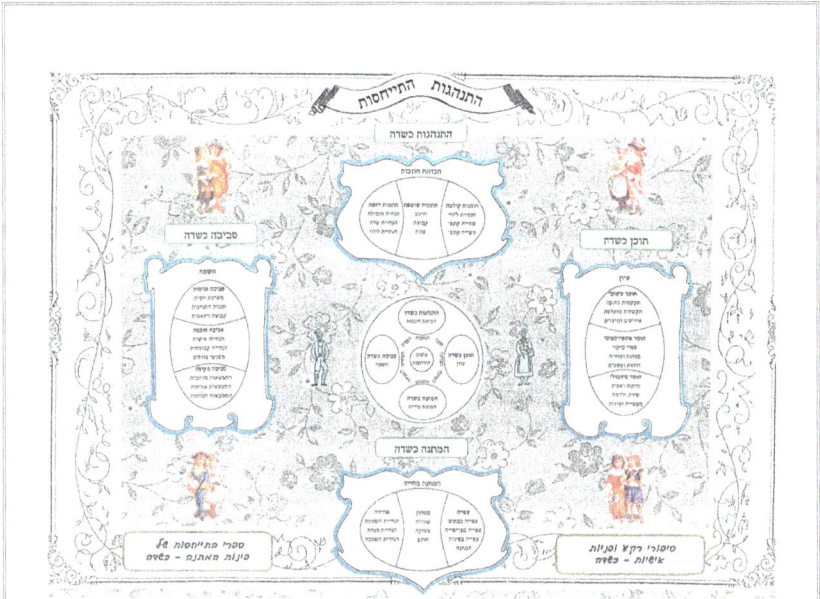

FIG. 9
THE PROSPECT OF RELATIONSHIP CENTER

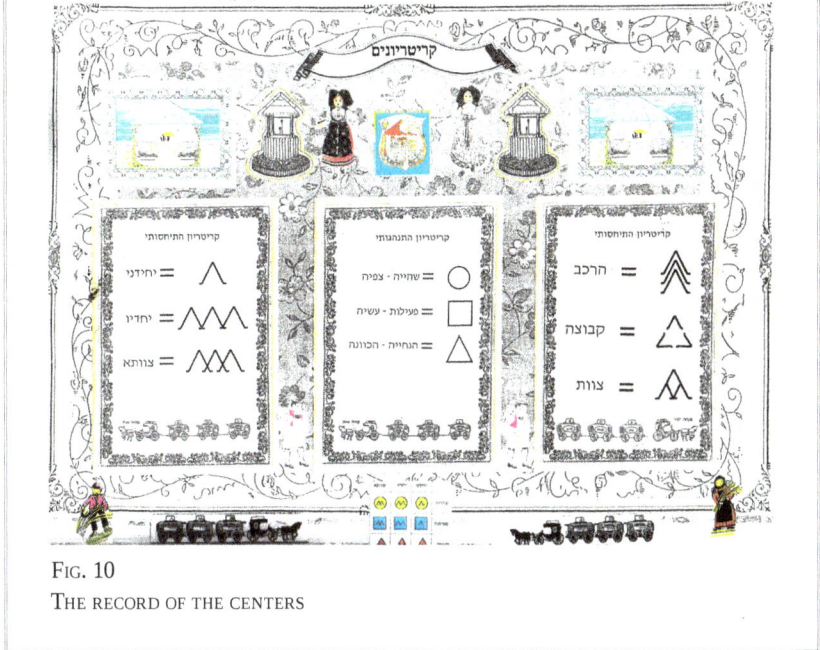

FIG. 10
THE RECORD OF THE CENTERS

Therapy in the Maon

Every child in the maon underwent psychological therapy. The therapists were clinical psychologists and social workers. A psychiatrist was permanently available for consultation. Besides traditional therapeutic work, the therapists were deeply involved in the lives of the children and with the rest of the working staff in the maon.

The therapists would meet the children in their office, even though most of the work was done outside the office: being involved in all the centers in the maon and being involved with all the people the child came into contact with. The therapist was informed about what happened to the child and took part in planning the child's activities in the maon; when needed, the therapist was called upon to provide consultation to those who were involved with the child. All therapists and instructors consulted with the head psychologist, Marion Baderian.

Family Involvement in the Maon

The parents and the kibbutz from which the child came were intensely involved in the treatment process. The parents were invited to come and visit and to participate in the activities at the maon once a week. There was constant contact with the relevant people from the kibbutz, including the child's peer group, to which he or she would return.

A Day in the Maon

It's difficult to describe a typical day in the maon because the dynamics of the maon's life was, and remains, so rich and versatile, and each child had his or her own individual plan for each day. Yet, there was a general basic structure, repeated daily and shared by everyone. Some of these features have changed since the emphasis turned from being Jungian/Neumannian to more generally social-psychological.

Most children would wake up at 7:00 a.m. They slept in meticulously decorated, shared rooms, which included unique features relevant to each child. Upon waking, the sound of classical music and the smell of breakfast came from the lobby of the house, where breakfast was served. The intention was to stimulate the children's senses as they woke up.

Breakfast was eaten in the company of the same adult every day—object consistency was considered very important.

Some of the children were "early birds" and woke up as early as 5:30 a.m. These children were chosen for the gardening group. There was great pride in belonging to this particular group. Landscaping and the aesthetics of the plants were very significant in the maon and in the children's lives.

After breakfast the children went to the morning meeting with the male director of the maon. This position was held by the same person over many years; he was involved in the lives of the children, and to many of them he was a significant father figure. The morning meeting was a ritual, which included reporting the activities of the previous evening and night, identifying possible distress signals that occurred during the night, and providing support and helpful solutions.

The morning meeting was hosted by a different center every day, with representatives of the respective centers present at the meeting. This was followed by a thirty minute discussion on a chosen topic. The discussion would turn into a conversation which dealt with realistic, relevant issues pertaining to the life of the maon, to worldly subjects, such as science, or something else relevant to the children's life, such as a story or a poem.

From 8:30 until 10:30 every child participated in the building and the maintaining of the maon. Every child belonged to a group responsible for a certain project, for which all the group members were involved in planning and executing. The groups were made up of children of all ages working together. There was a busy, hardworking atmosphere in the mornings. The motto was, "Start the day by amending yesterday."

In the morning, in addition to the manual work, some of the children were involved in preparing appealing sandwiches. Some of the work took place at the Animal Center, feeding and grooming the animals.

Upon finishing these activities, the groups would get together and everyone would write down what had been done. The moderator would read out all the groups' daily accomplishments so that the children could see a clear record of what they did, how they participated in the group, and how they contributed to the maon.

Many of the children had difficulties studying in the mornings. Thus, the daily structure was designed to allow them to come into their own through a group-shared physical experience. As the day progressed, activities gradually turned from group-related and physical activities to the more individual and learning-focused ones. After the more extraverted activity, and before starting the individual schedule of the day, a light meal of the sandwiches that had been prepared earlier by the children themselves was served. A restful morning break, accompanied by music chosen and operated by the children, served as a transition prior to the activity in the respective centers.

From here the children started their individual schedule. Every child sat in his or her place. There was a quiet and concentrated atmosphere. At the beginning there was a fatherly voice that dealt with some short story or poem, following which the children were asked to concentrate on their plan for the day. Along with the adult counselors, the children turned to plan the rest of the day's activities, which were to be done alone or in a group and initiated by the children themselves or by the counselor. The plan was always written down and included the geographic area and the relevant centers in which it was to take place. The plan was based on topics that the children took an interest in and were curious about. The children's daily plan included psychotherapy, study activity, sports, creative activity, music, participation in groups, other planned activities and initiated activities—life in the maon was always hectic.

The planning ended with an exit and an arrow that oriented the child where to go from this point.

The individual part of the day started at 11:00 a.m. The children went to the centers, where their arrival was expected and awaited. The child's work at the center would progress according to a predefined plan or based on curiosity and initiative. The children's activities in the centers were always documented. There was a description of the time, the length, the content, and the way the activity in the center took place; there was a symbol indicating whether the child was studying by themselves, or with someone else, or in a group.

Lunchtime meant gathering together and eating with the adult counselors, with each counselor always assigned to the same table. After lunch the children continued with their individual program. Every child had his or her unique schedule for the day, learning in one of the centers, and being involved in creative activities. Part of the day was devoted to more introverted activity, alone, while part of the day emphasized being and interacting with other children.

The children were accompanied during the day by the adults in the centers and the personal counselors, who were involved in and informed about everything that happened to the child and were in charge of counseling the children when difficulties were encountered.

The day ended with a summation ceremony. The children would get together, and each child, with the help of a counselor or an adult guide, would write down what they did during the day on a decorated piece of paper. The written daily summation would be placed in the child's personal folder in the Behavior Modification Center.

This was followed by a communal dinner, during which the children were informed about the evening's nightly activity. The nightly activities were sometimes regular and known and sometimes varied, based on the plan of the person in charge at that night. Some of the children sat by the fire, eating supper while hearing a story, some of them sat by themselves or with a friend, reading or playing, while others watched a movie chosen in advance.

During the evening there were rituals of preparing the place for the night. One group was the "Gate Keepers," a group of children who would check to see that all the gates of the maon were locked. Another group, responsible for the lanterns, would check that each lantern was working properly, to ensure that there was enough light for the children to feel safe. The atmosphere in the evening was quiet and introverted.

When all activities were completed, the children went to their rooms, where they participated in routines of washing, bedtime story, and going to sleep. The children went to sleep knowing who the adult in charge during the night was and feeling safe and secure in their space. All that happened during the night was written down the next morning and was the basis for sharing and relating, that is, for the beginning of the following day.

The maon provided a safe and therapeutic space, enabling development and creativity for the children who lived there, often for several years.

Conclusion

I hope I have managed to convey some of the experience we all—adults and children—shared in this unique place, while being a part of a field that possesses two simultaneous aspects: concepts as well as energy that are embedded in structure and images.

Erich Neumann's stages of development were conveyed in the philosophy of the maon. The child's development includes movement from the matriarch to the patriarch—from a caring and warm treatment to independence and responsibility. The goal of every child's journey of growth was to develop a functional ego, as expected from the first stage of life. The environment was very caring, but the children always had developmental missions, first within the maon, then within the close surroundings, and later on within the wider surroundings. Finally, they were meant to become a part of their society, graduate from school, serve in the army, and take part in life as adults, each one in his or her individual way.

PART VIII. ON RELIGION

Erich Neumann and Hasidism

Tamar Kron

O n a rainy Friday in July 1955, during an interview on the occasion of his eightieth birthday for the *National-Zeitung* (Basel), C. G. Jung made an astonishing revelation: "But do you know who anticipated my entire psychology in the eighteenth century? The Hasidic Rabbi Baer from Meseritz, whom they called the Great Maggid."[1]

Two decades earlier, Erich Neumann, after immigrating to Palestine at the age of twenty-nine, had begun to write a manuscript, as yet unpublished: "Hasidism and Its Psychological Relevance for Judaism." We know that the young Neumann had presented his wife-to-be, Julia, with a copy of Martin Buber's *Tales of the Hasidim* and had gone on to study Kabbalah and Hasidism at the university in Berlin.

This is how Neumann expresses his understanding of Hasidism, in the introduction to his manuscript, which he began to write a couple of years after his initial meeting with Jung in 1933:

> Certain formulations by Hasidic authorities match our own
> so precisely and in such great detail, one may correctly
> assume that they are present, at least latently, at the basis

---

1 C. G. Jung, *C. G. Jung Speaking*, ed. William McGuire and R. F. C. Hull (Princeton, NJ: Princeton University Press, 1987), 271–272.

of my own psychological interpretations. Of course, it goes
without saying that the formulations of Hasidic texts and
my psychological interpretations of them two hundred years
later move along different planes.[2]

Neumann apparently wrote the manuscript during his first years in
Palestine, 1934–1940, during which he was preoccupied with the
problems of the Jewish psyche and sought the mainspring for the creation
of a national Jewish culture in Zionism and Hasidism. Neumann never
published the unrevised three-hundred-page manuscript, and we cannot
be entirely certain why it never saw light. Some say that Gershom
Scholem, whom Neumann had met at Eranos, criticized his overreliance
on Buber and his inability to read the sources in Hebrew. It makes no
difference in my eyes whether or not this is so or whether Scholem in
fact ever read the manuscript. In any case, it is perfectly legitimate for
writers and researchers to choose their sources as they wish. Be that as it
may, although Neumann's presentation of Hasidism is Buberian in spirit,
the psychological understanding is original Neumann.

When he had finished writing the entire manuscript, Neumann
took up other subjects, not necessarily related to the Jewish psyche
and Jewish culture. One would be wrong to surmise that when he put
the manuscript away in his drawer and stopped teaching his seminars
on Judaism, Neumann also put away his reflections on the connection
between analytical psychology and Hasidism. What I will claim here
is that the same ideas and even entire passages from that manuscript
appear, though further developed and expanded, in the Eranos essays,
which he began writing in 1948, as well as in *Depth Psychology and the
New Ethic*. Moreover, I shall claim that the early stages of his original
thinking, which combined analytical psychology with existentialism

---

2   Erich Neumann, *Hasidism and Its Psychological Relevance for Judaism*, ed. Ann Lammers,
trans. Mark Kyburz (forthcoming). Translation of this quote, as well as all others from Neumann's
German manuscript, dated 1934–1940, is the responsibility of the author. —TK

and Buber's dialogue philosophy, are already present in the manuscript of "Hasidism and Its Psychological Relevance for Judaism."

Neumann's insights into Hasidism and the way in which they complement his psychology and figure in his Eranos essays are simply too numerous to discuss in this context. What I have chosen to focus on here is his unique interpretation of the Hasidic doctrine of the sparks and the doctrines of *tzimtzum* (contraction) and *ayin* (nothingness or the void) and, through them, to elucidate some Neumannian ideas that stem from them.

The Kabbalistic doctrine of *tzimtzum* is the divine contraction that gave rise to the primordial catastrophe of creation and the divine sparks that issued from it. Here is Buber's reading of the Hasidic interpretation:

> The sparks doctrine of the later Kabbalah has become in the hands of the Baal-shem-tov an ethical teaching, and has been amplified into a precept embracing the whole life of man. In a primordial catastrophe before the creation of our world (in the time when God set up worlds and tore them down), sparks of the divine fire fell into all things in the world. The spark is concealed in a material shell, in a mineral, in a plant, in an animal—a complete form similar to that of man, with the head on the thighs, unable to move hands or feet, embryo-like. Only through man is there redemption for him. It rests with men to purge the sparks of things and beings, which are met with every day, and to raise them to ever higher stages, to ever higher births, from mineral to plant, from plant to animal, from animal to man, until the holy spark can return to its high roots.[3]

Neumann wrote a great deal about the "creative point of nothingness" which is central to his thinking on creativity. He describes the Kabbalistic-

---

3   Martin Buber, *Hasidism*, trans. Greta Hort (New York: Philosophical Library, 1948), 54.

Hasidic concept of the void or nothingness (*ayin*) in the manuscript he began in 1934: "The world according to Hasidism rests upon God's creative *ayin*, the dynamics of which are not only latent in every element and object in this world, but also rhythmically animate and liberate this world."[4] Neumann elucidates the psychic component of *ayin* as follows:

> The *ayin* is the locus of the rebirth of consciousness which reemerges from it in a new, vitalized, and expanded form. What this means is that the concept of *ayin* and its identity with divine wisdom accords with the psychology and metaphysics of the creative process since all creativity arises out of the "unconscious," the deepest levels of the *ayin*, beyond the reach of ego-consciousness.[5]

Fourteen years later, Neumann wrote in his essay "Mystical Man": "Not only is the source of the creative nothingness—which is the point of departure for the autonomous, spontaneous, and unconscious activity of the creative, vital psyche—situated within the psychological domain of the *anthropos*, it is its very center."[6] In the same essay he writes:

> The creative void stands at the center of mystical anthropology as part of a depth psychology concerned with the nature of the creative process, but at the same time it stands at the center of all mystical experience which circles around the hiddenness of the godhead … . Analytical psychology calls this center the Self and thus enters into the very midst of the paradoxical truth that God and man are one image. In its individuation the personality no longer experiences itself as ego, or solely as ego, but at the same time as ego-self.[7]

---

4   Neumann, *Hasidism*.
5   Ibid.
6   Erich Neumann, "Mystical Man," in *The Mystic Vision: Papers from the Eranos Yearbooks*, ed. J. Campbell (Princeton, NJ: Princeton University Press, 1968), 377.
7   Ibid., 383–384.

And thus he writes in the essay "Man and Meaning," nineteen years after his completion of his manuscript on Hasidism: "The creative point of nothingness of the individual self, to which the world belongs, and that point to which the individual's unfolding destiny belongs, are one and the same."[8] These are merely examples. There are many other sections in Neumann's writings that refer to the concept of the creative point of nothingness.

Neumann, as we have seen, understands the creative point of nothingness as the origin of consciousness. Let us now consider the stages of developing consciousness in the process of individuation as Neumann presents them—mineral to plant, plant to animal, animal to human.

As he describes this process in the manuscript, the sparks that exist in the external world of animate and inanimate entities make demands on man irrespective of their quintessence or manifestation. They "desire" something from the individual, and this desire is matched by the human desires of the psyche. The demands of the external world transform the human into the great mediator and ruler, the "ladder" that connects the earthly with the divine, for it is between the world, humanity, and God that the great redemption is enacted. God is hidden and immanent, but the divine abundance and vitality of the sparks spread throughout the world of entities and creatures. The dynamic of the sparks is dependent upon human intention and consciousness. Neumann writes that man redeems the spiritual meaning of the spark by raising it to the conscious level. As he expresses the idea in his manuscript: "Clearly this is a gradual process of transformation wherein the movement of sentience from 'dead stone' to 'living man' likewise denotes the movement from 'mute stone' to 'speaking creature.'"[9] Neumann later refers to the rung of the speaking creature as the rung of man or the rung of meaning.

---

8   Erich Neumann, "Man and Meaning," in *The Place of Creation* (Princeton, NJ: Princeton University Press, 1989; "Mensch und Sinn," in *Der Schoepferische Mensch* (Zurich: Rhein Verlag, 1959), 242.
9   Neumann, *Hasidism*.

> The redemption of sparks lost in meaninglessness occurs when they are returned through relationship and connected to human consciousness. While contained in "mere-random-existence" (which reminds us of a later concept of Neumann's, "mere-ego") they are bound in spiritual-psychic wholeness and ascend to their roots, their original state.[10]

Consciousness redeems the unconscious spiritual kernel of an inanimate object or creature, the latent embryo imprisoned in the shell, into meaningfulness and leads it from the potential to the actual.

At the lowest rung, that of the inanimate, the spiritual-creative principle is latent. For primitive man the muteness of the inanimate sometimes takes the form of a "speaking" creature that calls to him. This becomes a sacred object, an abode of the divine. In such an object, the spark that has been revealed ascends to its root.

Another way in which the spark of the inanimate can be redeemed is when a mineral object is used by a human being and redeemed through its relationship with the psyche. The hewn stone has a different nature from the stone that lies somewhere on the hill. It is connected to man's consciousness, shaped and redeemed from the anonymity of existence. Likewise Neumann refers to the "act of naming" here as one that redeems the inanimate object from its existential anonymity. The spiritual act of naming which redeems the inanimate is not a magical one that endows the object with magical powers, but an act that connects the inanimate with consciousness and sublime spirituality. The most beautiful example I know of this act is found in the story of Jacob's great dream in Genesis 28:11, "And he lighted upon the place, and tarried there all night, because the sun was set; and he took one of the stones of the place, and put it under his head, and lay down in that place to sleep."

---

10 According to the sparks doctrine the sparks fell down to the material world from the spiritual, divine world. In the process of their liberation and redemption they ascend to their source and unite with their roots.

In the dream a ladder descends from the heavens with angels upon it, and Jacob hears God promising the land of his fathers to the people of Israel. When he awoke, he "took the stone that he had put under his head, and set it up for a pillar, and poured oil upon the top of it. And he called the name of that place Beth-el" (Gen. 28:18–19). Then he made a vow that when he would return to his father's house "this stone, which I have set up for a pillar, shall be God's house" (Gen. 28:22).

The stone was redeemed through Jacob's act of naming. One could say in Buber's dialogue language that the stone was transformed from "it" to "Thou" through Jacob's consciousness which connected with the spiritual totality, gave it a name, and thus redeemed the spark of the stone.

Next comes the rung of vegetation. Here the organism has a vitality of its own, yet is still directionless in terms of consciousness. The spark is closer to its essence here and reveals something formerly latent and locked, though it is still directionless from a human perspective. The world of vegetation represents life of a unique kind. It grows and lives in time, though it is restricted in movement by its roots. The realm of vegetation is more wondrous and enigmatic than the mineral realm. That is, it reveals more of the living secret of the divine.

It is in the animate rung, however, where for the first time intentionality and the creative urge reveal themselves as self-determining movement and instinct. Here the active aspect of the world appears and the desire of the spark is revealed in its movement toward the human psyche. The movement is expressed through affects and emotions.

These three rungs—mineral, vegetable, and animal—are inherent in nature, and their inner symbolism represents the path of transformation from the depths of the unconscious toward consciousness.

Above the animal rung is the rung of the "speaking creature" (the rung of man or meaning), where the sparks express themselves and their unique connection to the redeeming psyche is clarified. On this rung the self-redemptive process within the human psyche is unveiled. Man as representative of the spiritual in the world becomes self-reflective and bestows meaning on the world.

But is this not also the rung of the ego, in Neumann's metapsychology? Let us look at his last essay, "The Psyche as the Place of Creation," written nineteen years after the manuscript on Hasidism was completed.

> Only in man's self-formation does this double nature of the self become transparent: as the individual center of human destiny it is a creative and formative form, yet at the same time as the creative and formative agency at work everywhere and in everything it remains itself formless .... Individuation involves the inclusion of the ego as an essential pole of the ego-self axis, and destiny signifies just as much acceptance of the ego-self reality as an attempt by the creative and formative agency to realize itself in the uniqueness of the human psyche.[11]

Neumann continues:

> In this connection, I should like to refer to a Hasidic story which has occupied my mind for very many years. It is a story told by a rabbi about a simple Jew, to whom the prophet Elijah had appeared. But the appearance of Elijah "signifies the real initiation of the individual into the secret of the doctrine." [Martin Buber, *Die chassidischen Bücher* (Hellerau: Hegner, 1928), 690] The rabbi was asked how this could possibly be true, since the appearance of the prophet had never been vouchsafed to Master Ibn Esra, a man who was spiritually on an altogether higher plane. The rabbi replied that a larger or smaller part of the "allsoul" of Elijah enters into every child, according to his temperament and inheritance.

---

11   Erich Neumann, "The Psyche as the Place of Creation," in *The Place of Creation* (Princeton, NJ: Princeton University Press, 1989); "Die Psyche als Ort der Gestaltung," Top of Form *Eranos Jahrbuch 1960*, band 29: *Mensch und Gestaltung* (Zürich: Rhein Verlag, 1961), 373-374.

And if the person concerned, when he is growing up, trains his part of the soul of Elijah, then Elijah will appear to him. The simple man to whom Elijah had appeared had realized his small part of the soul of Elijah, whereas Ibn Esra had not realized his much larger part.

As I understand this story today, it means—in Jewish clothing—that what appears here as the soul of Elijah is the same as what we call the "'self." This self in a man is on the one hand the basis of his individuation and his destiny, but on the other hand the "smaller than small" and "greater than great" of the Indian *purusha* applies to it. This means that as something immeasurable and as a formless creator of form and images it is everywhere identical with itself.

From the standpoint of our meta-psychological enquiry this soul of Elijah is valid not only for the Jew and not only for humankind but for everything that lives and everything that exists, and the formless reality is the basis not only of all individual existence but of each thing that has been formed, in all its diversity, since it is everywhere one and the same reality. This means, however, that everything which fulfills its own nature is equal in rank and equal in radiance … . But this equality applies just as much to the inanimate that fulfills its inanimate nature by existing, as it does to the vital process which fulfills itself unconsciously as preformed form, and to the human reality that fulfills itself consciously as a form creating form and images. And so, just as we have to recognize man in this sense as "absolute man," so in this line of experience every animal, every plant, and every stone becomes "absolute."[12]

---

12   Ibid., 374–375.

Twenty years earlier, in his unpublished manuscript, Neumann had related the same story in connection to the rung of speaking creatures:

> At issue in this story is individuation. The development of Elijah's soul must be acknowledged as a basis for the fulfillment of every individual life. The spark, the latent spiritual content found in every object and creature as a locked kernel must be revealed. The revelation may take place in anything and anyone, depending on the manner, intensity and intention of the human psyche and its capability to be revealed. The greater the soul, the more the world demands to be revealed through it, and the more latent soul fragments exist in it which wait like the latent sparks in inanimate objects to be redeemed and raised on high.[13]

Above the rung of meaning is the rung of the symbolic. The subject of experience on this rung is not the speaking creature—the ego—but rather something transpersonal. The redemption of the sparks appears here not like the redemption of objects and creatures or human beings but as the redemption of the divine itself. At this rung the destiny of man and the world have become part of God's redemption. As an example of this Neumann relates the following Hasidic tale:

> A disciple of the Rabbi of Apt related this story: "Once I was present at a conversation my teacher carried on with a widow. He spoke to her of her widowhood in good, comforting words, and she allowed her soul to be comforted and found new strength. But I saw that he wept and I too began to weep. For suddenly I knew that he was speaking to the Divine Presence—the Shekhinah—that is forsaken."[14]

---

13   Neumann, *Hasidism.*
14   M. Buber, *Tales of the Hasidism: The Later Masters* (New York: Schocken Books, 1948), 118.

Here at the highest rung, writes Neumann, individual experience is symbolically elevated. The earnest manner in which the rabbi spoke to the widow reveals the symbolic aspect and their meeting becomes an instance of revelation. The occurrence is unveiled and transformed into an event between humanity and God Himself.

An everyday occurrence becomes allegorical. Though it remains worldly in content, it bears a different meaning, whether we speak of Enoch the righteous shoemaker, who by joining the sole to the shoe joins heaven and earth, or the Baal Shem Tov, who washes the vessels in his home and at the same time cleanses creation, which is also called "the vessels," or other figures from Hasidic tales. The world is always a symbol. It reaches the individual as a messenger of God in order to bring revelation which is the recognition of the symbolic nature of the act that brings about the redemption of the sparks. In his essay "Mystical Man" from 1948, Neumann returns to the story of the widow in relation to the highest level of mystical man:

> This level synthesizes two attitudes which at first seem mutually exclusive: one which takes seriously the concrete situation in the actual, given world, and another which looks on its encounter with the numinous substratum as the only authentic reality. Their synthesis constitutes "symbolic life."[15]

> If in everything and every situation a numinous background can break through, leading to the mystical encounter between the ego and the nonego and thence to illumination, everything in the world becomes a symbol and a part of the numinous, and the world becomes a symbol and a part of the numinous, and the world so pilloried by the uroboros mystics becomes prodigiously pregnant with God and godly. When there is light in man the light shines without and within; and when it

---

15 Neumann, "Mystical Man," 410–411.

becomes dark and opaque within him, the world too becomes dark and opaque, a world of dead things. The mission of living man is not to plunge himself into the white primal light and lose his identity, but to give transparency to the foregrounds of the world, in order that the primal light of the pleroma may become visible as a background and core of the world and thus become intensified in its radiation and efficacy. This he may do by experiencing a symbol, by raising a content to consciousness, by giving form to an archetype, through love for another human being, or in some other way, in any case, we are speaking of an encounter of the self with the self.[16]

Further on in his manuscript, Neumann uses the phrase "the actualization of Messianism," by which he means a radical shift from the future to the present, from there to here, from outside in. This actualization corresponds to the radical internalization of the problem of redemption. Redemption is not reliant on external factors but only on the individual here and now fulfilling the messianic rung of his soul. What is implied here is the enormous weight on the individual and his psychic work and its actualization in the world. Man's redemptive role in relation to the world is internal. He transforms himself through the transformation of the sparks of the world and thus transforms the world itself. In "Mystical Man" Neumann says almost exactly the same thing:

> The actualization of Messianism, a process that culminated in the popular mystical movement of Hasidism, overcame the provisional character of a life spent outside of history in waiting for a millennium. Redemption of the sacred sparks in every Now, in every Here, that is the essential task. And this task confronts not only the world, with its general need of redemption, but every individual, for each individual soul has its own particular sparks that demand to be redeemed ... .

---

16   Ibid., 410.

> This mission of the individual is in its profoundest meaning
> an actualization of Messianism.[17]

Here I would like to discuss another relevant passage from the manuscript "Hasidism and Its Psychological Relevance for Judaism," concerning the rungs of the sparks in which Neumann clarifies the psychological meaning of the transformation of the rungs as it relates to the transformation of the world. It is important to understand, says Neumann, that the transformation of the sparks occurs together with a transformation of perspective—either way, whether we say that the spark of something has been raised to the rung of meaning—from the perspective of the object—or that the world has become transparent through this object which has now reached the rung of man, or that the soul has raised itself to the rung of man, from man's perspective, all three are one and the same. Yet it would be a mistake to suppose that this is merely a shift in human perspective within man, for while man and his consciousness do indeed undergo a transformation, at the same time, the entire world is transformed, and not merely the human world.

Not only does the individual on the mineral rung have a different perspective from that of a man on the rung of meaning, but his reactions in and toward the world will also be different. The world actualizes itself in and through man at different rungs. The world at the mineral rung is obedient to the inanimate world. An event that man encounters at the mineral rung is blind, and man responds to it according to the principle of least resistance. The same event met at the rung of meaning will be entirely different. Here the event becomes transparent, and man is not blind to it but rather sees a meaning in it to which he responds. This event is a given but at one rung it is inanimate, meaningless, dead matter, while for someone else who encounters the same event the world may be revealed and actualized at a different rung. This process of transformation is continuous, and every person ceaselessly ascends and descends at every moment.

---

17   Ibid., 409–410.

Some fifteen years later, in 1952, in his important essay "The Psyche and the Transformation of the Reality Planes," Neumann articulates the same thing in the language of his metapsychology. He describes the paradigm of the ego-self axis centering in the psyche as it cuts through three planes of reality or fields of knowledge: the plane of reality, the archetypal plane, and the plane of the self. That such fields exist in parallel is Neumann's original idea, an idea that would appear to go well beyond the concept developed by Jung. I believe this idea is based on Neumann's reading of Hasidism. He writes:

> The transformation of the psyche manifests itself in the human being's changing relationship to the reality planes as they respectively become accessible to him or her, and the creative freedom of life as well as the extent and the luminosity of experience are directly dependent on the phase of transformation in which the personality of the human being happens to be.[18]

Neumann continues to describe the point of the personality's centroversion, "the world-encompassing self-field, and the central point within the psyche become identical. And the central self-form, the godhead within us, appears the same as the godhead who is the creator of the world."[19]

The central principle in these statements is that there is no longer any distinction between the personal self, responsible for the process of one's individuation, and the greater self that guides the whole world. What this means is, significantly, that the symbols of the self are not projections from the inner world to the outside and not the reflection of the outside in the inner world, but rather a union of outer and inner. For

---

18   Erich Neumann, "The Psyche and the Transformation of the Reality Planes: A Metapsycho-logical Essay," in *The Place of Creation* (Princeton, NJ: Princeton University Press, 1989); "Die Psyche und die Wandlung der Wirklichkeitsebenen: Ein metapsycholohischer Versuch," *Eranos Jahrbuch 1952*, band 21: *Mensch und Energie* (Zürich: Rhein Verlag, 1952), 54. Top of Form
19   Ibid., 59.

Neumann the question whether or not God is a projection of the self in the inner world to the outer world is extraneous. God is found both inside and outside and is revealed in centroversion.

I hope I have sufficiently clarified my claim that the symbolic rung and the rung of meaning as described by Neumann in the manuscript correspond to what he later calls the ego-self axis. In his last essay, "The Psyche as the Place of Creation," completed in 1959, he writes:

> It is an altogether different matter when man experiences himself as an ego-self structure, i.e., when he becomes aware, not of his inwardness but of his inner being. He experiences himself in his ego-self being as a creatively formative power which is alive in himself, in his ego and in his self; he is part of this power as an ego, and as a self he himself is this power.[20]

This great experience takes place in a state Neumann describes as "destiny" wherein man ceases to experience himself as "relative man" and can experience himself and his own numinosity as "absolute man." Or in Neumann's words: "This experience takes place in the midst of the world and the problems of the age and by no means in some remote 'free space' since 'to have a destiny' does not mean to exist outside time."[21]

This "absolute man" who experiences his ego-self as a creatively formative power is highly reminiscent of the *tzadik* in Hasidism, as we shall soon see. Neumann describes him in the manuscript thus:

> The *tzadik* as the epitome of wholeness actualizes the potential that exists as a kernel in every human being, and this is the meaning of creation "in God's image," that is Adam Kadmon (primordial man) who must be actualized in his entirety and all his parts. Such development and intentionality are natural to man, a part of his nature and correspond to his psychic make-up ... . His path is

---

20   Neumann, "The Psyche as the Place of Creation," 367.
21   Ibid., 369.

introverted and inward … . It is a path through the layers of
oneself, the shells of oneself, the distortions created by time,
race, nation and family, constitution and type … . It is not
merely the path from ego to self but the path of return from
outside to inside, from extroversion under the sign of ego and
world to introversion under the sign of Self and soul.[22]

Neumann quotes an unnamed Hasidic source which describes the *tzadik*
thus: "Just as a seed buried in the soil draws in all the powers of the earth
and brings forth fruit, so the *tzadik* in this world draws in the sparks
that are part of his soul from everything in the world and brings them
to God."[23] He comments that what is stressed here is the naturalness of
the process, for just as the plant draws its growth and development from
the powers of the earth and these powers spread when the plant grows,
so life on this earth is guided toward the *tzadik* and he is its growth
and development, and just as the plant grows from below to above and
between the two directions, and just as its vitality joins the air with the
soil, so the being of the *tzadik* in this middle space joins the higher and
lower worlds.

In the Hasidic texts the *tzadik* is frequently called the pillar or the
path. Neumann explains that this is the *tzadik*'s key position in relation
to the upper worlds of Godhead whose influence must pass through him.
The nature of the *tzadik* is to join or bind, and the aspect of totality and
unity is epitomized by the *tzadik* as one who links the elements of the
psyche at the inner subjective level and at the objective external level,
connecting God with the world, above and below. The *tzadik* stirs the
sparks of the soul in human beings and causes them to return, enabling
them to discover the rung of their own individual souls and to actualize
them. His mission is to lead man "to his own light, so he won't think the
Rabbi did it." This is the highest mission of the *tzadik* in early Hasidism.

---

22   Neumann, *Hasidism.*
23   Ibid.

The law that provides the basis for the *tzadik*'s influence is the dependency of the Godhead on the human realm of action.

Neumann's manuscript on Hasidism is a hidden treasure from which I have shared only a few gems. It has been a rare experience for me to discover the Hasidic sources of Neumann's thought and to trace their development over the twenty years that separate that manuscript from the Eranos essays. To paraphrase the allegory of the *tzadik* as a plant that draws sustenance from the soil and spreads through the world, one might say that Neumann drew his strength from the soil of Hasidism and flourished through the world of analytical psychology.

Theological Positions in the Correspondence between Jung and Neumann

Angelica Loewe

"I would like to eat some more fruit with you."

~ Erich Neumann, in a letter to C. G. Jung, June 4, 1946

Introduction

In this paper, I am going to address two themes that are representative of the intense correspondence between Jung and Neumann on a variety of theological issues. A complete overview is impossible here. The first thing to note about these two themes, which mark the beginning and the end of Jung's and Neumann's correspondence, is that they contain highly speculative thought. In the case of Neumann the tradition of thought is Jewish, in the case of Jung it is Christian. Both themes can be understood as an attempt at remythologization.

The subject of Jacob and Esau forms the beginning of a debate concerning the theme of "Tiefenpsychologie des jüdischen Menschen und das Problem der Offenbarung" ("Depth Psychology of the Jewish Man and the Problem of Revelation"), as Neumann called the first of his early (still unpublished) manuscripts. It is a debate that shows his quest for a theological-archetypal foundation of a specifically Jewish approach to individuation. The starting point is Neumann's review of an article by the Zionist Hugo Rosenthal entitled "Der Typengegensatz in der jüdischen Religionsgeschichte" ("The Type-Difference in the Jewish History of Religion"). Rosenthal's text had been published by Jung in 1934 in a volume entitled *Wirklichkeit der Seele*.[1]

The becoming conscious of God was a topic of discussion that Jung initiated. The theme was mentioned by Neumann early in the correspondence, in a manuscript enclosed with an undated letter that also included a reference to an analytical session with Jung ("a speculative hour with you").[2] The debate climaxed during an argument regarding Jung's book *Answer to Job*. In this latter discussion, Neumann held an opinion markedly different from Jung's.

As is well known, in *Answer to Job* Jung puts forward the thesis that God can become conscious of Himself only by means of the human being: "Because his creature has surpassed him he [God] must regenerate himself."[3] Neumann strongly objects to this thesis in his letter to Jung dated December 5, 1951. Jung answers him on January 1, 1952.

In Neumann's second to last letter to Jung (February 18, 1959) and Jung's last letter to Neumann (March 10, 1959), there is a heated argument on this topic again because of the last two chapters in *Memories, Dreams, Reflections*, which Jung had sent to Neumann for reading. In these chapters, Jung repeats the thesis from *Answer to Job*, and Neumann contradicts him once again.

---

1   Erich Neumann, "Review of Hugo Rosenthal, 'Der Typengegensatz in der jüdischen Religions-geschichte' ('The Type-Difference in the Jewish History of Religion')," *Jüdische Rundschau*, July 27, 1934; C. G. Jung, *Wirklichkeit der Seele: Anwendungen und Fortschritte der neueren Psychologie* (Zürich: Rascher, 1934).

2   C. G. Jung and Erich Neumann, *Analytical Psychology in Exile: The Correspondence of C. G. Jung and Erich Neumann*, ed. Martin Liebscher (Princeton, NJ: Princeton University Press, 2015), 67.

3   C. G. Jung, *Answer to Job* (1952), in *CW*, vol. 11 (Princeton, NJ: Princeton University Press, 1969), par. 640.

The Theme of Jacob and Esau

Jung writes to Neumann on August 12, 1934, answering an undated letter from Neumann that included a lengthy remark on Rosenthal's theses: "In reality, it seems to me, Jacob is the *quintessence* of the Jew and therefore a symbolic attempt at a collective individuation, or rather at individuation on a collective level."[4] This is a surprising statement. Presumably, the "Rosenthal debate" gave Jung the opportunity to reflect more on the myth of Jacob. Jung himself had commented on Jacob in his early work, *Wandlungen und Symbole der Libido*, in a footnote describing Jacob as a classical hero of the night sea journey.[5] In the later revised version, *Symbols of Transformation*, there is also a reference to Jacob.[6] Through the Rosenthal debate, new ideas came into play, particularly regarding the motif of the two opposed brothers. Rosenthal had already developed the idea that the opposition between the two brothers formed the basis of a fundamental intrapsychic Jewish conflict, in a Jungian sense. Neumann deepened this idea, and this evoked Jung's interest, who, as we know from his correspondence with Neumann, was greatly interested in the differentiation between archetypal Jewish and archetypal occidental thought in the years 1934 to 1938. Neumann, supported by Jung's interest and concern, worked from 1934 to 1940 on a two-part (still unpublished) manuscript entitled "Ursprungsgeschichte des jüdischen Bewusstseins" ("On the Origins and History of Jewish Consciousness"). The story of Jacob and Esau is about the tension between extraversion and introversion, and this also concerns the tension between the functions of intuition and

---

4   Jung and Neumann, *Analytical Psychology in Exile*, 54.
5   C. G. Jung, "Wandlungen und Symbole der Libido: Beiträge zur Entwicklungsgeschichte des Denkens" (1912/1916), in *Jahrbuch für psychoanalytische und psychopathologische Forschungen* 3–4; English edition: *The Psychology of the Unconscious*, trans. B. Hinkle (Princeton, NJ: Princeton University Press, 1991), 337, 61n.
6   C. G. Jung, *Symbols of Transformation* (1952), *CW*, vol. 5 (Princeton, NJ: Princeton University Press, 1967), par. 524.

sensation. In the attachment to his undated letter in 1934, spoken of by the two correspondents thereafter as the "Annotations," Neumann wrote:

> patriarchs and prophets ... were essentially introverted intuitives with thinking ... . This radical bias toward internal demands explains substantial parts of Judaism ... . Now the essential thing is that the inferior function of the introverted intuitive is an "extraverted sensation type of a lower, more primitive variety." ... The negative side of the Jew, an object-addicted, voracious sexuality, an obsession with power, money and acquisitiveness, and a murderous intent constitute the Jewish shadow.[7]

Neumann's conclusion is that "the Jacob-Esau conflict is, for sure, the mythological struggle of the patriarch as a representative of introversion with the natural inferior inherent extraversion."[8]

Encouraged by Jung, Neumann wrote an essay on Jacob and Esau that he finished in 1934, as we learn from a letter to Jung from December 10, 1934. After some hesitation, Neumann sent his paper on Jacob and Esau to Jung in 1935.[9]

I offer here a brief overview of this text. Neumann speaks of the "Jacob-Esau opposition," of the "hostile twin brothers." He depicts the polarity of the two brothers with reference to Bin Gorion's work, *Die Sagen der Juden* (*The Legends of the Jews*): Jacob is associated with the moon, the inner world, whereas Esau is associated with the sun, the outer world.[10]

> The essential hallmark of Esau's world is visibility, and it includes the outer, the ordinary, the unholy world.

---

7   Jung and Neumann, *Analytical Psychology in Exile*, 24–25.
8   Ibid., 25.
9   Ibid., 54.
10   M. J. Bin Gorion, *Die Sagen der Juden*, 5 vols, trans. Rahel Bin Gorion (Frankfurt: Rütten and Loening, 1913–1927).

> Jacob is neither like Esau nor like the peoples of the world,
> but instead he is turned toward that world which not only
> proves to be the coming world, the otherworld, but also
> the inner and invisible world. Jacob, the Jew, looks inward,
> toward YHWH and his inner demand.[11]

This interior realm that Jacob is turned to, says Neumann, "illuminates" crucial traits of Judaism. The realm manifests itself as a voice. It is "the radical prophetic demand for an orientation within the human heart toward the inner voice, toward the voice of God, toward the law that is placed within him."[12]

The claim that there is an inner voice that is not identical with the superego is crucial to Neumann's *Depth Psychology and a New Ethic*, and it is prefigured in his essay on Jacob and Esau. Through the descent of the inner voice as a word from God revealing itself to humanity, its sacred character becomes apparent. Neumann sees this as something different from the secular origin of laws and their reflection in the Freudian conception of the superego.

As the one turned to the inner realm, to the sacred, Jacob is, in accordance with Jungian typology, an introverted person, while Esau is an extraverted person. This typology is so valuable for Neumann because to him "the attitude of the Jew is introverted."[13] Neumann even thinks of the prospective psychic emancipation of Judaism in terms of introversion. He holds that the emancipation effected by regaining the original introversion is a possible rebirth of a mental and cultural, but also social nature in Judaism.

Jacob represents the prototype of a collective path of individuation. Through his connection with the "inward" and the "sacred" realm, he is the intrinsic son and legitimate heir of his father. Neumann turns to

---

11   Erich Neumann, *Jacob and Esau: On the Collective Symbolism of the Brother Motif*, ed. Erel Shalit, trans. Mark Kyburz (Asheville, NC: Chiron Publications, 2015), 4.
12   Ibid.
13   Ibid., 5.

the writings of Hasidism and kabbalistic mysticism, which had become accessible to him primarily through Martin Buber's writings. It is in the Jewish mystics that Neumann believes the inner voice that, as the voice of God had once spoken to the prophets, is heard.

The Theme of the Becoming Conscious of God

Now I want to consider two letters, the second-to-last letter from Neumann to Jung (February 18, 1959) and the last letter from Jung to Neumann (March 10, 1959). On the one hand, these letters give evidence of the high level of Neumann's and Jung's discussion of theological issues. On the other hand, they are indicative of a deep and steadfast inner affinity between the two men, which Neumann describes as follows: "My link with you is, as you know, not dependent on writing and speaking, or no longer dependent, I should say, but meeting with you always brings me a substantial affirmation that cannot be found anywhere else in the world."[14] This affinity never ceased, even in times when their relationship faced a crisis and even though their correspondence was interrupted in the war years 1940–1945.

The discussion concerns two chapters of the autobiographical *Memories, Dreams, Reflections* (*MDR*), which Jung had sent to Neumann to read prior to publication as he had done earlier with his *Answer to Job*. The two chapters were "On Life after Death" and "Late Thoughts." Both thinkers speak of myths in the context of their theological arguments, and in doing so they are not restrained by a commitment to any prevailing theological dogmas. Jung outlines the immense importance of myth in *MDR* and writes: "Unfortunately, the mythic side of man is given short shrift nowadays. He can no longer create fables. As a result, a great deal escapes him; for it is important and salutary to speak also of incomprehensible things."[15] He goes on: "The more the critical reason

---

14   Jung and Neumann, *Analytical Psychology in Exile*, 342.
15   C. G. Jung, *Memories, Dreams, Reflections*, ed. Aniela Jaffé, trans. Richard and Clara Winston (New York: Pantheon Books, 1962, 1965), 300.

dominates, the more impoverished life becomes; but the more of the unconscious, and the more of myth we are capable of making conscious, the more of life we integrate."[16]

It should be noted here that in philosophical-historical terms there is a close relationship between Jung's and Neumann's use of the notions "myth" and "mythology" and that of German idealism. "The Oldest Systematic Program of German Idealism" of 1797, ascribed variously to Hegel, Schelling, or Hölderlin, already voiced the demand for a new mythology, and even as late as 1842 Schelling postulated myths as products of the very essence of consciousness, seeing them as fundamental for human awareness.

Neumann shows his great affinity to Jung's mythological thought and recounts a myth that he had written at the early age of sixteen—a myth that prefigures his mental affinity to Jung. He had spoken about this myth during his analysis with Jung. About Jung's chapters from his forthcoming memoir, Neumann writes: "For me, it is the finest thing you have written ... I do not know anything else in writing that is closer to me and to my life experience ... you know well how closely the 'myth' I wrote when I was 16 led to all of this."[17] Neumann also objects, however, in several ways to Jung's theses as presented in these two chapters of *MDR*. His objections highlight the fundamental difference between their theological views. I want to single out what seems to me to be the central one.

Neumann explains the objections that he intends to advance, despite his proximity to Jung, as follows: "Some of it seems to me to be explained by my Jewish and more Eastern background that does not quite overlap with your Christian and more Occidental one."[18] This differentiation is a topos that both Neumann and Jung used from the beginning of their correspondence, thereby indicating a mutual acceptance of the

---

16   Ibid., 302.
17   Jung and Neumann, *Analytical Psychology in Exile*, 343.
18   Ibid.

fundamental differences between the Jewish and the Christian views of the world. As the correspondence reveals, the issue that Neumann is particularly concerned with is Jung's "thesis ... of the becoming conscious of God."[19]

For Jung, the God-image, which is what he is examining in *Answer to Job*, exists within the soul. It is something objective, indeed, something that we can explore empirically. According to Jung, it is this God-image that undergoes transformation. As a recent scholar puts it: "He [i.e., Jung] conceptualises this process ... as if this God-image were ... a subject that develops along certain psychological regularities ... and these developments find expression in the consciousness of individuals who then write them down in documents like the book of Job, the gospels, the apocalypse etc."[20]

The idea of the becoming God had been extensively discussed earlier in German romanticism, particularly in the philosophy of Schelling, and although it is evident that the romantic view is implicitly appealed to here, there is no explicit reference to it in Jung's work.[21] Presumably, Jung was familiar with this thesis from reading Jakob Böhme, an author whom he greatly admired. Böhme had been read by Schelling. Neumann, whose dissertation was on a poet of the romantic period (Kanne), explicitly cites Schelling's writings, as well as Böhme's, in his references.

Neumann had already objected to this thesis in his letter on December 5, 1951, immediately after reading *Answer to Job*.[22] Jung, however, held to his thesis. In *MDR*, he puts it as follows:

> In the experience of the self it is no longer the opposites "God" and "man" that are reconciled, as it was before, but rather the opposites within the God-image itself. That is the

---

19   Ibid., 344.
20   R. Lesmeister, "Eine Empörung im Grenzland von Religion und Tiefenpsychologie," *Analytische Psychologie* 176, no. 2 (2014): 202.
21   W. Lösch, *Der werdende Gott: Mythopoetische Theogonien der romantischen Mythologie* (Frankfurt a.M.: Peter Lang, 1996); Lesmeister, "Eine Empörung im Grenzland."
22   Jung and Neumann, *Analytical Psychology in Exile*, 271–276.

> meaning … of the service which man can render to God, …
> that the Creator may become conscious of His creation, and
> man conscious of himself … . If the Creator were conscious
> of Himself, He would not need conscious creatures.[23]

Neumann does not reject the idea of the becoming God; in fact, he completely agrees with Jung about that. But he takes exception to speaking of a "God-image." For him, the speaking of God is always linked with a transcendence that is incomprehensible to the human being. He argues that it is not the human being who helps God to become conscious. Rather, the reverse is the case: the human being is just a complex of God's unconsciousness, and through him God Himself gains consciousness of His very own unconsciousness. In order to support this view, he considers the dream Jung had described in *MDR* to illustrate the relationship between self and ego, namely, the famous dream in which a yogi, sitting in the lotus position, meditates Jung himself. Jung writes in *MDR*: "'Aha, so he is the one who is meditating me. He has a dream, and I am it.' I knew that when he awakened, I would no longer be."[24] Neumann writes: "If the Self contemplates you as the ego, then the Self is not unconscious."[25]

Neumann takes the reason as to why Jung emphasizes the position of the human being so much to be Jung's attempt to elevate human existence for narcissistic reasons—an existence so fragile, contingent, and often apparently meaningless.[26] Neumann argues that man plays no active role in God's becoming conscious, but he also wishes to maintain that this does not diminish the human role:

> If we humans are complexes of the divine unconscious, which
> he or it becomes conscious of while we make conscious our

---

23 Jung, *Memories, Dreams, Reflections*, 338–339.
24 Ibid., 323.
25 Jung and Neumann, *Analytical Psychology in Exile*, 344.
26 According to Lesmeister Jung until the end relies on "the narcissistic solution … . Not the approval of deficiency, but the totality of the opposite-united self"; Lesmeister, "Eine Empörung im Grenzland," 209.

individuality with our human consciousness, the accent on the individual would be still greater without our having to formulate the Self or God as unconscious.[27]

Earlier, in his letter on December 5, 1951, Neumann had phrased his objections in more drastic terms: "The problem is—why was an unconscious world created, but does not the omniscience that precedes it suggest a meaningful direction though, in which the Godhead can never be manifest in a different way from one that corresponds to humanity."[28]

Jung succinctly counters Neumann's objection in his reply to Neumann's critical letter regarding his chapters in *MDR*. With explicit reference to the aforementioned dream, he writes:

> The question: *an creator sibi conscious est*? [But is the Creator conscious of himself?] is not a "favorite idea" but a most painful experience of almost immeasurable impact that cannot easily be debated. If someone projects the Self … then it is an unconscious act, for projection arises empirically only out of unconsciousness.[29]

In this letter, Jung also refers to Neumann's second objection. This objection concerns the theme of incarnation. What did Jung mean by this term, and how did he express himself on this topic in *MDR*? There we find the following: "By this act of incarnation man—that is, his ego—is inwardly replaced by 'God,' and God becomes outwardly man … . If this God wishes to become man, an incredible *kenosis* (emptying) is required of Him, in order to reduce His totality to the infinitesimal human scale."[30] In his letter responding to Neumann's objections, Jung elucidates his view that the birth of God (incarnation) evolves in man as an unprecedented event. The birth of God he was speaking about was

27 Jung and Neumann, *Analytical Psychology in Exile*, 344.
28 Ibid., 273.
29 Ibid., 348.
30 Jung, *Memories, Dreams, Reflections*, 337.

to be seen as an experience of something absolutely new, the Christian paradigm for this being the birth of Jesus:

> *Incarnatio* describes in the first instance the birth of God, which took place in XPo [Christ], psychologically, therefore, also the realization of the Self was something new, not present before that. The previously created human is a "creature" even if "in the image of God," in whom the thought of *filiatio* and of the *sacrificium divinum* is not explicitly present. It is, as you say, a "new experience."[31]

Neumann had rejected the Christian term of incarnation in an earlier letter and had instead introduced the notion of the preexistence of a divine power that would subsequently evolve in man:

> It is not incarnation but its becoming conscious and its realization, which leads to the new phenomenon of the birth of God in which the divine as a divine individual and a unique singularity manifests itself in man. The incarnation is already preexistent in the ego-Self unity in which the numinous ego-nucleus has the capacity for consciousness.[32]

We can think of the possibility of contact with this "numinous ego-nucleus" according to Neumann's paradigm of the "inner voice" or "inner revelation."

Neumann's and Jung's diverging positions can now be summarized as follows: Jung, as a Christian, assumes the birth of Christ as the crucial theologoumenon: a transcendent God becomes immanent. In contrast, Neumann, as a Jew, is committed to a God that remains transcendent. God reveals Himself to man, but He does not become man.

As a last point, I want to elucidate a term that Neumann uses in his letter, thereby showing—despite all of his differences—a deep agreement with Jung. He speaks of an "actualized messianism," a term he had extensively discussed in the second manuscript that I mentioned earlier.

---

31 Jung and Neumann, *Analytical Psychology in Exile*, 348.
32 Ibid., 344.

This manuscript is a detailed presentation of the mystic foundations of Hasidism. In his letter, Neumann writes:

> the Jewish historical "development" in this mortal world is becoming ever more problematic for me, the "actualization of messianism" is becoming ever more crucial ... . What is relevant are the stages of development of consciousness in the development of the individual, otherwise everything "historical" belongs to the constellation of the ego as time, like family and constitution. The realization of the ego-Self unity is vertical.[33]

By alluding to the ego-Self axis as being vertical, Neumann makes reference to Jung's idea of a coordinate system for the formulation of fundamental cognitions, an idea that Jung expresses in *MDR* as follows:

> As I see it, the three-dimensional world in time and space is like a system of co-ordinates; what is here separated into ordinates and abscissae may appear "there," in space-timelessness, as a primordial image with many aspects, perhaps as a diffuse cloud of cognition surrounding an archetype.[34]

In his letter, Neumann emphasizes the importance of this vertical axis. Indeed, this vertical axis became much more crucial to him, compared to the horizontal axis of the contingency of historical existence. It is a theology of time that is virtually hidden in this complex reasoning of Neumann's. And, as Neumann states in part two of his unpublished manuscript, the account of time is intimately connected with the role that is assigned to the individual in Hasidism. What Hasidism had achieved, according to Neumann, was to have counteracted in a particular way the Jewish "resignation from history."[35] Neumann holds that through the loss of land and state, the course

---

33   Ibid., 345.
34   Jung, *Memories, Dreams, Reflections*, 308.
35   Jung and Neumann, *Analytical Psychology in Exile,* 172.

of history had become something irrelevant to the Jews. They considered their own lives as well as collective life as something preliminary, in expectation of the end time. In this apocalyptic expectation, a theocratic ideal was projected into the future, and thereby the present, the historical now, as a form of life and experience, became meaningless: "In the future, the time of the Messiah, the Zion to come, the upcoming rule of God lay all the brightness of hope, of justification. Yet the present, all present lay in the shadow of the squeezed-in preliminarity ... it was expectation and preparation at the best and most."[36]

According to Neumann, the theology of Hasidism abandons the view that our present existence is merely preliminary and that the end has already begun. Hasidism turns away from the future toward the present. It thereby effects an inward turn of messianism. The messianic element now presents a "stage of the individual that is to be fulfilled."[37]

Neumann's thought is permeated by this messianic element. We might even say that it became the central topic of his life.

Conclusion

In a letter to Jung dated November 15, 1939, Neumann mentions the doctrine of the *Pardes* in relation to a long dream of his. It is the Jewish version of the Christian doctrine of the fourfold sense of scripture.[38]

Moses de Leon wrote a now lost book some time before 1290 CE entitled *Pardes*, which literally means "paradise." Moses de Leon interpreted this nuanced term as an abbreviation of the four layers of meaning of the Torah. Each consonant of the word *pardes* refers to one layer of meaning. "P" stands for *Peschat*, the literal sense; "R" for *Remes*, the allegorical sense; "D" for *Derascha*, the Talmudic and Agadic interpretation; "S" for *Sod*, the

---

36   Erich Neumann, *Ursprungsgeschichte des jüdischen Bewusstseins* [*On the origins and history of Jewish consciousness*], 2 vols (unpublished typescript, 1934–40), 22.

37   Ibid., 23.

38   Jung and Neumann, *Analytical Psychology in Exile*, 150; Angelica Löwe, *"Auf Seiten der inneren Stimme ...": Erich Neumann—Leben und Werk* (München: Verlag Karl Alber, 2014), 151.

mystical sense.[39] While the Christian exegesis of scripture "practises an eschatological surpassing of the Old Testament by the New ... the Jewish learning community ... endlessly pursues the mysterious traces of an absence."[40] Or, to put it differently, Christian exegesis aims at *anagogé*, "a progress through time towards eternity," whereas Jewish exegesis aims at *eisagogé*, "an introduction of, and initiation into, the revelation of eternity in the midst of time."[41]

These two approaches are incompatible, yet we can imagine Neumann and Jung as two scholars who—on the basis of their different roots in Jewish and Christian religion—exchanged their controversial positions in a most inspired, even passionate, way in the garden of scripture (i.e., in their correspondence) and thus could enjoy the fruits of knowledge. Hence, the wish that Jung expressed in a dream of Neumann's—"I would like to eat some more fruit with you"—did in this way finally come to pass.[42]

---

39 D. Krochmalnik, *Vierfacher Schriftsinn in Judentum und Christentum: Sprache und Religion*, ed. U. Gerber and R. Hoberg (Darmstadt: Wissenschaftliche Buchgesellschaft, 2009), 77. This topic is at the core in the second part of Neumann's unpublished manuscript, *Ursprungsgeschichte des jüdischen Bewusstseins*.
40 Krochmalnik, *Vierfacher Schriftsinn in Judentum und Christentum*, 78.
41 Ibid.
42 Jung and Neumann, *Analytical Psychology in Exile*, 168.

PART IX. ON SYNCHRONICITY

Toward Psychoid Aspects of Evolutionary Theory

Joe Cambray

At the end of the Jung/Neumann correspondence, the last set of letters—from December 20, 1957 (115 N), to the penultimate letter (119 J) from March 1959—includes a discussion between the two men concluding with a rather bold statement by Jung on how synchronicity may have played a significant role in the origins and evolution of life on earth.[1] At the start of these four letters, Neumann picks up the subject of his lecture at the first IAAP congress in 1958, the genetic-phylogenetic aspect of analytical psychology. He raises Fordham's critique of Jung, claiming that "under pressure from the biologists, he abandoned the heredity of archetypal images" and offers a defense of Jung, stating that he had made this shift much earlier on. Neumann also complains of Fordham's dismissal of his own book, *Origins*.

Jung responds quickly, in less than two weeks, and immediately, in the first sentence, notes he "would like to hasten to correct Fordham's statement"—clearly this is psychoactive material for all concerned.

---

1 C. G. Jung and Erich Neumann, *Analytical Psychology in Exile: The Correspondence of C. G. Jung and Erich Neumann*, ed. Martin Liebscher (Princeton, NJ: Princeton University Press, 2015). Neumann's last letter of September 1959 refers to personal matters, not theoretical concerns, and Jung's last letter is to Julie Neumann after the death of Erich.

Jung feels Fordham "has been taken in by his own concretism" and decides to write him directly. He does this, which in turn stirs up a lively exchange between Jung and Fordham on the subject.[2]

This is followed by a hiatus of more than ten months until Neumann resumes the correspondence (in mid-October 1958), though in this letter he leaves off the topic of the biological dimension of the archetypes. It is not until his subsequent letter of February 18, 1959, that he raises the subject again. Although no letters from Jung are presented in the intervening time, apparently he had had some chapters from *Memories, Dreams, Reflections* sent to Neumann, as he was spurred to write Jung based on his response to these materials. In particular the material from the chapter "On Life after Death" causes Neumann to differentiate his views from Jung's on consciousness in the Self or God and to express his discomfort with incarnation versus realization of the ego-Self. These arguments could be read as debates on the "ultraviolet" end of psychoid phenomena.

What is remarkable is how Neumann then seamlessly follows Jung's argument in this same chapter to shift to the "infrared" pole of the psychoid. Jung had been arguing for consciousness as a "second cosmogony," beginning with "natural history" revealing a "haphazard and casual transformation of species," then going on to locate *meaning* as "concealed somewhere within all the monstrous, apparently senseless biological turmoil … found as if by chance, unintended and unforeseen, and yet somehow sensed, felt and groped for out of some dark urge."[3] Neumann challenges Jung to go further, seeing the evolutionary argument as true but inadequate, even though he himself is without "a counterthesis to hand."[4] He continues, speaking against the way the organs of consciousness are understood to have "been found by accident."[5]

---

2 See Jung and Neumann, *Analytical Psychology in Exile*, footnote 379, for the essential remarks; for the full text, see C. G. Jung, *Letters*, vol. 2, ed. Gerhard Adler, trans. R. F. C. Hull (Princeton, NJ: Princeton University Press, 1975), 494–495.
3 Jung and Neumann, *Analytical Psychology in Exile*, footnote 588
4 Ibid., 345.
5 Ibid., 346.

Neumann's intuition appears to have grasped that there is something still missing, but the solution seems lodged in the preconscious for both of them. From the exchange Neumann is in a quandary and cannot quite make the leap himself but believes and trusts Jung to be capable of doing this, and as we will see Jung does respond. I suspect Neumann is bringing Jung back here to a more complex aspect of the dilemma he faced when seeking an exit from the Red Book.

As I've written elsewhere, in 1914 Jung had been stuck on the horns of a personally distressing problem associated with meaning.[6] His precipitating visions, followed in time by the outbreak of World War I, had left him in terrible, unresolved tension between madness and prophecy. The transcendent exit only came fourteen years later when he received the manuscript of *The Secret of the Golden Flower* from Richard Wilhelm just at the time he was working on and puzzling over a mandala that bore, for Jung, striking resonance to the mandala associated with the text. The coincidence of inner imagery and outer text, as well the coincidence of the content of the text with the larger psychological problem Jung was wrestling with at the time, led him to the concept of synchronicity. The cosmological significance of the concept and corollary of objective meaning were not well articulated at the time.

Even with the publication of the full synchronicity essay in 1952, the cosmological relevance of the idea was still largely implicit. Neumann's February 1959 letter with its challenges served as a breakthrough. He pushed Jung beyond his usual cautions into the farther reaches of intuitive speculation. In this Jung realized that *he* indeed had a counterthesis to the classical Darwinian evolutionary narrative. In his final letter to Neumann (119 J, March 1959), he formulated some brilliant ideas on the subject; something that sadly never made it into publication—he did not have time to write it up in full detail.

---

6   Joseph Cambray, "*The Red Book*: Entrances and Exits," in *The Red Book: Reflections on C. G. Jung's Liber Novus*, ed. Thomas Kirsch and George Hogenson (London: Routledge, 2014).

In response to Neumann's activating letter, Jung wrote, in the midst of his reply and referring to mammalian and human evolution:

> In this chaos of coincidence, synchronistic phenomena were probably at work, which in contrast to and with the help of the known laws of nature were able to achieve syntheses in archetypal moments that appear amazing to us. Causality and teleology collapse here, for synchronistic phenomena behave like coincidences. But their being consists in the fact that an objective process coincides in a corresponding way with a psychic event, i.e., for example, a physical process has a meaning in common with an endopsychic one. This sentence implies not only a (ubiquitous?) *latent* meaning that can be recognized by consciousness but also, for that preconscious time, a psychoid process that coincides in a corresponding way with a physical process. But here, meaning cannot yet be recognized by any consciousness. It is through the archetype that we come closest to this early, irrepresentable, psychoid stage of conscious development; indeed, the archetype itself gives us direct intimations of it. Unconscious synchronicities are also, from experience, absolutely possible.[7]

By suggesting there are psychoid processes within evolutionary development, there is the possibility of more than an unconscious aspect to the psyche. The tendency for psyche to emerge, and with it the capacity for meaning, may precede, perhaps even shape, the evolution of consciousness.

My own speculations are that this passage can also be used to address the great biological question of what occurred prior to evolution, that is, the origins of life. Without repeating the arguments, the best theories of the origins of life center on self-organization and emergence in complex adaptive systems (CAS). Careful comparison reveals numerous parallels between synchronistic phenomena and these systems, especially at

---

7   Jung and Neumann, *Analytical Psychology in Exile*, 349-350.

critical moments, precisely when self-organization and emergence are occurring. These parallels strongly suggest overlapping if not identity between the concepts, so that we could speak of the observation of synchronistic phenomena as a form of CAS behavior.[8]

In exploring the writings of Jung and certain of those around him, we can find evidence of this approach, that is, complex systems, in their best intuitions, well in advance of the scientific articulation of these ideas beginning in the 1980s. Neumann's ability to value yet separate and differentiate himself from Jung at a theoretical level seems to have brought both of them to, and over, the speculative edge of the science of their day into a prescient dialogue that we are only recently able to bring to bear.

Using Ed Tronick's more general formulation of the cocreation of mind, I believe we can witness a "dyadic expansion of consciousness" in the correspondence.[9] Whether either Jung or Neumann intended this legacy is doubtful, and yet the letters reveal its occurrence. I believe they together were creating meanings that neither one of them was aware of in this exchange, in effect enacting another level of psychoid process.

The related question of latent meaning inherent in the universe was also raised in Neumann's February 1959 letter:

> Precisely because the psyche and the archetypes have developed with their meaning content in the development of nature, this meaning is not something foreign to nature but rather belongs to it from the outset.[10]

---

8   Joseph Cambray, "Synchronicity and Emergence," *American Imago* 59, no. 4 (2002): 409–434.
9   Edward Z. Tronick, "Multilevel Meaning Making and Dyadic Expansion of Consciousness Theory: The Emotional and the Polymorphic Polysemic Flow of Meaning," in *The Healing Power of Emotion: Affective Neuroscience, Development and Clinical Practice*, ed. Diana Fosha, Daniel J. Siegel, and Marion F. Solomon (New York: W. W. Norton, 2009). Ed Tronick is a developmental psychoanalyst, and he was not referring to the Jung/Neumann correspondence. But as you can see from the title of his paper he is discussing the way the cocreation of mind in the mother/infant dyad can be extended to ways we often expand awareness, as in the analytic vessel.
10   Jung and Neumann, *Analytical Psychology in Exile,* 346.

I would identify this as a form of objective meaning in the universe, that is, this is an argument in favor of "the strong Anthropic principle," that consciousness which is inherent in our world.[11] The possibility of objective meaning would be the resolution of Jung's Red Book dilemma, for synchronistic experience would be based on the possibility that such meaning exists in reality. Prophecy becomes an attempt to personalize this knowledge, and certain forms of madness a confused grasping at this.

In the last section of Jung's final letter to Neumann he discusses the psyche as a "higher synthesis," that is, a form of emergence and links the processes involved to synchronicities and to meaning:

> we ... need the hypothesis of a latent meaning to explain not only the synchronistic phenomena but also the higher syntheses. Meaning is always unconscious and can only be discovered post hoc ... . We do need the synchronistic experiences to be able to justify the hypothesis of a latent meaning that is independent of consciousness.[12]

Hence a latent objective meaning to the world, which preserved Jung's and perhaps modernity's sanity.

Finally, Jung wants to assert the myth of incarnation based on latent meaning. This he feels extends to humanity "a cosmogonic significance ... a true *raison d'etre*."[13] This is largely in response to Neumann's question of the way Jung plays with divine consciousness. In fact, Neumann holds a more philosophically stable position in his challenges to Jung's fascination with incarnation. One only has to remember the Leontocephalus fantasy from the Red Book to know how powerful this sort of myth was in Jung's imagination.[14]

---

11   Andrew Liddle and Jon Loveday, *Oxford Companion to Cosmology* (New York: Oxford University Press, 2008), 17–18.
12   Jung and Neumann, *Analytical Psychology in Exile*, 350.
13   Ibid.
14   C. G. Jung, *The Red Book: Liber Novus*, ed. Sonu Shamdasani (New York: W. W. Norton, 2009), 252–254.

Had Neumann outlived Jung where might he have taken these ideas? Obviously it is impossible to say, but I think there was a slightly greater psychological mindedness in Neumann's arguments.

PART X. *MEMORIES FROM MY (GRAND)FATHER'S HOUSE*

FIG. 1. LEFT TO RIGHT: MURRAY STEIN, RALLI LOEVENTHAL-NEUMANN, ANDREAS JUNG, NOMI KLUGER NASH, EREL SHALIT, DEBORA KUTZINSKI, MICHA NEUMANN, ULRICH HOERNI. PHOTO BY HUGH MILSTEIN HTTP://THEREDBOOKPRINTS.COM

Introduction to *Memories from My (Grand)Father's House*

O ne of the highlights of the Jung Neumann Conference at Kibbutz
Shefayim was an evening of "memories from my (grand)father's
house," which followed an exceptional dramatic reading from the Jung
Neumann letters performed by an ensemble of analysts from International
School of Analytical Psychology Zurich (ISAP Zurich)—Murray Stein
(narrator), John Hill (as Erich Neumann), Paul Brutsche (as C. G. Jung),
and Dariane Pictet (as various female figures). The fond memories shared
by two of Jung's grandsons and by Erich Neumann's children were
accompanied by reflections from several analysts who are children of
prominent first-generation Jewish Jungians.

In this section of the book, we have included, in addition to
words from Ulrich Hoerni, Andreas Jung, Micha Neumann, and Ralli
Loewenthal-Neumann, memories from Thomas Kirsch, Jacqueline
Zeller, and Nomi Kluger Nash. Thomas Kirsch, well known for his book
The Jungians and a past president of the International Association for
Analytical Psychology (IAAP), is the son of James and Hilde Kirsch,
acquaintances of Erich Neumann from their Berlin days onward and
founders of the Los Angeles Jungian circle and institute. Tom shares
his thoughts about aspects of the Kirsch-Neumann sibling rivalry for
Jung's attention as well as noting some of the connections between the
two already in Berlin, for example, Neumann's close friend Gerhard

Adler had been in analysis there with James Kirsch. Jacqueline Zeller, daughter of Max and Lore Zeller, tells of how her parents were able to escape from Germany after *Kristallnacht*, a few years after Neumann and Kirsch had left for Palestine, and how they later joined the Kirsches in Los Angeles. The section concludes with recollections shared by Nomi Kluger Nash, whose father, Yehezkiel Kluger, was one of the very first graduates of the Jung Institute in Zurich (and probably the only one who had his certificate signed by Jung himself). Her stepmother was Rivkah Schärf-Kluger, an early associate of Jung's in Zurich.

It is interesting to notice how a small group of Jews from Berlin became so significant in Jungian circles worldwide—Erich Neumann in Israel, James and Hilda Kirsch and Max Zeller in Los Angeles, Ernst Bernhard (an older cousin of Max Zeller) in Italy, and Gerhard Adler in England. The anecdotal recollections that follow add a personal dimension to the discussion of the creative dialogue between Jung and Neumann and with others among their associates.

Some Memories of My Grandparents

Andreas Jung

The year I was born, still in wartime, my parents moved from Zürich to Küsnacht, into a newly built house. Not far from our home, about ten minutes to walk, lived our grandparents Jung-Rauschenbach in a big old house on the shore of Lake Zurich. Three of my father's four sisters came with their families to stay nearby in Küsnacht or in the local area; at times there were sixteen of us cousins—fourteen boys and two girls. In summertime we used to meet up at 'Seestrasse', the home of our grandparents. We had great fun running around, plucking fresh carrots in the vegetable garden and jumping in the cool water! The friendly gardener tried to keep us in check, and Grandma offered us a tasty syrup. But Grandpa was not to be seen. Either he sat working with a client or his secretary somewhere hidden in the bushes—then we had to keep quiet!—or he was absent in his tower in Bollingen.

Every year we had our big children's party to celebrate Christmas, and during the year several other family events. Then Grandpa used to be present, and he knew what everyone was doing. But in a more intimate setting I saw him rather seldom. Therefore the little stories I'm going to share are not really about him but rather about his impact.

When I was a little boy, the mother of my mother invited me to spend holidays with her in Ascona in southern Switzerland. Rather unwillingly I went. Granny was writing at her desk, and I told her: "Listen, I don't like you that much, I prefer my Grandma in Küsnacht." She acted as if she wasn't listening, so I repeated: "Listen, I like my Grandma in Küsnacht more than I like you. You are rather like Grandpa [Jung] in Küsnacht." She got angry and phoned my mother to come take me home. My mother did not feel like traveling all that way, so I had to stay. But it was the beginning of a lifelong close relationship. What linked Granny with Grandpa in Küsnacht: he told you what he was thinking of you, not always flattering—obviously I was doing the same!

Once as a young boy I was in the big house on the lake. By chance I heard my grandparents Jung talking to one another and complaining about the house being quite a burden. I joined them and said: "Well, listen, whenever you don't want the house any longer, I will take it!"—they laughed, of course.

Years later, when both of my grandparents Jung had died, my father was in a position to move into the house with our family; but soon the four adult boys left home. Then in 1975 my mother got ill, and the house became too large for my parents. So they asked me and my young family to share the home with them. And now, after the passing away of my parents, my early wish was fulfilled—and the burden is ours!

Ten years ago we were asked to attend a conference in San Francisco. As I am not a psychologist but an architect, all I could do was to speak about the house. I prepared my lecture, and the evening before taking off everything finally was ready. Just by chance I inserted a CD my wife had been given that day in a fashion store. A sonorous voice sounded: *"Vocatus atque non vocatus, Deus aderit"*—this is the inscription over the doorway of my home! The two of us stared at each other spellbound and incapable of understanding: this was the voice of my grandfather! And even stranger—"Vocatus Atque Non Vocatus" was the title of my lecture! We listened for about fifteen minutes and felt highly encouraged after all.

Only much later I realized that I had made an operational error and released this testimony, which I had copied years before and lost in the system.

Memories

Ulrich Hoerni

I cannot share any professional memories of my grandfather, since I was a schoolboy, but I knew Seestrasse. C. G. and Emma Jung had five children, nineteen grandchildren—four girls and fifteen boys. And forty great-grandchildren. As boys, we were there often after school. The situation near the lake was very nice. When the weather was fine, we went swimming there. In between we went to the garden, where there were carrots. We took out the carrots and had them as a snack. If the carrots were too small, we put them back in the ground. We could also ride bicycles in the garden. There were paths all across the garden. Some of us learned to ride a bicycle there, in the garden. I especially remember, probably in 1955, when Jung planned an extension of the Bollingen tower. He made a mock-up of clay. He made the tower exactly as it existed then. He used the anatomical instruments that he had used as a student. He then painted the whole mock-up. As you know there is also a forest around the tower. So he needed trees. There was a shop in Zurich, the dream of all children, where you could buy every kind of toy. They had a toy train department. Jung sent me to the toy train department where they also had small trees. I had to bring him samples of different trees. I had to show them to him, and he then ordered a certain number of each tree. He then arranged the whole forest around the tower. Unfortunately, the mock-up has not survived.

I also remember certain people who have been mentioned today. I just experienced them from a child's perspective. The grandparents talked about them all the time. Sometimes they were invited for lunch. They might have said, "Ms. Jacobi will be here for tea next week," and "Ms. Jaffé wrote the letter in question," or "I asked Mr. Muller the gardener to give the cook five more eggs." This was the kind of memory I had. There were also piano concerts in the living room. My sister took piano lessons when I was in second class. We did not have a piano at home. We were allowed to use the piano. While she played, I looked at the books on the shelves. I also remember some splendid Christmas parties, when the whole big family was present. Mr. Muller, the gardener, arranged the whole landscape with the cradle, Jesus, the holy family, a number of animals, shepherds. The whole equipment. It was big. My feeling was that everything in the house was big. From the house itself to Jung's handkerchief—everything was big.

I also remember the person mentioned today, Mari-Jeanne Schmid, the secretary. Usually she was the first person we saw when we entered, because it was the first door after the entrance. Of course, she opened all mail, and I collected stamps as a boy. So she always gave me the envelopes with the stamps, and I took them home. I still have them in a box in a cupboard.

She was smoking all the time. So there were two people in the house who were smoking. The first one, of course, Jung himself. He smoked a pipe, and Mari-Jeanne smoked cigarettes. It belonged to the atmosphere.

These are some memories.

Memories

Micha Neumann

I could share a lot, and I believe the audience is very tired now. So I will start with the fact that I first met Erich Neumann on June 17, 1932. I have no memories, but my mother told me a very nice story that I want to share with you. I came with my mother to Tel Aviv when I was around two years old. And after three months, my father came. And my situation changed, not for the better. So, once, this is not my memory, but this is the story of my mother. I told her, "Mama, cannot the two of us kick this man out and send him to where he was before?" Excuse me for this oedipal story.

In our house in Tel Aviv, in the four-room apartment, it was totally German. We spoke German with our parents. My father was Papa, my mother was Mama, and everything was German. All books were in German. All the songs that my mother sang for me before I went to sleep were German.

My father told me stories of the Bible, which he liked very much. I don't remember at what occasion, probably not every Friday, but on special occasions, he painted for me the stories of the Bible. And I remember the paintings and the stories very well. I hope that sometime you will be able to see these pictures because one, for instance, I remember very well, about Joseph, who was the spoiled son of Jacob. He, of course, aroused a lot of sibling rivalry. So one day when he told his brothers about his dreams, the sun and the moon and the twelve stars that bow in front of him. He was very naïve and believed they would admire him for this. Instead, they threw him into the pit. My father painted how he ran with Arab camels back to Egypt, another painting was about him interpreting the dream of Pharaoh, and yet another one was about the ten plagues. It was very vivid for me to see these pictures and hear the stories.

But we also had fights. My parents had a very big bed. And in their sleeping room, my mother also worked with patients. There was also a place where my father and I could fight like lions. He was a big lion, I was a small lion, and I always won. This was my father's attitude. Our meetings especially were at *halb-zwei*, that is, 1:30. We ate lunch together. My father would listen to Ralli, to me. Conversation was very casual. Never about work or psychology. For me he was a regular father. It wasn't interesting for me what he was doing, though I knew patients came, and my father, as well as my mother, spoke with them. Sometimes my friends asked me, as did teachers, "What does your father do?" I did not know what to say, because what kind of work is that? I had a friend—his father was a physician, another friend's father was a bus driver, and yet another, his father was a pharmacist. What can I tell about my father? That he talks with people? What kind of work is that? So as a small child, my father's profession was very embarrassing for me.

Later, I also have memories of my father, with whom I also quarreled about political matters: because in my adolescent years, it was a time when a lot of things happened with the British. They didn't allow the refugees from the concentration camps to come to Palestine. I spoke against this, while my father was like a good citizen, very respectful to the government, like the Germans always were. He opposed all kind of acts carried out by the Jewish community against the British government. So we quarreled about this. He could often get very angry—my mother said, "He is a lion." My mother and I, we were like scales [balanced], but he could get very angry, though he quickly returned to being a nice person.

I experienced my parents, especially my father, as a very good father and parent. He had much confidence and trust in me. And he believed in me. This attitude of his, and of my mother, made me very self-confident and independent. I felt my parents allowed me much more than other parents allowed their children, which was very good to me.

I think this is enough for now to tell about Erich Neumann, my father.

FIG. 1. PAINTING BY ERICH NEUMANN (1936) FROM HIS STORY 'THE BEETLE ORCHESTRA' TO HIS SON MICHA. THE ORCHESTRA IS ARRIVING AT THE HOUSE OF SNOW WHITE AND THE SEVEN DWARFS. © MICHA NEUMANN.

Memories

Ralli Loewenthal-Neumann

I would like to talk first of all about my father. My father never talked about his youth. My mother talked a lot about her childhood. My father—never. We didn't know anything. But what I want to tell you is how it worked at Gordon Street One. We had an apartment of four rooms, which at this time was very big. Most people didn't live in four-room apartments. In one room my father worked, in the other my mother. One room was shared by Micha and myself, and there was also my grandmother. So how did everything work? My father said he didn't want to have a phone. "If I had a phone," he would say, "the patient would phone and cancel, preferring to go to the manicurist or the hairdresser. Without a phone, they have to come." So we didn't have a phone till after the death of my father.

So how did everything work? My father worked full hours—eight, nine, ten, and so on. My mother half an hour. We the children opened the door for the patients. Then we had to knock on the door and say, "One moment please," if someone wanted to arrange a meeting, or knock on the door and say, "The patient has come." So you need to know that the patients were everywhere. They were in our room, where the children were, where my grandmother was, sometimes they waited in the kitchen. I really don't know how it worked, without a phone. People came to my mother, wanting hand analysis. As a small child, I was very happy there, sitting in the lap of the patients. Some of them told me stories. You can't imagine. It wasn't the way it should be, but that's the way it was. Once I told a patient, "You don't know what I do with my father—I can turn him around my finger. He does whatever I want." That's how Gordon Street was working, more or less. I think we were educated in a very good way, because we ensured that people won't run into each other. I also called the patients with various names, to which my parents laughed. I would say, "Now comes the serious one," or "Here comes the one who drops his money on the stairs."

It was so different from the way things are nowadays.

Secondly, I believe I wasn't that clever, and my father wanted me to be more knowledgeable, to know more. I remember we were sitting together, and I had to write a work about Moses. So he explained to me how come Moses, as a child, stuttered, unable to express a complete sentence. He spoke about Moses' difficulty to overcome it, and initially always needing his brother Aaron to be with him. I remember this clearly, and it remains important to me, people who stutter or who have a speech difficulty.

Additionally, every Friday evening my father painted something from the Bible for Micha. He also then told me the stories of the Bible. He then decided I must also know something about the New Testament. I won't forget it. He took his many art books, and through the art books, a lot could be learned about the New Testament. He wanted to teach me, which he did in a very nice way. I never felt that he was a psychologist, because he never used psychological terms. He was a father, not a psychologist. As a girl I had asthma and wasn't allowed to eat egg whites. So he told a story about the sun and the moon, I received the cream of the sun, the others the moon. I was very spoiled. The atmosphere at home was very free.

When I was four, he wrote a story about the journey to the moon; I heard lots of stories.

PAINTING BY ERICH NEUMANN FROM HIS STORY 'THE MOON PRINCESS' TO HIS
DAUGHTER RALLI, WHO "SLIDES ON A RAY FROM THE MOON TO THEIR HOME AT 1
GORDON STREET, ACCOMPANIED BY MANET'S THE FLUTE PLAYER." © RALLI
LOEWENTHAL-NEUMANN.

Both parents worked from morning till evening, though after 7 p.m. my mother did not see any patients—she was entirely for us children, telling stories and singing songs. She was very special.

Memories

Debora Kutzinski

Erich Neumann founded the Israel Association of AΨ in January 1959. We were five people. The sixth member—there had to be six for the founding—couldn't make it on this day. So we were four women and Erich Neumann as the president. Neumann started by saying, "By this, ladies, we are founding ..." and here Julia interrupted him, pointing at me, or rather at my belly. I was eight months pregnant. Neumann stood up, made a ceremonial bow to the belly, and said, "By this, ladies and gentlemen, we are founding the Association." Well, one month later my daughter was born—who today is an experienced psychologist, what else!

I met Erich Neumann the first time in 1948. He made a great impression on me, for sure. He had a lion's mane of graying hair. He was very quiet, and then chain-smoking. I thought him to be seventy—he was forty-three, having just published his *Origins and History of Consciousness*. He sent me straight to Julia for analysis, which was a real blessing.

I now have to mention: we cannot talk about Erich Neumann without mentioning Julia, his heart and soul. She was my analyst, and till the end my friend. After some years in analysis, which was very painful—and analysis has to be painful, I understand—Neumann was my second analyst, then my supervisor, and then, with good fortune, he and Julia were good friends of my husband and me. Particularly we listened to classical music, chamber music and lieder, sometimes till two o'clock in the morning. And Neumann loved to eat Camembert and shrimps—which we had delivered.

I learned to know him better. This was a deeply religious man, humble vis-à-vis the numinous. Creativity was his essence. And yes, he did suffer fools gladly, which I just experienced with him. Once in supervision, he was late, which was unusual. I waited ten minutes, fifteen minutes, twenty minutes. Then he ended, and said, come in, I have a guest, I just want to end our conversation. You may have a cup of coffee.

The guest was evidently also a man of spirit, somewhat older than Neumann. The coffee was good, very good—but the conversation … what kind of conversation! It was much more a lover's tiff, both men being tense, in the grip of emotion, the atmosphere in the room was charged. They spoke in German, which is my mother tongue.

So I listened, but I just understood three words. In German—mysticism, *funken*, and *schalen*. In English: mysticism, sparks, and what I first understood as peels, like banana peels or potato peels. I did not understand what these two intellectuals are talking about peels. Only then did it dawn on me that "peels" are also "vessels." So it meant "mysticism, sparks, and vessels." But still, I didn't understand. A few minutes later, the guest stood up, he had to go back to Jerusalem. Neumann then asked me, "Do you know who this was?" It was Gershom Scholem. Then he asked me, "What do you know about mysticism?" I think my face showed that I had no idea. So he said, "I will help you. Do you love people?" Well, I wanted to be a Jungian analyst, so could I say no? I said, "Yes." "Do you love life?" This was much more difficult. I didn't love life. I had great reservations, because of my past. The past was four years in Auschwitz, and two other concentration camps, and the murder of my whole family; the extended family was fifty-nine people, because my father had seven sisters, all married, all with children. My mother had two brothers, married with children, and so on and so on. All of them went up … to heaven, I hope … as smoke.

So, understandably, I didn't love life. But I wanted desperately to be a Jungian analyst, hoping that this will give me some meaning in life. So I lied, and said "Yes." So Neumann said, "So at your age, you know enough about mysticism." I thought he was making fun of me. But shortly afterward I read his "Mystical Man" and saw that these are the important points. Neumann's mystic is no hermit in the desert. He loves people and loves life.

Another time, I brought a very difficult dream, of which I couldn't make heads or tails. I was sure that at the end of the session I would know more. For a long while, Neumann was quiet. Then he said, in a definite way, "I don't know. I don't understand the dream. What does it mean, what does he want?" I didn't like that. After all, he was the great Neumann. He had to know. You see, I don't know if I am talking to you out of transference or out of relatedness, but does it really matter? So I said, "Maestro, you don't know?" He terribly disliked being called "Maestro" by me. But since he could call me "Stupid sheep," I thought it was only fair.

So then he said, very seriously, "Tell me, how much do we know about the psyche? Ten percent? Fifty percent? How much?"

This one sentence has stayed with me for sixty years of my analytical work. It is of great help. How much do we really know about the mystery of the soul?

Let me share something about the humor of Neumann. In the summer of 1959, Neumann asked me to take over, for two months, his most difficult patient, who could not stay without a therapist. This was a twenty-eight-year-old, famously beautiful girl. He saw her every day for fifteen minutes and twice a week for therapy. Only afterward she told me that she was allowed to call him "Erich" and allowed to hold his hand. So she was very contained by him. Instead of being glad at Neumann's vote of confidence, I got terribly afraid. What would she tell him when he came back? When in supervision, I can choose what to tell him.

Her dominant symptom was a fear that she was going to go blind. It was quite serious. Neumann was her sixth psychologist. She had been hospitalized for a year before she came to him. What shall I tell you? She had already lived for five years with her boyfriend, a very serious man. After fourteen days, Neumann having gone to Zurich and Ascona, she told me she had left him and moved in with a new man, just on the spur of the moment. I got very afraid, what will I tell Neumann? Not only that, but ten days later, she told me she is pregnant. Well, I wanted to bury myself in the earth. What kind of irresponsible analyst am I? This is his most difficult patient, and in twenty days she has a new man and is pregnant. Well, Neumann returned and asked me, "How did it go?" I said, "*Comme ci comme ça*; there is news." "What?" I said, "A new man." To my astonishment, Neumann answered, "Maybe this is good. The old one was very introverted." "There is more," I said. He immediately understood and pointed to his belly, and I said, "Yes." I asked him, "What should I have done?" With a very serious face, Neumann answered, "You should have been lying under the bed." I was so afraid of him that I took it seriously, "What!!" He, of course, burst out laughing. Only later, when Neumann was already dead, did I understand that this was no accident. Evidently I didn't contain her as much as Neumann did, which allowed her to move. And she found a more suitable man, with whom she is married, with two grown-up children. Ten years ago she came for a visit—they now live in Paris—and to this day, she is grateful to Neumann.

Thank you very much.

A Response

Thomas B. Kirsch

O verall, this correspondence is of immense importance to the history of the Jungian movement. Neumann was considered by many, but by no means all, especially in Jung's inner circle in Zurich in the 1940s, to be Jung's intellectual and spiritual son. Jung certainly implies as much in his foreword to *The Origins and History of Consciousness* (1949/1954), where he writes, "he arrives at conclusions that are among the most important ever to be reached in this field." In an interview recently available from the Library of Congress in the United States in which Kurt Eissler interviewed Jung on Freud in 1953, Jung discusses the difficulty of being a leading figure but then having a student continuing in a creative way one's most important thoughts. Jung thought that he was doing that with Freud's ideas of "archaic vestiges" into archetypes. Freud could not accept that. Jung has the same feeling about Neumann furthering his work. It is not easy when a student makes a real contribution to one's own most cherished work, but Jung says, "I have a very talented student, Neumann, in … Tel Aviv. He is truly a significant person! And, he took hold of some of my material and did something with it. You know, when one is overtaken in this manner, it is not easy for someone who has been in front." High praise, indeed!

So, given the importance Jung attributed to Neumann's work, it is perhaps a little surprising that two of his central contributions to analytical psychology are not given as much space in the correspondence as I had expected to find. Maybe I am mistaken in this impression, and I would appreciate the views of the Neumann specialists on this point. I am thinking of the concept of centroversion, that is, the coming together of introversion and extraversion, and the concept of the ego-self axis.

There has been much criticism coming from Michael Fordham and his followers in the SAP of Neumann's book *The Child* (this was published in German in 1963 and in English in 1973, but Fordham's stinging critique did not reach its crescendo until the early 1980s). Fordham was scathing because, he said, Neumann never treated children. However, what is little known is that for many years he ran a consultation group for child therapists and developed his ideas about children from this long-standing experience, as I learned in 1997 when I interviewed Geula Gat, a Jungian-oriented child therapist who lived and worked in a kibbutz below the Golan Heights. Regularly, she traveled to Tel Aviv, where she was part of a group of child therapists to discuss their cases with Neumann in his apartment. In addition, I believe there is still in existence a child treatment facility using Neumann's ideas and approaches.

A big part of the early correspondence with Jung concerned Neumann's difficulties with my father, James Kirsch. I hadn't realized they had had such a competitive, "sibling rivalry" relationship when they were both in Palestine.

It is clear to me from the limited reading that I have done so far that the small mandatory Palestine, later to become Israel, would never have been big enough to contain both my father and Erich Neumann. In fact, I don't think that there were many Jungian communities that could have contained both of them. Each needed to be a singular leader of his own Jungian group!

Another question is, did my father and Neumann know each other in Berlin? The editor seems to think that they had very little contact prior to going to Palestine. I wasn't born yet so I can't make a definite statement. However, Neumann's friend from childhood until his death, Gerhard Adler, was in analysis with my father beginning in 1929. I cannot imagine that Gerhard did not talk about his analysis to some degree with his good friend Erich. It also seems that they were all part of a liberal Zionistic movement in Berlin, and even if he and my dad were not good friends, it is hard for me to imagine that their paths did not cross in this larger social context.

The next issue I want to raise concerns about is my father's *seniority* to Neumann. As Ann Lammers has pointed out, James Kirsch received his medical degree in 1923 and had a solid practice in Berlin. He had already contacted Jung in 1928 and began his analysis in 1929. He'd lectured twice to the Analytical Psychology Club in Zurich in 1930. Neumann never officially got his medical degree because by that time the Nazis did not permit Jews to get diplomas. He didn't meet Jung and begin analysis until 1933. So I can see that at the beginning my father, who had arrived a few months earlier than Neumann and established his practice, would've felt that he deserved the status of the senior Jungian analyst in Palestine and saw Neumann as his junior. Also to be noted is the fact that Jung's first letter to Neumann in Palestine was sent to my father's address. Knowing my father as I did, I can't imagine that he was very happy that Jung chose Neumann over him to have a dialogue about the Jewish questions.

I find it interesting that my father's first wife, Eva, gets involved with the whole situation between the two men. It was 1935, and my father was already deeply involved with his patient Hilde Silber, who was soon to become his second wife and my mother. James and Eva were already in the process of getting a divorce. Why did she rush to his defense? Fortunately, James and Hilde left for London and were married on September 11, 1935. I was born June 14, 1936. You can do the math. According to Jo Wheelwright, I was considered a love child.

I must say that I found it very charged that Neumann wrote to Jung about my father's lack of clinical boundaries. As those of you who have read my father's correspondence with Jung will already know, my father certainly did a lot of acting out with female patients. However, Neumann speaks of his concerns about six patients. These concerns include sexual acting out but also involve disagreements with the way in which my father handled the "religious problem" of the patient. I am surprised to see Neumann writing critically about my father to Jung. I wonder if it was also, in a sense, tactical, in order to gain Jung's respect in some way. Certainly Neumann refers to my father as being a warm man at the same time as sending Jung these negative reports. Was this genuine or was there an element of "damning with faint praise"?

On a personal note, when Erich Neumann was still in Berlin, my favorite aunt was engaged to his older brother Franz, before marrying my favorite Uncle Walter, my mother's older brother. This is another piece of evidence that the German Jews in Berlin were quite involved with each other.

People may be interested to know that my parents always read Neumann, and I never heard a bad word about him at home! My mother read him avidly, and so did my dad. I have often wondered what my life would have been had my parents stayed in Palestine in 1935. I could have been a Sabra. Hebrew would be my mother tongue. What would I be saying today, at this conference, about Erich Neumann? A path not taken.

Remembering the Mamas and Papas

Nomi Kluger Nash

As the daughter of Yehezkel Kluger and the stepdaughter of Rivkah Schärf-Kluger, I have been asked to share some memories. They would be delighted (perhaps are?) that this is being done in their final home, Israel, having in 1967 kept the promise to themselves to return to this country.

What seemed like only yesterday is now many a yesteryear, in fact, eight decades, since our (collective) parents began work as Jungian analysts under the tutelage and inspiration of C. G. Jung—the biological grandfather of two gentlemen on this stage and the spiritual grandfather of us, his "offspring."

How sweet it is that our celebration of the Jung/Neumann letters is here in Israel where my father and mother, Yehezkiel and Tovah Kluger, both New Yorkers, came to live in 1935 (and where I was born the following year). It is to Israel that another Jungian Berliner, James Kirsch and his wife Hilde, came to live after escaping Germany. Adding to this Israel grouping in the more recent years of the 1980s is David Zeller, a rabbi who raised a family here and whose spiritual sensibilities were inherited from his father Max Zeller, yet another Jungian Berliner who left that city in the 1930s, escaping internment in a concentration camp largely due to the efforts of his wife, Lore.

I say "how sweet" because this cluster of Jungian Jews who directly studied with the living Jung, and who had some living connections to Israel, flies in the face of the *surety* of those accusations against Jung of being anti-Semitic ... as does the close connection between Jung and Neumann.

This land, both spiritual and material, was an essential presence for my parents, as it was to Zionism in general. My father, in lecturing on the archetypal reality of daily life in Israel, would quote a line in an old Zionist song, [phonetically] *"Anu banu Artza, livnot ulhibanot ba,"* loosely translated as, "Let us build up the Land and therein/thereby, become rebuilt" that is, within ourselves.

I am reminded of a letter Jung wrote to Neumann in 1935.

> I am extraordinarily interested in what the Jews are doing on their own archetypal soil ... . I find your very positive conviction that the soil of Palestine is essential for Jewish individuation most valuable.[1]

It took a while for my father and Rivkah to return to Israel, not moving there until 1967. The final push came with a short but strong dream of my father's in which he is driving his car in Israel and throws a piece of paper out the window, which paper is a deed for ownership of a parcel of land. The next day he made the arrangements for their long-postponed *Aliyah*.[2]

Living in Haifa they joined the tightly knit group of Neumann's students, of which another Swiss analyst who had studied with Jung, Gustav Dreifuss, had a bit earlier become a member.

My father was in the first class of the newly formed C. G. Jung Institute in Zurich (1948) and upon his graduation he took the gift of marrying his Swiss teacher, Rivkah Schärf. She obediently followed him to Los Angeles (not a city beloved by her) where they joined the

---

1   C. G. Jung, *Letters*, vol. 1, ed. Gerhard Adler, trans. R. F. C. Hull (Princeton, NJ: Princeton University Press, 1973), 206f.
2   "Immigration," but the literal meaning of the word is "ascent."

newly formed Jung Institute among whose founding members were Max Zeller with James and Hilde Kirsch, which organization grew from the Kirsches' Psychology Club.[3]

Today three of us children of the Los Angeles Jungian analysts are present, each of whom has pursued the profession of Jung's psychology, each in his and her individual way, to a greater or lesser fame. Here is Tom Kirsch, looming large on the screen on stage, myself, and in the audience, Jacqueline Zeller Levine, a Jungian analyst, is sitting alongside her nephew of Israel, Mordechai, son of David Zeller. Not attending is Daniel Zeller, a therapist in Canada.

Oh these generations radiating from my childhood in Los Angeles in the '40s and '50s when it was Tommy and Danny who were my friends, for we were the same age and shared many giggles. Jacqueline and David were too young to be our playmates, though they were a part of the Seder celebrations at the Klugers. The Kluger celebrations were traditional and oh so lively, both my father and Rivkah having been raised in orthodox homes with Hassidic backgrounds, his from Poland and Austria, hers from Bukovina (now in Romania).[4] I miss the long evenings of Sabbaths, Seders, all holidays, hearing my father's melodic baritone chanting of prayers and Rivkah's rich voice in our singing of the songs well into the night.

In being at this conference with the children of Kirsch, Kluger, and Zeller, I am visited by another gathering, when Danny, Tommy, and I were in our teens. It was a lecture by James Whitney (San Francisco), a child of two Jungian analysts (the first in America, or so I recall). He told of evenings at the dinner table listening to his parents speak of Mr.

---

3   See C. G.Jung and J. Kirsch, *The Jung-Kirsch Letters: The Correspondence of C. G. Jung and James Kirsch*, ed. Ann Conrad Lammers, trans. U. Egli and Ann Conrad Lammers (London: Routledge, 2011, 2016).

4   See my brief biography, "Rivkah Schärf Kluger (1907–1987): A Life Filled with Intensity of Spirit and Rare Depth of Soul," in C. G. Jung, *The Solar Myths and Opicinus de Canistris: Notes of the Seminar given at Eranos in 1943*, ed. Riccardo Bernardini, Gian Piero Quaglino, and Augusto Romano (Einseideln, Switzerland: Daimon Verlag, 2015), 116.

X or Mrs. X, being curious as to all this attention being given to these mysterious beings. We three turned to one another and nodded knowingly. Once again we turned to each other, nodding our heads, oh so strongly in agreement when Whitney told of his parents never scolding him with the usual statement of "You are a bad boy," but rather would say, "You should raise your inferior function!"

Yes, we were raised with Jungian terminology; mainly, however, we were raised with the spirit of Jung's mode of viewing life and in that we were gifted.

Memories of Max Zeller (1904–1978)

Jacqueline Zeller

Attending the Neumann-Jung Conference in Israel stirred up many feelings and memories of my father, Max Zeller.

My parents were German Jews from Berlin. My father, Max, my mother, Lore, and my older brother, Dan, at that time two and a half years old, emigrated from Berlin after my father was arrested on *Kristallnacht*, November 9, 1938, and sent to Sachsenhausen, a concentration camp outside of Berlin, where he was subjected to hard labor and unbearable living conditions for two months.

Because of the courage and persistence of my mother, who was only twenty-three years old at the time, the family's visas were issued in late January 1939. Max was released from the camp and within four months they left Germany and their families to live in London for two years during the frightening years of the bombing of London, the Blitz. Both my father's and my mother's family were forbidden to emigrate, and they were all murdered in 1941 in the concentration camps. Only my mother's two brothers survived. My parents and brother emigrated from England to Los Angeles, California, in 1941 where my father worked as a graphologist and analyst and my mother as a housekeeper. Within a few years, my father and James and Hilde Kirsch (with my mother at their side) founded the

C. G. Jung Institute of Los Angeles. This was a fulfillment of the dreams of these Jungians in their new lives in a new country.

Both Erich Neumann and James Kirsch, Jungian analysts and German Jews, had long-term correspondence with Jung, regarding Jungian psychology and the question of Jung's alleged anti-Semitism, both trying to "educate" Jung about Jews and religion, Jewish images, questions and reflections about the individual and the collective. My father, who became a Jungian analyst in the late '30s, did not have that personal relationship with Jung, nor, I believe, did he question Jung. He was a profoundly sensitive, introverted individual, who was, as my younger brother David once described him, an Orthodox Jungian and a Reform Jew. Jung was his lifeline and his life, and it colored our entire family life.

From the trauma of Nazi Germany, and the concentration camp, Max found his soul and hope through his relationship with Jungian psychology and his work as an analyst as well as with his family. He was dedicated to Jung, and from my earliest memories he comes asking, "What did you dream last night?" Jung was as integrated into our lives, from dreams to terms—"Ah, your negative animus is present" (to me as a teenager)—as was his love of being a Jew, the holidays. The stories, the music, and the rituals touched his heart and his soul. He passed that on to his children and now to the grandchildren through us.

It is thirty-seven years since his death and almost a decade since my mother passed away. It is now that I, as a Jungian analyst, can appreciate the depth of his love and identification of being a Jew *and* a Jungian. To my father, the two fit together and gave him a home for his soul, he who had been made homeless because of the Nazis. His family and Jung and his identification as a Jew were his nurturance as was my mother, who was his anchor in a world that had betrayed him and destroyed his life as it was in the 1930s. His life in Los Angeles was full of Jungians who were Jews, classical music (to which we *had* to listen every Sunday afternoon), and his love of nature. I am now deeply grateful that he "forced" me to learn from him to love classical music and Jung, even if at the time when I was young, I felt rebellious and did not want to be included in those things that he loved.

I was embarrassed that he spoke with a German accent, that as an analyst he didn't have a nine-to-five job like my friends' fathers. We didn't have a television until well into the '50s, and he wore a suit and tie at almost all times except when he was hiking with us or at his beloved beach on Sundays. I was again embarrassed, when I began to bring boyfriends home before a date, that my father was always such a European, in his suit and tie. My home was very different from my American friends'.

In 1957, having received reparation from Germany, we went to Switzerland for my father to study with Jung and intensify his analysis (as did my mother). My younger brother and I were in boarding schools in the French part of Switzerland. Another symbol of being different— living in Europe while all my friends were dating and wearing makeup and I was in a girls' school. In the end I did not want to come home, and I believe that it was that time, in "Jung Land," that I began to integrate Jung and being Jewish, as well as accepting and even able to be amazed and proud of my parents who were so different from the collective in which I yearned to fit.

Max and Lore's determination to live beyond survival, always deepening and responding to psyche, enabled them to emigrate from Nazi Germany and make a profoundly meaningful life in America.

The love of my father for my mother, my father's love for us children, my mother's steadfast presence and love, the house we lived in all our young lives and where my mother lived until 1994, gave me a security to find my own way in life. It has led me back to a deepening of relationship with my father, with my mother, and with being Jungian and Jewish. Recently I participated in the republication of my father's book *The Dream: The Vision of the Night* (Fisher King Press).

I am now able to live my life, *with* my father and his dreams, and it has become a deeply meaningful connection for me.

Bibliography

Abramovitch, H. "Erich Neumann and the Search for a New Ethic," *Harvest: International Journal for Jungian Studies* 52(2): 130–47.

Abramovitch, H. "Erich Neumann as My Supervisor: An Interview with Dvora Kutzinski." *Harvest: International Journal for Jungian Studies* 52(2): 172.

Abramovitch, H. "Ethics: A Jewish Perspective." In *Cast the First Stone: The Ethics of Analytical Therapy*, edited by L. Ross and M. Roy. Wilmette, IL: Chiron Publications, 1995.

Abramovitch, H. "The Influence of Martin Buber's Philosophy of Dialogue on Psychotherapy: Lasting Contribution." In *Dialogue as a Trans-Disciplinary Concept*, edited by P. Mendes-Flohr. Berlin: De Gruyter, 2015.

Abramovitch, H. "Stimulating Ethical Awareness," *Journal of Analytical Psychology* 52: 449–461.

Abramson, Larry. *Eventus Nocturnus*. Haifa: Haifa Museum of Art, 2001.

Adler, G. "Erich Neumann: 1905–1960." *Spring* (1961): 6.

Anonymous. "The Unfolding and Healing of Analytic Boundary Violations: Personal, Clinical and Cultural Considerations." *Journal of Analytical Psychology* 50, 661–91.

Anzieu, D. *Le Corps de l'Art*. Paris: Gallimard, 1981.

Baer, B. *Picasso: Gravures 1900–1942*. Paris: RMN, 1996.

Bair, Deirdre. *Jung: A Biography*. Boston: Little, Brown, 2003.

Bänziger, H. "Das Eranos-Archiv," *Du* 15, no. 4 (1955): 62.

Bernardini, R. "Guest Editor's Introduction." *Spring: A Journal of Archetype and Culture*, special issue, *Eranos—Its Magical Past and Alluring Future: The Spirit of a Wondrous Place* 92 (2015): 9–11.

Bernardini, R. *Jung a Eranos: Il progetto della psicologia complessa*. Milan: FrancoAngeli, 2011.

Bernardini, R. "Jung nel giardino di Eranos: il paesaggio dell'analisi." In *L'Ombra del Flâneur: Scritti in onore di Augusto Romano*, edited by F. Vigna. Bergamo, Italy: Moretti & Vitali, 2014.

Bernardini, R. "La corrispondenza Carl Gustav Jung–Henry Corbin." *Historia Religionum* 5 (2013): 97.

Bin Gorion, M. J. *Die Sagen der Juden*, 5 vols., translated by Rahel Bin Gorion. Frankfurt: Rütten and Loening, 1913–1927.

Bly, Robert. *Iron John: A Book about Men.* Cambridge, MA: Da Capo Press, 2004.

Buber, M. *Eclipse of God: Studies in the Relation between Religion and Philosophy.* Translated by M. Friedman. New York: Harper and Row, 1975.

Buber, M. *Hasidism.* Translated by Greta Hort. New York: Philosophical Library, 1948.

Buber, M. *Tales of the Hasidism: The Later Masters.* New York: Schocken Books, 1948.

Buber, Martin. "Sinnbildliche und sakramentale Existenz im Judentum." In *Martin Buber Eranos Jahrbuch 1934*, 340–67. Zürich: Rheinverlag, 1935.

C. G. Jung Institute. *Evil: Studies in Jungian Thought.* Translated by R. Manheim and H. Nagel. Evanston, IL: Northwestern University Press, 1967.

Cambray, Joseph. "*The Red Book*: Entrances and Exits." In *The Red Book: Reflections on C. G. Jung's Liber Novus.* Edited by Thomas Kirsch and George Hogenson. London: Routledge, 2014.

Cambray, Joseph. "Synchronicity and Emergence." *American Imago* 59, no. 4 (2002): 409–434.

Cocks, Geoffrey. *Psychotherapy in the Third Reich: The Göring Institute*, 2nd ed., revised and expanded. London: Transaction Publishers, 1997.

Cunningham, Adrian. "Victor White: A Memoir." In C. G. Jung and Victor White, *The Jung-White Letters*, edited by Ann Conrad Lammers and Adrian Cunningham, 307–336. London: Routledge, 2007.

de Angulo-Roelli, X. "Eranos 1950. August 21–August 29" (typescript, 1959, Eranos Foundation Archives).

Dreifuss, Gustav. "Erich Neumanns jüdisches Bewusstsein." In *Kreativität des Unbewussten. Zum 75. Geburtstag von Erich Neumann (1905–1960)*, edited by H. Dieckmann, C. A. Meier, and H. J. Wilke. Basel: S. Karger, 1980.

Ehrenzweig, A. *The Hidden Order of Art.* London: Weidenfeld and Nicholson, 1967.

Eliade, M. "Eranos." *Nimbus* 2 (1954): 58.

Eliade, Mircea. *Journal II (1957–1969)*. Translated from French by Fred H. Johnson Jr. Chicago: University of Chicago Press, 1989.

Ellmann, R. *James Joyce*. New York: Oxford University Press, 1959.

Feuchtwanger, E. *Erlebnis und Geschichte als Kind in Hitlers Deutschland—Ein Leben in England*. Berlin: Duncker und Humblot, 2010.

Fichte, Johann Gottlieb. *Sämtliche Werke*. Edited by J. H. Fichte. Berlin: Verlag von Velt, 1845.

Fierz, Heinrich. "Memory of C. G. Jung," Carl Jung Depth Psychology, July 15, 2014; accessed at http://carljungdepthpsychology.blogspot.ch/2014/07/memory-of-cg-jung-by-henry-k-fierz.html.

Fierz-David, H. E. *Die Entwicklungsgeschichte der Chemie*. Basel: Birkhäuser, 1945.

Folini, M., and L. Zaza-Sciolli. "La collezione Barone Eduard von der Heydt al Monte Verità." In *Dal Seicento olandese alle avanguardie del primo Novecento: La collezione Eduard von der Heydt al Monte Verità*, edited by M. Khan-Rossi. Zurich: Museo Cantonale d'Arte/Pro Litteris, 1996.

Fraser, J. A. "ARAS: Archive for Research in Archetypal Symbolism." *Spring* (1964): 61.

Fraser, J. A. "Archive for Research in Archetypal Symbolism of the C. G. Jung Foundation (ARAS)." In *International Encyclopedia of Psychiatry, Psychology, Psychoanalysis and Neurology*, vol. 2, edited by B. B. Wolman. Indiana, PA: Aesculapius, 1977.

Fraser, J. A. "Report on the Archive for Research in Archetypal Symbolism." *Quadrant* 6 (1970): 21–24.

Fraser, J. A. ed. *The Bollingen Catalogue and Indexes to the Eranos Archive*. New York: privately printed, 1958.

Freud, S. *The Future of an Illusion*. New York: W. W. Norton, 1975.

Freud, S. *Leonardo da Vinci and a Memory of His Childhood*. New York: Norton, 1989.

Freud, S. *Moses and Monotheism*. New York: Vintage, 1955.

Freud, S. *The Moses of Michelangelo*. London: Hogarth Press, 1955.

Freud, S. *New Introductory Lectures on Psychoanalysis. Standard Edition of the Complete Psychological Works*, vol. 22. London: Hogarth Press, 1953–1973.

Freud, S. "Obsessive Actions and Religious Practices" (1907). *Standard Edition of the Complete Psychological Works*, vol. 9. London: Hogarth Press, 1953–1973.

Freud, S. *Totem and Taboo*. Translated by James Strachey. London: Routledge and Kegan Paul, 1950.

Freud, S., and K. Abraham. *The Complete Correspondence of Sigmund Freud and Karl Abraham*. Edited by Ernst Falzeder. London: Karnac, 2002.

Freud, S., and C. G. Jung. *The Freud/Jung Letters: The Correspondence between Sigmund Freud and C. G. Jung*. Edited by William McGuire. Translated by Ralph Manheim and R. F. C. Hull. Princeton, NJ: Princeton University Press, 1974.

Fröbe-Kapteyn, O. "In Memoriam Erich Neumann." *Eranos-Jahrbuch* 29 (1960): 7.

Fröbe-Kapteyn, O. "The Psychological Background of Eranos" (1939). *Spring: A Journal of Archetype and Culture* 92 (2015): 31–38.

Fröbe-Kapteyn, O., ed. *25 Jahre Eranos: 1933–1957.* Zurich: Rhein-Verlag, 1957.

Gaillard, C. "The Egg, the Vessels and the Words: From Izdubar to Answer to Job, for an Imaging Thinking." *Journal of Analytical Psychology* 57, no. 3 (2012).

Gaillard, C. "Jung, Picasso et le Bleu." *Revue de Psychologie Analytique* 1, no. 1 (2013): 33–75.

Gaillard, C. *Le Musée Imaginaire de C. G. Jung*. Paris: Stock, 1998.

Gaillard, C. "Le regard presbyte de C. G. Jung." *Cahiers Jungiens de Psychanalyse* 82 (1995).

Gaillard, C. "Psychanalyse à l'Ecole?" In *La Mémoire de l'Art*, edited by J. Gatard and P. Tilman. Paris: Sgraffite, 1984.

Gaillard, C. "Transcendance et croyance en psychanalyse jungienne à la lumière du *Livre Rouge*." *Cahiers Jungiens de Psychanalyse* 134 (2011): 61–91.

Gaillard, C. "Ulysse et Moïse. Première Partie." *Cahiers de Psychologie de l'Art et de la Culture* 3 (1978): 39–62.

Gaillard, C. "Ulysse et Moïse. Deuxième Partie." *Cahiers de Psychologie de l'Art et de la Culture* 5 (1979): 31–66.

Gilman, S. *Freud, Race, and Gender*. Princeton, NJ: Princeton University Press, 1993.

Gimbutas, M. A. *The Language of the Goddess: Unearthing the Hidden Symbols of Western Civilization*. New York: HarperCollins, 1989.

Gioni, M. *La Biennale di Venezia: Il Palazzo Enciclopedico* [*The Encyclopedic Palace*]. Venice: La Fondazione La Biennale, 2013.

Graf-Nold, Angela. "C. G. Jung's Position at the Eidgenössische Technische Hochschule Zürich (ETH Zurich): The Swiss Federal Institute of Technology, Zurich." *Jung History* 2, no. 2 (Fall 2007): 12–15.

Green, A. *Révélations de l'inachèvement: A propos du carton de Londres de Léonard de Vinci*. Paris: Flammarion, 1992.

Green, M. *Mountain of Truth—The Counterculture Begins: Ascona 1900–1920*. Hanover, NH: University Press of New England, 1986.

Green, M. *Otto Gross, Freudian Psychoanalyst, 1877–1920*. Lewiston, NY: Edwin Mellen, 1999.

Green, M. *Prophets of a New Age—The Politics of Hope from the Eighteenth through the Twenty-first Centuries*. New York: Charles Scribner's Sons, 1992.

Green, M. "Una Nuova Era. New Age e nuovi "Centri di vita" dal 1890 al 1920." In *Senso della vita e bagni di sole: Esperimenti di vita e arte al Monte Verità*, edited by A. Schwab and C. Lafranchi. Ascona: Fondazione Monte Verità, 2001.

Green, M. *The von Richthofen Sisters—The Triumphant and the Tragic Mode of Love: Else and Frieda von Richthofen, Otto Gross, Max Weber, and D. H. Lawrence, in the Years 1870–1970*. New York: Basic, 1974.

Gronning, T., P. Sohl, and T. Singer. "aras: Archetypal Symbolism and Images." *Visual Resources* 23, no. 3 (2007): 245–267.

Hakl, H. T. *Eranos: An Alternative Intellectual History of the Twentieth Century*. Montreal: McGill-Queen's University Press, 2013.

Hasenfratz, D. *Das Schicksal der Brissago-Inseln—Le Isole di Brissago e la loro storia: Vom Venustempel zum Eukalyptusbaum*. Ascona, Switzerland: Ferien-Journal, 1994.

Hasenfratz, D. "Il destino delle Isole di Brissago: dal tempio di Venere all'albero di eucalipto." Ascona, Switzerland: Ferien-Journal, 1994.

Haumann, Heiko, ed. *Acht Jahrhunderte Juden in Basel*. Basel: Schwabe Verlag, 2005.

Häussermann, Friedrich. *Wortempfang und Symbol in der alttestamentlichen Prophetie* (1932).

Henderson, J. L. "Introduction." In *An Encyclopedia of Archetypal Symbolism. The Archive for Research in Archetypal Symbolism*, vol. 1, edited by B. Moon. Boston: Shambhala, 1991.

Hill, J. "The Venom Destiny: Reflections on the Jung/Joyce Encounter." *Spring Journal* 79 (2008).

Hölderlin, Friedrich. *Hölderlin: Selected Verse.* Introduction and prose translations by Michael Hamburger. London: Anvil Press Poetry, 1986.

Humbert, E. G. *C. G. Jung: The Fundamentals of Theory and Practice.* Wilmette, IL: Chiron, 1987.

Hurwitz, E. "Conflitto e verità: La dimensione politica della psicanalisi per Otto Gross." In *Senso della vita e bagni di sole: Esperimenti di vita e arte al Monte Verità,* edited by A. Schwab and C. Lafranchi. Ascona: Fondazione Monte Verità, 2001.

Hurwitz, E. "Otto Gross: Dalla psicanalisi al Paradiso." In *Monte Verità. Antropologia locale come contributo alla riscoperta di una topografia sacrale moderna,* edited by H. Szeemann. Milan: Armando Dadò/Electa, 1978.

Hurwitz, E. *Otto Gross's "Paradies"—Sucher zwischen Freud und Jung: Leben und Werk.* Zurich: Suhrkamp, 1979.

Irigaray, L. *Ce sexe qui n'en est pas un.* Translated by D. Lieber. Tel-Aviv: Resling, 2003.

Jacoby, Mario. "Erich Neumanns Konzept der Urbeziehung im Lichte der neueren Kleinkindforschung" (pp. 38–48). In *Zur Utopie einer neuen Ethik. 100 Jahre Erich Neumann. 130 Jahre C. G. Jung.* Vienna: Mandelbaum Verlag, 2005.

Jaffé, A. "C. G. Jung and the Eranos Conferences." *Spring* (1977): 202.

Jaffé, A. *C. G. Jung: Bild und Wort.* Olten und Freiburg in Breisgau: Walter Verlag, 1978.

Jaffé, A. *From the Life and Work of C. G. Jung.* Einsiedeln, Switzerland: Daimon Verlag, 1989.

James, D. Lee. "The Archive for Research in Archetypal Symbolism." *Visual Resources* 1, no. 1 (1980): 10–11.

Jamme, Christoph, and Helmut Schneider, eds. *Mythologie der Vernunft: Hegels "Ältestes Systemprogramm des deutschen Idealismus."* Frankfurt a.M.: Suhrkamp, 1984.

Jehle-Wildberger, M. *C. G. Jung und Adolf Keller.* Zurich: Theologischer Verlag, 2014.

Jones, E. *Life and Work of Sigmund Freud, Vol. 2: The Years of Maturity, 1901–1919.* New York: Basic Books, 1955.

Jung, C. G. "After the Catastrophe" (1945). In *CW*, vol. 10. Princeton, NJ: Princeton University Press, 1970.

Jung, C. G. *Analytical Psychology: Notes of the Seminar Given in 1925 by Carl Gustav Jung.* Princeton, NJ: Princeton University Press, 1989.

Jung, C. G. *Answer to Job* (1952). In *CW*, vol. 11. Princeton, NJ: Princeton University Press, 1969.

Jung, C. G. *Aspects of the Feminine.* London: Routledge, 2008.

Jung, C. G. *Bericht über das Berliner Seminar von Dr. C. G. Jung, 26 Juni–1 Juli 1933*; forthcoming as: *C. G. Jung's Berlin Seminar 1933*, edited by Giovanni Sorge. Princeton, NJ: Princeton University Press.

Jung, C. G. "Bruder Klaus." *Neue Schweizer Revue* 1, no. 4 (August 1933). English translation: "Brother Klaus" (1933). In *CW*, vol. 11. Princeton, NJ: Princeton University Press, 1969.

Jung, C. G. *C. G. Jung Speaking.* Edited by William McGuire and R. F. C. Hull. Princeton, NJ: Princeton University Press, 1987.

Jung, C. G. "Die Erdbedingtheit der Psyche." In *Mensch und Erde.* Edited by Hermann Keyserling, 83–137. Darmstadt: Otto Reichl Verlag, 1927.

Jung, C. G. "Diskussionsvotum von Dr. Jung (über Halluzination)." Lecture at the Swiss Association of Psychiatry, Prangins, Switzerland, October 7–8, 1933; published in *Schweizer. Archiv für Neurologie und Psychologie* 32(2):382. English translation: "On Hallucination" (1933). In *CW*, vol. 18, Princeton, NJ: Princeton University Press, 1976.

Jung, C. G. *Dream Analysis.* Princeton, NJ: Princeton University Press, 1984.

Jung, C. G. *The Earth Has a Soul.* Edited by Meredith Sabini. Berkeley, CA: North Atlantic Books, 2008.

Jung, C. G. "Epilogue to *Essays on Contemporary Events*" (1946). In *CW*, vol. 10. Princeton, NJ: Princeton University Press, 1970.

Jung, C. G. "The Fight with the Shadow" (1946). In *CW*, vol. 10. Princeton, NJ: Princeton University Press, 1970.

Jung, C. G. "Flying Saucers: A Modern Myth of Things Seen in the Sky" (1958). In *CW*, vol. 10. Princeton, NJ: Princeton University Press, 1970.

Jung, C. G. "Foreword to Adler: *Entdeckung der Seele*" (1933). In *CW*, vol. 18. Princeton, NJ: Princeton University Press, 1976.

Jung, C. G. "Geleitwort des Herausgebers." *Zentralblatt für Psychotherapie* 6:3. English translation: "[ ]" In *CW*, vol. 10. Princeton, NJ: Princeton University Press, 1970.

Jung, C. G. "Introduction to the American Eranos Volume." *Spring*; reprinted *Spring: A Journal of Archetype and Culture* 92 (2015): 58.

Jung, C. G. *Letters*, 2 vols. Selected and edited by Gerhard Adler. Translated by R. F. C. Hull. Princeton, NJ: Princeton University Press, 1973, 1975.

Jung, C. G. "The Meaning of Psychology for Modern Man" (1934). In *CW*, vol. 10. Princeton, NJ: Princeton University Press, 1970.

Jung, C. G. *Memories, Dreams, Reflections*. Recorded and edited by Aniela Jaffé, translated by Richard and Clara Winston. New York: Pantheon Books, 1962, 1965.

Jung, C. G. "Mind and Earth" (1931). In *CW*, vol. 10. Princeton, NJ: Princeton University Press, 1970.

Jung, C. G. *Mysterium Coniunctionis* (1955–1956). *CW*, vol. 14. Princeton, NJ: Princeton University Press, 1963.

Jung, C. G. "On the Nature of the Psyche" (1954). In *CW*, vol. 8. Princeton, NJ: Princeton University Press, 1969.

Jung, C. G. "On the Relation of Analytical Psychology to Poetry" (1922). In *CW*, vol. 15. Princeton, NJ: Princeton University Press, 1966.

Jung, C. G. "Paracelsus" (1934). In *CW*, vol. 15. Princeton, NJ: Princeton University Press, 1966.

Jung, C. G. "Paracelsus as a Spiritual Phenomenon" (1942). In *CW*, vol. 13. Princeton, NJ: Princeton University Press, 1967.

Jung, C. G. "Paracelsus the Physician" (1942). In *CW*, vol. 15. Princeton, NJ: Princeton University Press, 1966.

Jung, C. G. "Picasso" (1934). In *CW*, vol. 15. Princeton, NJ: Princeton University Press, 1966.

Jung, C. G. "A Psychological Approach to the Dogma of the Trinity" (1948). In *CW*, vol. 11. Princeton, NJ: Princeton University Press, 1969.

Jung, C. G. "Psychologie und Dicthung" (1930); in English, "Psychology and Literature" (1933). In *CW*, vol. 15. Princeton, NJ: Princeton University Press, 1966.

Jung, C. G. "The Psychology of the Transference" (1946). In *CW*, vol. 16. Princeton, NJ: Princeton University Press, 1966.

Jung, C. G. *Psychological Types* (1923). *CW*, vol. 6. Princeton, NJ: Princeton University Press, 1971.

Jung, C. G. "A Psychological View of Conscience" (1958). In *CW*, vol. 10. Princeton, NJ: Princeton University Press, 1970.

Jung, C. G. *Psychology and Alchemy* (1944). *CW*, vol. 12. Princeton, NJ: Princeton University Press, 1953.

Jung, C. G. *The Red Book: Liber Novus*. Edited by Sonu Shamdasani. New York: W. W. Norton, 2009.

Jung, C. G. "A Rejoinder to Dr. Bally." *Neue Zürcher Zeitung*, March 13–14, 1934.

Jung, C. G. "Rezension von: G. R. Heyer: Der Organismus der Seele." *Europäische Revue* 9:10. English translation: "Review of Heyer: *Der Organismus der Seele*" (1933). In *CW*, vol. 18. Princeton, NJ: Princeton University Press, 1976.

Jung, C. G. "The Role of the Unconscious" (1918). In *CW*, vol. 10. Princeton, NJ: Princeton University Press, 1970.

Jung, C. G. "Sigmund Freud in His Historical Setting" (1934). In *CW*, vol. 15. Princeton, NJ: Princeton University Press, 1966.

Jung, C. G. *Symbols of Transformation* (1952). *CW*, vol. 5. Princeton, NJ: Princeton University Press, 1967.

Jung, C. G. *The Solar Myths and Opicinus de Canistris: Notes of the Seminar given at Eranos in 1943*. Edited by Riccardo Bernardini, Gian Piero Quaglino, and Augusto Romano. Einseideln, Switzerland: Daimon Verlag, 2015.

Jung, C. G. "The State of Psychotherapy Today" (1934). In *CW*, vol. 10. Princeton, NJ: Princeton University Press, 1970.

Jung, C. G. "The Structure of the Psyche" (1931). In *CW*, vol. 8. Princeton, NJ: Princeton University Press, 1969.

Jung, C. G. "A Study in the Process of Individuation" (1950). In *CW*, vol. 9i. Princeton, NJ: Princeton University Press, 1968.

Jung, C. G. "Über Psychologie." *Neue Schweizer Rundschau* 1, no. 1 (May 1932): 1–28 and no. 2 (June 1932): 98–106. Updated and revised as "Die Bedeutung der Psychologie für die Gegenwart." In *Wirklichkeit der Seele: Anwendungen und Fortschritte der neueren Psychologie*, 32–67. Zürich: Rascher, 1934.

Jung, C. G. "Ueber die Beziehungen der Analytische Psychologie zum dichterischen Kunstwerk" (1922); in English, "On the Relation of Analytical Psychology to Poetic Art" (1923). In *CW*, vol. 15. Princeton, NJ: Princeton University Press, 1966.

Jung, C. G. "'Ulysses': A Monologue" (1934). In *CW*, vol. 15. Princeton, NJ: Princeton University Press, 1966.

Jung, C. G. *Visions*. Princeton, NJ: Princeton University Press, 1997.

Jung, C. G. "Vorwort zu Neumann *Ursprungsgeschichte des Bewusstseins*" (1949). In *GW* XVIII/2, pp. 556–557; "Foreword," in Erich Neumann, *The Origins and History of Consciousness*," translated by R. F. C. Hull. Princeton, NJ: Princeton University Press, 1954; reprinted in *CW*, vol. 18. Princeton, NJ: Princeton University Press, 1976.

Jung, C. G. "Wandlungen und Symbole der Libido: Beiträge zur Entwicklungsgeschichte des Denkens" (1912/1916). In *Jahrbuch für psychoanalytische und psychopathologische Forschungen* 3–4; English edition: *The Psychology of the Unconscious*, translated by B. Hinkle. Princeton, NJ: Princeton University Press, 1991.

Jung, C. G. *Wirklichkeit der Seele: Anwendungen und Fortschritte der neueren Psychologie*. Zürich: Rascher, 1934.

Jung, C. G. "Wotan" (1936). In *CW*, vol. 10. Princeton, NJ: Princeton University Press, 1970.

Jung, C. G., and Erich Neumann. *Analytical Psychology in Exile: The Correspondence of C. G. Jung and Erich Neumann*, edited by Martin Liebscher. Princeton, NJ: Princeton University Press, 2015.

Jung, C. G., and J. Kirsch *The Jung-Kirsch Letters: The Correspondence of C.G. Jung and James Kirsch*. Edited by Ann Conrad Lammers. Translated by U. Egli and Ann Conrad Lammers. London: Routledge, 2011; 2nd ed. London: Routledge, 2016.

Jung, C. G., and Victor White. *The Jung-White Letters*, edited by Ann Conrad Lammers and Adrian Cunningham. London: Routledge, 2007.

Kalff, D. M. *Sandplay: A Psychotherapeutic Approach to the Psyche*. Boston: Sigo Press, 1980.

Kant, Immanuel. *Religion and Rational Theology*. Translated by Allen W. Wood and George di Giovanni. Cambridge, UK: Cambridge University Press, 1996.

Kirsch, J. "Das Problem des modernen Juden." Lecture at the Psychological Club, Zurich, October 4, 1930. Unpublished typescript, Library of the Psychological Club, Zurich.

Kirsch, J. "Die Judenfrage in der Psychotherapie: Einige Bemerkungen zu einem Aufsatz von C. G. Jung." *Jüdische Rundschau*, no. 43, May 29, 1934, Berlin.

Reprinted as: "The Jewish Question in Psychotherapy: Some Remarks on an Essay by C. G. Jung." Translated by A. C. Lammers. *Jung Journal: Culture & Psyche* 6, no. 4 (2012) 78–84.

Kirsch, J. "The Jewish Image of the World" ["Das Weltbild des Juden"] (1931). In *The Jung-Kirsch Letters: The Correspondence of C. G. Jung and James Kirsch*, edited by Ann Conrad Lammers, translated by U. Egli and A. C. Lammers, 15–16. London: Routledge, 2011.

Kirsch, J. (1986). "Reflections at Age Eighty-Four." In *A Modern Jew in Search of a Soul*, edited by J. M. Spiegelman and A. Jacobson, 147–55. Phoenix, AZ: Falcon Press, 1986.

Kirsch, T. B. *The Jungians: A Comparative and Historical Perspective.* London: Routledge, 2000.

Kristeva, J. *Desire in Language: A Semiotic Approach to Literature and Art.* New York: Columbia University Press, 1980.

Krochmalnik, D. *Vierfacher Schriftsinn in Judentum und Christentum*: Sprache und *Religion*, edited by U. Gerber and R. Hoberg. Darmstadt: Wissenschaftliche Buchgesellschaft, 2009.

Kron, T., and D. Wieler. "Erich Neumann: A Jungian Dialogical Existentialist." Lecture delivered at the IAAP Congress, Copenhagen, August 2013. Unpublished typescript.

Lammers, Ann C. "C. G. Jung und die Gesellschaft für Psychotherapie." *Jungiana* 18(2014): 50–86.

Laplanche, J., and J. B. Pontalis. *The Language of Psychoanalysis.* London: Hogarth Press, 1973.

Lesmeister, R. "Eine Empörung im Grenzland von Religion und Tiefenpsychologie." *Analytische Psychologie* 176, no. 2 (2014): 202.

Lessing, Gotthold. *Lessing's Theological Writings*, trans. Henry Chadwick. Stanford, CA: Stanford University Press, 1956.

Liddle, Andrew, and Jon Loveday. *Oxford Companion to Cosmology.* New York: Oxford University Press, 2008.

Lo Russo, M. *Otto Gross: Psiche, Eros, Utopia.* Rome: Editori Riuniti University Press, 2011.

Lori, Aviva. "Jung at Heart." *Haaretz*, January 28, 2005.

Lösch, W. *Der werdende Gott: Mythopoetische Theogonien der romantischen Mythologie*. Frankfurt a.M.: Peter Lang, 1996.

Löwe, Angelica. *"Auf Seiten der inneren Stimme . . .": Erich Neumann—Leben und Werk*. München: Verlag Karl Alber, 2014.

Maercker, Andreas. "Geschichte des Psychologischen Instituts der Universität Zürich." Online paper, June 15, 2007; accessed at http://www.maerckerwebsite.ch/images/data/Gesch_Psych_Instituts_260607.pdf.

Maidenbaum, A., ed. *Jung and the Shadow of Anti-Semitism*. Berwick, ME: Nicolas-Hays, 2002.

Maidenbaum, A., and Stephen A. Martin, eds. *Lingering Shadows: Jungians, Freudians, and Anti-Semitism*. Boston: Shambhala, 1991.

McGuire, William. *Bollingen: An Adventure in Collecting the Past*. Princeton, nj: Princeton University Press, 1982.

McGuire, William. "Editorial Note." In E. Neumann, *The Place of Creation—Six Essays*. Princeton, NJ: Princeton University Press, 1989.

McGuire, William. "Firm Affinities: Jung's Relations with Britain and the United States." *Journal of Analytical Psychology* 40, no. 3(1995): 301–326.

McGuire, William. "Jung and Eranos in America." *Spring* (1984): 51–59.

Meier, Carl Alfred. *Antike Inkubation und moderne Psychotherapie*. Zurich: Rascher, 1949; English translation: *Ancient Incubation and Modern Psychotherapy*. Evanston, IL: Northwestern University Press, 1967.

Meier-Seethaler, Carola "*The Child*, Erich Neumann's Contribution to the Psychopathology of Child Development." *Journal of Analytical Psychology* 27 (1982): 357–379.

Mellon, P., with J. Baskett. *Reflections in a Silver Spoon—A Memoir*. New YorkY: William Morrow and Company, Inc., 1992.

Mellon, P., W. McGuire, K. Coburn, and J. Campbell. *To Celebrate the Life of Jack Barrett: 1903–1981*. New York: Pierpont Morgan Library, 1981.

Merlini, F. "Eranos: A Space and a Time for Thought." *Spring: A Journal of Archetype and Culture* 92 (2015): 41–55.

Meyer, Werner. *D a v erfiele B asel ü berall: D as B asler E rdbeben v on 1 356*. Basel, Switzerland: Schwabe Verlag, 2006.

Michaels, J. E. *Anarchy and Eros—Otto Gross' Impact on German Expressionist Writers—Leonhard Frank, Franz Jung, Johannes R. Becher, Karl Otten, Curth Corrinth, Walter Hasenclever, Oskar Maria Graf; Franz Kafka, Franz Werfel, Max Brod, Raoul Hausmann and Berlin Dada*. New York: Peter Lang, 1983.

Michaels, J. E. "Otto Gross und das Konzept des Matriarchats." In *2. Internationaler Otto Gross Kongress. Bürghölzli, Zürich 2000*, edited by G. Heuer. Marburg an der Lahn: Literatur Wissenschaft.de, 2002.

Mondada, G. *Le isole di Brissago nel passato e oggi.* Locarno: Amministrazione delle Isole di Brissago/Tipografia Stazione S.A. 1975.

Nagel, H., ed. *Eranos Archive: Images of the Great Mother Throughout the Ages.* New York: Analytical Psychology Club, 1938.

Nagel, H., ed. *The Eranos Conference 1938: Papers of the Analytical Psychology Club of New York.* New York: Analytical Psychology Club, 1939.

Neumann, Erich. *Amor and Psyche.* Princeton, NJ: Princeton University Press, 1973.

Neumann, E. *The Archetypal World of Henry Moore* (1961). Princeton, NJ: Princeton University Press, 1985.

Neumann, E. *Art and the Creative Unconscious.* Princeton, NJ: Princeton University Press, 1959.

Neumann, Erich. *The Child.* Translated by R. Manheim. Boston: Shambhala, 1990.

Neumann, Erich. *Creative Man: Five Essays.* Translated by Eugene Rolfe. Princeton, NJ: Princeton University Press, 1979.

Neumann, Erich. *Depth Psychology and a New Ethic.* Boston: Shambhala, 1990.

Neumann, Erich. "Die Judenfrage in der Psychotherapic." *Jüdische Rundschau,* no. 48, June 15, 1934, Berlin. Reprinted in *Analytical Psychology in Exile: The Correspondence of C. G. Jung and Erich Neumann.* Edited and with an introduction by Martin Liebscher, 355–56. Princeton, NJ: Princeton University Press, 2015.

Neumann, E. *The Fear of the Feminine and Other Essays on Feminine Psychology (1950–1959).* Princeton, NJ: Princeton University Press, 1994.

Neumann, Erich. *The Great Mother.* Princeton, NJ: Princeton University Press, 1981.

Neumann, Erich. *Jacob and Esau: On the Collective Symbolism of the Brother Motif.* Edited and with an introduction by Erel Shalit. Translated by Mark Kyburz. Asheville, NC: Chiron Publications, 2015.

Neumann, E. "The Magic Flute." *Quadrant* 2 (1978): 6.

Neumann, Erich. "Man and Meaning." In *The Place of Creation.* Princeton, NJ: Princeton University Press, 1989.

Neumann, Erich. "Mystical Man." In *The Mystic Vision: Papers from the Eranos Yearbooks*, edited by J. Campbell, 375–415. Princeton, NJ: Princeton University Press, 1968.

Neumann, Erich. *Origins and History of Consciousness*. Princeton, NJ: Princeton University Press, 1970.

Neumann, E. "The Psyche and the Transformation of the Reality Planes: A Metapsychological Essay." In *The Place of Creation*. Princeton, NJ: Princeton University Press, 1989.

Neumann, Erich. "The Psyche as the Place of Creation" (1960). In *The Place of Creation*. Princeton, NJ: Princeton University Press, 1989.

Neumann, E. "Review of Hugo Rosenthal, 'Der Typengegensatz in der jüdischen Religionsgeschichte' ('The Type-Difference in the Jewish History of Religion')." *Jüdische Rundschau*, July 27, 1934.

Neumann, Erich. *Ursprungsgeschichte des jüdischen Bewusstseins* [*On the origins and history of Jewish consciousness*], 2 vols. Unpublished typescript, 1934–40.

Neumann, E. "Zur psychologischen Bedeutung des Ritus." *Eranos-Jahrbuch* 19 (1950): 120.

Noth, Isabelle, ed. *Sigmund Freud—Oskar Pfister: Briefwechsel 1909–1939*. Zürich: Theologischer Verlag, 2014.

Ofrat, G. "Tumarkin: The Father, the Son and the Spirit of Sculpture." In *Bikurei omanut*. Tel Aviv: Hakibutz Hameuchad, 2005.

Paglia, C. "Erich Neumann: Theorist of the Great Mother." *Arion* 13(6): 9–10.

Paris, J. *Joyce par lui-même*. Paris: Seuil, 1957.

Portmann, A. *Animals Are Social Beings*. New York: Viking Press, 1961.

Portmann, A. "Vom Sinn und Autrag der Eranos Tagungen." *Eranos-Jahrbuch* 30 (1961): 7.

Prokop, H. "Erich Neumann in Israel." *Psychologie des 20: Jahrhunderts* 3, no. 2 (1977): 850.

Rank, O. *Beyond Psychology*. New York: Dover, 1958; originally published in 1941.

Reich-Ranicki, Marcel. *The Author of Himself: The Life of Marcel Reich-Ranicki*. London: Weidenfeld & Nicolson, 2001.

Reid, J. C. *Jung, My Mother and I: The Analytic Diaries of Catharine Rush Cabot*. Einsiedeln, Switzerland: Daimon, 2001.

Rosen, R. *Saving the Jews: Franklin D. Roosevelt and the Holocaust.* New York: Basic Books, 2007.

Rosenthal, Hugo. "Der Typengegensatz in der jüdischen Religionsgeschichte." In C. G. Jung, *Wirklichkeit der Seele: Anwendungen und Fortschritte der neueren Psychologie.* Zurich: Rascher, 1934.

Rosenzweig, Franz. *Der Mensch und sein Werk. Gesammelte Schriften*, part 3: *Zweistromland. Kleinere Schriften zu Glauben und Denken.* Dordrecht, Netherlands: Martinus Nijhoff, 1984.

Rosman, M. *Stories That Changed History: The Unique Character of Shivhei Ha-Besht.* Syracuse, NY: Syracuse University Press, 2007.

Rowland, S. *C. G. Jung and Literary Theory: The Challenge from Fiction.* Basingstoke, England: Macmillan Press, 1999.

Rowland, S. *Jung as a Writer.* London: Routledge, 2005.

Rowland, S. *Psyche and the Arts: Jungian Approaches to Music, Architecture, Literature, Painting, and Film.* London: Routledge, 2008.

Sacks, Oliver. "Sabbath." *New York Times*, August 16, 2015.

Samuels, A., B. Shorter, and F. Plaut. *A Critical Dictionary of Jungian Analysis.* London: Routledge and Kegan Paul, 1987.

Schelling, F. W. J. *Historical-Critical Introduction to The Philosophy of Mythology.* Translated by Mason Richey and Markus Zisselsberger. Albany, NY: State University of New York Press, 2007.

Schoenl, W. *C. G. Jung—His Friendships with Mary Mellon and J. B. Priestley.* Wilmette, IL: Chiron, 1998.

Scholem, G. "Identifizierung und Distanz: ein Rückblick.," *Eranos-Jahrbuch* 48 (1979): 463.

Shalit, E. *The Hero and His Shadow: Psychopolitical Aspects of Myth and Reality in Israel.* Rev. ed. Hanford, CA: Fisher King Press, 2012.

Shalit, E. *Requiem: A Tale of Exile and Return.* Hanford, CA: Fisher King Press, 2010.

Shamdasani, Sonu. *C. G. Jung: A Biography in Books.* New York: Norton, 2012.

Sorge, Giovanni. "Jung's Presidency of the International General Medical Society of Psychotherapy: New Insights." *Jung Journal: Culture & Psyche* 6, no. 4 (Fall 2012): 46.

Sorge, Giovanni. "Psicologia analitica e anni Trenta: Il ruolo di C.G. Jung nella Internationale Allgemeine Ärztliche Gesellschaft für Psychotherapie, 1933–1939/40" (PhD thesis, University of Zurich, 2010).

Sperling, H., and M. Simon. *The Zohar.* London: Soncino Press, 1931, 1934.

Stein, M. *Minding the Self: Jungian Meditations on Contemporary Spirituality.* London: Routledge, 2014.

Stein, M. *Solar Conscience/Lunar Conscience.* Wilmette, IL: Chiron Publications, 1993.

Szeemann, H., ed. *Monte Verità: Antropologia locale come contributo alla riscoperta di una topografia sacrale moderna.* Milan: Armando Dadò/ Electa, 1978.

Tacey, D. *The Jung Reader.* New York: Routledge, 2012.

Tronick, Edward Z. "Multilevel Meaning Making and Dyadic Expansion of Consciousness Theory: The Emotional and the Polymorphic Polysemic Flow of Meaning." In *The Healing Power of Emotion: Affective Neuroscience, Development and Clinical Practice.* Edited by Diana Fosha, Daniel J. Siegel, and Marion F. Solomon, 86–111. New York: W. W. Norton, 2009.

van de Berk, Tern. *Jung on Art: The Autonomy of the Creative Drive.* London: Routledge, 2012.

Vitolo, A. "The Analytical *Leitmotif* of the Eranos Conferences." *Spring: A Journal of Archetype and Culture* 92 (2015): 109 ff.

Vitolo, A. "Erich Neumann e la prospettiva mitica." In *Psicologia analitica contemporanea,* edited by C. Trombetta. Milan: Bompiani, 1989.

von Franz, Marie-Louise. *A Psychological Interpretation of the Golden Ass of Apuleius.* New York: Spring Publications, 1970; published in German as *Die Erlösung des Weiblichen im Manne: Der Goldene Esel des Apuleius in tiefenpsychologischer Sicht.* Zurich: Walter Verlag, 1980.

von Mangoldt, U. *Auf der Schwelle zwischen Gestern und Morgen.* Weilheim: Otto Wilhelm Barth, 1963.

Wasserstrom, Steven M. *Religion after Religion: Gershom Scholem, Mircea Eliade, and Henry Corbin at Eranos.* Princeton, NJ: Princeton University Press, 1999.

Wehr, G. *An Illustrated Biography of C. G. Jung.* Boston: Shambhala, 1989.

Wirtz, U. "The Symbolic Dimension in Trauma Therapy." *Spring: A Journal of Archetype and Culture* 82 (2009): 33.

For Further Reading

Kirsch, Jean and Tom. "A Visit to Hildemarie Streich." *Jung Journal: Culture and Psyche* 3, no. 2 (2009): 59–62.

Kirsch, Thomas B. *The Jungians*. London: Routledge, 2000.

Lammers, Ann C. "James Kirsch's Defense of Jung: Jüdische Rundschau, 1934." *Jung Journal: Culture and Psyche* 6, no. 4 (2012): 74–84.

Rasche, Jörg. "C. G. Jung in the 1930s: Not to Idealize, Neither to Diminish." *Jung Journal: Culture and Psyche* 6, no. 4 (2012): 54–73.

Röhm, Eberhard. *Sterben für den Frieden: Spurensicherung Hermann Stöhr* [Dying for Peace: On the Traces of Hermann Stöhr]. Stuttgart: Calwer Verlag, 1985.

Streich, Hildemarie. "Music in Dreams." *Jung Journal: Culture and Psyche* 3, no. 2 (2009): 63–73.

Citations to Unpublished Collections

AJP   Aniela Jaffé Papers, ETH Zurich University Archives, Swiss Federal Institute of Technology

CFB   Cary F. Baynes Papers, Contemporary Medical Archives, Wellcome Trust Library for the History of and Understanding of Medicine, London

EA   Eranos Archive, Ascona

JA   C. G. Jung Papers Collection, ETH Zurich University Archives, Swiss Federal Institute of Technology

MFP   Michael Fordham Papers, Contemporary Medical Archives, Wellcome Trust Library for the History of and Understanding of Medicine, London

NP   Neumann Papers (private collection of Rali Loewenthal-Neumann, Jerusalem)

RA   Rascher & Cie (publisher's archive) 1910–1970, Zentralbibliothek, Zurich

About the Contributors

Henry Abramovitch, PhD, Jungian analyst, clinical psychologist and anthropologist, is founding president and senior training analyst at the Israel Institute of Jungian Psychology as well as a professor at Tel Aviv University Medical School, where he teaches the "human" side of medicine. He has served on the Ethics and Program Committees of the International Association of Analytical Psychology (IAAP), as president of The Israel Anthropological Association, and as a co-facilitator for the Interfaith Encounter Association group. He supervises "Routers" in the IAAP Developing Groups in Poland and Moscow. He is author of *The First Father* (2010); *Brothers and Sisters: Myth and Reality* (2014), which has been published in English, Russian, and Hebrew; and *Psychotherapy as Performance Art* (forthcoming from Routledge).

Riccardo Bernardini, PhD, PsyD, serves as the scientific secretary of the Eranos Foundation. He is the founding president of the postgraduate Institute of Analytical Psychology and Psychodrama (IPAP) in the Olivetti University District of Ivrea. He is an associate of the Association for Research in Analytical Psychology (ARPA) in Turin, Italy, and a member of the board of the Fellow Traveller Foundation in Lugano, Switzerland. His research interests focus on the history of the Eranos phenomenon. His writings in this field include *Carl Gustav Jung at Eranos 1933–1952*, edited with Gian Piero Quaglino and Augusto Romano (2007), and *Jung at Eranos: The Complex Psychology Project* (2011), with an upcoming English edition. He edited the correspondence between Carl Gustav Jung and Henry Corbin (2013) and Carl Gustav Jung's *The Solar Myths and Opicinus de Canistris: Notes of the Seminar Given at Eranos in 1943*, with Gian Piero Quaglino and Augusto Romano (2014). For the Eranos Foundation, he is now editing, among other works, Olga Fröbe-Kapteyn's *Visions*, Emma von Pelet's *Analytic Diaries*, and Alwine von Keller's *Paintings of the Unconscious*. He serves as coeditor of the Eranos Yearbooks, together with Fabio Merlini, and of *Spring: A Journal of Archetype and Culture*.

Batya Brosh Palmoni, Jungian analyst, is a training and supervising analyst at the Israel Institute of Jungian Psychology (IIJP), where she currently serves on the Certifying Board. In the past she was honorary secretary and served on the Training Committee. Currently, she works in private practice, but for over thirty years she has also worked in public mental health clinics. She teaches in two different programs in Jungian psychotherapy in Israel. For the past five years, she has acted as supervisor and lecturer to the Developing Group in Kiev, where her work has enormously expanded her understanding of the great contribution of Jung and Neumann for clinicians living far from the traditional centers of analytical psychology.

Joe Cambray, PhD, is provost of Pacifica Graduate Institute, past president of the International Association for Analytical Psychology, and has served as the U.S. editor for the *Journal of Analytical Psychology*. He is on the editorial boards of the *Journal of Analytical Psychology*, *Jung Journal: Culture and Psyche*, and *Israel Annual of Psychoanalytic Theory, Research and Practice*. He was a faculty member at Harvard Medical School in the Department of Psychiatry at Massachusetts General Hospital, Center for Psychoanalytic Studies, and former president of the C. G. Jung Institute of Boston. He is a Jungian analyst in Santa Barbara, California. His numerous publications include *Synchronicity: Nature and Psyche in an Interconnected Universe*, based on his Fay Lectures, and a volume edited with Linda Carter, *Analytical Psychology: Contemporary Perspectives in Jungian Psychology*.

Thomas Fischer, PhD, studied history, political science, and public and international law at the Universities of Zurich and Brussels, with a specialization in international political and diplomatic history of the twentieth century. He has been a university lecturer and a visiting researcher at various institutes in Zurich, Beirut, Vienna, Helsinki, and Geneva, before becoming director of the Foundation of the Works of C. G. Jung, Zurich, in 2013. He is a great-grandson of C. G. and Emma Jung.

Nancy Swift Furlotti, PhD, is a Jungian analyst in Los Angeles and Santa Barbara. She is a past president of the C. G. Jung Institute of Los Angeles, founding member and past co-president of the Philemon Foundation, a long-term ARAS board member, founding member of the Kairos Film Foundation, and on the board of Pacifica Graduate Institute. She is co-chair of the C. G. Jung Endowment at the Semel Institute at

UCLA, where she includes the Jungian perspective through dialogue. She also serves on the board of the Foundation for Anthropological Research and Environmental Studies (FARES), in Guatemala, where she has a long-standing interest in Maya mythology and culture. She lectures in the United States and internationally, has written numerous articles, and is coeditor of *The Dream and Its Amplification* with Erel Shalit. She recently founded Recollections, LLC, to edit and publish first-generation Jungian materials.

Christian Gaillard, PhD, is a doctor of psychology (Sorbonne and EPHE), a training analyst, supervisor and former president of the Société Française de Psychologie Analytique (SFPA) and of the International Association for Analytical Psychology (IAAP), a lecturer at several universities and, until 2007, professor at the National Academy of Fine Arts in Paris. He founded and directed the *Cahiers de Psychologie de l'Art et de la Culture,* was for a long time co-chief editor of the *Cahiers Jungiens de Psychanalyse,* and is now a member of the international editorial teams of several international journals. Among the works he has published, translated into various languages, are *Le Musée imaginaire de Carl Gustav Jung* (Stock, 1998), *Donne in mutazione. Saggi di psicoanalisi dell'arte* (Moretti, 2000), *L'Inconscient créateur: A propos du* Libro dei sogni *de Federico Fellini* (Moretti, 2009), and *Jung,* in its sixth edition (Presses Universitaires de France, 2013).

Ulrich Hoerni earned a degree in architecture at the Swiss Federal Institute of Technology Zürich (ETH) in 1967 and went on to work as an architect in Denmark and Switzerland before retiring in 1994. In 1981 he joined the Executive Committee of the Community of Heirs of C. G. Jung and served as its manager from 1997 to 2007 and as its chair from 2004 to 2007. In 2007 he became the first president and director of the newly established Foundation of the Works of C. G. Jung, Zurich, where he was a board member until 2016. In his various functions first with the Community of Heirs and then with the Foundation of the Works of C. G. Jung he has been involved for the past thirty years in the planning and preparation of new Jung publications, most notably, *The Red Book* in 2009.

Andreas Jung was educated in the classics, Greek and Latin, in Zürich and Davos, and studied architecture, receiving a degree from the Swiss

Federal Institute of Technology Zürich (ETH) in 1970. He practiced at the architectural firm of Hertig Hertig Schoch from 1970 to 1974. He was the assistant conservator for the Historic Preservation Department, City of Zürich, from 1974 to 2006. He has served as secretary of the Foundation C.G. Jung Küsnacht and as conservator for the Jung Family Archive. He has lectured and published on family history, building history, and antique texts. He is the grandson of C. G. Jung and lives in Jung's former family home.

Tom Kelly, Jungian analyst, completed his training at the C. G. Jung Institute in Zurich in 1986. He is a member of the editorial board of the *Journal of Analytical Psychology* and has lectured widely in Canada, the United States, and Europe. He is currently president of the International Association for Analytical Psychology (IAAP). He lives and has a private practice in Montreal, Canada.

Thomas B. Kirsch, MD, is a graduate of Yale Medical School, Stanford University's Department of Psychiatry, and the C. G. Jung Institute of San Francisco. He has been president of the Jung Institute of San Francisco and vice-president and president of the International Association for Analytical Psychology (IAAP). He is the author of *The Jungians* (2000) and *A Jungian Life* (2014), and of more than one hundred articles on clinical and historical subjects in analytical psychology. He is currently retired from analytic practice.

Nomi Kluger-Nash is a Jungian psychologist and therapist and writer. She completed her doctoral studies at International College in Los Angeles in 1977 and previous graduate courses at the New School of Social Research in philosophy, history, and psychology in 1970. At the University of California–Los Angeles she studied anthropology and theater arts, then worked as an actress, worldwide, for five years. After a brief career in politics, she kept her promise to study at a Jung Institute (Los Angeles and Israel) upon reaching the age of forty. She trained informally with her father, Yehezkel Kluger, with whom she coauthored a book, *A Psychological Interpretation of Ruth/Standing in the Sandals of Naomi* (Daimon Press), and with her stepmother, Rivkah Scharf Kluger, both parents being of Jung's inner circle. She lived in Jerusalem for sixteen years, where she worked as ombudsperson with the Arabs of the West Bank. She currently teaches at the C. G. Jung Institute of Zurich.

Tamar Kron, PhD, Jungian analyst, is professor emeritus of the Hebrew University and head of the clinical psychology graduate program at the Academic College of Tel Aviv-Yafo. She integrates her clinical-analytical work with teaching and research. She has published numerous articles, chapters, and books and presented at international conferences. One of her main areas of interest is the metapsychology of Erich Neumann. Together with David Wieler she has translated three of Neumann's Eranos papers from German into Hebrew and is engaged now in translating Neumann's unpublished manuscript, "Roots of Jewish Consciousness," into Hebrew.

Debora Kutzinski, Tel Aviv, Israel, writes: "I was born in Prague in 1925. Until age thirteen, I was a happy daughter to good parents, with an older brother. From an early age, I loved sport—and dreams. Already at five, I told my brother my dreams. He ran to my father, telling him I was crazy . . . and my father told me, dreams are meaningless, though I did not believe him. Dreams constituted the experience in depth of my childhood.

"In 1942, my family and I were deported to the Theresienstadt concentration camp. In 1944, I was deported to Auschwitz, and from there, together with another two hundred girls, to a concentration camp near Dresden. On May 13, 1945, I returned to Prague, to the sound of the bells that were ringing in honor of the liberation of the city. Eventually I learned that my entire, extended family had been killed in the Shoah.

"In 1946 I arrived in the land of Israel, and my life changed. Through a friend I came to Erich Neumann. I asked him if my frequent dreaming was a sign of insanity. He calmed me but sent me for analysis with his wife, Julie. I did not believe him and did not calm down, since most people at the time thought that if you were in treatment, you were not psychologically balanced or, rather, crazy.

"I remained for eighteen years in analysis with Julie, and with Erich Neumann in supervision and studies, eventually becoming a Jungian analyst. During those years I married, and gave birth to a son and a daughter, both of whom are psychologists. I see my work as the realization of a vocation. Every day I am happy that at the age of ninety-one I continue my analytical work, as well as teaching and supervising younger generations."

Rivka Lahav has been a clinical psychologist and Jungian analyst since 2000. She worked for twelve years in Neve Tzeelim and for ten years in the mental health clinic of Ramat Chen. She now runs a private clinic.

Ann Conrad Lammers, MDiv, PhD, LMFT, earned her master of divinity at the General Theological Seminary and her doctorate at Yale. In the 1980s, before being licensed in California as a marriage and family therapist, she taught theology and ethics at the Church Divinity School of the Pacific and the Graduate Theological Union. She spent the next ten years in private practice in California as a Jungian psychotherapist. Lammers is the author of *In God's Shadow: The Collaboration of Victor White and C. G. Jung* (Paulist, 1994); the lead editor of *The Jung-White Letters* (Routledge, 2007); and editor and cotranslator of *The Jung-Kirsch Letters* (Routledge, 2011/2016; German edition, Patmos, 2014). Recently retired from the practice of psychotherapy in New Hampshire, she is presently editing and, together with Mark Kyburz, collaborating on the translation into English of Erich Neumann's work, *The Roots of Jewish Consciousness*. This major work, written in Tel Aviv between 1938 and 1945 and previously unpublished, will be forthcoming in 2018.

Martin Liebscher, PhD, is a senior research associate at the School of European Languages, Culture and Society and an honorary senior lecturer at the Health Humanities Centre at University College London. His research interests lie in nineteenth- and twentieth-century German philosophy, in the conceptual history of the unconscious, and in the historical and philosophical foundations of Jungian psychology. His publications include *Thinking the Unconscious: Nineteenth-Century German Thought* (2010) and *Libido und Wille zur Macht: C. G. Jungs Auseinandersetzung mit Nietzsche* (2011). He is the editor of *Analytical Psychology in Exile: The Correspondence between C. G. Jung and Erich Neumann* (2015). His current work for the Philemon Foundation consists of the publication of Jung's lectures at the Polytechnicum Zurich. He is a collaborator on the translation of Jung's Black Books.

Angelica Löwe, PhD, Jungian analyst, studied philosophy, German literature, and history in Heidelberg, Tübingen, and Vienna. She has lived in Vienna since 1977, lecturing in literary studies, philosophy, and psychoanalysis. Trained in Vienna as a Jungian analyst, she is a member of Österreichische Gesellschaft für Analytische Psychologie (ÖGAP), also of the C. G. Jung Institute Munich and of Deutschen Gesellschaft für Analytische Psychologie (DGAP). She works as a psychoanalyst in private practice in Vienna and is editor in chief of the journal, *Analytische Psychologie,* and author of *On the Part of the Inner Voice: Erich Neumann—Life and Oeuvre* (Karl Alber, 2014). She works with the Hungarian Developing Group in Budapest.

Paul Mendes-Flohr, PhD, is professor emeritus of the Hebrew University of Jerusalem and currently teaches at the University of Chicago. His major research interests include modern Jewish intellectual history, modern Jewish philosophy and religious thought, philosophy of religion, German intellectual history, and the history and sociology of intellectuals. Together with Bernd Witte, he serves as editor-in-chief of the twenty-two-volume German edition of the collected works of Martin Buber, sponsored by the Berlin-Brandenburgische Akademie der Wissenschaften, the Israel Academy of Sciences and Humanities, and the Heinrich Heine Universität, Düsseldorf, Germany. He has recently published *Progress and Its Discontents* (in Hebrew), *The Jew in the Modern: A Documentary History* (with Jehuda Reinharz), and *Encrucijadas en la Modernidad* (Buenos Aries). He is the editor of a series on German-Jewish literature and cultural history for the University of Chicago Press. He is completing a biography of Martin Buber to be published by Yale University Press and is the editor most recently of *Gustav Landauer, Anarchist and Jew* (Walter de Gruyter-Oldenbourg Verlag, 2014) and *Dialogue as a Trans-Disciplinary Concept* (Walter de Gruyter Verlag, 2015).

Micha Neumann, MD, is the son of Erich and Julie Neumann. He is a psychiatrist and Freudian psychoanalyst, trained in Israel and in the United States. He is the former president of the Israel Psychiatric Association and the former medical director of the Shalvata Mental Health Center, a teaching hospital for psychiatrists and mental health workers. He was a professor in the Tel Aviv University Medical School, where he also served as the director of all the teaching and training programs of the psychiatric department. He has researched and published papers about Holocaust survivors and Israeli soldiers with posttraumatic stress disorder and was an expert witness with the Israeli court regarding victims of violence, accidents, and abuse.

Being the son of Erich Neumann, he has lectured and published about the relationship between Neumann and Jung, based on their long correspondence and on his personal knowledge. He is the author of *The Relationship between C. G. Jung and Erich Neumann Based on Their Correspondence* (Chiron, 2016).

Ralli Loewenthal Neumann is the daughter of Erich and Julie Neumann. She resides in Jerusalem where she is a Jungian psychotherapist and, like her mother, a chirologist.

Gideon Ofrat, PhD, earned his doctorate at the Hebrew University in 1974. He has been deeply involved in Israeli art both as a historian and theoretician. A graduate of Tel Aviv University, Brown University, and the Hebrew University, he has taught at various Israeli universities and art academies and also lectured as a guest professor in many universities in Europe and America. Ofrat has curated many historical and contemporary Israeli art exhibitions, mostly in Israel, but also in the United States and at the Venice Biennale. He has published hundreds of articles, art catalogues, and about fifty books on Israeli art, Israeli culture, philosophy of art, and more, mostly in Hebrew, but a few in English, including *The Jewish Derrida* and *100 Years of Art in Israel*. Recently he published a large trilogy on Israeli art's historical connections with Berlin, Paris, and New York. On his widely read Internet site he has published hundreds of essays in Hebrew that tackle contemporary Israeli art.

Rina Porat, Jungian analyst, was born in Bulgaria and has lived in Israel since 1949. She is married and has three daughters and nine grandchildren. She is a psychologist with degrees from Hebrew University in Jerusalem and a senior training analyst at the Israel Institute of Jungian Psychology (IIJP). She is a member of the International Society of Sandplay Therapy (ISST) and cofounder and former president of the Israel Sandplay Therapists Association (ISTA). She works in private practice and is involved in training, teaching, and supervising professionals in the Israeli Institute of Jungian Psychology, at Bar Ilan University, and in sandplay therapy training programs. She writes and lectures in Israel and abroad, mainly on the subjects of Erich Neumann's writings and developmental theories, sandplay images of peace, war, and terrorism, collective and personal traumas, and victims of prolonged traumas.

Joerg Rasche, MD, is a Jungian analyst trained in Berlin and Zurich and as a sandplay therapist with Dora Kalff. He teaches at the C. G. Jung Institutes in Berlin and Zurich and elsewhere. He is the former president of Deutschen Gesellschaft für Analytische Psychologie (DGAP), former vice president of the International Association for Analytical Psychology (IAAP), and currently president of the German Association for Sandplay Therapy. He has published on psychoanalysis, sandplay, music and psyche, and the history of Jungian analysis. He coedited, with Tom Singer, *Europe's Many Souls: Exploring Cultural Complexes and Identities* (Spring Journal Books, 2016). Currently he is writing a reconstruction of the early interreligious dialogue between St. Francis of Assisi and the Sultan al-Kamil during a crusade in 1219. Rasche is also a musician. For his engagement with psychotherapy in Poland and people's reconciliation he was honored in 2012 with the Golden Cross of Merit by the president of Poland.

Erel Shalit, PhD, is a Jungian psychoanalyst in Tel Aviv. He is a training and supervising analyst and past president of the Israel Society of Analytical Psychology. He is founder and past director of the Jungian Analytical Psychotherapy Program at Bar Ilan University and past director of the Shamai Davidson Community Mental Health Clinic. He has served as honorary secretary of the Ethics Committee of the International Association of Analytical Psychology (IAAP) and as its liaison with the Bulgarian Jung Society. He is a member of the Council for Peace and Security. He has lectured widely and is the author of several books, including *The Cycle of Life: Themes and Tales of the Journey, Requiem: A Tale of Exile and Return, Enemy, Cripple, and Beggar, The Complex: Paths of Transformation from Archetype to Ego,* and co-edited, with Nancy Furlotti, *The Dream and its Amplification.* He has edited and introduced *Jacob and Esau: On the Collective Symbolism of the Brother Motif* by Erich Neumann.

Murray Stein, PhD, Jungian analyst, is a graduate of the C. G. Jung Institute of Zurich (1973) and of Yale University (1965), Yale Divinity School (1969), and the University of Chicago (1985). He is a founding member of the Inter-Regional Society of Jungian Analysts and the Chicago Society of Jungian Analysts. He was president of the International Association for Analytical Psychology (IAAP) from 2001 to 2004 and president of the International School of Analytical Psychology

Zurich from 2008 to 2012. He has lectured internationally and is the author of *In Midlife*, *Jung's Map of the Soul*, *Minding the Self*, and *Soul: Retrieval and Treatment* as well as numerous articles on analytical psychology and Jungian psychoanalysis. He is the Jungian editor for the *Edinburgh Encyclopedia of Psychoanalysis* and the editor of *Jungian Psychoanalysis*. He lives in Switzerland, where he has a private practice and is a training and supervising analyst with ISAPZurich.

Jacqueline Zeller Levine is a Jungian analyst at the C. G. Jung Institute of Santa Fe, New Mexico. She is the past president of the institute and is currently the training director.

She specializes in grief, depression, change of life and getting older in this world, and disabled children in the family. She has a PhD from Pacifica Graduate Institute and has written on children of the Holocaust, secrets and silence, and countertransference in the analytic process. Her parents, Max and Lore Zeller, were two of the founders of the C. G. Jung Institute of Los Angeles, and she dedicates her writings and presentations on the Holocaust to them.